SPINOZA CONTRA PHENOMENOLOGY

Cultural Memory
    in
    the
    Present

Hent de Vries, Editor

SPINOZA CONTRA PHENOMENOLOGY

French Rationalism from Cavaillès to Deleuze

Knox Peden

STANFORD UNIVERSITY PRESS
STANFORD, CALIFORNIA

Stanford University Press
Stanford, California

© 2014 by the Board of Trustees of the Leland Stanford Junior University. All rights reserved.

No part of this book may be reproduced or transmitted in any form or by any means, electronic or mechanical, including photocopying and recording, or in any information storage or retrieval system without the prior written permission of Stanford University Press.

Printed in the United States of America on acid-free, archival-quality paper

Library of Congress Cataloging-in-Publication Data has been requested.

ISBN 978-0-8047-8741-3 (cloth)
ISBN 978-0-8047-9134-2 (pbk.)
ISBN 978-0-8047-9136-6 (electronic)

Typeset by Bruce Lundquist in 11/13.5 Adobe Garamond

Contents

Acknowledgments		ix
List of Abbreviations		xiii
	Introduction Spinozism: A Source of Enthusiasm	1
1.	From Consciousness to the Concept: The Spinozism of Jean Cavaillès	17
2.	Spinoza Contra Descartes: Martial Gueroult versus Ferdinand Alquié	65
3.	From Stalinism to Asceticism: Jean-Toussaint Desanti between Spinoza and Husserl	95
4.	Recuperating Science: The Sources of Louis Althusser's Spinozism	127
5.	Redefining Philosophy: The Development of Louis Althusser's Spinozism	149
6.	Toward a Science of the Singular: Gilles Deleuze between Heidegger and Spinoza	191
7.	Nothing Is Possible: The Strange Spinozism of Gilles Deleuze	219
	Conclusion The Sense of Spinozism	257
	Notes	267
	Bibliography	319
	Index	341

Acknowledgments

Work on this book has taken me from California to Australia by way of France, and I have accumulated a number of debts along the way. Material support at Berkeley came from the Department of History, the Institute of European Studies, and the Mabelle McLeod Lewis Memorial Fund. Carla Hesse and David Bates were judicious readers and encouraging interlocutors throughout the project. I am pleased to join a chorus of students who express gratitude for the distinctive blend of probity, severity, and above all generosity that Martin Jay brings to the task of advising. Amid all the talk of the crisis of the humanities, his contribution to the debate in a July 2013 edition of the *Daily Cal* also expresses something of the model of intellectual history he promotes, one grounded in ruthless self-scrutiny and an appreciation of the benefits that accrue when you cherish what you criticize.

Beyond Berkeley, three mentors share a measure of responsibility for this book. Monty Holamon set me on this path when he took me to Paris in 1994 along with other classmates in French, and he ensured that the path would be absurd when he cast me as Pa Ubu in a production of Alfred Jarry's Ubu plays the next year. At Penn, Marc Trachtenberg introduced me to the tasks, protocols, and joys of historical scholarship. My interests have taken me afield from the diplomatic history that I studied with him, but his lessons about how to read critically—and to think historically—have proved foundational for all of my work. Though I knew him for only several months, the last of his life as it turned out, Richard Popkin shaped my thinking about the history of philosophy and helped me realize that, especially when it comes to Spinoza, skepticism and enthusiasm are not antithetical sentiments but in fact prerequisites of one another.

The bulk of the research for this project was conducted in France, and it is a pleasure to acknowledge the librarians and archivists who assisted my efforts at the Bibliothèque nationale de France, the École Normale Supérieure at rue d'Ulm, the Institut d'éditions de memoire contemporaine in Caen, and the Institut Desanti at the École Normale Supérieure–LHS in Lyon. I am also grateful to the scholars who took time to discuss this project with me. My chief debt is to Chantal Jaquet, who, in addition to indulging my earliest musings on this subject, wrote a letter of recommendation that helped me secure a Chateaubriand Fellowship to support my time in Paris. Others who met with me in cafés and bureaus to discuss Spinoza's rationalism include Alain Badiou, Étienne Balibar, Pierre Cassou-Noguès, Pierre Macherey, Pierre-François Moreau, Bernard Pautrat, and Frédéric Worms. Hourya Sinaceur read my chapter on Cavaillès with a discerning eye and gave fruitful advice on how to approach his philosophy of mathematics. I thank Vincent Gerard and Dominique Pradelle for welcoming me to their reading group of Desanti's *Idéalités mathématiques*, and remain grateful to Dominique Desanti for responding to my queries about her husband's life and work. I was saddened to learn of her death in 2011 and am honored that Christine Goémé has authorized a treasure from the Desantis' estate to serve as the cover for this book. Michel Tort kindly permitted the reproduction of a sketch he likely had no idea had been preserved. A special word of thanks is due Quentin Meillassoux for alerting me to an interview with Jean-Luc Marion in *Le Monde*.

The book was completed during my time as a postdoctoral research fellow in the Centre for the History of European Discourses (CHED) at the University of Queensland (UQ), and I am grateful to the Faculty of Arts for so generously supporting my work through the UQ postdoctoral fellowship scheme. I am also pleased to thank the two directors of the center I have known, Peter Cryle and Peter Harrison, along with my colleagues at CHED, for creating such an impossibly ideal venue for research in European intellectual history in its myriad forms.

The final draft of the manuscript benefited enormously from the insightful remarks and initially anonymous criticisms that Stanford University Press solicited from Samuel Moyn and Peter Gordon. I am grateful to Emily-Jane Cohen at Stanford for her support for the project and helpful advice, as well as to Hent de Vries for including the book in a series I have long admired. Emily Smith's diligence and patience have been instrumental in turning the manuscript into a book, and the sharp eyes and sound advice of my copyeditor Cynthia Lindlof have spared me much embarrassment.

For a publication that has been so long in the making, I have naturally accumulated a sizable debt to friends and colleagues who have discussed this project with me in various settings. There is not space—in this book or my memory—to name them all, but I am happy to acknowledge the audiences who responded to my claims at the following institutions: the Australian National University, the University of New South Wales, the University of Queensland, the annual meeting of the Australasian Society for Continental Philosophy, the Consortium for Intellectual and Cultural History at CUNY, the École Normale Supérieure, the annual meeting of the American Comparative Literature Association, Cornell University, and the Centre for Research in Modern European Philosophy in London.

Among the many friends who have supported my work, a handful read portions of the book and responded with invaluable criticism and feedback. A special acknowledgment on this score is due Nathan Brown, who read the initial manuscript in one heroic sitting and expressed an enthusiasm for the project that has sustained me in periods of heightened skepticism. My debt is no less great to these other readers who responded to various sections of the book: Ed Baring, Giuseppe Bianco, Ray Brassier, Marija Cetinic, Stefanos Geroulanos, G. M. Goshgarian, Martin Hägglund, Peter Hallward, Ian Hesketh, Ian Hunter, Rob Lehman, Ozren Pupovac, Joel Revill, Audrey Wasser, and Ben Wurgaft. This book would not be the reality it is without the critical advice of these readers. And despite Spinoza's contention that perfection and reality are one and the same, its imperfections are still my doing.

Some readers will recognize that the title of this book pays homage to Gillian Rose's classic *Hegel Contra Sociology*. Though I admire many things about Rose's book, in particular her focus on the persistence of neo-Kantianism in European thought and her insistence on the value of speculative philosophy, this homage also includes an emotional component. In 1991, three years before Rose died from ovarian cancer at the age of forty-eight, and thirteen years before I even knew who she was, my mother died at the age of forty-nine in similar circumstances. I have read enough Lacan to appreciate that the acknowledgment of a debt typically does not go without a measure of transference, and I'm happy to be explicit about that here. I'm also pleased to experience the merits of Spinoza's insistence that our affective inclinations acquire a richer meaning when we seek to form an adequate idea of them.

My family in Texas has been a constant source of sustenance and a site of joyful reprieve from the stresses work on this book has involved. As for my father, there really is no way to give an adequate idea of my love for him and my gratitude for his support for all of my intellectual adventures, from Pa Ubu to this one.

Leslie Barnes has lived with this book and its author for ten years and on three continents. Here my debt is incalculable. This book is dedicated to her.

. . .

For the most part, I cite from English translations of French texts where they are available, but in some cases I have seen fit to cite from both the French original and the English translation. Instances where the translation has been modified have been identified as such. Unless otherwise noted, translations from the French are my own, though I am pleased to acknowledge David Webb for his contribution to the translated portions of Cavaillès's *Sur la logique et la théorie de la science* and to thank him for productive exchanges grappling with this difficult text. I am also grateful to Cambridge University Press and the editors of *Modern Intellectual History* for allowing my article "Descartes, Spinoza, and the Impasse of French Philosophy: Ferdinand Alquié versus Martial Gueroult" to be reproduced here in a revised form.

Abbreviations

BT   Heidegger, *Being and Time*
CC   Deleuze, *Essays: Critical and Clinical*
Découverte   Alquié, *La Découverte métaphysique de l'homme chez Descartes*
Destin   Desanti, *Un Destin philosophique*
DR   Deleuze, *Difference and Repetition*
Encounter   Althusser, *Philosophy of the Encounter*
ESC   Althusser, *Essays in Self-Criticism*
FM   Althusser, *For Marx*
Future   Althusser, *The Future Lasts Forever*
GDFG   Dosse, *Gilles Deleuze et Félix Guattari*
Humanist   Althusser, *The Humanist Controversy and Other Writings*
ID   Deleuze, *Desert Islands and Other Texts*
IHP   Desanti, *Introduction à l'histoire de la philosophie*
IP   Desanti, *Introduction à la phénoménologie*
Lenin   Althusser, *Lenin and Philosophy and Other Essays*
Liberté   Droit, *La Liberté nous aime encore*
LS   Deleuze, *The Logic of Sense*
LTS   Cavaillès, *Sur la logique et la théorie de la science*
Matrice   Moulier Boutang, *Louis Althusser, une biographie: La Formation du mythe, 1918–1945: La Matrice*
Nostalgie   Alquié, *La Nostalgie de l'être*
OC   Cavaillès, *Oeuvres complètes de philosophie des sciences*
"Path"   Desanti, "A Path in Philosophy"
PC   Desanti, *Une Pensée captive*
PH   Althusser, *Politics and History*
PM   Cavaillès, *Philosophie mathématique*

PSPS   Althusser, *Philosophy and the Spontaneous Philosophy of the Scientists and Other Essays*
Rationalisme   Alquié, *Le Rationalisme de Spinoza*
RC   Althusser and Balibar, *Reading Capital*
Ruptures   Moulier Boutang, *Louis Althusser, une biographie: La formation du mythe, 1946–1956: Ruptures et plis*
SPE   Deleuze, *Expressionism in Philosophy: Spinoza*
Spectre   Althusser, *The Spectre of Hegel*
TEI   Spinoza, *Treatise on the Emendation of the Intellect*
VM   Canguilhem, *Vie et mort de Jean Cavaillès*

SPINOZA CONTRA PHENOMENOLOGY

Introduction

Spinozism: A Source of Enthusiasm

In April 2008, *Le Monde* published an interview with Jean-Luc Marion in which the philosopher and soon-to-be-elected member of the Académie française discussed the enduring fascination with Benedict de Spinoza (1632–77) in modern intellectual life.[1] For Marion, Spinozism's capacity to accommodate a host of positions is its main source of appeal. Reflecting on Henri Bergson's remark that every philosopher in truth has two philosophies, Spinoza's and his own, Marion observes:

One can just as easily become a convinced Spinozist (or a firm opponent) with a materialist and atheistic interpretation of the *Ethics* as with a mystical-religious one. A vitalist interpretation works just as well as a logicist one, a scientific and modern interpretation just as well as one that makes it Neoplatonist, Jewish, or even Christian. You start to suspect that Spinozism accompanies the philosophy of each philosopher precisely because it is not a philosophy itself but an ideological complement to all, the refuge of faith for nonbelievers.

Marion is struck that a philosophical system committed to exposing "our irrepressible need for ideology" can nourish so many ideological abuses. "It is above all the *Ethics*," he says, "in its ahistorical extraterritoriality, its splendid abstraction and its unbridled ambition, that fascinates us because it poses the question of the power and limits of philosophy itself." But Marion wonders whether going to such extremes does not end up revealing philosophy's limits as an enterprise. "Spinoza can disappoint his reader because he leaves him suspecting that philosophy doesn't have the means for its own ambition. But he delights the thinker because he keeps intact all of his ambitions for philosophy, even the imprudent ones." In the end, Spinozism posits a transgressive role for rational thought, "an irrational belief in reason" that makes philosophy itself an object of quasi-theological affirmation. "Whence the perverse impression that we must believe in the *Ethics*, and that if we don't, then the *Ethics* itself will explain which mental disorder is preventing us from doing so."

Marion's discussion of Spinoza was consistent with the other interviews that appeared under the rubric "Le Monde des philosophes" in the newspaper's book section throughout 2008. In each instance, the apparent idea was to have a contemporary philosopher speak on a canonical figure with whom he or she had, if not an antagonistic relationship, at the very least a fraught or conflicted one. For example, André Glucksmann, the author of a series of antitotalitarian polemics in the 1970s, had been asked to discuss Plato, a conversation that found its counterpoint the next month when the arch-Platonist Alain Badiou set his sights on Aristotle.[2] The editorial decision to solicit Marion's views on Spinoza was particularly inspired, not simply because Marion has long been recognized as France's leading expert on Descartes, a familiar target of Spinozistic criticisms, but also because of his status as arguably the preeminent living inheritor of the phenomenological tradition in France.[3] *Le Monde*'s choice was serendipitous for this book as well, since it resulted in an interview that clarified its core thesis at a time when it was still very much a work in progress. In their elegant simplicity, Marion's comments not only manifested a set of irreconcilable differences between phenomenology and Spinozism; they also made clear that those differences resulted from a fundamental disagreement about the value of rationalism as a philosophical ethos.

By insisting on Spinozism's core liability as one of transgression, a failure to respect the limits of rational thought, Marion lent his remarks a striking historical resonance. Despite their casual delivery, his censures recapitulated those Immanuel Kant leveled against Spinozism in the pages of the *Berlinische Monatsschrift* in 1786. Responding to suggestions that his own philosophy would lead, like Spinozism, to the ruin of morality, Kant insisted that whereas Spinoza claimed to possess knowledge of "supersensible objects," such as God, "the *Critique* completely clips dogmatism's wings."[4] For Kant, the value of the "rational faith" on offer in his philosophy was that it did not mistake itself for knowledge, a value that was especially clear when counterpoised to Spinoza's demonstrative insistence on the role of determinant necessity throughout existence. Against Spinoza's rationalist conviction, rational faith in God, the source of morality, was a matter of presupposition, not demonstration. With its claims about God arranged in the manner of a geometrical proof, Spinoza's philosophy resulted in an enthusiasm or *Schwärmerei* of reason to rival if not exceed the fanaticism of religious zealots.[5]

Kant's *Critique of Pure Reason*, in name and principle, led to a decisive shift in European intellectual history, a "Copernican Revolution" in his famous phrase, whereby reason itself became the object of critique rather than the unproblematic source of metaphysical speculation or empirical inquiry. The critique of reason assumed many guises in the nineteenth century, from Marx's historico-political approach to Darwin's naturalism on to Nietzsche's "transvaluation of all values." It was only with the political catastrophes of the twentieth century, however, that the philosophical rejection of rationalism acquired a new ethical and political force. Faced with Nazism, Stalinism, and imperialism, any historical confidence in reason's beneficent role seemed misplaced. What's more, the critique of rationalism spanned the left and right of the political spectrum, from Max Horkheimer and Theodor Adorno's *Dialectic of Enlightenment* to Michael Oakeshott's *Rationalism in Politics*. In all cases, an overweening confidence in reason and its capacity to divine some truth about the world, or to introduce some true order into the world, seemed to verify Kant's concerns about Spinozistic *Schwärmerei* and its deleterious moral and political effects.

In France, the main vehicle for the critique of reason was the reception and reworking of German phenomenology over a period of decades, from the existentialism of Jean-Paul Sartre to the deconstruction of Jacques Derrida. Consequently, when France's leading phenomenologist reiterates the critique of Spinozism in the pages of *Le Monde*, he evokes something more than Kant's foundational concerns. His comments are also reflective of the manner in which Spinozism and phenomenology came to be regarded as antagonistic approaches to philosophy in France. Over the past decade, a series of major studies has established phenomenology's crucial role in the innovations of twentieth-century French thought, placing particular emphasis on the impact of Martin Heidegger's existential and ontological reconfiguration of Edmund Husserl's transcendental phenomenology. Much of this history has focused on how phenomenology was reshaped—or indeed deconstructed—by a French engagement that sought to decouple the method from the nefarious implications of Heidegger's indulgence in Nazism in order to salvage it as the basis for a contemporary philosophical ethos and ethics.[6] This book is a history of a countervailing strand of development in which a series of French thinkers sought to salvage rationalist philosophy from its phenomenological denigration by reconfiguring it in Spinozist terms. In their view, the travesties of modern life were not instances of rationalism run amok; they were instead consequent upon a dearth of rationalism, to the profit of myth. For the Spinozists discussed in this book, phenomenology was likewise a stimulus to thought: a negative stimulus.

. . .

Louis Althusser deployed military metaphors often and would no doubt have recognized that this book seeks to intervene on two fronts. First, it participates in the resurgence of interest in Spinoza's philosophy in contemporary scholarship, a diverse enthusiasm that runs from Jonathan Israel's promotion of Spinoza as the theoretical progenitor of democratic modernity to various "new materialisms" that find in Spinoza's metaphysics the resources for an emancipatory politics of affect.[7] Second, the narrative that follows aims to develop a fuller picture of twentieth-century French intellectual history, one that builds on the scholarship that has established the reception of phenomenology as the main arc in the story.

In addition to highlighting the central role of philosophy, one further consequence of this recent work has been to confirm what has long been recognized, if not explicitly thematized: "French Theory" is best regarded as a transatlantic if not global entity rather than a French one. In other words, the history of French Theory is a history that took place mainly outside France's borders in a variety of cultural and disciplinary contexts in the Anglophone world.[8] What this means is that the history of French Theory is not strictly commensurable with the history of philosophical and theoretical developments that were later disseminated under that name. In this regard, the emphasis on the local reception of phenomenology in France has yielded a more accurate historical picture of this body of thought in its original formulation, insofar as we understand historical accuracy here to mean correlating as closely as possible to what the subjects in question understood themselves to be doing. It is often remarked, for example, that the French make no distinction between structuralism and poststructuralism, the former term alone sufficing to name a gamut of critical interrogations of philosophy and the human sciences that dominated French intellectual life in the 1960s and, to an extent, into the 1970s.[9] In the American history of French Theory, the famous 1966 Johns Hopkins symposium "The Languages of Criticism and the Sciences of Man," which included presentations from such luminaries as Jacques Lacan and Roland Barthes, began as an episode in the reception of structuralism and ended with the advent of poststructuralism.[10] The turning point occurred when Derrida presented his famous deconstruction of the elements of "play" in Claude Lévi-Strauss's otherwise austere formalism. Events such as this established the initial terms of intelligibility for Derrida abroad, presenting him as a thinker concerned mainly with the vicissitudes of structuralist poetics.[11] Recent work has made clear, however, at least until the next wave of revisionism, that Derrida is best understood as a philosopher, one responding to the challenges inherent in the phenomenological enterprise.[12]

None of this is to deny that there was something called "structuralism" in France or that it unified a variety of theoretical projects. But the picture of the 1960s as a moment when structuralism burst onto the scene to render existentialism obsolete, only to be replaced in turn by a poststructuralism in which leading figures of existentialism—Nietzsche and Heidegger chief among them—reemerged in a more theoretically sophisticated light is too crassly Hegelian in its form to be satisfactory. Much as recent work has established the roots of deconstruction in a longer story of phenomenology's reception, this book provides a different view of the genealogy of structuralism by focusing on the rationalist resistance to phenomenology that reached its pinnacle in the 1960s with the philosophical projects of Louis Althusser and Gilles Deleuze. To be sure, the postwar introduction of linguistic formalism into the human sciences, from anthropology to psychoanalysis, was a transformative moment in twentieth-century French thought. But one of the main implications of this book is that this formalism acquired the purchase it did because it resonated with the insights of a rationalism rooted in the initial French response to phenomenology in the interwar years.[13]

Here, some preliminary questions insist: Isn't France's native son René Descartes typically regarded as the father of modern rationalism? And did Paul Ricoeur not identify a "latent rationalism" as "one of the fundamental springs of Husserl's thought?"[14] In a sense, this book uses "rationalism" as a term of art, although it joins others in emphasizing the extent to which structuralism as a diverse theoretical phenomenon was grounded in a more basic philosophical rationalism, the lineaments of which are beginning to come into view.[15] As an investment in rationalism as an ethos—understood as a commitment to the capacity of reason, however it is conceived, to supervene on the spontaneous insights of lived experience—becomes a more clearly discernible trait of modern French thought, developing a fuller and more nuanced account of that rationalism becomes a more urgent task.

The traits that distinguish Spinozist rationalism from Cartesian rationalism are of special importance to what follows; an ongoing debate about the distinction is in fact one of the central threads of the story. For Husserl certainly did consider his phenomenology to be a new kind of rationalism, and he readily claimed Descartes' patronage by naming the lectures in which he introduced phenomenology to a French audience the "Cartesian Meditations." But Husserl's choice of title also indirectly points to the significance of Spinozism. For phenomenology was quickly assimilated to a Cartesian framework in France, which meant that it became a matter of focusing on the phenomenon of subjectivity and a subject's encounter with, or embeddedness in, the world. A Spinozist rationalism, by contrast, refused the notion of a "subject"—the *cogito* of Descartes' immortal phrase "I think therefore I am" (*cogito ergo sum*)—as the starting point for philosophy. Ricoeur helps us specify our terms here as well in his description of Lévi-Strauss's structuralism as a "Kantianism without a transcendental subject."[16] The demotion of the subject to a consequence of other, more fundamental forces, rather than a founding instance, is one of the unifying themes of postwar French thought, common to projects as disparate as Althusser's Marxism and Levinas's ethics. At issue is whether those anterior processes or forces are in principle amenable to a rational elucidation, however abstract or incomplete. A Spinozist thinks they are.

. . .

The specific ways in which Spinoza's rationalism came to be regarded as an antidote to phenomenology is the stuff of what follows. It should be noted, however, that readers seeking a comprehensive account of twentieth-century French Spinoza scholarship—there must be a few—

will appreciate that such is not the aim of this inquiry. Like any canonical figure, Spinoza has garnered a more or less continuous stream of attention since the institutionalization of academic philosophy in the late modern period, and twentieth-century France is no exception to a trend that spans multiple national cultures. Key figures include Sylvain Zac and Robert Misrahi, both of whom published important assessments in the postwar period that focused on Spinoza's moral and religious writings, precisely those aspects of his thought overlooked in the reception that is the focus here.[17] And while Léon Brunschvicg, a towering figure of Third Republic philosophy, plays an important role in what follows, his contemporary Victor Delbos, who authored two major studies of Spinoza, receives no attention.[18] The most striking absence to readers familiar with the field will be Alexandre Matheron, whose book *Individu et communauté chez Spinoza* is often cited alongside Gueroult and Deleuze's major studies as helping to usher in a "Spinoza Renaissance" in France at the end of the 1960s.[19]

The issue of genre partly explains these omissions. With the possible exception of Martial Gueroult, none of the authors covered in this book could be regarded as "Spinoza specialists." Rather, they are thinkers for whom aspects of Spinoza's thought played an instrumental role in their own projects. Beyond the specialists, however, it will also be noted that there is no engagement with the works of Étienne Balibar, Pierre Macherey, or Antonio Negri, the Italian Marxist whose writings on Spinoza came to form a core component of contemporary French Spinozism.[20] The rationale for neglecting these important figures is at once historical and theoretical. In the first place, it's true that, following upon the open secret of Spinoza's importance to Althusser and his students, the near-simultaneous publication of Gueroult, Matheron, and Deleuze's studies helped bring about an efflorescence of political engagements with Spinoza's thought that persists in France to this day.[21] The intensity of this shift alone marks it as the beginning of a separate story, although the sheer volume of scholarship it has generated would also make writing an intelligible history of this contemporary period very difficult. More important is the genuine transformation in the content of Spinozism that accompanies this turn and that points to the substantive reasons for terminating the inquiry at this point. For it is only after 1968 that Spinoza's political writings and the later sections of the *Ethics*, containing his writings on affect and emotion, begin to merit wider attention in France. Zac's works notwithstanding, prior to

1968 Spinoza is a rationalist metaphysician and epistemologist. The relevant texts of his corpus are the first two books of the *Ethics*, containing his foundational metaphysics of substance and his theory of the mind or soul, and his incomplete early writing, the *Treatise on the Emendation of the Intellect*, a popular text for French philosophy exams due to its incomplete nature and its status as a foil to Descartes' *Discourse on Method*.

To be sure, Spinoza's other writings begin to get a hearing largely because of the success with which Althusser and Deleuze reestablished his philosophical importance. But the tools that Althusser and Deleuze used to do this were inherited from a previous generation of thinkers who first used Spinoza's rationalism to combat the influence of phenomenology in philosophy of science and the history of philosophy as a discipline. Beginning with the foundational work of Jean Cavaillès, the first three chapters tell the story of how and why Spinozism came to be seen as a privileged intellectual resource for demonstrating the nominally "irrationalist" tendencies of phenomenology. Specialists in early modern metaphysics may be familiar with Ferdinand Alquié and Martial Gueroult as authors of seminal works on Descartes, Spinoza, Leibniz, and Malebranche. And although Cavaillès is beginning to procure an intrepid readership keen to understand the role played by the philosophy of mathematics in recent French thought, his student Jean-Toussaint Desanti has garnered scarcely any attention beyond the hexagon.[22] By and large, these philosophers remain unknown quantities to an Anglophone audience. Consequently, the chapters that detail the uses of Spinozism in their thought also serve as more general introductions to their ideas and projects.

The second part of the book looks at the ways that two very familiar thinkers, Althusser and Deleuze, deepened and began to develop the broader implications of this work. In this regard, their efforts form the hinge that connects the history recounted in this book with contemporary Spinozism. But their efforts were not the same effort, and the discrepancies between the transformations they wrought in Spinozism have had lasting effects.

With Althusser, we witness the ne plus ultra of a rationalist resistance to phenomenology. To be sure, Marxism serves as the terrain on which Althusser will draw his line in the sand, but the substance of his argument is consonant with variants of Spinozist rationalism developed elsewhere by Cavaillès and Gueroult. Where their concerns were, for lack of a better word, academic, in Althusser's intransigence we find a rationalist critique of any political thought grounded in phenomenology, an intransigence shaped and politicized to a degree by the negative example of Desanti, an underappreciated figure in the development of Althusser's thought. In breaking with various precedents internal to French Marxism, Althusser's intransigence paves the way to the theoretical exhaustion of Marxism as a positive political platform, to the extent that it offers no constructive, much less programmatic, guidance for a transformative political agenda. As an alibi for his bravura, Althusser liked to cite Lenin's remark that when a stick has become warped, sometimes excessive force is required to straighten it out.[23] I want to suggest that, in applying this force, he broke the stick. But given that the stick in question was an eschatological Marxism, the results were eminently salutary. For if it was mainly a series of historical events that steered French intellectuals away from Marxism into various "post-Marxisms,"[24] it was Althusser's theoretical project that brokered a significant reworking of Marxism among intellectuals reluctant to jettison the Marxist tradition altogether—not just theoretically but politically. In other words, if Althusser's Marxism was a "failure," it was a glorious one. Philosophically robust, it ushered in a variety of projects, acting as an inspiration in some cases and a provocation in others.[25]

With Deleuze, the story is different. Whereas Althusser endowed Spinozism with a political valence that was thoroughly negative and antiprogrammatic, Deleuze fundamentally transformed the philosophical meaning of Spinozism in the French context and, more than any other thinker, ushered in the vitalist Spinoza—the Spinoza of affect—that has become the dominant Spinoza in the humanities today. Deleuze's place at the end of this inquiry is thus not simply a consequence of chronology. Rather, if the guiding thread of this book concerns an antagonism between Spinozism and phenomenology, the ultimate significance of Deleuze is that his metaphysics achieves a synthesis—a disjunctive synthesis, in his vernacular—that finally brings these strands together. Indeed, Deleuze's philosophical project in the 1960s, which culminates in his major work *Difference and Repetition*, is precisely to develop a post-Heideggerian rationalism that does not simply evade Heidegger's critique of metaphysics but accounts for Heidegger's ontology in turn. The resultant system purports to describe a scenario that is more fundamental than Heidegger's fundamental ontology, the "groundless ground" of Spinozan Substance. In Foucault's oft-cited discussion of an opposition between philosophies of consciousness and of the concept in twentieth-century French thought—an opposition first conceived by Cavaillès and later glossed by Elisabeth Roudinesco as Cartesians versus Spinozists—he also suggests his generation saw as its task to overcome this opposition.[26] We also know that elsewhere Foucault remarked, in a fawning if no doubt jocular vein, that "perhaps one day the century will be known as Deleuzian."[27] If it was Deleuzian, its philosophical content lay in this reconciliation. This explains, too, why the Spinozism recounted in this book bears a critical relation to contemporary Spinozism. Grounded as much of it is in Deleuze's thought, Spinozism today contains elements of the very Heideggerianism that was targeted by the Spinozists of a previous generation.[28]

Making this case, which goes against a prevalent notion that Deleuze is opposed to Heidegger when he is not simply indifferent to him, requires an extensive engagement with the details of Deleuze's philosophical arguments, just as it requires attention to the care with which Spinoza's earlier partisans developed their uses of his thought. It might be justly wondered, if Heidegger is an important condition for Deleuze's thought, then why does he not number among the heroes of Deleuze's counterhistory of philosophy, one that runs from Duns Scotus, via Spinoza, Hume, and Nietzsche on to Bergson? Here context is key. For even if Deleuze felt "bludgeoned to death" by the history of philosophy as an academic institution,[29] the questions and concerns he brought to these unsung heroes were shaped by his quintessentially French philosophical education and the same shock wave of phenomenology that galvanized the rest of his generation. To put it bluntly, Deleuze's counterhistory of philosophy is something of a red herring, and his own remarks about the acts of ventriloquism that informed his writings in the history of philosophy are perhaps best taken with less salt than his colorful descriptions of philosophical "buggery" might otherwise suggest. It could be that reading Deleuze in this way somehow compromises his singularity. But this seems a small price to pay to emphasize his exemplarity. By focusing on Deleuze's metaphysics, and taking seriously his own lack of compunction in describing what he does as metaphysics, this book contributes to a growing appreciation for the substance, ambition, and depth of Deleuze's philosophy. To be sure, the "Capitalism and Schizophrenia" project that he coauthored with Félix Guattari remains an important moment in French political thought, one that continues to pay dividends in a variety of projects. But as Guattari becomes increasingly regarded as the main political force in the pairing, the one who gave political teeth to a metaphysical rethinking of power and desire in dispersed interpersonal terms, Deleuze is acquiring a hearing as a philosopher whose commitment to abstraction is regarded less as a liability than a source of theoretical fecundity far beyond the political fortunes of "desiring machines" and nomadic "lines of flight."

As for Althusser, to decouple, even for heuristic purposes, his philosophical thought from his political agenda—a move that runs contrary to some of his own pronouncements on the matter—requires a sustained inquiry into his arguments if it is to be justified. If Althusser's philosophy is irreducible to his Communist commitments, it must be demonstrably so. But such a case is plausible only in light of the renewed hearing that Althusser is receiving today. Indeed, if a reception shift is discernible in estimations of Deleuze, with Althusser the shift is even more dramatic. Multiple reasons account for this change, not least the outpouring of publications from his archive that yield a fuller picture of his intellectual project and its development. The continued importance of the work of his students and collaborators—from Badiou to Balibar—also elevates Althusser's status. The irony is that as Althusser becomes a more historical figure, his thought becomes more relevant. It also becomes amenable to a more sober assessment, for arguably no other thinker in recent French thought has been as controversial as Althusser. First is the defining tragedy of his personal life: the murder of his wife, Hélène Legotien, during a psychotic episode in the autumn of 1980, an event that Althusser describes in harrowing detail in his memoir, *The Future Lasts Forever*. The second factor was his continued allegiance to the French Communist Party (PCF) at a time when its project seemed bankrupt and the deference to Soviet apologetics that his membership implied struck many as unconscionable. Adding insult to injury was the fact that just as Eastern European dissidents were invoking the language of humanism and various other themes of the "early Marx" for their cause, Althusser was targeting humanism as the philosophical enemy. Charges of Althusser's "Stalinism" are reflective of this context for his reception in the Anglophone world, a context shaped both by a more general notion of "Western Marxism" opposed to the Leninist legacy and a dissidence movement that sought to put paid to the travesty of "really existing socialism."[30]

Historical distance has tempered this assessment of Althusser in myriad ways. It has become clear that, if hostile reactions abroad to Althusser's antihumanism are intelligible only in light of the local vicissitudes of a more general crisis of Marxism in the 1960s and 1970s, the gestation of Althusser's ideas on the subject are intelligible only in light of the specific and admittedly insular context in which they developed: the space of postwar French philosophy and the internecine quarrels of French party politics. Recent work has focused on the internal debates of the PCF that shaped Althusser's interventions, and editors of Althusser's posthumous publications have helpfully situated these writings and others in the context of various institutions of French philosophy.[31] At the summit of these developments is Warren Montag's remarkable *Althusser and His Contemporaries*, which has set a new standard of interpretation for Althusser's work. Montag's title suggests the point: Althusser makes sense and remains relevant only in light of a contextual determination of his thought, one that places it alongside other tendencies and developments in French philosophy. Althusser's Spinozism is no exception in this regard.

As for the calamity of Althusser's personal life, no amount of hand-wringing or schadenfreude would suffice to establish a relationship between this event and Althusser's philosophy. Althusser's lifelong struggle with manic depression is a matter of record, and the facts of the event and its aftermath, which resulted in no trial and Althusser's being committed to a mental hospital for an extensive period, are not disputed. The analysis of Althusser's thought in this book presumes no relation between his ideas and this tragedy, which raises the question of why it is important to bring something up only to insist that is irrelevant. First, and most basically, the endnotes did not seem an appropriate place to speak about Hélène Legotien's death. But if the event is not relevant to the contents of Althusser's thought, it is certainly relevant to the vagaries of its reception. Given that Althusser's reception history is embroiled with his personal biography, in a way that is not the case, for example, with twentieth-century receptions of Spinoza, the key factors of that biography are all relevant for making sense of the initial reception and consequently for the different reception that Althusser is getting today. That he killed his wife is typically the first or second biographical fact that new readers learn about him and fades in relevance for making sense of his thought and commitment to Marxism alongside other biographical factors, for example, his upbringing in Algeria, his experiences as a foot soldier and prisoner of war, and the particulars of his position as a student and later instructor at the École Normale Supérieure.

These biographical factors are certainly germane to understanding the origins of Althusser's political commitments and theoretical investments. But there is a difference between understanding ideas and understanding where they came from, however much the one may illuminate the other. This distinction is operative in this book and leads on to one final rationale for its method and structure, and for its focus on philosophical argument.

Like many disciplines, intellectual history thrives on internal debates about its methodology. That said, it is easily observed that methods tend to become incoherent the moment they become articulated as such. While this book has some "contextualist" elements—contextualist in the dual sense that it considers both how thinkers worked with inherited discourses and how they were responsive to institutional and political pressures (including the pressures of "academic politics")[32]—the arguments it pursues are basically "internalist," in the sense that the real drama of this history takes place in the theoretical efforts of the Spinozists in question. This means taking arguments seriously as arguments, irrespective of the ostensible purposes for which they may have been initiated or fashioned.

Not coincidentally, this kind of internalism, which insists that philosophical arguments have an integrity and transmissibility that are irreducible to their context, biographical motives, or strategic purposes, also has its own Spinozist imprimatur, for few philosophers in the canon are as ahistorical as Spinoza. Indeed, this was Hegel's fundamental grief against Spinoza, whose most pointed injunction was to see things "under the aspect of eternity." Writing the intellectual history of Spinozism thus results in a dilemma. The dilemma is not so much that historicizing Spinoza's ideas necessarily betrays them, for there are many ways to historicize. One way, the one Jonathan Israel has pursued in his gargantuan history of the Radical Enlightenment, is to take Spinoza's word as gospel and to catalogue its dissemination. Another way is to regard Spinoza's ideas as exemplary of a recurrent challenge to orthodoxy, one that needs to be either resisted or endorsed wherever it arises.[33] Still another is to treat Spinozism as a kind of floating signifier that serves as a vehicle for various ideological commitments. The more sophisticated versions of this approach—such as the one Marion flirts with—ground this pliability in Spinoza's ostensibly monistic metaphysics; if everything is in everything else, then Spinozism can mean anything—because it all means the same thing in the end.

This book takes its subjects' philosophical engagement with Spinoza very seriously. In fact, it considers this engagement to be the substance of the history in question. The philosophers under consideration here spent the lion's share of their professional lives thinking, so to write the history of what they were doing is to write the history of their thinking. This requires using the available means of the historical record—correspondence, institutional data, private notes, and public performances—but it means focusing mainly on the texts in which their ideas took form and were expressed. But to take this thinking seriously also requires that it be approached sympathetically rather than skeptically or, to put it even more emphatically, enthusiastically rather than suspiciously. It means taking seriously a conviction shared by all the protagonists of this volume—that in the end philosophical arguments are regarded as persuasive not because they seem useful but because they seem right.

. . .

Here, however, we alight on the driving tension of the narrative: the desire nevertheless to derive something useful from a philosophy that seems to be correct. For with the exception of the dispute between Alquié and Gueroult, which serves as a kind of abstract distillation of the philosophical disagreement at the heart of the story, each valorization of Spinozist rationalism is accompanied by a problematic attempt to generate a politics out of this rationalism. In the case of Cavaillès, the effort to derive a politics is not his own but that of his theoretical inheritors. With Desanti, it is more properly speaking the struggle between Spinozism and phenomenology that plays a role in his shifting political convictions. Althusser's effort has been noted, but in regard to Deleuze, suffice it to say that, prior to his collaboration with Guattari, the political implications of his arguments were by and large held in abeyance or obscurely encoded in his arguments. Taken together, what these episodes suggest is that using Spinozism to identify the troubling political consequences of phenomenology—which are deemed to be consequential to its philosophical inconsistencies—winds up producing no positive alternative of its own. The consequence of this follows in an almost syllogistic way. If Spinozism is regarded by these thinkers as the most compelling rationalism available, and if it generates no politics, it suggests that a compelling rationalism is not equipped to generate a politics. What it is especially well equipped to do, evidently, is to reveal the problems that result from any effort to derive a politics from a philosophy, especially but not exclusively, when that philosophy is a phenomenological ontology. Continental philosophy has been bridled for several generations by efforts to comprehend how such a gripping philosophy—Heidegger's—could be complicit with such troubling ends. Shielding the insights of Heidegger's thought from political instrumentalization has consequently become something of an imperative.[34] Yet when it comes to Spinozism, it is evidently unnecessary to shield philosophy from its political instrumentalization; the philosophy does it for us.

This claim must seem bizarre in light of the proliferation of Spinozisms today, with their variously liberal and emancipatory inflections. It seems to be a lesson one can draw from the philosophical efforts recounted in this book all the same. To argue that Spinoza's rationalism—his metaphysics and epistemology as they were understood in this specific context—entails no politics is not to suggest that Spinoza did not write many cogent things about politics. His political treatises are rightly acquiring the place in the history of political thought they deserve.[35] But it is to suggest that Spinoza's philosophy can be used to undermine the pretensions of any mode of political thought that seeks a metaphysical foundation—even if that metaphysics is Spinoza's. Such a formulation no doubt tests the boundaries between the paradoxical and the obnoxious, and there is little to be gained in attempting to justify it in advance. Kant shunned Spinozism because it "leads directly to enthusiasm." Consequently, his critique erected roadblocks to a concept of reason that "transgresses all boundaries" in search of a shortcut to the absolute. It is ironic, then, that the history of Spinozism suggests the virtues of a more circuitous route. Perhaps this is what Spinoza himself meant when, following upon scores of definitions, axioms, and digressions, he concluded his *Ethics* with the proposition that "beatitude is not the reward of virtue, but virtue itself."[36]

1

From Consciousness to the Concept

The Spinozism of Jean Cavaillès

> Scientific faith, which is an active faith, can take Spinoza as its precursor, its model, its prophet.
>
> Gaston Bachelard, "Physique et métaphysique," 1933[1]

The history of Spinozism's critical relationship to phenomenology in twentieth-century French thought properly begins with Jean Cavaillès for two reasons. As a philosopher of mathematics, Cavaillès was attuned to modern developments in the mathematical sciences that posed a challenge to philosophical accounts of transcendental subjectivity grounded in a priori theories of consciousness or intuition. The mathematics of the transfinite inaugurated in the late nineteenth century by Georg Cantor's set theory produced a conceptually operative account of the infinite and its function in mathematical sequences. For the most part, mathematicians working in Cantor's wake relied more on conceptual demonstration than empirically grounded insights. Post-Cantorian mathematics proved its theoretical mettle in the physical sciences, but it remained a conundrum for philosophers in that it showed the utility and apparent truth content of a mode of rational thought that was not only irreducible to but by and large incommensurable with an intuitive grasp of lived experience. Cavaillès, who was born in 1903, was one of the first French philosophers to consider this problem, and his efforts to work through the implications of transfinite mathematics involved an extensive and critical engagement with Husserl's phenomenology throughout the interwar years. In the course of this engagement, Cavaillès invoked Spinoza's rationalism as a potential antidote to the excessive reliance on a concept of consciousness, or *cogito*, in Husserl's effort. In the final work of his attenuated career, Cavaillès concluded that "it is not a philosophy of consciousness, but a philosophy of the concept that can yield a doctrine of science."[2] With this statement, Cavaillès effectively codified Spinozism as a rationalist alternative to phenomenology, thus setting the terms for the critical confrontation to be explored over the following chapters.

The contents of Cavaillès's philosophical thought are the first reason for his inaugural status in this study. The second concerns why his project was attenuated. In addition to being one of the leading philosophical minds of his generation, Cavaillès was one of the most active leaders in the French Resistance during the Second World War. He was called up for military service as an officer in 1939 and was captured during the German invasion of France in June 1940. He escaped from prison later that summer and returned to the University of Strasbourg, which had been moved to Clermont-Ferrand as a result of the Occupation, to resume his duties as a professor of philosophy. In the autumn of 1940, Cavaillès founded, along with Emmanuel d'Astier de la Vigerie, the Resistance movement Libération-Sud, which was designed to combat and destabilize the Vichy government in the south of France. In 1941, he was called to the Sorbonne in Paris to serve as a professor of philosophy and logic. Once there, Cavaillès made contact with the then barely existent group Libération-Nord, serving as a kind of emissary for Libération-Sud. While employed as a professor at the Sorbonne, and thus in full public view, Cavaillès took on a range of pseudonyms and conducted a series of clandestine missions throughout France. He was arrested in Narbonne in September 1942 and imprisoned by Vichy authorities. In December he escaped again and made his way back to Paris before undertaking a mission to London, where he sought to intervene in the political quarrels among the Resistance leadership in order to demand more focus on strategy. In the months after his return to France in the spring of 1943, Cavaillès took on a greater role in military action himself; among his many missions was a particularly dangerous operation wherein he placed and detonated a series of hidden explosives in the German submarine base at Lorient, on the Atlantic coast of Brittany. In September 1943, Cavaillès was arrested as he was walking along the boulevard Saint-Michel in Paris. After a series of efforts on his behalf by sympathetic countrymen who were collaborating with the Germans, Cavaillès was judged and sentenced to death on February 17, 1944, whereupon he was immediately executed by a firing squad.[3]

While in London, Cavaillès met with other French intellectuals who were taking part in the struggle against Nazism in one capacity or another, such as Simone Weil and Raymond Aron. In a preface written for a posthumous collection of Cavaillès's writings, Aron recounts a memorable exchange in London with his erstwhile classmate at the École Normale Supérieure (ENS). Whereas others invoked partisan imperatives, be they communist, socialist, or democratic, to justify their Resistance activity or pointed instead to a general notion of national honor, for Cavaillès the Resistance was simply a question of necessity: "'I'm a Spinozist,' he said; 'we must resist, fight, and confront death. Truth and reason demand it.'"[4] This was Aron's recollection in 1963. In December 1945, Aron had relayed the same conversation in a commemorative ceremony for Cavaillès at the Sorbonne. Cavaillès told Aron, "I'm a Spinozist; I believe we submit to the necessary everywhere. The sequences of the mathematicians are necessary; even the [historical] stages of mathematical science are necessary. This struggle that we carry out is necessary as well."[5]

In recounting these words, Aron manages the peculiar feat of politicizing and depoliticizing Cavaillès's moral example in the same stroke. On the one hand, Aron connects Cavaillès's heroism to his philosophical Spinozism. Just as Cavaillès believed, following Spinoza, that rational thought was governed by necessity regardless of whether or not a thinking individual was cognizant of it, so, too, did he describe his commitment to struggling against the Occupation. On the other hand, Aron explicitly decouples Cavaillès's example from politics—"be they communist, socialist, or democratic"—by insisting that Cavaillès was an exceptional figure who thought necessity "had command over practical imperatives as well as scientific propositions."[6] In effect, then, Aron explains Cavaillès's heroism in terms of his Spinozism, even as he also evacuates that Spinozism of any specific political content. Cavaillès was exceptional precisely because his motives were not "political." This is a politics that is logical and pure; in a word, it is above politics.

If Cavaillès the philosopher is responsible for figuring Spinozism as a rationalist alternative to phenomenology in the French context, his actions and fate are responsible for imbuing Spinozism with an ambiguous political valence. Despite eschewing references to "national honor," Aron's account clearly ties Cavaillès's heroism to the republican ideal as something worth dying for. A child of the Third Republic who was deeply influenced by its leading intellectual defenders, Cavaillès fought to preserve the French nation-state and the abstract ideal it incarnated. His actions were conservative in this limited sense. In later years, however, the idea of Cavaillès as a historical character will come to be expressive of the desire that there be a prescriptive or revolutionary politics of Spinozism, or if not Spinozism per se, of rationalism and a commitment to formalism and logic that is at the very least inspired by Spinoza. Indeed, Cavaillès has been a touchstone for radical French thinkers from Althusser to Foucault to Badiou.[7] In each instance, there is the intimation of a link between Cavaillès's philosophy, which, to be clear, was in no way a political theory, and his manifest heroism in the face of death. But even when Cavaillès is invoked, no political content is ascribed to his example. At best there is an allusive equivocation between Nazi forces of Occupation and the contemporary enemies of the political left. In other words, Cavaillès's Spinozist commitment to necessity merely gives the form of Resistance and the contours of tenacity. Yet, because Cavaillès was philosophically opposed to philosophies of consciousness, it is as if one might perform a logical deduction that then establishes the political superiority of a philosophy of the concept to the proliferation of subject-centered philosophies of meaning that followed upon the arrival of phenomenology in France.[8]

The mobilization of Cavaillès's example against philosophies of consciousness is one of the main themes of Georges Canguilhem's *Vie et mort de Jean Cavaillès*, a short book that best illustrates the ambiguities of Cavaillès's legacy. First published in 1976, this volume is a collection of three commemorative talks Canguilhem gave in 1967, 1969, and 1974. Though its contents are primarily exercises in hagiography, they also advance a set of arguments. On each occasion, Canguilhem describes Cavaillès's increasing hostility to Husserl's philosophy and "its exorbitant use of the *Cogito*" in terms of a growing attachment to Spinozism.[9] "It is because Spinoza's philosophy represents the most radical attempt at a philosophy without *Cogito* that it is so close to Cavaillès's." But Canguilhem goes much further and connects Cavaillès's affinity for Spinozist necessity to his political fate as a "Resistant *by logic*." "Cavaillès always read, studied, and one could say practiced Spinoza," Canguilhem writes. More suggestive still is Canguilhem's take on Simone Weil's misgivings over the fact that Cavaillès appeared "to have abolished the intellectual in himself" in favor of pure action. In Canguilhem's view, Cavaillès's severity was the result of philosophical rigor. His words and decisions were not those of a lapsed intellectual; they were those of "a Spinozist mathematician who conceived action under a certain aspect of universality, of nonsubjectivity, we might say." Speaking in 1969, Canguilhem refers to the contemporary "cries of indignation" on the part of those distressed to see that some "have formed the idea of a philosophy without a personal subject." Cavaillès's example evidently puts paid to the claims of other "intellectual resistants who talk about themselves so much because only they can talk about their Resistance, discreet as it was." "Jean Cavaillès, this is the logic of Resistance lived until death. Let the philosophers of existence and the person do as well next time if they can."[10]

With conclusions like this, Canguilhem's commemorative efforts indulge something akin to the rationalist fanaticism that Kant feared. There is indeed a degree of violence in Canguilhem's description of Cavaillès as "a philosopher mathematician packed with explosives, a lucid temerity, and a resolution without optimism. If this is not a hero, what is?" Cavaillès's tenacity has "something terrifying" about it: "A philosopher terrorist, that's Cavaillès." To be sure, the rhetorical register of Canguilhem's speeches must be borne in mind. Even so, concurrent with his evocations of a Cavaillèsian *Schwärmerei*, there is, perhaps fittingly, also a case made for the universality of reason. Canguilhem cites Cavaillès's own description of *Mein Kampf*, which he read in Germany in 1934, as a pathetic exercise in "pseudo-philosophy." "As for myself," Canguilhem adds, "I prefer 'counter-philosophy' insofar as the principle of this systematization, which was improvised to achieve a kind of collective conditioning, consisted in hate and the absolute refusal of the universal." This view is further elaborated in another instance: "Nazism was unacceptable insofar as it was the negation, savage rather than scientific, of universality, insofar as it announced and sought the end of rational philosophy. The struggle against the *unacceptable* was thus *ineluctable*."[11]

Canguilhem's remarks about the universality of reason against the historical advent of Nazism acquire a deeper sense when they are considered in light of the long-standing critique of Hegelianism that informed his own philosophical work. In a 1948 review of Jean Hyppolite's translation of the

Phenomenology of Spirit, Canguilhem also makes reference to Cavaillès's fate.[12] He considers the consequences if we were to read the defeat of France by Nazi forces in June 1940 as "the Judgment of the World" in the Hegelian sense. In this reading, Cavaillès's Resistance would then be understood as the refusal of this "Judgment." But, Canguilhem asks, were Cavaillès's refusal and ultimate death undertaken "in order to verify the Negativity of History or in order to overcome History with Reason?"[13] It is clear that Canguilhem thinks in terms of the latter formula. If "History" might explain the advent of Nazism, just as it accounted for Napoleon's arrival in Jena, then what explains Cavaillès is the force of reason *against* history.

It is this subtle critique of "History" as a metaphysical and political warrant that gives Canguilhem's commemoration a peculiar twist. For even as he celebrates Cavaillès in no uncertain terms, he also limits the political lessons that might be taken from his example by refusing to tether Cavaillès's fate to anything other than a resistance to the historical negation of "reason." Canguilhem reads Cavaillès's comments on mathematics' relationship to physics in these terms. In Amersfoot in 1938, Cavaillès remarked: "Whatever the importance of physics' suggestions for the positing of new mathematical problems and the edification of new theories, the authentic development of mathematics under the accidents of history is oriented by an internal dialectic of notions." Canguilhem develops the implications of this downplaying of the "accidents of history" as follows:

> Cavaillès thus refuses in advance the interpretation that Marxist philosophers of good will, and no doubt good faith, have wanted to give the last sentence of the posthumous text, *Sur la logique et la théorie de la science*, as if, by invoking a dialectic of concepts, Cavaillès had brought the water to the mill of this dialectic that makes all thought, including mathematics, arise from the sensible world. [...] According to Cavaillès, the development of a mathematical essence owes nothing to existence.[14]

Although Canguilhem's assessment of the efforts of Althusser and his collaborators is questionable—after all, their goal was to move beyond the vulgar base to superstructure model invoked here—the point is clear enough. Reason is not in the service of History, and it is not History that accomplishes Reason's tasks for it. Much as Aron placed Cavaillès's Resistance "above" politics, Canguilhem places it "outside" history. The valorization of the universality of reason against its attempted historical negation by Nazism is Canguilhem's main polemic point. It is surely ludicrous, if not obscene, to suggest that there is a rational necessity that "elected" Cavaillès to resist and determined others to collaborate or perish. What Canguilhem aims to illustrate, however, is that reason cannot be reduced to a historical agenda. This suggests that it is irreducible to a political one as well, if politics is to be understood as a means for accomplishing goals attributed to History or any other external criterion that might bring the essential "water" to the "mill" of social existence. That there remains an air of elitism, if not "election," in Canguilhem's portrait of Cavaillès is in fact perfectly consistent with the latter's Spinozism. For Spinoza recognized that viewing existence "under the aspect of eternity," that is, *not* of history, was a difficult task. But "all things excellent are as difficult as they are rare."[15]

Cavaillès's example, as digested and presented by Canguilhem, thus presents a host of problems, rather than solutions, concerning what the political and ethical implications of a Spinozist "philosophy of the concept" might in fact be. If the sources of the slogan within Cavaillès's work were narrow and technical, however, its broader significance for French philosophy becomes clear in a historical perspective. In Cavaillès's work, the sense of Spinozism transforms from an idiosyncratic feature of French neo-Kantianism to a key resource in the battle against phenomenology and its apparently solipsistic and irrationalist tendencies. Appreciating this historical development thus requires a grasp of Cavaillès's theoretical concerns and investments. In this regard, coming to terms with Cavaillès's Spinozist hostility to phenomenology in its original discursive context—a context that was thoroughly based in the philosophy of mathematics—allows us to develop an at once critical and historical perspective on others' attempts to mobilize his example for their own political ends, academic or otherwise.

What follows begins with a reconstruction of Cavaillès's intellectual itinerary as a student, which will show how his early exposure to Husserl's ideas conflicted with the rationalism he had absorbed from Léon Brunschvicg. Indeed, the roots of Cavaillès's Spinozism lay in elements of Brunschvicg's teaching. But as Cavaillès pursues his engagement with set theoretical mathematics, his Spinozist rationalism sharpens and results in a move away from Brunschvicg's neo-Kantianism and the historical philosophy of consciousness that it promotes. With a sense of Cavaillès's philosophical investments established, the chapter concludes with a close reading of his most lasting philosophical statement, *Sur la logique et la théorie de la science*, a text written in prison in the winter of 1942. Here, Cavaillès's effort culminates in the call for a Spinozist philosophy of the concept that can supervene on Husserl's phenomenology, in which Cavaillès ultimately finds the same solipsism that compromised Kant's philosophy of science and that of his neo-Kantian avatars.

Philosophy and Mathematics: Husserl, Brunschvicg, Spinoza

The Allure of Phenomenology

The reception of phenomenology in France has done much to obscure its origins in a philosophical consideration of modern mathematics and its relationship to science.[16] The first French article on Husserl's thought, written in 1911 by Victor Delbos, amounted to a summary of Husserl's critique of psychologism in the *Logical Investigations* and focused primarily on the restoration of objective science portended there.[17] However, the first French book concerning Husserl's new method was Jean Hering's *Phénoménologie et philosophie religieuse* in 1926. The early appearance of this volume suggests that, *pace* Dominique Janicaud, French phenomenology was not devoid of a theological register from the outset.[18] Beyond the bibliographic record, the anecdotes concerning phenomenology's arrival in Paris are manifold. Virtually all attest to phenomenology's complicated liaison with French traditions and other imports, such as existentialism and Marxism, from the outset. Alexandre Kojève's Hegel seminar of the 1930s delivered to a French audience the three H's—Hegel, Husserl, and Heidegger—in one politically charged package.[19] But Kojève's audience was an eager one, its appetite whetted by earlier whiffs of Husserlian phenomenology that had found their way into the hexagon. Simone de Beauvoir recounted in her memoirs Sartre's joy in 1932 at finding a method that would allow him to make philosophy out of a cocktail glass; according to de Beauvoir, he dove into Emmanuel Levinas's book on Husserl as he exited the bookstore, before the pages were cut.[20] Stories also abound from the celebrated Davos encounter in 1929 between Ernst Cassirer and Heidegger, where young emissaries from France were amazed at the success with which Heidegger dismantled the presuppositions of his neo-Kantian interlocutor.[21]

One might plausibly locate phenomenology's official debut in France in the winter of 1928–29. Brunschvicg invited Husserl to deliver a series of lectures at the Sorbonne under the aegis of the Institut d'études germaniques and the Société française de philosophie. These lectures were to serve as "an introduction to phenomenology" for a French audience, and Husserl's choice of subject matter was ultimately prophetic in this regard. The "Cartesian Meditations" ensured that German phenomenology would serve less as a riposte to the limits of Descartes' philosophy than as testimony to its enduring legacy as the dominant mode of rationalist thought in modern France.[22]

That Husserl's invitation would come from Brunschvicg is ironic, given that the latter's neo-Kantianism would come to be crushed under the volume of innovative French work that followed phenomenology's arrival. In 1932, Paul Nizan, skeptical though he was of phenomenology, set his sights on Brunschvicg in his excoriation of bourgeois republicanism in philosophy, *Les Chiens de garde*. Numerous French intellectuals followed Nizan's lead in turning their backs on neo-Kantianism, chief among them Sartre and de Beauvoir, along with Maurice Merleau-Ponty, Jean Hyppolite, and Raymond Queneau.[23] But it should not be surprising that Brunschvicg's interest was piqued by Husserl's project, despite the former's reputation as a nationalist in philosophy. Brunschvicg was a notorious assimilator of competing philosophical projects; that he cited Kant and Spinoza as his two primary authorities is testimony to this trait.[24] Husserl's project was attractive to Brunschvicg because it proposed to maintain for philosophy a foundational role as eidetic science. His attraction was nonetheless mitigated by a certain skepticism, which had been stimulated by his friendship with Alexandre Koyré.[25] Koyré saw phenomenology as the superior fruition of the philosophical methodology portended by Henri Bergson, Brunschvicg's philosophical nemesis. That Husserl presented his own project as a renewal of Descartes' was thus comforting to Brunschvicg, for whom rationalism was a fundamental philosophical precept.

According to the phenomenological movement's official historian the French philosophical establishment in fact responded rather coolly to Husserl's "Paris Lectures."[26] All the same, Brunschvicg's invitation of Husserl opened a Pandora's box in Paris. For example, Merleau-Ponty attended Husserl's lectures, although he did not yet know German, and he found in them inspiration for reconciling a transcendental methodology with the concrete world of perception.[27] French philosophy largely assimilated imports from its neighbor, and Merleau-Ponty's reaction was no exception. While his efforts to articulate a phenomenology of perception based in embodied experience bore an existential cast and were averse to idealism, they were, like Husserl's lectures, more an internal critique of Descartes' legacy than a rejection of it. Phenomenology provoked a reconsideration of the *cogito* in myriad ways, most of which were conceived as "concrete" alternatives to the idealist consciousness of neo-Kantianism. This movement toward the concrete resonated with a more general crisis of political identity in interwar-years France and the search for political alternatives to the abstractions of republicanism.[28]

Whereas many French auditors were apparently indifferent to the idealist turn of Husserl's thought, Cavaillès was fully cognizant of Husserl's reliance on the figure of the *cogito* as a crucial component of his methodology's infrastructure. Like Merleau-Ponty, Cavaillès heard in the Paris Lectures "a warmth and simplicity of the true philosopher."[29] Yet what Cavaillès detected in Husserl was not an overcoming of Cartesian idealism through a radicalization of Descartes' project; instead, he heard the sketch of a methodology that preserved Descartes' original errors. Although Husserl pointed to the insufficiency of Cartesian doubt and criticized Descartes for his refusal to follow through with his own logic to include the doubting subject itself, he maintained with Descartes that any transcendental grounding of philosophy must begin with an interrogation of the knowing subject. Even as Husserl reconceived the concept of philosophical evidence as that which is apodictic, in other words unassailable and immediately graspable, he nonetheless located the site of apodicticity *in* the field demarcated by the subject's consciousness. To be sure, Husserl's conscious subject is distinct from the Cartesian one because it is marked by its constitutive intentionality; in Husserl's vocabulary, "noetic" consciousness as act is always in an intentional relationship with a "noematic" object. That an object was not a given but instead something constituted was an attractive idea for Cavaillès, who saw mathematics as a theoretically generative activity. But Husserl's emphasis on the phenomenological regard or gaze as the determinant pole in the process of constitutive intentionality effectively put the cart before the horse in Cavaillès's view. Husserl's logical investigations, taken alongside his Cartesian meditations, did nothing to secure the rational integrity of mathematical objects, even as they helped to explain their origins. Whereas the logical positivists could account for logic's necessity but not its genesis, Husserl, like Kant and Descartes before him, could account for its genesis but not its necessity.[30] For Cavaillès, Husserl's move toward the transcendental ego, far from securing knowledge against the threats of psychologistic relativism, threatened it even more by accentuating—in spite of Husserl's own intentions—the absolute *contingency* of apodictic certainty over the intrinsic *necessity* of the rationality it sought to establish.[31]

The spring of 1929 was a heady time for Cavaillès. In the weeks following Husserl's talks, he accepted the ENS director Celestin Bouglé's offer to send him and other young French scholars along with Brunschvicg to Davos, Switzerland, for a meeting of German and French philosophers.[32] Attending Davos was a formative event for Cavaillès, in that it led to the struggle with phenomenology that would mark the rest of his brief career.[33] His formal recounting of the proceedings was diplomatic and emphasized the convivial "spirit of Locarno" that permeated them.[34] He observed that although the meeting made clear "a persistence of the spirit of national identity in the Universities, [. . .] French rationalist reflection and German phenomenology are expressed in the same spiritual universe."[35] He admitted that he found the confrontation between Cassirer and Heidegger "hard to follow."[36] Still, he recognized the seductiveness of Heidegger's arguments and the historical significance of the encounter. In a letter to his sister, he referred to the "discussion between Cassirer, the last but still influential representative of the neo-Kantian tradition, and the new star Heidegger."[37] He knew that the conflict between Heidegger and Cassirer would inaugurate a conflict among those attending. The "spirit of Locarno" notwithstanding, Cavaillès came away from Davos with a sense of the stakes involved and the tendency among his generation to take sides:

> There was a defender of Husserl and Heidegger there, Levinas, a Lithuanian who's going to publish an article on Husserl in the *Revue philosophique*. And there was another who at the beginning, when I asked him where he studied, answered: "Bei Cassirer." This attachment to a master is almost like a civil position for them—he represented neo-Kantianism for us.[38]

Cavaillès's presence at Husserl's lectures as well as the Davos encounter places him at two key turning points in French thought at the time when his own scholarly plans were first taking shape. What distinguishes Cavaillès's perspective is the degree to which he refused to take sides with the contending schools but instead saw the dispute between neo-Kantianism and phenomenology as evidence of the impasse of both positions.

Cavaillès's reflections also shed light on the relationship between Husserl's thought and Heidegger's as it was understood in the French context. In contrast to those who regarded Heidegger as rescuing Husserl's effort from idealism and developing it further,[39] Cavaillès saw in Heidegger the fulfillment of the unsettling tendency in Husserl's project to undermine the immanent nature of rationality. The primacy accorded to subjectivity was the common source of an error in their respective approaches. However, this error pulled in different directions; where Husserl forsook the *immanent* in his quest for the transcendental constitution of the subject, Heidegger forsook the *rational* in his critique of the transcendental ego.

Although Cavaillès was more engaged with Husserl's writings, we have evidence of his familiarity with Heidegger's as well, primarily in his correspondence with his friend and fellow philosopher of mathematics Albert Lautman in the late 1930s. Though he shared Heidegger's critique of transcendence, Cavaillès refused to disavow rationality's immanence in mathematics. Lautman was more sympathetic to Heidegger and sought to translate the latter's notion of the ontological difference between Being and beings into a rubric for making sense of mathematics as a historically grounded mode of thought.[40] Where for Cavaillès mathematics was nothing outside its own autonomous conceptual production, for Lautman mathematical concepts stood in relation to the dialectical Ideas that were their conditions in a way not unlike the merely ontic entities of Heidegger's formulation in their relation to the ontological processes constitutive of them. Lautman attempted to translate Heidegger's framework for understanding the ontological *question* as anterior to the ontic *answer* into a mathematical account of the dialectical *problem's* ontological primacy over its conceptual *solution*. After reading Lautman's exploration of these themes, Cavaillès responded as follows:

Heidegger vigorously rejects the opposition between essence and existence and wouldn't like that you even seem to be comparing him with Plato. I'd thought before that you allowed an immanence of ideas to their mathematical actualization. This doesn't seem to be the case now, at least if you go with Heidegger. Too bad—but you might be right in the end. For my part, I am so stuck in the similar problem (at root the same) of mathematical experience that I cannot see the link with any other way of posing it. But perhaps we'll wind up agreeing in the end— I'd like that very much.[41]

Cavaillès's effort to provide a philosophical account of mathematical experience also countenanced no opposition between essence and existence, but, as will become clear, his resource was Spinoza and not Heidegger. It is not that essence was rational and existence irrational for Spinoza; rather, he affirmed that essence was effectively coextensive with existence itself. Heidegger's refusal of essence, as Cavaillès understood it, was not simply a critique of the metaphysical category of presence but a refusal of the rational *tout court* as a key component of the world described in his ontology. For Cavaillès, this feature of Heidegger's project was a natural extension of the impasse to which Husserl's project inexorably led once it committed itself to exploring the apodictic qualities of the thinking subject instead of the apodicticity of mathematical thought itself as a kind of rational imposition. Recourse to consciousness per se as a foundational trope led either to solipsism, in Kant's case, for example, wherein the structures that determine rationality are not themselves rationally accounted for, or instead to a devaluation of the rational as such. The "exorbitant use of the *Cogito*" in Husserl's philosophy,[42] as Cavaillès would later put it, meant that phenomenology was either spinning its wheels in Kantianism or escaping the trap only with Heideggerian recourse to irrationalism. Cavaillès's cognizance of this dual "threat" meant that his engagement with the implications of Husserl's thought would be as serious as his ultimate rejection of it would be emphatic.

The Paris Lectures were Cavaillès's first substantive exposure to Husserl's project, and it was this experience, combined with the Davos encounter, that led him to consider Husserl's written work seriously. Cavaillès was in Freiburg in June 1931, during his Rockefeller year in Germany, and he took the occasion to meet Husserl in person. He attended one of Husserl's seminars but found it uninspiring, even as he picked up some knowledge on useful subjects.[43] Cavaillès worked through Husserl's *Formal and Transcendental Logic* that summer, "only unfortunately," because despite his own initial sympathies for Husserl's general method, Cavaillès found the system drawn from it to be "so far from all that Brunschvicg & Co. have imbued in [him]" that he could regard it only as some "strange thing."[44] In August 1931, Cavaillès wrote to a colleague: "Inspired by certain passages in his *Logik*, I had wanted to try its application to my problem, but he led me to the Rubicon."⁴⁵

Cavaillès's correspondent in this exchange was Étienne Borne, a philosopher sympathetic to phenomenology who would later play a role in French personalism. In an earlier letter, Cavaillès had professed his misgivings over the *Cartesian Meditations*, but he addressed more pertinently the subject that had occasioned their correspondence in the first place: Borne's suggestion that he read the existentialist Catholic philosopher Gabriel Marcel. We have only Cavaillès's side of the correspondence with Borne, but we can gather that Borne would have imagined Cavaillès to be sympathetic to Marcel's Christian approach to philosophy, given that this was the period of Cavaillès's own most strident "Christian militancy [*militantisme chrétien*]."⁴⁶ Marcel, who had converted to Catholicism in 1929, was, like Koyré and Levinas, emblematic of the French tendency to read phenomenology as the "answer" to the failed promise of Bergsonism, a mode of philosophy for which Cavaillès displayed no interest, much less sympathy.⁴⁷ Marcel's existentialism, as expressed in his 1935 book *Être et avoir*, made use of a Heideggerian vocabulary, although the communitarian impulses in his own thought were less ominous than Heidegger's.⁴⁸

At any rate, Cavaillès told Borne that he read Marcel with "a holy horror," recoiling before Marcel's placement of the intelligible in a transcendent beyond. Cavaillès said that all one finds in Marcel "is the reign of the contradictory and the joy of sin against spirit, which he caricatures in a kind of bogus judgment." Marcel fails to consider that "true reason, the absolute of thought, is the essence of Being but immanent elsewhere, in mathematical invention for example."⁴⁹ This dialogue with Borne concerning Marcel's work provides the most succinct expression of Cavaillès's take on the proper relationship between the immanent and the transcendent. For Cavaillès, who was very much a devout Protestant at this time, love was an experience of transcendence, and thought an experience of immanence. 'Philosophy only works in the light," he wrote to Borne on another occasion, "between rational clarity and the obscure night of religious life."⁵⁰ If Cavaillès evinced a certain hostility to empiricism throughout his work, he was more hostile still to a mode of philosophical thought that turned to the transcendental as a source of its justification or legitimacy.⁵¹ Ultimately, Cavaillès declared that his "grief against Marcel" derived from Marcel's "misrecognition of the absolute value of the intelligible, of the rational."⁵² Cavaillès expressed his own position in no uncertain terms:

> There is something of the divine even in the concept, at least in the passage of one concept to another. And it is here that we have the genuine *Spinozist ontology*, incomplete, but definitive in what it affirms. To put Being and value above or below this caricature of thought, to reduce philosophy to a simple description or recognition of the exterior, all of this is to renounce philosophizing: I believe that, outside of rationalism, philosophy can only be self-defeating [*ne peut être qu'un suicide*].⁵³

Here Spinozist ontology is opposed explicitly to Marcel's thought. But it is also implicitly mobilized against Cavaillès's understanding of Heidegger with the addition of the words *en dessous* (below) to a phrase that would otherwise apply solely to the transcendentalizing moves of Marcel's Catholic existentialism. Being is not transcendent, nor is it prior or "below." It is fully immanent, coextensive with existence itself. In 1938, Cavaillès would express his misgivings over Lautman's flirtation with Heidegger, but already in 1930 Cavaillès is emboldened enough to express his commitment to rationalism in unequivocal terms. Over the course of the 1930s, Cavaillès would prepare his twin doctoral theses to be published in 1938, the minor thesis on the history of set theory preparing the groundwork for the major thesis on axiomatics and mathematical formalism. Husserl offered Cavaillès no methodological purchase on the mathematical developments attendant to Georg Cantor's theories of transfinite numbers. Set theory—the more general term for the mathematics inaugurated by Cantor—drove a rift between demonstrable justification and intuitive experience by privileging the conceptual, and interminable, development of mathematical knowledge over the fixed categories, be they transcendental or existential, of a priori intuition.

The next section addresses how and why Cavaillès's fidelity to Spinozism only grew in intensity over the course of his doctoral research, but it will also consider its sources. In 1930, Cavaillès was advocating a Spinozist ontology in his private correspondence with Borne. In 1938, he would, in his own words, "reclaim Spinoza's patronage" in the defense of his doctoral work before a committee at the Sorbonne.⁵⁴ Understanding Spinoza's centrality to Cavaillès's effort requires a confrontation with some of the technical aspects of his research. But it also requires an assessment of the impact of the single most determinant, and proximate, influence on his intellectual career. In his correspondence, Cavaillès attributed his ambivalent relationship to Husserlian phenomenology to its distance from all he had imbibed from "Brunschvicg & Co." If we are looking to uncover the sources of Cavaillès's fidelity to Spinoza and his belief in the immanence of reason in its own works, we have to consider his fidelity to another philosopher, one whose lessons his colleagues were all too eager to escape in their search for a new inspiration.

Brunschvicg: Between Kant and Spinoza

Léon Brunschvicg set the initial terms for the French reading of Spinozism in the twentieth century by emphasizing the primacy of the rational in Spinoza's philosophy and the fully immanent nature of its own development.[55] The author of several sweeping histories of philosophical thought, focusing on the development of mathematics, physics, and moral consciousness, as well as an array of writings on specific thinkers, Brunschvicg exerted a powerful influence over French philosophy in the interwar years.[56] As the main representative of French neo-Kantianism and a philosopher deeply committed to the republican ideal, Brunschvicg was an easy target for thinkers, like Nizan, who saw a link between Kantian philosophy and the ostensibly bankrupt political ideology of the Third Republic. Nizan's verdict against Brunschvicg has meant that he has been regarded more as the obstruction that, once removed, cleared the way for the innovations of twentieth-century French thought than as a source of those innovations. Recently, however, there have been signs that Brunschvicg is emerging as something more than a historical curiosity.[57] A close look at his writings suggests that there was something "proto-structuralist," not simply about his writings in the history of science but even in his very conception of republicanism. For Brunschvicg read the history of science as exemplary of the republican ideal. Science in his view was a collective endeavor, pursued according to rules, that was conceived without a metaphysical telos yet produced genuinely novel insights about the world. Philosophical reflection on this history was, for Brunschvicg, instrumental in the formation of a properly republican citizenry. The goal was to produce citizens invested in the success of the republic, an entity that conceptually mediated the domains of the abstract and the concrete, not unlike the objects constitutive of the history of scientific thought.

The philosopher with whom Brunschvicg is most closely associated is of course Kant, and with his focus on the history of science and epistemology as keys to the Kantian system it is easy to see how Brunschvicg served as a French counterpart to the Marburg School of neo-Kantianism led by Hermann Cohen. For Cohen, Kantianism became neo-Kantianism when it did away with the metaphysical vestiges of the "thing-in-itself" and other concepts that compromised Kant's contemporary utility. For Brunschvicg, too, the "thing-in-itself" was a liability in Kant's thought. But this makes it all the more striking that Brunschvicg turned to Spinoza to develop a critique of this aspect of the Kantian project. If for Cohen, the move "from metaphysics to method" required a modernization of the Kantian paradigm,[58] for Brunschvicg, the main resources for overcoming Kant's limitations lay elsewhere in the philosophical tradition. In light of Kant's own assurances that his critical method is what sets him apart from Spinoza's dogmatism, it is ironic to find Brunschvicg suggesting that if there is incompatibility between Kant's and Spinoza's philosophies, it is not to be found in the critique but in the metaphysics that kept Kant tethered to Leibniz and Wolff. Brunschvicg turns to Spinoza to argue that there can be no limits to thought imposed by a figurative "thing-in-itself," which is deemed an incoherent concept. "Since the thing-in-itself is never given in the world of knowledge," Brunschvicg writes, following Spinoza, "the concept of thing-in-itself must not play any role, even a negative or a limiting one; *for there is no possible concept of a thing-in-itself.*"[59]

Even if Brunschvicg had his misgivings about the noumenal sphere, he nevertheless found that Kantian restrictions were particularly useful for his battles against psychologism and Bergsonian spiritualism. In this case, however, critique was deployed not in order to limit reason but to extend it. Brunschvicg disliked the expression "philosophy of science" because of the connotation that philosophy had something to teach science.[60] The inverse was the case; philosophy comes to understand reason by attending to science and its history. Spinoza, in his unmitigated praise for the power of mathematical reasoning, inspired Brunschvicg. For Brunschvicg, scientific reason was typically a step ahead of the evidence of the physical world, and here the limits of his Kantianism are starkest. For example, Brunschvicg saw Einstein's theory of relativity as a paradigmatic case of theoretical science's ability to "blithely ignore" (*jouées comme à plaisir*) Kantian or positivist limits.[61] One could say that Brunschvicg preferred crowing roosters to night owls that wait until dusk to take flight; to take Althusser at his word, Brunschvicg thought Hegel had "the mental age of a twelve year old."[62]

In an exchange with the Marxist philosopher and later sociologist Georges Friedmann concerning his work in progress, *Leibniz et Spinoza*, Cavaillès made clear his preference for the latter over the former. Between Leibniz and Spinoza, Cavaillès suggested it was clear that the latter was the "true Christian," and this was the case not despite but *because* of his severity.[63] In his valorization of this quality, Cavaillès found a kindred spirit in Brunschvicg. The relationship between Cavaillès and Brunschvicg was personal as well as professional. The Cavaillès papers at the ENS contain a moving letter that Brunschvicg sent to Cavaillès following the outbreak of war in the fall of 1939. There we see Brunschvicg clinging to his faith in philosophy's progressive mission, lamenting the "quasi- or pseudo-philosophical façade" regnant in a brutal Germany, different from the one of 1914, now masquerading behind a veil of so-called culture.[64] Brunschvicg's letter responds to Cavaillès's own queries to him, seeking insight on the significance of the war's opening weeks. That Cavaillès would turn to Brunschvicg for solace suggests Cavaillès's admiration for the man. The war would be as tragic for Brunschvicg as it was for Cavaillès; Brunschvicg's Jewish heritage meant that he was forced into internal exile in the south of France, and he died in isolation in 1944.

The relationship between *maître* and student began in 1923 when Cavaillès matriculated at the ENS after placing first on the *concours* in the "promotion littéraire." Cavaillès's role at the ENS as *cacique*, an intermediary of sorts between the faculty and the student body, accounts for his closeness with numerous ENS and Sorbonne faculty (often the same professors taught at both institutions), even as it partially explains his isolation from other students.[65] Cavaillès developed close relationships with Celestin Bouglé and Emile Bréhier, but his strongest attachment was to Brunschvicg. An anecdote he shared with his sister says as much:

In the middle of a discussion at Bréhier's Saturday, I suddenly felt the need to intervene with an ardent profession of faith in Brunschvicgian idealism. I realized afterward that this was a little ridiculous; it is at any rate strange to see how naïve you appear once you fall in line with a certain party. Neither Bréhier nor the classmates contradicting me had a solution for the problem we were discussing, but they maintained an air of obvious superiority over me, precisely because they were affirming nothing. You always have the advantage over someone when you're making objections—he plays the role of the accused; he defends himself.[66]

For Brunschvicg, the historical and theoretical connections between mathematics and philosophy were a matter of course. Cavaillès was rare among the philosophers of his generation in that his philosophical studies were connected to an interest in mathematics from the outset of his career. Indeed, he was committed to a degree of mathematical detail that would even surprise his doctoral committee when he defended his theses in 1938. In that confrontation, which, in addition to Brunschvicg, included the mathematicians Henri Cartan and Arnauld Denjoy, Cavaillès was pressed on his refusal to include a historical account of philosophical speculation on the nature of mathematics in his relentlessly technical study. Cavaillès's response was internalist in inspiration: he claimed that his work was concerned solely with set theory itself, not with its influence on the conceptions of philosophers.[67] This internalist approach dates back to 1928 when Cavaillès first decided to pursue doctoral work on set theory after consulting with Brunschvicg on the subject. Initially, Cavaillès had considered doing work on probability theory, but he was concerned that the history of probability theory, unlike set theory's, was more a history of mathematical application than innovation. Set theory was gaining increased scholarly attention at this time, as it lay at the foundations of the logicist movement associated with Bertrand Russell. Apparently, Brunschvicg thought of Russell's logicism as "a parasitic and quasi-monstrous excrescence,"[68] and Cavaillès was unsure if Brunschvicg would support the project. According to Cavaillès's testimony, Brunschvicg allayed his concerns, urging him to go ahead with a project on set theory with the observation that "our agreed-upon method has never been applied there."[69] The "method" was Brunschvicg's own, which, in the primacy it accorded to history, was opposed to the clean-slate logicism of Russell and the logical positivist movement. Ten years later, when Cavaillès was defending the theses that resulted from this conversation with his mentor, he offered that he had taken his inspiration and his model from Brunschvicg's first major work of philosophy, *Les Étapes de la philosophie mathématique* (1912).[70]

Les Étapes is a sweeping history of mathematics and its relationship to philosophy from Zeno to the twentieth century. In it we see at once the methodological precursor for Cavaillès's own project as well as the source of the differences that will ultimately distinguish it from Brunschvicg's. The heroes of Brunschvicg's study are Plato, Descartes, Leibniz, and Kant, primarily because their respective philosophical projects were acutely sensitive—or in Leibniz's case, coextensive—to mathematical achievement. Near the volume's end, Brunschvicg takes stock of Bertrand Russell's intervention in this history, paying particular reference to the latter's *Principles of Mathematics*, the plain-language text that would serve as a precursor to the monumental *Principia Mathematica*. Brunschvicg saw in Russell's work the advent of a latter-day Aristotelian Scholasticism that threatened to sap mathematics of its historicity by positing immutable "types" (which would become "classes" in the *Principia Mathematica*) that constrained rational thought by virtue of the theory of types' own reductive and legislative method. Russell was inspired by Frege, and Russell's own efforts would play a crucial role in Rudolf Carnap's logical positivism. The tendencies were clear to Brunschvicg in 1912: "the Logicist Movement" sought to reduce mathematics to mere description,[71] a language among others whose "truths" were hardly worthy of the name, in Brunschvicg's estimation, since "truth" itself was reduced to an effect of analytic accordance with an agreed-upon system. Brunschvicg was taken aback by the ease with which Russell would, "with a dogmatic temerity," deem things "*totally irrelevant*."[72] Like Kant, Brunschvicg thought the truths of mathematics to be truly synthetic, not merely analytic. The crucial aspect of Brunschvicg's example, however, insofar as it was a source of inspiration for Cavaillès, was its commitment to developing a philosophically significant historical reading of mathematics that could resist both historicist relativism and the desire to foreclose historical mathematical development evident in the ambitions of the *Principia Mathematica*. Brunschvicg sought to maintain a nonhistoricist and nonlogicist conception of truth. The sources of his own concept are clear from a pivotal segment of *Les Étapes* titled "The Spinozist Conception of Truth."[73]

Spinoza's privileged place in Brunschvicg's project is different from Leibniz's, for example, because, although Spinoza did not produce any properly mathematical work, it is his rationalism that provides the architectonic for Brunschvicg's historical methodology. Spinoza's genius, according to Brunschvicg, was to show that intuition, if it was to remain a viable concept, could not be located in the historical contingency of an individual's thought; instead, "intuitive science is self-sufficient";[74] and the internal and interminable dynamism of scientific thought reveals its own "*spiritual automatism*."[75] To be sure, Brunschvicg expresses qualms over the "technical limits" of Spinoza's thought, for example, its refusal to countenance the mathematical viability of infinitesimals.[76] But he lauds Spinoza's essential insight, which was developed in his concept of substance as an idea that locates a network of rational relations that is deemed constitutive of existence itself. As Brunschvicg writes, "[T]he unity of substance guarantees that no obstacle in the nature of things or in the nature of spirit will arise to halt the blossoming [*essor*] of intellectual science."[77] The most illuminating passages are those that place Brunschvicg's contemporaries in his sights; we see here a critical response to Bergsonian themes that seeks to restore the centrality of the rational and is a rebuttal of the demarcative strategies of the logical positivists as well. According to Brunschvicg, what marked the "radical originality of Spinoza, not only in relation to the thinkers who preceded him, but in relation still to those who would follow, until even our own days" was the following:

He alone was capable of going all the way with the exclusion of the scholastic notion of *faculty*. Intelligence is an activity coextensive with the life of man; it is *judgment* and *will*. Every idea affirms itself and produces its consequences from itself. Verification is nothing other than the awareness [*conscience*] of the synthetic power that establishes the coordination and connection of ideas. [. . .] Truth is indeed [. . .] accord [*convenance*] between the idea and the object [. . .]; only this accord is an effect, not a principle. In the external adequation of the thing to the idea we must see the corollary of this internal adequation that makes ideal products equal to the activity deployed in order to produce them.[78]

We garner several insights into Cavaillès's Spinozism by consulting Brunschvicg's example. The emphasis on the unity of the judgment and will, the coextensive nature of intelligence and morality, was a central tenet of Brunschvicg's oeuvre. With Spinoza invoked as the authority for this position, we can see why Spinoza would be a reference for Cavaillès in the justification of his Resistance activity. More pertinently, however, we see in Brunschvicg's recourse to Spinoza two themes that will be central to Cavaillès's doctoral work. The first is an abrogation of intuition conceived as a synthetic act that might be discretely located *in*, or referred back to, a given consciousness or faculty along Kantian lines. In his assessment of contending mathematical schools, Cavaillès will opt in general for the formalism of David Hilbert over the intuitionism of L. E. J. Brouwer. Brouwer's intuitionism is profoundly indebted to Kant in that it requires recourse to a conceptual "absolute consciousness," or transcendental subject, in which to ground the otherwise spontaneous moments of mathematical innovation."[79] The reasons for Cavaillès's preference for Hilbert over Brouwer are seen most clearly in Cavaillès's Spinozist take on the revolutionary concept of number central to set theory's development, which is addressed in the following section. The second theme concerns the differential temporality that Brunschvicg imputes to rationality's development as a historical process irrespective of subjective contingencies. To be sure, Brunschvicg's sweeping history of mathematics takes care to examine its liaisons with various philosophers, and his own assessment of Russell's contribution shows that, for Brunschvicg, personality counted for something. But the rational core of the project, the lesson that Cavaillès took from it, is evident in these passages inspired by Spinoza. Finally, we should note that in his doctoral defense, when shortly before reclaiming Spinoza's patronage Cavaillès claimed to take *Les Étapes* as the model for his work, Brunschvicg saw the opportunity to push his student a little further. Brunschvicg took Cavaillès to task for the murky definition of intuition he employed in his doctoral work, but he was concerned above all that Cavaillès paid absolutely no attention to the psychology that interfered in mathematics' own history. Cavaillès told his father that he responded to Brunschvicg "dryly": "But, Monsieur, this problem is in no way the one I am examining and has no relevance to it."[80]

Abstract Set Theory and Axiomatic Method

True to a French educational tradition that we will see again in Deleuze's case, Cavaillès received his doctorat d'État as a result of two works that were complementary in their aim. His minor thesis was titled *Remarques sur la formation de la théorie abstraite des ensembles* (*Remarks on the Development of Abstract Set Theory*); its historical argument laid the groundwork for Cavaillès's broader engagement with the problem of mathematics' foundations presented in the major thesis, *Méthode axiomatique et formalisme* (*Axiomatic Method and Formalism*).[81] Set theory, given its initial expression in Georg Cantor's work in transfinite mathematics, compelled Cavaillès's concern because it presented a powerful expression of a crisis lurking at the heart of mathematics. As mathematical methods, geometry and arithmetic had peacefully coexisted for centuries by leaving a series of mathematics' thornier issues unresolved, primarily those pertaining to the status of irrational numbers, including the most irrational "number" of them all: the infinite.[82] Whereas geometry relied on the intuitive concept of space, arithmetic did not concern itself with spatial models, opting instead for analytical precision. Infinitesimals, for example, could be preserved in geometrical expression with the graphing of functions as lines that converge or diverge in their tendencies. But the arithmetical expression of similar phenomena relied on algorithmic notations, signs that often functioned as stopgap measures to cover the lack of numerical exactitude.[83] Kant holds a key place in the history of this problem because of his effort to secure mathematical knowledge and its geometric representation in the synthetic a priori, thus grounding all mathematics in the intuitive concepts of space and time.

Among mathematicians, Kant's critique did not convince for very long. Making good on a tendency inaugurated in the early years of the nineteenth century by the Czech philosopher and mathematician Bernard Bolzano, and continued in the efforts of Karl Weierstrass, Richard Dedekind, and Gottlob Frege, Cantor's complementary theories of cardinal and ordinal numbers saw the virtual completion of "the arithmetization of analysis" first portended in Bolzano's work.[84] Radically anti-Kantian, Bolzano was among the first to argue that mathematical truths could not rely on any sort of intuitive foundation but must result from purely conceptual analysis. Bolzano could be a precursor to so many—from Russell to Husserl—because he was hesitant to make any ontological claims. Despite this evident modesty, he accomplished a veritable divorcing of all truth claims from any foundation in the subjective apprehension of that truth, thus laying the groundwork for Frege's own *Grundlagen der Arithmetik*: "a truth does not cease to be a truth because it is not thought or apprehended."[85] For Bolzano, subjective confirmation was a pale substitute for demonstrable justification.

Arguably the most important consequence of this post-Bolzanian history was that the concept of "number" became divorced from any intuitive measure of temporality or size.[86] The significance of cardinality as a mathematical concept was that it expressed a number's value in solely arithmetical terms, irrespective of the order of constitutive members that constituted that set's (i.e., that "number's") value. It is in this sense that Cantor could talk about $\aleph^0$ (aleph-null)—the first *cardinal* transfinite number—as being equivalent to the *ordinal* number that resulted from adding up all of the rational numbers of the number line. Cantor's "continuum hypothesis" was that the *next* consecutive cardinal transfinite number after $\aleph^0$, $\aleph^1$, was then equivalent to the ordinal value of the *real* number line, which contained all the irrational numbers as well, making it infinitely larger, or denser, than the standard number line that included only rational numbers. Cantor's challenge was to show how a set could be "well-ordered"—that is, its contents could be mathematically verified—without those contents being "known" in themselves as discrete components added one upon the other in an interminable ordinal accumulation. With Cantor's notion of the transfinite, analysis firmly supersedes (or at least departs from) our imaginative understanding of the infinite as an intuitive item.

Though critical of certain aspects of Cantor's work, Cavaillès was by and large deeply sympathetic to Cantor's "discovery." Cavaillès's first major scholarly endeavor was a collaboration with the German mathematician, and student of David Hilbert, Emmy Noether, which led to the publication of Cantor's correspondence with Richard Dedekind. Cantor had built upon Dedekind's theory of irrational numbers in the elaboration of his own project, and Cavaillès was inspired by Cantor's ability to pursue rationally a mathematical development that was unimaginable in the most literal sense of the term. The drama of Cantor's work was captured in his confession to Dedekind, following his own proof of the parity between infinite points on a line and those on a plane. Interrupting their German conversation, Cantor wrote in French: "[J]e le vois, mais je ne le crois pas! [I see it, but I don't believe it!]."[87]

Spinoza's rationalism illuminates Cavaillès's investments in Cantor's project. In a key text, his "letter on the infinite," Spinoza attacked the concept of number as the essential hindrance to our rational grasp of the infinite as an actuality.[88] One of Brunschvicg's several enemies, Aristotle, had legislated centuries of mathematical and philosophical confusion by positing a strict cleavage between the *actual* infinite and the *potential* infinite. Making use of the evident contradiction between infinity and totality, Aristotle argued that the infinite could only ever be discussed as something to come, as something potential, but never as something fully present or graspable in its entirety. The problem with Aristotle's approach was that it conceived the concept of the infinite in purely quantitative, or in Cantor's language, *ordinal*, terms. This meant that any reckoning with the infinite would eventually concede before what was, by definition, an interminable process of accumulation. In his letter on the infinite, Spinoza, in a reference to the Aristotelian legacy, castigated the thinkers who had preceded him and who falsely conceived of substance as made up of discrete parts. Whether conceived spatially or temporally in terms of duration, this imaginary belief in cumulative parts led to all sorts of confusion. Spinoza pointed to the absurdity of all "those who, having convinced themselves that a line is made up of points, have devised many arguments to prove that a line is not infinitely divisible."[89] Similarly, he argued, "[T]o say that Duration is made up of moments is the same as to say that Number is made up by adding noughts together."[90] Spinoza drove to the heart of the matter:

> [I]f you ask why we have such a strong tendency to divide extended Substance, I answer that we conceive quantity in two ways: abstractly, or superficially, as we have it in the *imagination* with the help of the senses; or as substance apprehended solely by means of the *intellect*. If we have regard to quantity as it exists in the *imagination* . . . it is found to be divisible, finite, composed of parts, and multiplex. But if we have regard to it as it is in the *intellect* and apprehend the thing in itself (and this is very difficult), then it is found to be infinite, indivisible, and one alone.[91]

Though Spinoza is working with a pre-Cantorian notion of number, his argument in fact provides support to Cantor's use of cardinality as a means for making sense of the infinite in its actuality. Spinoza's "number" in this letter is meant in what will later be recognized as a decidedly ordinal sense. The most important element of this passage is the opposition Spinoza forges between the "imagination" and the "intellect." The "number" that Spinoza abhors is that which is imaginatively construed, the one that is a product of sensory experience and the accompanying intuitive forms—which are on the side of the imagination in Spinoza's philosophy—that make sense of our *experientia vaga*. As Martial Gueroult has argued, Spinoza's claim that the infinite can be understood *only* by the intellect and *not* the intuitive imagination is in marked contrast to a philosophical tradition that conceives of the infinite in precisely the opposite terms: as an intuitively available phenomenon to be felt or lived but that the intellect can in no way apprehend. According to Gueroult, this latter take finds its fullest contemporary expression in Bergsonism, to which Spinoza's model should be opposed in no uncertain terms.[92] Gueroult sheds more light on this matter in his speculative comparison of Spinoza's philosophy with Cantor's transfinite mathematics. Taking his lead from Frege's qualified praise for Spinoza in the *Grundlagen der Arithmetik*, Gueroult argues that, notwithstanding Spinoza's apparent disdain for the finitude inherent in the concept of number from his epoch, we find common ground for Spinoza "by recognizing with the mathematicians of today that number is founded in the understanding and involves nothing within it of the finite."[93]

Gueroult's Spinozism receives treatment in the next chapter, but it is useful to introduce his observations here because they help clarify Spinoza's utility in Cavaillès's own project and the latter's sympathies with Hilbertian formalism.[94] Cavaillès's support for Hilbert and his followers was not unequivocal, however. Though he agreed with the formalist instinct to privilege arithmetical demonstration, he was uncomfortable with the tendency in any axiomatic system to disregard as irrelevant the prior mathematical processes that served as the conditions of axiomatization. This brings us to the second Spinozist feature of Cavaillès's doctoral work: the emphasis on rational thought conceived as an interminable process. Just as Cavaillès's distaste for intuitionism accords with the disparagement of the "lived" in Spinoza's own project for the "emendation of the intellect," so too does Spinoza's distrust of originary foundations account for Cavaillès's only qualified respect for the formalist enterprise. A key terminological distinction for Cavaillès was that between *histoire* and *devenir*. *Histoire* was the realm of the contingent, the world as experienced, in short, the lived. Cavaillès did not deny that mathematics had an *histoire*; more important, however, was the need to uncover the *devenir*, the becoming or evolution, that subtended that history and that possessed a rational integrity independent of historical contingency. In this regard, Cavaillès saw in mathematics—the paragon of rational thought—a privileged site for contemplating the philosophical problem of philosophy's and mathematics' intercalated history. What his two doctoral works show, in anticipation of the more ambitious argument of *Sur la logique et la théorie de la science*, is that Cavaillès understood the internal arithmetical and analytical operations of mathematical thought to be not only formally consistent with but also revelatory of *how* rational thought manifests itself in its own differential historical time.

Cavaillès's commitment to a pure rationalism that manifests itself in its own historical enactment finds its authority in Spinoza's principle of "the idea of the idea." Spinoza posits this formulation as the generative motor that advances rational knowledge, and he insists that when an idea takes another idea as its object, this relation is exactly the same as when an idea takes an object in the domain of Extension as its object.[95] This Spinozist concept, although articulated in the *Ethics*, finds its clearest expression in the *Treatise on the Emendation of the Intellect*, which Brunschvicg referred to as "Spinoza's Logic."[96] This text was a staple of the *agrégation* in philosophy in the first third of the past century and was well known by all of France's aspiring philosophers.[97] Cavaillès will refer explicitly to the "idea of the idea" in *Sur la logique et la théorie de la science*, but the strict rationalism that derives from this Spinozist proposition and allows no recourse to criteria beyond the ideas in question, is already evident in his doctoral work. The intimations of this position were clear in Cavaillès's thesis defense when he deemed philosophical assessments and psychological factors irrelevant to his study. But the most pointed expression of Cavaillès's Spinozist rationalism at this stage took place in a more public venue.

In February 1939, the Société française de philosophie invited Cavaillès and Albert Lautman to discuss their doctoral works in a common forum. Juxtaposing elements of Cavaillès's concise presentation alongside passages from Spinoza's *Treatise on the Emendation of the Intellect* puts the Spinozist quality of Cavaillès's rationalism into sharp relief. Cavaillès began his presentation with a survey of the contemporary mathematical terrain. Kurt Gödel's incompleteness and undecidability theorems of 1931 had exposed the inadequacy of both Russell's logicism and John von Neumann's radicalization of Hilbert's formalism by showing the impossibility of inserting mathematics into any unique formal system. In either case, the "impossibility of a regression procuring an absolute beginning" was made manifest.[98] For Cavaillès, Gödel's intervention was an exemplary answer to the "crisis of set theory" that had occasioned the search for new foundations on the part of various mathematical and philosophical schools. The three essential lessons to be taken from the history of this quest were the three key arguments of Cavaillès's project. They were presented to the audience as follows: (1) "Mathematics constitutes a singular becoming [*devenir*]." (2) "The resolution of a problem possesses all the characteristics of an experiment [*expérience*]: Any construction is submitted to the sanction of a possible failure, but it is accomplished conforming to a rule (that is to say, it is *reproducible* and thus a *non-event*), and it is ultimately developed in the domain of the sensible. Operations and rules only have meaning [*sens*] relative to an anterior mathematical system." (3) "The existence of objects is correlative to a method's actualization, and, as such, this existence is not categorical, but is always dependent upon the fundamental experience of effective thought. [. . .] Objects represent [*figurent*] projections in the representation of the steps of a dialectical development: there is, each time, a criterion of evidence for them conditioned by the method itself (for example: the evidence unique to the transfinite induction). These objects are thus neither in themselves [*en soi*] nor in the world of the lived; they are the reality itself of the act of knowledge."[99]

Together these claims constitute the most succinct statement of the agenda pursued over the course of Cavaillès's doctoral studies. We see Cavaillès's debts both to logical positivism (a construction must be reproducible, i.e. a "non-event") and Husserlian phenomenology (the existence of objects is correlative to their actualization), but we also see the effort to distance himself from the ahistorical search for origins qua foundations attendant to each agenda. More important, however, we see three interlocking arguments that share a common authority in Spinozism. For Cavaillès, the *nature* of mathematics and the *progress* of mathematics were one and the same thing.[100] In Cavaillès's mathematical intervention we see his intransigent commitment to rationalist immanence most clearly in the refusal to countenance the intervention or surety of any outside legitimizing or foundational force independent of mathematics' autonomy. Cavaillès avoided reference to consciousness or a discrete subject, and his repeated use of the term *expérience* is to be understood primarily in the French sense of the term as experiment. But it is equally clear that Cavaillès sought to maintain the polyvalence of the word whenever he referred to *l'expérience mathématique*. The signal philosophical importance of this unique experience was that it was, properly speaking, an experience without a subject, in the sense that its own development as an experience was not contingent upon the idiosyncrasies of a given consciousness. In his presentation, Cavaillès addressed his use of the term: "By 'experiment' [*l'expérience*], I mean a system of actions [*gestes*] governed by a rule and submitted to conditions independent of these actions."[101] He admitted that his definition was vague and that it required mathematical examples. But he elaborated nonetheless: "By that I mean that every mathematical method is defined in terms of a prior mathematical situation. If it is dependent on that situation in part, it is also to a certain extent independent of it, in that the result of applying the method can be determined only after the fact. That is what I mean by a mathematical experiment [*l'expérience mathématique*]."[102]

In the *Treatise on the Emendation of the Intellect*, Spinoza's "logic," it is said that "method [. . .] is the understanding of what is a true idea, distinguishing it from other kinds of perception and examining its nature, so that we may thereby come to know our power of understanding and may so train the mind that it will understand according to that standard all that needs to be understood."[103] In Spinoza's view, we must recognize that "method is nothing but reflexive knowledge, or the idea of the idea; and because there is no idea of an idea unless there is first an idea, there will be no method unless there is first an idea."[104] The nature of this "idea" is a historically contentious aspect of Spinoza's philosophy, linked to disputes over the meaning of the four Latin words *habemus enim ideam veram* (for we have true ideas, *or* we have a true idea) Spinoza inserted parenthetically in another instance to qualify the expression "a true idea."[105] In our view, Spinoza's main point is to insist on the factic nature of thought in a purely formal sense. At any given moment, there is the experience of an idea, and this experience is anterior to the theoretical gesture that "places" this experience in a given consciousness or subject. What is primary is the idea itself. "[I]n respect of its formal essence the idea can be the object of another objective essence, which in turn, regarded in itself, will also be something real and intelligible, and so on indefinitely."[106]

Cavaillès's claims in February 1939 translate Spinoza's rationalist methodology into a post-Cantorian epistemology that manages to be at once historical and formalist. The "anterior situation" (Cavaillès's words) on which thought operates is a formally determinant condition, yet what arises from it by the operation of the rational is "something real and intelligible" (Spinoza's) and in its way, a development simultaneously indebted to, and autonomous from, the preexisting situation. The procedural temporality at the heart of "mathematical experience" is to be distinguished from the spontaneous felt temporality of the *vécu*, or "lived," to which both Cavaillès and Spinoza oppose their own rationalisms. "Since truth," according to Spinoza, "needs no sign [. . .] it follows that the true method does not consist in seeking a sign of truth after acquiring ideas; the true method is the path whereby truth itself, or the objective essences of things, or ideas (all these mean the same), is to be sought in proper order."[107] Again truth is immanent to its own historical production. Some of Cavaillès's interlocutors at the Société, chief among them the mathematician Maurice Fréchet, found this version of mathematical history to be bizarre indeed.[108] To quell dissent, Cavaillès offered that it was possible that certain problems may not be resolved, either because mathematicians are lazy or because external circumstances may interfere. But for Cavaillès none of this denied "the role of internal necessity" in mathematical thought.[109] On another occasion, Cavaillès argued that Cantor's personal psychology, which led to his lingering desire for an intuitive grasp of the infinite, impeded him from seeing the true importance of his own discoveries.[110]

Brunschvicg once observed that what was called "method" in the *Treatise on the Emendation of the Intellect* will come to be called "consciousness" itself in the *Ethics*.[111] But consciousness in the Spinozist universe is not the name for a transcendental or empirical subject; it is a name for the process of thinking itself, conceived as an equally synthetic and genetic activity. The absence of concern for an intuitive or empirical confirmation of the rational is ultimately what gives Cavaillès's thought a more Spinozist bent than a Platonist one.[112] Cavaillès did not deny the crucial role of the sensible as the domain in which mathematical objects were effectuated. Indeed, in his talk, and again in *Sur la logique et la théorie de la science*, he affirms that mathematics essentially proves its mettle in physics. But his point is not to provide an image of empirical verification where theories are simply tested in a world of indifferent matter; rather, his claim is that the rational that inheres in mathematical thought, that is immanent to it, develops in such a way that its own synthetic operations synthesize the mathematical objects of theoretical physics. This kind of mathematical thinking has only become possible in a scientific world wherein *objects themselves*—such as atoms and subatomic particles—are no longer a matter of empirical presence but are essentially determined by the theoretical and material instruments of thought. Cavaillès's philosophy of mathematics does not search out forms that will themselves be indicators of a "Being" that remains transcendental, and thus obscure. Rather, the philosophy on offer is the thinking of essence, an "*immediate* thought of essence and not by exterior recognition."[113] This process is historical because it is interminable, though it is devoid of teleology. It is genetic, and not constructivist, insofar as both its necessity and the impossibility of plotting its course in advance are elements internal to the process and not contingent upon any transcendental criteria.

Taking a page from Brunschvicg, Cavaillès sees dynamism as the essential trait of scientific thought, a dynamism that escapes prerequisites but not rules altogether.[114] The past conditions the thought of the present, no doubt. But the concern to preserve a sense of irreducible innovation and true novelty is at the heart of Cavaillès's immanentist view of the rational's *devenir*. In this regard, Spinozism functions as the methodological sine qua non of Cavaillès's project in a manner similar to Spinoza's authoritative role in Brunschvicg's project in *Les Étapes*. Where Cavaillès differs from Brunschvicg is in his abandonment of concern for the extra-mathematical contingencies attendant to mathematics' historical development, be they social and moral or transcendental or empirical. In other words, Cavaillès takes leave of Brunschvicg's Kantianism in order to achieve a radicalization of the "Spinozist conception of truth" at the heart of Brunschvicg's historico-philosophical account of mathematics. Finally, in his insistence on the truth content of mathematical "becoming," Cavaillès also distinguishes his position from logical positivism.

The figure most notably absent from Cavaillès's doctoral works, and the proceedings inspired by them, is Edmund Husserl. After Husserl left him at the Rubicon in the early 1930s, Cavaillès moved on from the Husserlian problematic in the course of his mathematical scholarship. This is not to say that the criticism of phenomenology inherent to Cavaillès's work is not still present but simply that Husserl is not the privileged interlocutor he was in the earlier years of Cavaillès's intellectual formation. But Cavaillès was aware of intellectual trends in both France and Germany. His ongoing engagement with German philosophy and mathematics lasted the duration of his career, with much time spent in Germany over the course of the 1930s. In France, Cavaillès had a privileged view of the intellectual concerns of the moment. From 1931 to 1935, well after passing the *agrégation* himself, Cavaillès remained at the ENS. During those years he held the position of *agrégé-répétiteur*, or *caïman* in ENS slang, a post Merleau-Ponty would hold between 1935 and 1939 and that would later be the institutional base for Althusser's influence. Cavaillès developed close relationships with many students over those years, notably Desanti, whose work is addressed further on. Cavaillès also taught Tran Duc Thao, the Vietnamese émigré who would be the first French scholar to attempt a reconciliation of Husserl's project with dialectical materialism.[115] In a letter to Brunschvicg, Cavaillès communicated how impressed he was with Thao's initial work on Husserl: "Thao did an excellent *mémoire* on Husserl for me, a Husserl a little Hegelianized—or Fink-ized."[116] In this same letter, Cavaillès complained that professional duties and articles here and there were preventing him from resuming work on his major research project, *L'expérience mathématique*, in which he would pursue "an old quarrel against transcendental logic, especially Husserl's, which Thao's *diplôme* gave me the occasion to return to."[117]

Cavaillès was writing in 1941, from his own position in the Sorbonne to Brunschvicg in internal exile in Aix-en-Provence. He would never complete his work on *L'expérience mathématique*. But he would nonetheless resume his old quarrel with Husserl in *Sur la logique et la théorie de la science*, Cavaillès's most substantial theoretical statement. According to Gabrielle Ferrières, her brother experienced something of a crisis in his faith in the late 1930s, one that the outbreak of war only intensified. It is not only suggestive, then, but altogether fitting in light of Cavaillès's philosophical Spinozism, that when he delivered the manuscript to his sister, he included the following affirmation in the accompanying note: "In numbers, I find God again [Dans les nombres, je retrouve Dieu]."[118]

Sur la logique et la théorie de la science

The manuscript Cavaillès delivered to his sister in the summer of 1943 was untitled and without citation notes. In addition to providing references where possible, and rendering the prose more readable in certain places, the work's editors, Canguilhem and Charles Ehresmann, also gave the manuscript its title, *Sur la logique et la théorie de la science* (hereafter *LTS*).[119] The long essay is composed of three sections. The first part explores the legacy of the "philosophy of consciousness" to be found in Kant's critical philosophy. It begins with a comparison of Kant's logic with that of Port-Royal and then identifies two philosophical tendencies emanating from Kant's example. One finds in mathematics an *organon* for a philosophical theory of science, whereas the other is more concerned to develop a theory of science grounded in systematic demonstration. Brunschvicg and the intuitionist mathematician L. E. J. Brouwer are exemplars of the first tendency; the second is attributed to Bolzano and Husserl, each of whom will receive greater attention in Cavaillès's work than either Brunschvicg or Brouwer.

The middle section of *LTS* contains Cavaillès's engagement with logical positivism. Here he introduces his own distinction between two logical phenomena, what he terms the "paradigm" and the "thematic." The key interlocutors for developing this distinction are Rudolf Carnap and Alfred

Tarski. The final section of the volume is where Cavaillès deals most extensively with Husserl, whose project he reads as an attempted synthesis of logicism and a philosophy of consciousness. Focusing mainly on Husserl's *Formal and Transcendental Logic*, Cavaillès develops a sympathetic, though increasingly robust critique of phenomenology. He concludes, ultimately, that as long as phenomenology remains reliant on the concept of consciousness as an explanatory, transhistorical category, it will be unable to provide a philosophy of science that transcends the limits of Kant's own problematic. Cavaillès's concern is that Kantian categories are viable only for a science that remains within the domain of finite mathematics; but since "genuine mathematics begins with the infinite" (73), a philosophy of consciousness that attempts to ground the forms of the understanding in the empirical forms of experience itself will be unable to make philosophical sense of the developments in mathematics and physics from Cantor to Gödel and beyond. As a result, Cavaillès concludes that "it is not a philosophy of consciousness but a philosophy of the concept that can yield a doctrine of science" (78).

In 1947, the philosopher and epistemologist Gilles-Gaston Granger produced a review of *LTS* titled "Jean Cavaillès, or the Ascent toward Spinoza."[120] Noting the text's "astonishingly Spinozist atmosphere," Granger argued that Cavaillès's effort could be read as an effective renewal of Spinozism that also helped make sense of Spinoza's own philosophy in turn. Cavaillès's work showed how and why phenomenology had to "stop at the threshold of logical entities."[121] In other words, with its reliance on a concept of consciousness blind to its own empiricist bias, phenomenology could not account for the viability of mathematical objects, or "logical entities," such as those within Cantor's continuum hypothesis, which transgressed the structural criteria of the transcendental ego. For Granger, Cavaillès's work signified a renewal of Spinoza's project in that it reasserted the primacy of reason itself against attempts to locate it in a *cogito* and, as a consequence, legitimate its operations by defining its contours, limits, and possibilities in advance. With Cavaillès "the rationality of consciousness in its labor of constructing science is thus revealed as 'genuine immanence,' which is to say that no requirement or preliminary definition can guarantee it."[122]

This chapter has thus far sought to establish the generalized Spinozism of Cavaillès's philosophical outlook. What accounts for Cavaillès's signal historical and philosophical importance is that, in the concluding section of *LTS*, the set of rationalist convictions that Cavaillès himself deemed to be Spinozist is for the first time posited as an explicit alternative to phenomenology. Before we turn to Cavaillès's critique of Husserl, Cavaillès's recourse to Spinozist positions in the book's first two sections must be identified. In the first part, Cavaillès, in his sole reference to Spinoza by name, identifies the Spinozist principle of the "idea of the idea," which confers upon science an "absolute intelligibility," as one of the two tendencies evident in Brunschvicg's own theory of science, the other being reference to a "generative consciousness" as the foundation of scientific work. Cavaillès suggests that in either case the epistemological formula must be supplemented by an ontological analysis. But immediately after characterizing Brunschvicg's example in such terms, Cavaillès turns his attention to Bolzano, underlining his "predominant concern [. . .] to put the accent on the necessary character of science" (19). Though it is not explicitly identified as such, the option for "absolute intelligibility" that Cavaillès read as a Spinozist element in Brunschvicg's example is an apt distillation of what is found to be most pertinent in Bolzano's case as well. In the second part, Cavaillès develops his own concept of "thematization" with reference to the "traditional principle" of the "idea of the idea." Moreover, in this section Cavaillès invokes Alfred Tarski's semantics as a complement to Carnap's emphasis on syntax in order to show how, in any logical or mathematical system, *sens posé* (posited sense) can only ever be heuristically, and temporarily, isolated from *sens posant* (positing sense). Cavaillès's juxtaposition of the past participle with the active present recalls Spinoza's conceptual distinction between *natura naturata* (roughly, nature natured) and *natura naturans* (nature naturing). Spinoza's argument for the fundamental unity of the two phenomena in a singular idea of self-caused Substance was essential to his philosophy's efforts to establish the genetic, immanent, and procedural qualities of the rational. Cavaillès's assessment of logical sense proceeds along the same lines.

LTS opens with a reference thus: "In Kant's *Course on Logic*, it is said that recourse to psychology would be 'as absurd as drawing morality from life. It is not a question of contingent rules (how we think) but necessary rules, which must be drawn from the necessary usage of the understanding [*entendement*] that one finds without any psychology'" (1). Cavaillès reads in Kant a fundamental innovation in the theory of science in the emphasis he puts on the at once necessary and normative nature of logical rules.

But he quickly notes the debts to Port-Royal logic insofar as Kant seeks to locate these rules in an "initial term." Ultimately, the necessity of the rules themselves is subordinated "to an absolute consciousness whose presence and essential structure—what consciousness itself is—are irreducible, and which no rational content can define" (2). Cavaillès agrees with the importance that Kant attributes to form: "the formal coincides with the act of thinking in general, i.e., the act of unifying diverse representations under one alone" (5). But he also notes a fundamental irony in Kant's example. In trying to deduce a transcendental logic from a general logic, that is, an account of synthesis grounded in analysis, Kant produces a formal logic that is ultimately vacuous in that its very abstraction forsakes the object itself.[123] In other words, Kant's formal account of the unifying synthesis is grounded in an empty category of "any object" (*tout objet*) that treats matter as a simple limit concept for the constitution of singular objects, which, when viewed through Kant's logic, are indistinguishable from one another.

"The application of synthesis as an act on a given presupposes a definition of the given, some possibility that it be thought independently of the act, and is therefore already in consciousness, an element that is positively perceived and in a certain relation with the act—otherwise, the act alone is thought" (4). For Cavaillès, as will become clear over the course of *LTS*, it is precisely the case that thought is an act that cannot be grounded in a categorically marked concept of consciousness whose structures are determined in advance. Cavaillès's point is that Kant's problematic is ultimately circular, because in his efforts to escape psychologism by securing transcendental logic in immutable, given structures, Kant must invoke "consciousness" as the site of these structures. In its desire to transcend the empirical, Kant's logic turns to consciousness itself; yet the contents of this concept are themselves borrowed from the intuitive notions of space and time that serve to make experience possible. "Since it is a question of arriving at pure consciousness through a rejection of the empirical, there would have to be a way to bind consciousness to something else; but this something else [*cet autre*] is, by its very essence, not consciousness. It thus escapes all attempts to grasp it, and the suspicion arises that this pseudo-empirical is only consciousness itself once again" (4). Cavaillès notes that Kant has successfully shown that "collaboration with traditional ontology is impossible." As a result, "in a philosophy of consciousness logic is transcendental, or there is no logic" (10). But since Kant's account of the synthetic act of judgment is grounded in a more primordial account of the unity that inheres in intuition, he assumes, without demonstrating, that this formal intuition somehow essentially relates to the "extra-intellectual character" of space (13). The recourse to this "extra-intellectual character" is functionally similar to the recourse one finds in "traditional ontology" to an "extra-intellectual" principle that magically ensures logic's theoretical purchase. What is more, in seeking to ground logic in this intuition of something extra-intellectual—the intellection of something that is not in the intellect—Kant cannot but take recourse to a pure abstraction of this form that evinces an "indifference to the object" (14). Ultimately, with Kant, "there is no science qua autonomous reality, describable as such, but rather a rational unification of diversity that is already organized by the understanding according to a set pattern, or gleaned from a body of evidences with neither plan nor discovery" (14).

In Cavaillès's balance sheet, Kant's intervention in the history of efforts to develop a theory of science is decisive in that it seeks the framework for the theory in science itself. But its commitment to a "philosophy of consciousness" attenuates its efficacy. Moving forward, Cavaillès identifies two predominant pathways opened by Kantianism, one emphasizing demonstrative systematization and another seeking a mathematical *organon* that might serve the sciences most generally. Brunschvicg and Brouwer will be two manifestations of the latter tendency, and Cavaillès will identify Bolzano and Husserl as the two figures emblematic of the first, more open-ended process. Cavaillès's engagement with Brouwer is cursory at best; his main concern is that both Brouwer and Brunschvicg wind up reducing philosophy to a simple explication of the intentions of the scientist. In effect, Brouwer is uninterested in developing a philosophical account of science's integrity, settling for mathematical science's auto-justification in "the spontaneous movement of mathematics' becoming" (16). Cavaillès finds this recourse to the "spontaneous" to be untenable, since a viable theory of science must account for the necessity that inheres in genuine scientific development, even if that necessity is only legible ex post facto.

With regard to Brunschvicg, as noted, Cavaillès reminds readers of the Spinozist "superposition" of "the idea of the idea" that was integral to Brunschvicg's reflexive methodology. Pierre Cassou-Noguès has argued that it is in fact against Brunschvicg's "authentic Spinozism" that Cavaillès will elaborate his own "paradoxical Spinozism" and that the passages in this section should be read as a rupture with Brunschvicgian Spinozism.[124] But what Cavaillès criticizes in Brunschvicg's example is precisely not the Spinozist concept of "absolute intelligibility" expressed in the formula "the idea of the idea" but instead Brunschvicg's vague invocation of the "being of the world" as the adjudicative standard of science's progress: "The being of the world—of a world posited as outside and that it is the task of thought to reduce to the terms of interiority—persists as the determinant condition of science. To know [connaître] the world, to understand the world, this is a program that already represents the abandonment of creative autonomy, the renunciation of a necessity attached to nothing other than itself" (19). In other words, what Cavaillès is critical of in Brunschvicg is his Kantianism, not his Spinozism. It is the recourse to the posited "world" that plays a role similar to Kant's posited "consciousness" as the adjudicative standard; and the link that assures the consonance between the two poles is again assumed, not demonstrated. When Cavaillès turns to Bolzano in the paragraphs following this assessment, he jettisons the Brunschvicgian notion of a "generative consciousness" whose authority comes from the "world" itself to consider a rationalism more faithful to the Spinozist model.[125] But in his account of Bolzano, Cavaillès nevertheless references the authority of Brunschvicg's *Les Étapes*, a book in which the influence of Spinoza's rationalism was in full force (19).

What Cavaillès praises in Bolzano above all is the recognition that science is not an intermediary between human spirit and "being-in-itself" (*être-en-soi*), devoid of its own reality, but rather is "an object sui generis, original in its essence, autonomous in its movement" (21). A proper "theory of science can only be a theory of the unity of science," but "this unity is movement," concerning not a scientific ideal but a science in its actuality wherein "incompleteness and the demand for progress are part of the definition" (22). In this autonomous progress, dynamism closes on itself; "with neither absolute beginning nor term, science moves outside of time—if time means reference to the lived [*vécu*] of a consciousness" (22). Again we see here a distrust of the "lived" of any given "consciousness." These concepts were disparaged in Cavaillès's defense of his doctoral works wherein he sought to decouple mathematics as a rational enterprise from the contingencies of mathematicians as historical actors. But in *LTS*, this attempted decoupling is pushed beyond the domain of mathematics to consider its implications for science *tout court*. No longer concerned for the laziness of mathematicians alone, Cavaillès expands the scope and argues that "the true sense of a theory is not in an aspect that the scientist understands as essentially provisional but in a conceptual becoming [*devenir*] that cannot be stopped" (23). In the concluding passages of the first part of *LTS*, Cavaillès endorses Bolzano's call for demonstration as the essential practice of scientific thought. "If there is to be science, it is in its entirety demonstration, which is to say logical" (25). Bolzano's virtue is twofold: he avoids subordinating science per se to the insights of a particular historical moment, and he makes no recourse to "an absolute consciousness" (which is not to be confused with the Spinozist injunction for "absolute *intelligibility*"). But the problem that remains unresolved in Bolzano's example is how the principle of demonstration can be grasped as an essentially "generative movement" (which, again, is distinct from a "generative consciousness"). Bolzano's analysis remains too static and must be complemented by an analytic account of the constitution of objects and an ontology that relates these objects to being itself. Part 2 of *LTS* considers this first concern through an assessment of logical positivism; ontology is held in abeyance until part 3, when Cavaillès turns to Husserl.

Cavaillès begins his discussion of logicism with the claim that the unity of science is in no way to be confused with a wish for its uniformity (26). In its efforts toward a unified theory of science, the middle section of *LTS* introduces the key distinction between two concepts: the "paradigm" and the "thematic." Both terms are introduced as concepts, but they will come to refer to processes; the first process is "longitudinal" and the latter is "vertical." "The paradigm is characteristic of actualization [. . .] an actualization required by the sense of what is posited, that is, it is a relation that is only affirmed as such in the singularity of the realization of the sequence" (27). The process of "paradigmatization" describes the extension of an arithmetical or mathematical operation to new terms beyond those of the initial operation. It is a process of formalization, and here we see Cavaillès's ongoing debts to David Hilbert's formalist account of mathematics. Formalization, actualization, and paradigmatization all describe the extension of form, and thus the extension of sense, to new terms and objects. What is essential is that the constitution of a new term or terms is a result of the requirements of "what is posited [*ce qui est posé*]" and not an effect of the application of tools that inhere in a speculative subject distinct from the operation itself.[126] "Thus synthesis is coextensive to the engendering of the synthesized" (28). Moreover, "there is no sense without an act, but no new act without the sense that engenders it" (29).

Cavaillès ultimately reads in this formalist account of the paradigm the contours of Rudolf Carnap's own account of syntax and its paradigmatic role in logic. Logical syntax, for Carnap, is a matter of extension; it is a transposition of formalism in mathematics to the more generic domain of logic. Yet "to formalize is to ground [*formaliser c'est fonder*]" (33). In other words, it is essentially generative. In his account of this process, Cavaillès indirectly invokes Spinoza's authority again, with a formulation evocative of the distinction that Spinoza forged within the singular concept of nature between nature conceived actively and nature conceived passively, *natura naturans* and *natura naturata*. For Cavaillès, however, the matter at hand is not nature but mathematical sense or meaning, the essential content of mathematical reasoning:

> Positing sense [*le sens posant*] is, like all sense, an act of longitudinal development, which is to say that all positing sense [*sens posant*] is at the same time the posited sense [*sens posé*] of another act (this reminds us of the traditional principle that any idea has a formal reality). Thus the deepening movement, once initiated, gives rise to a new sequence of the first type: the idea of the idea manifests its generative power on the plane that it defines without the prejudice of an unlimited superposition. (32)

Cavaillès's concern, however, is that with Carnap's syntax what we find is in fact not an enrichment or deepening of sense but a tendency toward further abstraction lacking theoretical purchase. A process of thematization that develops the *semantic* content of what would otherwise simply be an increasingly abstract *syntax* must supplement the longitudinal, actualizing process of paradigmatization. Cavaillès invokes Alfred Tarski's theory of semantics to articulate his own version of thematization. In effect, Tarski halts the infinite regress of increasing syntactical abstraction by introducing an element of reflexivity into the process. The reflexive moment expresses the "generative power" of the "idea of the idea." "The secondary act," Cavaillès writes, "for which the positing sense of the primary act serves as sense posited thus coincides with the effective action of formalism itself; here formal thought turns back on itself in a way that would have been impossible to predict before its accomplishment" (35). But this reflexivity is not to be confused with an abstraction projected beyond the immediate: "to abstract in this way is not to fix the essence but to stop" (36). What an exclusively syntactical formalism—be it of a Hilbertian or a Carnapian variety—"takes for an absolute beginning is only the surreptitious evocation of anterior actions and sequences" (39).

Formalism helps clarify and specify what is taking place in science, but it cannot generate a theory of it because, "as a system of actions, the experience itself is internally organized in such a way that it is impossible to interrupt its development except through a superficial abstraction" (40). Cavaillès concludes his critique of the excessive formalism of logical positivism by returning to the crucial status of the object for mathematics and mathematical physics. In Cavaillès's reading, the combined operational processes he has described—the syntax of the paradigm and the semantics of the thematic—converge toward the object itself as a kind of "ideal pole." But the object itself never intervenes in their development; all of its "reality" as an object is simply contained in these processes. The danger here is that the object vanishes in a way not unlike it did in Kant's logic, as a category of pure abstraction. For Cavaillès, the status of the object has become an urgent problem for mathematics precisely because mathematical science has moved beyond a point where it can rely on the domain of the empirical to ensure the presence and integrity of discrete objects: "The notion of the object, an immanent necessity to the sequences of physics, is imposed ipso facto on those of the mathematicians" (43).

It is the utter destitution of the object itself that one finds in logical positivism that leads Cavaillès to the conviction that a viable theory of science must develop an ontology in which the "object" ceases to vacillate between being a void category and an "ideal pole" excluded from the theoretical sequences themselves. This does not mean a return to empiricism but rather an ontological account of the logical sequences that have been described throughout the preceding section. Dissociating *sens posé* and *sens posant* is merely a heuristic stopgap measure that should not obscure the fundamental ontological unity of these phenomena along the lines of Spinoza's "nature." In this conviction, and the theoretical program it inspires, we witness the resurgence of Cavaillès's Spinozism. Thinking the union of these phenomena means thinking the constitution of objects in a way that reduces them neither to the operations of an "internal" consciousness nor to an "external" world that is mysteriously ordered in itself. It means considering the *relation* itself, between the substantial attributes of Thought and Extension in Spinoza's language, or the act of thought and the material upon which it operates in Cavaillès's, as an interminable process that refers back to no originary legislative moment that ensures their unity in advance.[127] In other words, the unity is purely one of continuous relation and emphatically not a nonrelational union that collapses all theoretical activity in a primordial experience or lifeworld. The object's autonomy and ontological status, its discrete existence as either subsisting, persisting, or vanishing, can be grasped only in the procedural nature of the relation itself: "The representation of the object, chased away, reappears elsewhere, be it as the formal system object or the operative action object; object, this is to say a reality sufficient unto itself and manifesting in some way a duality with the pure action immerged in the very sequence it develops" (43). In the concluding section of *LTS*, Cavaillès turns to Husserl to see if his fundamental emphasis on a relation between "authentic meanings" and "independent beings," wherein each remains an irreducible element, can provide the ontological ground for a theory of science that is sorely lacking in logical positivism.

Though Cavaillès's desire to conceive of the constitution of objects in terms of equally ontological and epistemological synthetic processes is of Spinozist inspiration, it is also what accounts for his sympathy with Husserl's effort to understand consciousness as a noetic process rather than as an immutable fact or structure. Cavaillès's critique of Husserl is all the more potent given the proximity of their respective points of departure. Commentators have observed that Cavaillès's engagement with Husserl, at least as expressed in *LTS*, is for all its depth and rigor limited in its reference.[128] For Cavaillès the key text of Husserl's oeuvre was his *Formal and Transcendental Logic*, a work that opens by seeking to develop a formal ontology rooted in an account of apophansis (44). *Apophansis* is a keyword of phenomenology that refers to a kind of ur-judgment, a predicative act of assertion that is coterminous with the "showing forth" of evidence. By focusing on apophansis as a process, Husserl provides a theory of the constitution of objects as rooted in acts of judgment. "Since knowledge of the object is expressed in judgments, it sets forth the indispensable prelude to all knowledge; it is first ontology" (48). But Cavaillès immediately explores the implications of this approach: "The aim here is not the object but the judgment of the object; and as it is only a question of its structure, nothing proves that we reach anything other than the extrinsic conditions of an expression or thought that determines nothing in the structure, but only the accidental quality of its actualization in a consciousness. The proper theme remains irreducibly the pure apophantic entity" (48). In other words, the object that is reached in this process is not the "undetermined x that would represent the individual irreducibly individuated in the physical world, void of any particular qualification, but rather what Husserl calls the *categorial entity*" (48–49). In effect, Husserl develops an ontology of categorial entities understood not as objects per se but as "qualifications of objects." Cavaillès finds this model alluring because it puts the ontological emphasis on a process of theoretical effectuation. "Outside of applications, there is no mathematical knowledge," he writes. Moreover, "knowing has only one meaning; it is to reach the real world" (53). The value of the relation that Husserl establishes is that it is imbued with an essentially *necessary* framework; Husserl provides the fundamental tools for articulating the discrete qualities of objects.

At this point in his analysis, however, Cavaillès takes a sharp turn. He argues that Husserl is able to establish this necessary framework only by grounding it in the "primacy of consciousness." In seeking the resolution to the problems of objective constitution in "the correlation of the noetic and the noematic," Husserl nonetheless locates the process of reflexivity itself inside a kind of absolute consciousness: "The independence of objects is not affirmation of their being, in relation to consciousness, a heterogeneity that would entail subordination and a polymorphism of corresponding kinds of knowledge as a consequence of their diversity. Rather, consciousness is the totality of being; what it affirms *is* only because it affirms it, as long as it affirms with full confidence in itself" (55–56, emphasis added). Husserl is even more radical than Kant in his affirmation that subjectivity itself is the source and foundation of objects: "the problem posed by logic is transformed into a problem of the transcendental constitution of objective entities" (59). Husserl's virtue, with regard to logical positivism and neo-Kantianism, is to have shown the "vanity of a transcendental philosophy that departs from pure logic: the source and justification of apophantic unity must be sought in the preliminary affinity of the experimental contents it organizes" (61). But ultimately Husserl himself is no less "vain" because he locates the norms for the "constitution of the *constituted* being," or object, without providing an account of what norms the "constitution of the *constituting* being," or subject (64, emphasis added). With Husserl, "there is a stoppage of progress by a kind of *coup de force*." Creative subjectivity is deemed transcendental, but in the same stroke it is exempted from history and from the possibility of transformation. "If transcendental logic truly founds logic, then there is no absolute logic (which is to say, one that governs this absolute subjective activity). If there is an absolute logic, it can draw its authority only from itself, which means it is not transcendental" (65). Cavaillès had said of Kant that in a philosophy of consciousness, logic must either be transcendental, or it is not at all. The same perspective applies here.

In the remainder of this final section of *LTS*, Cavaillès returns to the post-Cantorian mathematics that was the subject of his doctoral work. Husserl's phenomenology is simply unable, in Cavaillès's view, to provide any kind of purchase on these scientific developments. Phenomenology "limits itself to analyzing the acts and constitutive intentions of transcendental subjectivity, that is, to dissecting the muddle of motivations and elementary subjective actions without questioning the logical entity itself. [. . .] Phenomenological analysis will only ever operate in the world of acts wherein [. . .] contents' architectures are dissociated, [. . .] halting itself before simple elements, which is to say, those realities of consciousness that refer to nothing else" (75). The problem with this perspective is that, in the conceptual development of mathematics as an interminable sequence, there is effectively *no* reality of consciousness that does not refer to something else. In moving beyond the domain of empirical reference or intuitive sensibility, mathematics effectively discovers its own intrinsic historicity as a rational process for which there is no foundation and no ultimate goal. Cavaillès's critique of phenomenology becomes increasingly oracular in the final pages of *LTS*, but its general contours remain clear. He writes that "lived impossibility and distinct actualization are the last instances of phenomenological analysis" (76). Several lines later, he evokes this sense of lived impossibility again: "The foundation of all necessity [in phenomenology] is this 'I can do no other' of the eidetic variation, which, however legitimate it may be in itself, is an abdication of thought" (77). Cavaillès's point here is that, in the necessary sequences of a mathematical operation, it is strictly speaking incorrect—"an abdication of thought"— to say "*I* can do no other." It is not *you*, as a set of fixed structures and categories, that can do no other; it is the necessary sequence of the rational itself that *does* no other.

This critique of the subject compressed into the final feverish paragraphs of *LTS* is interspersed with gestures toward a new way to think the historical nature of scientific thought. Cavaillès grants phenomenology its due on the score, citing Eugen Fink for his efforts to develop phenomenology in a way that makes it a kind of historical archaeology of sense. "History," Cavaillès writes, "reveals authentic meanings insofar as it allows us to rediscover lost links, to first of all identify automatisms and sedimentations as such, and then to bring them back to life and allow us to dive back into them in a conscious actuality" (76). Phenomenology is imbued with an "indefinite plasticity" that allows it to organize various types of evidence. But ultimately, "this authority has but one source [. . .]: if there is consciousness of progress, there is no progress of consciousness" (78). The excavation and organization of evidence are not enough, Cavaillès argues. Scientific "progress is not an augmentation of volume through juxtaposition, the anterior subsisting with the new, but is rather a perpetual revision of contents by deepening and erasure" (78). A philosophy of consciousness cannot account for this process:

The term consciousness does not entail a univocal application—no more than the thing or the isolatable unity does. There is not one consciousness generating its products or simply immanent to them; rather, it is in the immediacy of the idea each time, lost in it and losing itself with it and only connecting with other consciousnesses (which we would be tempted to call other moments of consciousness) through the internal links of the ideas to which they belong. Progress is material, or between singular essences; the demand that each one be surpassed is its driving force. (78)

Cavaillès then concludes: "It is not a philosophy of consciousness but a philosophy of the concept that can yield a doctrine of science. The generative necessity is not that of an activity but of a dialectic" (78).

How are we to make sense of this final compacted formula? It seems plausible to regard the disparagement of "activity" here as the disparagement of the activity *of consciousness*. The claim that there is no absolute subject, or absolute consciousness that is the active subject of science, is perfectly consistent with the argument that Cavaillès has been developing over the course of *LTS*. The use of the term "dialectic" is more perplexing, but it is likely a belated effect of Cavaillès's long-standing dialogue with Lautman. For Lautman, the dialectic referred to the ideal processes and relations among mathematical problems anterior to their conceptual, "ontic" solutions. Cavaillès expressed his misgivings over Lautman's tendency to search for the sense of "mathematical experience" beyond "mathematical experience" itself, but insofar as Lautman's use of dialectic connotes an ideational play independent of an active subject, we can grasp why the term may have seemed useful to Cavaillès in this context. Finally, the word cannot but evoke Hegel's philosophy. During the writing of *LTS*, Cavaillès made a request for a copy of Hegel's *Logic*, "if possible in the Berlin edition,"[129] but it seems that this volume never made it into his hands as he was preparing his essay. Jean Hyppolite, for his part, was keen to note the closeness of many of Cavaillès's arguments with those of Hegel's logic.[130] In contrast, Desanti maintained that Cavaillès always "distrusted" Hegel.[131]

What Cavaillès would have thought of Hegel's logic must remain a speculative matter. What is clear is that the conclusion of *LTS*, with its call for a philosophy of the concept to replace a philosophy of consciousness, was a decisive moment in French intellectual history in that the fundamentals of Spinozist rationalism were for the first time posited against those of phenomenology. To be sure, Cavaillès's conclusion is oracular. The "philosophy of consciousness" has been subjected to pages of critical scrutiny—*LTS* is in any event best read as a critical prolegomenon—but the "philosophy of the concept" that would be its alternative is simply introduced on the last page. This chapter has sought to establish the breadth and depth of Cavaillès's Spinozism in order to make a claim that the "philosophy of the concept" is Cavaillès's own Spinozist response to Husserl's "exorbitant use of the *Cogito*." Because Cavaillès leaves the Spinozist philosophy of the concept undefined, his attenuated project stands as the first word in the history of Spinozism's critical relationship to phenomenology in twentieth-century French thought, not the last.

The next chapter shows how the operative alternative between rationalism and phenomenology in Cavaillès's project would come to be institutionally codified in France as an opposition between Spinozism and Cartesianism. Chapter 3 turns to Jean-Toussaint Desanti, the most direct inheritor of Cavaillès's philosophical project. But it seems germane, before taking leave of Cavaillès, to offer a few final words about his complicated legacy as at once a philosopher and a Resistance martyr. One of the most striking features of Cavaillès's Spinozist philosophy of science is the extent to which it both is, and apparently aims to be, a philosophy without normative content in itself. In effect, what Cavaillès develops throughout *LTS* is an attempted historicization of formalism that preserves what is, in Cavaillès's view, formalism's signal virtue as a philosophical position.

The virtue of formalism is what one finds in Bolzano, and above all Spinoza: on the one hand, there is never any suturing of science per se to the scientific contents of a given historical moment; but, on the other hand, there is never any attempt to tether science to an originary consciousness or subject that might legislate or determine its results. In other words, the Spinozist rationalism Cavaillès seeks to develop is, if not quite an *organon*, a primarily dispositional and methodological "philosophy." The whole thrust of Cavaillès's critique of the philosophy of consciousness is that it attempts to legislate the *contents* of science in advance through a recourse to *formal* restrictions. For Cavaillès, forms are never restrictive; they are essentially enabling.

But if Cavaillès's philosophy is essentially "without content," then what is equally striking is that his moral and political example is without content as well. This is not to trivialize Cavaillès's heroism—far from it. The point, rather, is to emphasize that if we are to remain true to Cavaillès's own philosophical insights in his written works, then we cannot extrapolate the "content" of his moral example in order to apply it elsewhere. All Cavaillès gives us is the "form" of Resistance: determination, commitment, tenacity. But it is no use looking to Cavaillès for any kind of moral insight into the contents of a political or ethical situation that is historically other than the one in which his own "Resistance by logic" was embedded, the Nazi occupation of France. To do so would be as futile an effort as trying to use the tools of Kantian logic to make sense of the contents of transfinite mathematics.

In this regard, the deep ambivalence of Canguilhem's commemoration, its vacillation between holding Cavaillès as an exemplar and, at the same time, prohibiting its appropriation for other political or historical agendas, acquires its own philosophical sense, as does Canguilhem's observation that Cavaillès "always read, studied, and one could say practiced Spinoza."[132] But the extent of Cavaillès's Spinozism must be given its full due. This means recognizing in Cavaillès's heroism a "rational object" like any other in Spinoza's system and thereby granting its status as the incommunicable "discrete singularity" that it was and remains. The Spinozist rationalism informing Cavaillès's thought emphasized the primacy of form over the contingencies of an always changing meaning, or *sens*, subjected to an interminable process of "deepening and erasure." With his commitment to the necessity inherent in this framework, Cavaillès followed Spinoza's lead in committing himself to the power of rational thought to supervene on the contingencies of lived experience and "the accidents of history." Yet in moving beyond the contingent or accidental "contents" generated by life or history, the capacity of philosophical thought to address their equally contingent meaning—be it ethical, moral, or political—was, for better or worse, attenuated as well. It is not solely in its commitment to philosophical rationalism that Cavaillès's Spinozism was prophetic.

2

Spinoza Contra Descartes
Martial Gueroult versus Ferdinand Alquié

The previous chapter sought to establish that, with Cavaillès's project, Spinozist rationalism was for the first time promoted in France as an alternative to the phenomenological currents of philosophy descending from Husserl's inaugural effort. In this regard, the incompleteness of Cavaillès's case for a "philosophy of the concept," along with the oracular quality of its presentation, only accentuates its historical significance. Thinkers working in Cavaillès's wake did not have a ready-made "philosophy of the concept" that they could deploy for various ends. Rather, with Cavaillès it is the problematic itself that is established.

This chapter takes a much wider view, in effect panning out to develop a broader assessment of French philosophy in the postwar era before returning to the inheritors of Cavaillès's critique of phenomenology. If Cavaillès provides us with a sketch of a rationalist critique of phenomenology, and is the first to frame that critique in terms of Spinoza's philosophy, it is only after the Second World War that the critique will become codified and effectively institutionalized as a stand-off between Cartesianism and Spinozism in French thought. To demonstrate this point, the focus here will be on two scholars who remain little known to readers outside France but who, given their privileged institutional standing, nonetheless had a decisive impact on the trajectory of French philosophy: the Sorbonne professor, and self-proclaimed Cartesian, Ferdinand Alquié; and the Collège de France professor, and "radical idealist" responsible for one of the most ambitious assessments of Spinoza's rationalism anywhere in the twentieth century, Martial Gueroult.

The dispute in question began over Descartes in 1951, the year of Gueroult's appointment to the Collège de France, and it ended with the publication of Alquié's *Le Rationalisme de Spinoza* in 1981,[1] five years after Gueroult's death. Their quarrel over the proper methodology for the history of philosophy, and by implication, of philosophy itself, serves at once as a metonym for conflicts central to postwar French philosophy and as an exemplar of their historical development. Alquié, an erstwhile surrealist and friend of Jacques Lacan's, once conceded to a classroom that he was "a Cartesian, as everyone knows."[2] Gueroult's rigorous historical methodology—what he termed a *Dianoématique*, a "study of doctrines"—has been described as an attempt to do for the history of philosophy what Spinoza did for philosophy.[3] Following Spinoza, Gueroult sought to eliminate from philosophy the insights of first-person experience in favor of a proliferation of structurally interconnected concepts indifferent to their source. Herein lies the metonymic quality of their conflict, for it gives historical content to Elisabeth Roudinesco's gloss on Foucault's distinction between philosophers of rationality and the concept and philosophers of experience and the subject as, in effect, a conflict between Spinozists and Cartesians.[4]

This opposition between Cartesian purveyors of consciousness and Spinozist partisans of the concept is no doubt too schematic to account fully for the ideas in question. For instance, when Gueroult mobilizes his reading of Descartes, which purports to be the most faithful one, against Alquié's, a strong case can be made that Gueroult has already "Spinozized" Descartes. Beyond this context, there are plenty who would find more "mystical vitalism" in Spinoza than in Descartes.[5] Also surprising is the notion that Descartes would be the celebrant of a mediated first-person experience against the rationality of the concept, a suggestion that runs counter to a Heideggerian critique that sees Cartesianism as the modern reinstatement of Plato's original sin of representational idealism. Nonetheless, the suggestion here is that Roudinesco's heuristic is largely just insofar as it designates the function of the appellations "Cartesian" and "Spinozist," particularly with regard to the currency they acquired following the introduction of phenomenology in France.

French and Anglophone observers alike have long viewed German thought as the key stimulus for the most innovative French thinking from

Sartre to Derrida. But only recently has it become evident the extent to which philosophical imports to France were subjected to naturalization procedures upon arrival. As noted in the previous chapter, this phenomenon is clear in the case of phenomenology, especially in its Husserlian variant and the way it was "Cartesianized" by French interpreters, with assistance from Husserl himself when he delivered the "Cartesian Meditations," his lectures at the Sorbonne in 1929. Though Sartre's project is the most popular example of a persistent Cartesianism at the heart of French thought, Alquié's scholarship was most essential in making Descartes a phenomenologist *avant la lettre*, thus inspiring the line of French phenomenology that has found its greatest fruition, and its most obvious debts to Descartes, in Jean-Luc Marion's work.[6] Conversely, for French thinkers in the interwar years such as Cavaillès, who were distrustful of what they regarded as the irrationalist tendencies of phenomenology, the appeal of the logicism being developed in England and by the Vienna Circle was at least partially rooted in the family resemblances between this nascent mode of thought and the rigorous rationalism of Spinoza. For Spinoza, the productive capacities of conceptual thinking were given pride of place over the dubious insights garnered from intuition or lived experience. It might be objected that Spinoza, unlike Descartes, is not a French native son. But then again centuries of assimilation have worked toward Spinoza's adoption in France, starting with the earliest readings of his philosophy as a "post-Cartesian" materialism and continuing up to Brunschvicg's celebration of Spinoza as the standard-bearer of rationalist temerity against whom all philosophers must measure themselves.[7] When Gueroult's massive volumes on Spinoza, the product of his lectures at the Collège de France, appeared in 1968 and 1974, they were the capstone of this reading.[8] In contrast to Spinoza's reception in twentieth-century Germany, the issue of Spinoza's origins, much less his relationship to Judaism, has until recently been of marginal interest at best. An exception proves the rule; the opening chapter of Geneviève Brykman's *La Judéité de Spinoza* (1972) is a profession of incredulity that French scholars have not deemed this subject of interest.[9]

The academic quality of Alquié's and Gueroult's readings of Descartes and Spinoza is ultimately a virtue, as it allows for a consideration of the antagonistic relationship between Cartesianism and Spinozism in French thought at a philosophical level shorn of its imbrications with other disciplinary agendas. And it is on this score that the metonymic pairing of Cartesian/Spinozist needs to be supplemented with a second claim about their conflict. The quarrel between Alquié and Gueroult took place over thirty years, and as such it was a process with its own history, and that took place within a broader history. At this level, the quarrel serves as an exemplar of broader commitments in the second half of the twentieth century to preserve philosophy's autonomous status and disciplinary integrity despite the encroachments of rival modes of thinking.

Though the disagreement began as one over Descartes and ended over Spinoza, and Alquié and Gueroult each remained intransigent on their fundamental positions, a shifting set of concerns subtends the continuity. In the earliest phases, each protagonist accuses the other of pursuing a methodology that is complicit with historicism, understood as any attempt to reduce a philosophical position to its contextual trappings. In the later phases of their argument, however, once the terrain of Descartes' texts has been abandoned for a concern with Spinoza's, the chief threat to philosophy's universalist pretensions is no longer historicism but theology. Here Spinoza serves as the medium for their countervailing charges of theology and "occultism." Alquié will accuse Spinoza, and by extension Gueroult, of offering a covert naturalist (or pantheist) theology masquerading as rationalism. Gueroult will come to celebrate Spinoza against Descartes, and by extension Alquié, for pursuing an "absolute rationalism" that overcomes the "occult qualities" of the Cartesian framework.[10]

What follows is divided into three parts. The first section adds to the introduction of Gueroult and Alquié, biographically and in terms of the basic features of their methodologies. This section also addresses their readings of Descartes. From there, we turn to their heated confrontation at a colloquium devoted to Descartes' philosophy in 1955 and also provide an account of their second key public meeting, a 1972 colloquium in Brussels on method and the history of philosophy. The organizers of this conference deliberately intended it to be a resumption of the unfinished conversation from seventeen years earlier. The assessment of these two confrontations provides the framework for assessing Gueroult's and Alquié's studies of Spinoza, in which their discord comes to be expressed in its highest intensity. Indeed, it is in their incommensurable accounts of Spinozism that, to borrow a phrase from Jean-François Lyotard, the Alquié/Gueroult "différend" acquires its greatest clarity.

Descartes and the Challenge of Historicism

According to the sociologist Jean-Louis Fabiani, the Collège de France's decision in 1951 to appoint Martial Gueroult instead of the rival finalist, Alexandre Koyré, is best understood as a reactionary move to forestall the spread of historicism in French higher education.[11] A historian and philosopher of science, the émigré Koyré had made a name for himself with studies of Galileo that firmly situated the advent of Galilean science in the broader cultural context of sixteenth-century Europe.[12] Gueroult's major work at this point, a massive study of Fichte's *Wissenschaftslehre*, could not have made for a more striking contrast.[13] Whereas Koyré's modus operandi was one of contextualization, Gueroult pursued a methodical reading of Fichte's system that emphasized its inherent qualities and that, more to the point, conceived of the autonomous development of rationality as the systematic elimination of contingency from the finished product.[14] In other words, if for Koyré a thinker's thought acquired its full sense only in its context, for Gueroult the full sense of a philosophical system manifested itself only in a break with the contingencies of its original context.

Born in 1891, Gueroult was very much a product of Third Republic idealism, though minus the optimism. His main influences were Brunschvicg and Émile Bréhier, but his career advanced in fits and starts chiefly as the result of a dramatic experience as a soldier in the First World War. Having managed to survive a gunshot wound to the head in the war's opening weeks, Gueroult spent the remainder of the conflict in a German prisoner-of-war camp, wherein he discovered what would come to be two lifelong passions: the piano and Fichte.[15] As indicated, Fichte would be the subject of his first major study, which served as his major thesis, in 1930; the accompanying minor thesis was on Salomon Maimon.[16] These works secured Gueroult a post at the University of Strasbourg, where he would teach until being called away to the Sorbonne in 1944 to replace Brunschvicg, who was in internal exile in Aix-en-Provence. At the time of his appointment to the Collège seven years later, Gueroult had not produced a major study in twenty years. In fact, he had spent the majority of this time attempting to elaborate his own methodology, a brand of self-styled "radical idealism" he called the *Dianoématique*, the "study of doctrines."[17] Though the texts of this project were published posthumously, Gueroult did publicize the fundamental contours of his method on at least one occasion. Indeed, his inaugural lesson at the Collège de France could not have failed to delight those concerned to keep historicism at bay.[18]

In an implicit reference to Sartre, Gueroult began his lesson by thanking the Collège for providing respite from the imperious orders to "engage in the world" that were commonly heard at the time. He went on to justify the renaming of his post "the chair in the history and technology of philosophical systems." In contrast to his predecessors, Henri Bergson and Étienne Gilson, Gueroult maintained the irreducibility and singularity of philosophical works. Where Bergson had a tendency to reduce philosophy to the subjective experience of the philosopher—Gueroult called this tendency "subjectivism"—Gilson judged philosophies according to an immutable and ideal, though unarticulated, standard foreign to the philosophies themselves. In both instances, Gueroult detected a disparagement of the work itself, which alone was the locus and sole expression of a philosophy's meaning or sense. The main virtue of philosophy as a practice, in Gueroult's view, was its ability to check the gratuitousness of opinion and mere appearance. In the lesson, Gueroult defined appearance as that which "gives itself as real without being able to prove itself as such," hence the importance of irrefutable demonstration. For Gueroult, all philosophies were demonstrative in their essentials. But, evidently, this notion of demonstration is meant to be intrinsically rational: "The rationality that grounds any philosophy—whether that philosophy is rational or not [. . .] has a constitutive function: since the philosophy is not already finished before it is developed, only existing after its completion despite numerous obstacles [. . .] a double end in one is thus realized: the construction of a monument, the demonstration of a truth." Truths were plural in history; they were singular and eternal in a given philosophical system. Accordingly, then, the historian of philosophy was to be "skeptical as a historian, but dogmatic as a philosopher."[19]

Gueroult's call to "vanquish historicism" at the end of his inaugural lesson, which, in addition to Bergson and Gilson, called Dilthey and Heidegger in for sharp scrutiny, drew from his belief that the scholar's conception of philosophy and its history must not be conceived prior to an engagement with anterior philosophical systems, each of which must be granted its autonomy as a "philosophical reality." On this view, the problem with historicist modes of study was that they were not historical enough, making philosophy's history subservient to the perspective of the philosophical present. This charge was more fully fleshed out, and more emphatically linked to the German philosophical tradition, in the pages of the *Dianoématique*.[20] There Gueroult elaborates his idiosyncratic distinction between "doctrine" and "system." It was taken as given that multiple philosophical doctrines existed in history, a doctrine being defined as the "apprehension of the system or the Idea in subjective thought."[21] The doctrine might be marked by innumerable particularities of the author's contingent circumstances, but the "system or the Idea" subtending it was, according to Gueroult, the site of that philosophy's "reality." A dogged emphasis on plural "philosophical realities," each to be accorded its status as universally true, runs through the *Dianoématique*. The term *réel* or a derivation appears some 1,615 times in the methodological core of the *Dianoématique*, an average of nine appearances per page,[22] a repetition that suggests Gueroult's difficulty in articulating the precise content of this philosophical reality or where it might lie.

But this obsession with "reality" points us to the key ambition of Gueroult's "radical idealism." He desired his own method to be nothing less than the "reversal of Hegelianism."[23] Where Hegel had made his subjective apprehension of philosophy's history serve as the very basis for his account, Gueroult wanted to effect an inversion, thus making "the reality of philosophy's history" the foundation for our systematic assessment of it. This method would dictate a militant fidelity to the letter of philosophical texts and a practice of reading devoid of hermeneutic intentions. For Gueroult, a philosophical system was not a representation of a truth or reality extrinsic to that system. Thus, not only would a hermeneutic approach be of no avail; it would be disastrously misleading. Because a philosophical system could be judged only on its own terms, it could not be held accountable to some deeper truth of which that system was but one aspect. Against Hegel's historicism, Gueroult was insistent that philosophical truth exists in the plural in history, as do plural versions of the rational or the real. Gueroult targeted Kant as well for positing the synthetic a priori as an immutable structure that, while perhaps useful for the pursuit of scientific truths, laid the groundwork for the return of a "radical subjectivism" in philosophy and metaphysics.[24] Finally, Gueroult contrasted his position with Husserl's in similar terms, arguing for an efflorescent pluralism against a reductive essentialism whose criteria were located more in the vagaries of a contingent encounter than in the fixed integrity of the philosophical text. Intentionality was Husserl's concept, borrowed from Franz Brentano, for describing the way that all consciousness is always consciousness *of* something, an object, ideal or sensibly perceived, that said consciousness "intends" in its apprehension of it. But for Gueroult, intentionality was nothing more than a "mysterious deux ex machina" on the level of philosophical argumentation,[25] forsaking analysis and conferring legitimacy upon what might well be the vague and gratuitous insights of a purely contingent encounter between a given consciousness and its "intended" object.[26] In other words, there was nothing in Husserlian phenomenology to prevent the rampant "subjectivism" that had also marred Bergson's philosophy. Phenomenology provided no safeguards against the tendency toward what Gueroult called "unconscious objectivation,"[27] the misrecognition as objective of what is subjective through and through.

In contrast to this "tendency," in which Husserlian phenomenology is deemed the latest episode of a German trajectory, Gueroult presents his own project as the essence of rational philosophy. Rational philosophy is to be a flight from the gratuitous in the systematic construction of the work; by extension, the history of philosophy should be conducted in the same way. In this, the conduct of the historian of philosophy is not unlike that of art historians. Works of art are not assessed by how well they represent some extrinsic reality; moreover, it is taken for granted that multiple works all partake of the name "art" and that the concept "art" does not exist independently of its historically produced constituent components, works of art themselves. The same goes in philosophy, except with the caveat that an art critic need not master the physical techniques of painting in order to assess a painting. According to Gueroult a rational assessment of a given philosophy does require "mastery" of the techniques that "render operational" the "monument" itself, the work.[28] The *Dianoématique* was a delicate balancing act in that it wanted to simultaneously affirm a rational pluralism in the history of philosophy alongside a pluralistic rationalism on the level of method, that is, a sole methodology that would have infinitely plural applications and remain true to the singularity of multiple systems, all the while maintaining internal consistency as a method.[29] In the end, it would seem Gueroult opted to focus his energies on the prior concern, as he abandoned the attempt to articulate his methodological principles. Several readers have suggested that Gueroult himself realized the inadequacy of his efforts and that his time would be better spent doing his work and letting it justify itself rather than justifying it in advance.[30] One could add that this development is not only consistent with but also emblematic of Gueroult's guiding conviction: to grant the history of philosophy its cacophonous reality against the last word of a singular, overarching interpretation.

Descartes was the first "monument" considered after Gueroult's appointment to the Collège. This decision was not entirely contingent. Eleven months before his inaugural lesson, Gueroult had sent a letter to his junior colleague Alquié to share some of his thoughts on the latter's recently published study, *La Découverte métaphysique de l'homme chez Descartes*. In this work, Alquié argued that, in the discovery of the *cogito* following the experience of radical doubt, Descartes articulated a universal concept of the human as predicated upon a conscientious fortitude in the face of radical absence, an absence of certainty or confidence in the surrounding, existent world.[31] Voicing his displeasure with this reading, Gueroult pleaded with Alquié to abandon this "novelistic philosophy" in which the philosophers of the past serve as mouthpieces for one's own philosophical convictions. He implored Alquié to make a decision, either for "pure philosophy where you express yourself directly, or the history of philosophy, where you will merely serve the thought of a genius, rather than enlisting him, willy-nilly, to your own service."[32] In 1953, Gueroult published the result of his courses: *Descartes selon l'ordre des raisons*. The title drew its authority from Descartes' injunction to be read in such terms; its polemical force lay in its riposte to Alquié's interpretation. In the opening pages, Gueroult cited Alquié's statement that "we do not believe there is a system in Descartes," only to follow with the rejoinder: "Descartes thought otherwise."[33]

As Alquié was fifteen years younger than Gueroult, there must have been something both harrowing and flattering in being taken to task by such an authority. The contrast between Gueroult's and Alquié's educational trajectories is revealing. Though no less influenced by Brunschvicg and Bréhier than Gueroult was, Alquié's philosophical itinerary was much less restricted. Too young to have seen action in the First World War, Alquié came of age in the interwar years, during which time he was deeply affected by his close friendship with André Breton and his involvement in the surrealist movement.[34] These formative experiences would impress upon Alquié a concern to preserve a space for the mysterious and the ineffable in his subsequent work. Our sensory experience of art or of the world was, for Alquié, allusive in its essentials and thus more suggestive than satisfactory. The task of philosophy was to offer an account of our experiences that would retain this sense of ineffability and provide its own kind of satisfaction as a result. These convictions are fully evident in his critical review of Gueroult's study of Descartes, which served as Alquié's first public response to Gueroult's disparagement of his work.

Alquié conceded all manner of brilliance to Gueroult's exquisite reconstruction of Descartes' philosophy according to the "order of reasons," but he maintained that the truth Gueroult sought to articulate was merely "scientific." As a result, the Descartes presented therein was not "satisfying."[35] In striking contrast, Alquié's book had argued that the eternal value of Descartes' philosophy, and the source of its satisfaction for anyone who encountered it, was the lesson in ontological experience dramatized in the *Meditations*: man's ability to move beyond the world of objects gaining closer proximity, not to say convergence, with Being itself. In general, for Alquié, "system" was a term foreign to true philosophical experience. Access to the eternal required an "ontological démarche."[36] Along these lines, in his short book *Qu'est-ce que comprendre un philosophe?*, the result of a lecture conceived as a response to Gueroult's inaugural lesson, Alquié argued that one is not born a philosopher but becomes one as a reaction against nonphilosophical thought and the lack of satisfaction to be found there.[37] Philosophy is defined as this "démarche" that moves one toward philosophy's essential discovery of a "subjective universality." "Philosophers," Alquié argues, "by showing that the world does not contain its own conditions, go toward a Being that is not a world." More emphatically, "[N]othing disorients us more than philosophy precisely because it takes us out of the world to something that is not a world." Alquié contrasts his position with Gueroult's, arguing that the constitution of a system has never been the goal of philosophy. Just as the knights of the Middle Ages did not know they were living in the Middle Ages, Descartes did not know that he was "Cartesian." "In effect," Alquié writes, "Descartes did not want to establish a system that would be Descartes' system; he wanted to find the truth, which is totally different, and he sought this truth with complete sincerity."[38]

In a move that drives to the heart of Gueroult's project, Alquié casts Gueroult's method in the same league as those methodologies—psychological or historicist—that Gueroult so distrusts. According to Alquié, what all of these methodologies have in common is that they make an *object* out of philosophical truth.[39] True, the philosopher must express himself in some way, and this he usually does according to the norms and procedures of the epoch. "For the system is always the interpretation of evidence in the name of that which is not obvious [*évident*]." But in this systematization Alquié sees the greatest risk for the author to express "despite himself, his time and the errors of his time."[40]

The notion that the philosopher's errors, whatever they may be, conceal some deeper immutable truth is central to Alquié's conception of philosophy. This conviction was given its clearest expression in Alquié's *La Nostalgie de l'être*, where it was argued that an "eternal relation" exists between our consciousness and Being. Against Hegelianism, and historicism more generally, in which Alquié saw a lack of respect for the "impassible totality of each man," Alquié claimed, like Gueroult, that philosophies exist in history to be accepted or refused but never "exceeded [*dépassé*]."[41] In each true philosophical gesture, Alquié detected a profound "nostalgia for Being."

The certainty of Being is thus, above all, certainty of its absence: as such, it is inseparable from the desire to rediscover it, because, as it is not objective knowledge, it can only be manifested in the feeling of our separation, which is itself born from our inclination not to be separated. In this sense, every consciousness is nostalgia for Being, an indissoluble union of certitude and will, and it is no easy task to distinguish in philosophers what responds to the will and what expresses the certitude, ontological construction and metaphysical critique.[42]

Even if it is no easy task, Alquié will present as heroes those who can withstand the painful sense of separation, responding to this fact rather than the desire to suture some lost wholeness.[43] Indeed, "the nostalgia for being is at the origin both of critical philosophies, which describe it with exactitude and accept it with courage, and ontologies, which set out to soothe it."[44]

Throughout Alquié's project one can detect echoes of Heidegger's critique of metaphysics insofar as conceptual thought is seen as grounded on a more primordial experience of incompletion, be it as "separation" or "thrownness." And Heidegger does make it into Alquié's account, but more as a derivative specimen of Kierkegaardian courage before the nostalgia for Being than as a philosophical authority in his own right.[45] In Jacques Derrida's recollection, Alquié thought himself a worthy rival to Heidegger, whom he believed had stolen his idea.[46] But the fact remains that if there is a Heideggerian quality to Alquié's project, it is a strange Heideggerianism that posits Descartes as an exemplary figure and nevertheless develops a project of authenticity grounded in radical absence. The démarche central to Alquié's effort "calls upon an *unconceptualizable* ontological experience, which cannot be replaced by anything that derives from it."[47] Philosophy "makes explicit a fundamental experience, a *nonconceptual* presence of being to consciousness, common to the philosopher and everyone. This universal presence is what makes philosophy at once legitimate and necessary."[48] Here Alquié aligns himself in the camp of philosophers who, according to Gueroult, make the philosophical work derivative of an ineffable experience, a trend that Gueroult associates with the "excess of subjectivism" infecting Bergsonism and its phenomenological legacy in France.[49] More important still, this démarche of Alquié's own points to the fundamental disagreement between his and Gueroult's positions: the primacy of subjective experience or conceptual thought.[50]

Confrontations

Nowhere was the dispute between the two scholars clearer than in the confrontation that took place between them at the 1955 colloquium on Descartes in Royaumont, an event largely inspired by their conflicting readings. Alquié began the proceedings with a concession to Gueroult's emphasis on demonstration in Descartes' philosophy but nevertheless maintained that the demonstrative is important only in Cartesian science, which, as the domain of the homogeneous, merely explains, whereas the heterogeneous realm of metaphysics, Descartes' "philosophy," discovers and "observes."[51] Alquié suggests that, despite the myriad avenues by which Descartes can logically lead us to a concept of God, what Descartes really wants to provoke is the ontological experience of separation similar to his own.[52] Gueroult's response to Alquié follows a similar rhetorical tack, ceding ground in its acknowledgment of the "ontological experience" that inaugurates Descartes' project. But he then launches into an unforgiving offensive against Alquié's position, centered above all on the issue with which Alquié closed his talk: the location of truth in Descartes.[53]

Gueroult maintains that, for Descartes, the quest for certainty is essential and what takes him "above the plane of the simple lived." We can too easily be duped by the "multitude of intuitions" present in experience.

"In a word," Gueroult says, "Descartes is absolutely hostile to a philosophy of gratuitousness," fearing above all to be a victim of "poetic intuition."[54] From this opening gambit, the conversation between Gueroult and Alquié traverses the text of Descartes' corpus and quarrels by turns over the status of the "extended thing" versus "extension" or the "thinking thing" versus "thought." Alquié wants to maintain a metaphysical distinction within both sets of terms where Gueroult sees none; Gueroult claims that Alquié imputes a fundamental "extra-intellectual support" with an "occult quality" to Descartes' argumentation, "a being that is unable to be reached by thought since it would not be thought," and thus a move that effectively achieves a "negation of Descartes, who fought all his life against those who would place an occult quality either in exterior things or in oneself."[55] A dizzying exchange then ensues concerning the difference between "a thinking thing" and "thinking being" and the relationship of both to "Thought" as such. Eventually Alquié breaks with the banter to avow the following:

My whole thesis consists in affirming that, with Descartes, being is not reducible to the concept. Yet the question you are asking me is the following: but what is it, this being that is not reducible to the concept? As I can express myself, by definition, only by concepts, I am unable to respond. But this doesn't prove I am wrong, because my thesis consists in saying that being is precisely not reducible to the concept. If you are asking me what is this being in the plane of concepts, then I cannot tell you or provide you with an "attribute" that is adequate to being. I believe that being [and] existence reveal themselves to thought only in an experience that is familiar but untranslatable. The evidence of the *sum* [i.e., of being] is primary and exceeds [*dépasse*] the idea of thought.[56]

But Gueroult maintains his position all the same, ultimately refusing the phrase "reducible to the concept" as relevant to the meaning of concept in Descartes' philosophy.[57] He also attacks further Alquié's slippery usage of Cartesian concepts, as if they are flexible placeholders for intuitions rather than products of rational deduction. As the discussion nears exhaustion, with the hope of any sort of agreement already gone, Gueroult declares the following:

We are in a period where many do not like mathematics and mathematical certainty very much, but the problem that Descartes poses for himself, everyone knows, is that of certainty; it is not that of ontological experience. What is important at bottom to know [*savoir*] is not what we know [*connaît*], but to be sure that we can know [*connaître*]. It is to be sure that we can have a science, to have the certainty that the certainty that we grant to science or to metaphysics or to anything whatsoever is not deceptive.[58]

The Aristotle scholar Victor Goldschmidt no doubt spoke for many in attendance when he noted the "disconcerting impression" left by Gueroult and Alquié's dispute at Royaumont. "That agreement between two philosophical positions might be difficult, that is no problem," Goldschmidt wrote. "But that two interpreters could not come to agree upon the meaning, or even the letter of the Cartesian texts, that's what's disturbing, humiliating even, for any listener who believes in the universality of the intellect."[59] But universality was indeed at stake in the interlocutors' disagreement. As Alquié said, the evidence of the *sum* in *cogito ergo sum* is primary, apodictic even, and exceeds all conditions that might intervene to obscure it. Gueroult's untimely celebration of mathematical certainty is directed against the "gratuitousness" he sees at work in this obscure "evidence" and in Alquié's presentation. For Gueroult, Alquié serves as an avatar for the same liabilities he discerns in phenomenology—the threat of "gratuitousness" chief among them—and the abrogation of rationalism it ostensibly threatens. For Gueroult, the concept is what serves as a check on the "occult qualities" he finds lurking in Alquié's Descartes, qualities that countenance the elision that substitutes the first evidence of the *sum* for the first evidence of the *cogito*.

In the vehemence of Gueroult's critique as it was presented, however, we see the intimations of this conflict's move from the terrain of Cartesianism to that of Spinozism. For Spinoza the factic immediacy of thought has priority over the evidence of the *sum*. What is clear from Gueroult's contribution to the debate at Royaumont is that, regardless of the potential justification for his claims in Descartes' texts, Gueroult is infusing Descartes with a position that he will attribute to Spinoza more emphatically later on. He persistently downplays the location of Cartesian certainty in the *cogito*, and the element of discreteness and indeed isolation that this localization implies. The primacy accorded to thought itself as a generalized attribute, opposed to the murky "evidence of the *sum*," leads Gueroult to his refusal to distinguish as to their cause among "a thinking thing," "thinking being," and "Thought" altogether. This move amounts to giving "attributes" in Descartes' philosophy a degree of discrete substantiality more strongly affirmed by Spinoza. As noted, many respondents to

Gueroult's work have pointed to the general accord between Gueroult's hard-line rationalist outlook in the postwar years and Spinozism as a rational system.[60] This assessment is provocative, but its implications are of course deeply problematic for Gueroult's general method. Gueroult's reading of Descartes is in fact strangely similar to Spinoza's own, at least in the fact that it uses structural coherence as a benchmark and manages to express the coherence of Descartes' system, but finds it implicitly inadequate nonetheless. Gueroult and Spinoza both recognize that one effect of Descartes' philosophy is the limitation of reason, one that makes God—if not being—truly incomprehensible.[61] If, as Spinoza argued, truth is its own sign, and the *more geometrico* gives us the eyes to see this sign, what are the stakes for Spinoza's intentions and Gueroult's method if variable truths can be expressed with the same tools?[62] Can truth retain its constitutive and universal qualities in such circumstances?

Alquié and Gueroult would meet again in 1972 at a colloquium in Brussels on method and the history of philosophy where these issues would be addressed more directly. Chaïm Perelman orchestrated this event, which also involved contributions from Michel Serres and Henri Lefebvre, among others, to be a deliberate resumption of the debate begun at Royaumont seventeen years earlier.[63] At this stage, the positions of both thinkers have modified slightly, reflecting their scholarly accomplishments in the intervening years. Alquié's study of Malebranche has taught him the value of historical work that considers a philosophy's implications beyond its intentions; for example, he sees a strong line of Malebranchist thought stretching into the secular Enlightenment.[64] Gueroult for his part maintains his distrust of phenomenology—which he claims locates philosophy's value in an inaccessible interiority—and rehashes his insistence that a philosophy's construction is "commanded" by the "reality" at its source, even if that reality is one that "requires of reason its own detriment."[65] A new emphasis on plurality nevertheless appears in Gueroult's contribution to these proceedings. Indeed, Gueroult stresses the "multiplicity of paths, rational or irrational, that give access to philosophy."[66] Once there, however, each philosophy calls upon a "philosophizing reason [*raison philosophante*]" to justify the reality it discovers.[67] In this way, Descartes' foreclosure of reason's reach can be justified by his own "philosophizing reason," and his philosophy is now understood to be effectively self-caused and sensible in its own immanent terms. Gueroult also suggests a new relationship between reality and truth in the exchanges at this conference, yet rooted still in his *Dianoématique*. "The truth of a philosophy is the affirmation of a certain reality, which it estimates truly to be reality."[68] The systematic philosophical text is not a means of "communication" of a reality independent of it, as if intuitions could be communicated as such; the chef d'oeuvre is rather that philosophy's "optimum" and "maximum" expression.[69]

Perelman, a proponent of Gueroult's method, presses Alquié on how a démarche, which in and of itself is not a proposition, could ever be "true." Alquié concedes a plurality of truths but maintains that truth in this sense is merely logical, the effect of a proposition. His reference in support of his own position—and his hesitation to present it as such—is significant. Philosophical truth, for Alquié, is "in the same sense" as Christ's response to Pontius Pilate that he is "the Truth, the Way, and the Life."[70] The point of this reference, directed against Gueroult's lecture, is that Christ did not say "truth*s*," because the genuine referent of truth cannot be pluralized. But Gueroult will persist: though philosophies contain an element of truth in a scientific sense, this truth is only that of a judgment; the truth he is talking about, the one that can exist in the plural, is "an intrinsic truth."[71] The implication of Gueroult's response is that the scientific concept of truth is more in line with Alquié's patently religious example; here truth results from assent. The truth that is intrinsic, that is attendant to philosophical reality as Gueroult understands it, must be recognized as such. That this recognition must take place from the outside is obvious to Gueroult; but this recognition does not involve, or require, assent.

In the course of their exchange at Brussels, Alquié argues that even though Descartes, Kant, and Husserl all say "something different" when the first says, "I think, therefore I am," or the second establishes the transcendental subject, or the third performs his phenomenological reduction, "it is equally true that, in a certain manner, they are saying the same thing. And it is that, before whatever objective given, there is a way for the mind [*l'esprit*] to come back to itself and to consider itself as primary in relation to the object."[72] It is this reduction to singularity that Gueroult finds intolerable, even within the confines of a sole philosopher. If Descartes was satisfied with his intuition of the *cogito*, Gueroult asks, why didn't he stop there? "The *cogito* is not the unique truth of Descartes; it is one of the truths of Descartes, a truth to which, from all evidence, his philosophy cannot be reduced."[73] Moreover, the suggestion that with the *cogito* Descartes is expressing the same truth as "Saint Augustine, Kant, Fichte, Maine de Biran, or Husserl, etc." is not only impossible to endorse or refute; it is irrelevant. "Descartes' philosophy, that is to say, his system, incites a world of productive reflections that the *cogito* alone would be unable to incite."[74]

Although Gueroult and Alquié find themselves here on the familiar battleground of Descartes' philosophy, it is clear that the terms of their dispute have shifted somewhat. Where previously the argument had concerned the location of immutable truth in Descartes' philosophy, in the depths of his conscious experience or in the proliferation of his conceptual apparatus, at this stage the dispute concerns the status of "philosophical truth" as either singular or plural, even within a unique philosophical system. As noted, the meeting in Brussels took place at a time when each scholar had moved beyond Descartes to engage with other rationalist philosophers. The first volume of Gueroult's study of Spinoza had already appeared in 1968, and Alquié's work on Malebranche would be published six years later in 1974, the same year as Gueroult's second volume on Spinoza. The last foray in their protracted conflict would be Alquié's major study of Spinoza, published in 1981, five years after Gueroult's death. In their respective readings of Spinoza, we see that theology is regarded as the privileged threat to philosophical activity. In Gueroult's study, theology goes by the name of the "occult," which is regarded as the target of Spinoza's absolute rationalism. For Alquié, Spinozism is itself nothing but a hyperrationalized theology that is by turns naturalist or negative. Alquié's hesitation to invoke a theological analogy at Brussels belies his own effort to maintain that the separation constitutive of the immutable truth at work in Descartes, Kant, or Husserl is *not* theological just because it brackets a space in the beyond as unknowable. But it also prefigures his later concern to color Spinozism as theological precisely in its privileging of God, however naturalized, as a fully available object of inquiry.

Spinoza and the Threat of Theology

Though Gueroult's study can be situated amid the upsurge of interest in Spinozism among French thinkers beginning in the late 1960s, *Spinoza I: Dieu* is an anomaly in this field. Where for Althusser and his students, Spinoza became the privileged theoretical resource for rethinking the Marxist project, the concerns of the political, and indeed the ethical, were far from central or even relevant to Gueroult's study. Similarly, where Deleuze found in Spinoza a concept of ontological univocity that would be foundational for his later, more engaged work with Félix Guattari, for Gueroult the peculiarities of Spinoza's ontology were subservient to the elaboration of the rational epistemology, or gnoseology, to use the Scholastic term Gueroult favors, that was Spinoza's chief aim.

In one sense, however, Gueroult's project was of a piece with this broader return to Spinoza. In addition to elaborating the contours of an absolute rationalism, Gueroult's exegesis is also an attempt to rescue Spinoza's philosophy from the misreading it has suffered historically, chiefly in the hands of Hegel and those who read Spinoza through a Hegelian lens. Gueroult devotes nearly two hundred pages to the opening propositions of Book I of the *Ethics* in order to refute Hegel's interpretation of Spinozism as a negative theology wherein the "attributes" serve as determinations of a Substance that would otherwise remain indeterminate without them. Gueroult argues that Spinoza's decision to have "substance" and "attribute" operate as equivalent, that is, synonymous, terms in the first eleven propositions of the *Ethics* is "genetically" essential for his overall project. Though Substance will later be capitalized to refer to the idea of the infinity of attributes in one concept, the establishment of the "substantial" quality of the attributes in these early steps is necessary to prevent the speculative persistence of an *arrière-monde* that exists prior to its determination in this world. The error of "classical rationalism" as Spinoza saw it was its reliance on a foundation that was elsewhere, outside the world itself. It is for this reason that Gueroult insists that the concept of "creation," which necessarily involves a "creator" and a "created," is evacuated of sense in Spinoza's philosophy.[75]

At one point in his study, Gueroult gives a striking clue as to the complicity of his methodology with his scholarly object in his description of Spinoza's concept of Substance as "genetic, in other words synthetic" (457). The central paradox of Spinoza's philosophy that Gueroult's work seeks to clarify is how there can be a synthetic operation, indeed any concept of synthesis at all, without a foundation for that synthesis that is elsewhere or at the very least external to the synthetic operation itself (e.g., a transcendental subject or a creator-God). The model for the equivalency that Spinoza establishes between "genesis" and "synthesis" is mathematical. Mathematics provides Spinoza a method of reasoning that is intrinsic, driven by wholly internal conditions. A genetic definition, according to

Gueroult, is one that expresses the efficient cause of the object in question; in this it is opposed to a definition that merely offers a property. A circle is not to be defined by its roundness; it is a figure described by a straight line of which one end is fixed and the other is mobile (170). In this example, the "comprehension" of a circle as a "being of reason" is predicated not on an exhaustive account of all the qualitative differences among all the possible or existent circles, large or small, or red or blue, or whatever properties any given circle may bear (413–24). It is "comprehended," rather, *only* in terms of its genetic cause.

Gueroult pursues his interpretation of the role of the infinite in Spinoza's philosophy in the same regard (500–528). Seeking to avoid the consignment of the Spinozist infinite to the "bad infinity" of Hegel's critique, Gueroult positions Spinoza against an anachronistic adversary, Bergson. Bergson's claim that the intellect cuts apart what is experienced as continuous is presented as the complete *inversion* of the Spinozist position on this subject (504n17). Spinoza argues that the affective imagination is what leads the human mind to conceive of the world as parts, and that only the intellect, which breaks from lived experience, is able to conceive of the infinite as actuality. Spinoza's genetic understanding of the infinite, as irrespective to the imaginative trope of number, is rooted in the genetic definition of Substance as the idea of the necessary coexistence of the attributes. Gueroult must deal, however, with the fact that Spinoza calls the mental operation by which this concept of the infinite is grasped "intuition," a term that, at the time of Gueroult's writing, had become fraught with Bergsonian connotations. The point Gueroult presses is that for Spinoza intuition involves nothing external to ideas; the immediacy of intuition derives not from its ability to break through the gauze of the reasoning intellect to something external to it. To the contrary, it is simply the immediacy of an idea conceiving of another idea. This is "radical idealism," indeed.

This whole operation, however, has the potential to remain purely analytical given that it is rooted in a mathematical concept of concepts. And it is certainly difficult to conceive of a purer example of precritical tautology than the Spinozist formula of *Deus sive Natura*. To understand how the ontological descriptor "genetic" provides some purchase on the epistemological notion of "synthesis," and vice versa, it is essential to come to grips with Gueroult's handling of the relationship between modes, on the one hand, and Substance/attributes, on the other, in Spinoza's philosophy. Here Gueroult's reading is at its most challenging. Though Spinoza insists upon an infinity of attributes, because of his own genetic definition of Substance, the only two that figure into the *Ethics* are those able to be perceived in their essence by the human intellect. These are the two distinct halves of Cartesian dualism, Thought and Extension. In Spinozism, however, although these two attributes are "absolutely different," that is, distinct as to their essence, they are "absolutely identical" because they share the same immanent cause, Substance. "There is no juxtaposition of the attributes, since they are identical as to their causal act," Gueroult writes, "but neither is there fusion between them, since they remain irreducible as to their essences" (238).[76]

The modes are an even more elusive category in Spinoza's typology. Modes are defined as "affections of substance," which Spinoza unpacks as meaning "that which is in something else and is conceived through something else."[77] But it is clear that the modes include all the various experiences and contingencies of existence; these, not the attributes, are the sites of qualitative determination and change. Yet in order to be rationally accounted for, they must be conceived with reference to the attributes of which they are at once the determinations and the effects. More problematic still is the distinction Spinoza makes between finite and infinite modes. God's intellect is an infinite mode: infinite because its essence necessarily involves existence; modal because, as "intellect," it requires the attribute "Thought" in order to be adequately conceived in a qualitatively distinct way. In contrast, the intellect of a discrete human mind is a finite mode, because its essence does *not* necessarily involve existence. That said, this finite mode of intellect is "part of" the infinite mode of intellect in that they partake of the same essence; the qualitative distinction of "intellect" from other modes is quantitatively dispersed throughout the infinite attribute of Thought. At this point we see why the infinite as such is so problematic for Spinozism. How can the finite be "part of" the infinite if the concept of the infinite that Spinoza seeks to promote is wholly antithetical to number?

In this regard, it is crucial to follow Gueroult's insistence that the intellect as infinite mode, that is, the divine intellect, must never be confused with Thought as an infinite attribute, the latter of which is the rational "cause" of the former "effect."[78] This is the case even though the two categories are absolutely coextensive. The infinite mode of the "intellect" is absolutely coextensive with the attribute Thought; but the attribute Thought also grounds all the other modal expressions of thought apart from the intellect (e.g., desire, love, and various other states). The intellect is a mode, which by definition means it is qualitatively distinct from these other modes; Thought is an attribute, which means it is, along with Extension, at once the *formal* and *substantial* condition for modal change and relation in general. As Gueroult has shown in the opening sections of his volume, the attributes Thought and Extension are absolutely distinct from each other as to their essence. But they are also epistemologically or cognitively distinct from the modal effects of which they are the cause. The qualitative changes that occur on a modal level can never be completely reduced to their ground in the attributes; modal change occurs through relations among the modes. But these relations nonetheless require the fundamental relation between Thought and Extension as their rational ground, even if this ground in no way provides us with an exhaustive account of modal qualities or properties.[79] Substance, as a rational concept, is nothing more than the name for the permanent relation of these essentially distinct attributes, each of which is infinite in its essence. Gueroult recognizes full well that the relationship of the intellect as finite mode to the divine intellect as infinite mode is problematic; but he maintains that as each mode, being an "effect" in Spinoza's system, is placed on the side of *natura naturata* rather than *natura naturans* (the site of Substance as cause), there is an identity of essence between the infinite and the finite.[80] Here "identity" does not mean analogous by a supposed doubling but identical as in one and the same, just as attributes and Substance are the same. In this move, the murky analogy of a part to a whole, which attends to the comparison of the finite to infinite and which is the bane of any rationalist metaphysics, disappears.

The only ontological distinction in Spinoza's philosophy is that between the attributes. The relation established in Spinoza's understanding of cause and effect is a purely gnoseological (or epistemological) one; but this gnoseological relation makes sense only if it is predicated upon the ontological distinction at the heart of Spinoza's metaphysics. The thought of the cause/effect relation is, in its own essence, an *idea*, and it is an idea that in effect "transcends" the ontological distinction that is its condition. Gueroult has no qualms playing the heretical Spinozist when he argues that the relation from cause to effect necessarily involves an element of transcendence. Spinoza's idea of Substance, which manifests itself as an insistence on God's immanence, is marshaled against a concept of God as a *transient* cause only, *not* as a *transcendent* cause. Gueroult says:

[B]y virtue of the definition of cause, all things that God causes being incommensurable with him as to essence and existence, God is in this regard exterior to his effects; and, moreover, by reason of the definitions of substance and mode, they [modes] are in him, but as one is in an other. Thus, just as much from the point of view of his causality as from his essence, God appears as absolutely distinct from his effects or from his modes. In this sense, he is transcendent to them. The immanence of God to things does not go without a certain transcendence. (299–300)

It is this radical distinction between cause and effect—the gnoseological relation made possible by the ontological distinction of the attributes—that allows for the elision from genetic construction to an understanding of synthetic reality. The distinction between Substance/attributes and modes maps on to that between cause and effect; but this distinction is possible only because the attributes themselves, Thought and Extension, are distinct from each other. The attributes can relate only *because* they are distinct. And it is their permanent "relation" that is the genetic cause of all modal effects, that is, the universe of qualitatively variegated existence itself. For Gueroult, the incommensurability in play here is integral and constitutive: "The incommensurability is not between the divine intellect [infinite mode] and ours [finite mode], but between God [Substance/attributes] and his intellect [mode]" (279). These modal effects, however, which in essence are radically distinct from their cause by virtue of being effects, do not emanate from, nor are they expressive of, a prior substance; rather, each effect is the result of a rational procedure whose genetic operation mirrors the synthetic process to which it attends. "The incommensurability between God as cause and his intellect as effect *coincides therefore* with the incommensurability between God as object and his intellect as idea." More important, "this incommensurability, *far from excluding knowledge or the truth of the idea, is on the contrary their condition*, for the conformity of the idea to its object, which defines the idea, or truth, *would be impossible without their fundamental distinction*" (285, emphasis added). The opposition of the object and its idea, their essential distinction, even when the idea's "object" is in fact another idea, is what renders synthetic knowledge possible. Here, the *concept* is forged not in the overcoming of a radical opposition, and a consequent forgetting of this moment, but rather in a militant attentiveness to the eternal and insistently repeated opposition between the idea and its object.

In the insistence on the incommensurability of an idea with its object as a condition for the emergence of a "true idea," Spinozism becomes for Gueroult not the site of a singular truth in and of itself but rather an epistemology (gnoseology) that allows for the articulation and understanding of a plurality of "true ideas" to be produced ad infinitum. This investment acquires its full remit only in light of Gueroult's methodology, which is geared in each instance toward producing the fully adequate "idea," that is, his study, of the "object" in question: a textually extant philosophical system. In his wholesale refusal to tolerate any chiasmic intertwining between ideas and their objects, or a hermeneutics in which the ideas of the reader and the text are ultimately rendered indistinct, Gueroult is at pains to make Spinozism a rigorous antidote to the "mysterious deus ex machina" of phenomenological intentionality that assures their fundamental union. In this regard, the resonance of Gueroult's Spinozism with the general current of French structuralism is patent. At the heart of Saussurean linguistics was the insistence on the pure difference among linguistic signs as constitutive of meaning. At no point was a signifier deemed meaningful due to an essential content to be found in the signified; rather, it was the incommensurability among signs, signifiers, and phonemes that allowed for a proliferation of sense. Gueroult's reading of Spinozism in terms of its integral incommensurability is not only redolent of structuralism; it is exemplary of it.

We can thus see why Spinozism is so convenient for Gueroult's method and how formally similar the two "systems" are in their essentials. This proximity turns on the distinction in French between knowing as *savoir* or as *connaître*, a distinction we have seen was important to Gueroult in his defense of the rationalist Descartes. Spinozism is a philosophy purely on the side of *savoir*; Gueroult writes of *savoir absolu*, not *connaissance absolue* (11). Just because God, or Substance, is "unknowable" in an exhaustive sense does not mean that an "adequate" comprehension of the idea of Substance is impossible. To know in the sense of *savoir*, which involves an abstracted and genetic understanding, is predicated on the impossibility of knowing as *connaître*, which involves an intimacy and familiarity, a kind of burrowing out of the object in question. In Gueroult's reading, the attempt to know God in the sense of *connaître* came to be the hobgoblin of Descartes' otherwise rationalist project (9). This same epistemological distinction is in play in Gueroult's reading of past philosophical systems. As conceptual systems, they can be known in the sense of *savoir*; but it is impossible to "know" a philosopher's consciousness, his inner or lived experience, in the latter sense of *connaître*. Against a fusion of an idea with its object, or mind with world, that would allow for an interminable intuition of properties, Gueroult maintains that it is the immutable incommensurability between the two that is generative of rational concepts qua true ideas. To be sure, this fully "rational" version of the world is arguably anemic, in that it is conceived at a maximal level of abstraction that provides minimal purchase. Indeed, this abstracted world is belied daily by the multitude of feelings and intuitions that are attendant to lived experience. It is for this reason that Alquié finds Spinozism, and in particular the version of it exquisitely presented by Gueroult, completely unacceptable as philosophy.

It is a testament to the challenge of Gueroult's reading, and to the persistence of their dispute, that Alquié saw fit to make the last major study of his own career an eminently critical work. The advantage of Alquié's study over Gueroult's is readily apparent. Where Gueroult concentrated on the first two books of the *Ethics*, containing Spinoza's metaphysics and his theory of the soul, Alquié takes the whole of the *Ethics* for his object. As a result, where the limitations of Gueroult's study, cut short by his death, offered the convenience of remaining silent on the questions of beatitude that inform the conclusion of the *Ethics* in Book V,[81] for Alquié it is these promises of salvation that structure his interpretation of Spinoza's philosophy as a whole. In other words, where Gueroult read each book of the *Ethics* in "Spinozistic" terms, as structured proofs devoid of teleology, Alquié reads the *Ethics* in terms of the text's own material telos, the promise of beatitude. In his Sorbonne courses twenty years earlier, Alquié offered that his failure to understand Spinoza was perhaps a personal one.[82] At this later stage, Alquié professes to be more empowered in his critique given that, in his lifetime, he has never met or heard of anyone living a life of beatific salvation as a result of reading the *Ethics*. What is more, Alquié maintains that his assessment is most faithful to Spinoza's demands in that other so-called Spinozists must somehow be disingenuous by Spinoza's own standards. If Spinoza's philosophy "works," where is their evidence of the everlasting contentment promised at the end of the *Ethics*?

Spinoza's readers were not the only disingenuous ones. In fact, the heart of Alquié's exposé is an accusation of Spinoza's own disingenuousness in his attempts to produce a rationalism more "absolute" than Descartes'. The myriad discrepancies in the *Ethics*, for example, those between a God as Nature and a God that remains "personal" in its benevolence, or those inherent in a realist concept of knowledge that produces salvation as a result, draw from Spinoza's misguided attempt to make fully rational his own fundamental naturalist intuition concerning God's immanence. Spinoza's failure lies less in his intuition per se than in his effort to conceptualize his own inaugural ontological experience. Spinoza's desire to banish the unknown from the domain of human experience by way of mathematical certainty serves to produce a philosophy more mystifying in spite of itself.[83] Where rationalism as a method led Descartes to a concept of God as precisely that which was incomprehensible, in Spinoza rationalism ceases to be a method and becomes a doctrine that is in itself incomprehensible (325–26). In this move, Spinoza effectively creates a "new theology" whose insistence on God's full presence paradoxically reinforces a Judeo-Christian image of the *Deus absconditus* (160–62). The argument runs that Spinoza's intransigent avowal that God is fully immanent and thus knowable is belied on two counts. First, turning Gueroult's gnoseological argument against itself by testing its ontological implications, Alquié notes that the attributes are effectively transcendent to the modes in Spinoza's universe, as causes are to effects, despite impressions some passages may give to the contrary. Where for Gueroult this "transcendence" operated in our epistemological grasp of the relation of cause to effect, for Alquié this admission of God qua attributes as functionally transcendent clearly shows that Spinoza's insistence on God's immanence fails by his own lights. The second issue is revelatory of the persistent confusion at work in Gueroult and Alquié's argument over what it means to "know" or to "understand." Alquié emphasizes that the modes and the attributes are both infinite in number; as such, not even Spinoza himself claims that a complete inventory of these categories could ever be accomplished. For this reason, "the universal intelligibility that his rationalism affirms remains a promised intelligibility. This promise of intelligibility does not cause the transcendence of Being, which remains forever beyond our grasp, to disappear" (160). But the insistence on intelligibility, minus the evidence of it, infuses Spinozism with a "promesse du bonheur" that is essentially theological (352). As Alquié remarks at the outset of his study, Spinoza's version of salvation never comes.

Spinoza's dissimulation does not stop there, however. In his dogged pursuit of his pantheist conviction, Spinoza achieves a curious slippage that compromises the foundation of his entire system. In Alquié's reading, Spinoza's intolerance for the "incomprehensibility" of God in Descartes' philosophy leads him to strategically displace the "I think," which inaugurates Descartes' philosophy and which Alquié believes is the essence of the *sum* as first evidence, with his own formula: "I am thought *by God*" (325–26). The subjective act of thinking does not evaporate in this transition; it is merely transposed to God, which is precisely contrary to the evidence one experiences when one thinks oneself, in Alquié's view. "With Spinoza, the *cogito* extends itself, universalizes itself, and eternalizes itself." The result is a certainty that a Cartesian can always throw into doubt, not with recourse to logic or ontology but according to the necessary itinerary available to any human being, the "'I think,' first discovered and affirmed" (326). Hence, even worse than being a theology masquerading as philosophy, Spinozism is effectively a doctrine in bad faith. The roots of Alquié's critique of Spinozism are evident in *La Nostalgie de l'être*: the exigencies of critical thought and the virtue of rationalism qua method are submitted to the demands of a will that finds the constraints of existence to be intolerable. Much as Gueroult's Spinozism resonated with the currents of French structuralism, we can see here Alquié's proximity to the general line of French phenomenology from Levinas to Marion. There is an "otherwise than Being" or a "without Being," and any attempt to incorporate this "Other" into an ontological or conceptual continuum with worldly existence cannot but collapse into incoherence.[84]

In Alquié's view, the central event of Spinoza's philosophy is the dissolution of the "I" and its finitude contrary to all evidence. Thus, the "seduction of Spinozism" is that it answers man's eternal desire to escape finitude and achieve immortality. This seduction aims for the derealization of man "to the profit of God alone" (110).[85] In effect, Alquié reduces Spinoza's philosophy to fidelity to an inaugural instinct. He considers Spinoza's philosophy in light of Spinoza the man's own desires, elements that Gueroult would no doubt call "gratuitous" and irrelevant to the "reality" of Spinoza's philosophy. More important, however, in terms of Alquié's own philosophy, he judges Spinozism's failure against a singular truth of separation, a once-and-for-all moment to be infinitely reaffirmed that, by virtue of its emphasis on a singularity that trumps the efforts of rational thought to comprehend it, arguably possesses a theological quality in its own right. Alquié made a confession of this sort at Brussels, and it is thus no small irony that with *Le Rationalisme de Spinoza* Alquié reverses the charge against Gueroult, making the affirmation of "absolute rationalism" a surreptitious replacement of philosophy with theology.

In the juxtaposition of their studies, the incommensurability of their respective philosophical agendas is thrown into the sharpest relief. Most revealing is the way that incommensurability itself figures into each thinker's defense of his own position. For Gueroult, it is the incommensurability of idea and object, modal intellect and God/Nature (Substance/attributes), that is itself generative of absolute understanding. For Alquié, it is this same incommensurability that is evidence of the failure of any project that seeks to overcome it. The fact that Gueroult levels charges of occultism at Alquié, and that Alquié returns the charge, effectively calling Gueroult's Spinozism antiphilosophical in its theological aims, points to the fundamental short circuit at the heart of their dispute. Anything that smacks of completeness is theological in Alquié's account; theological for Gueroult signifies the persistence of a domain that is off-limits to rational thought. Each thinker wants philosophy to be autonomous and eternal, yet not theological. But there is nary an agreement between them over what it means to *be theological*. In fact, their respective versions of this persistent threat to philosophy are mirror images of one another. In the end, their dispute over rationalism appears to collapse into a kind of philosophical decisionism. Alquié, for his part, is perfectly cognizant of this. He writes,

> The sage of the *Ethics* "thinks of nothing less than death." Thus Spinozism can be constituted only by excluding from itself the anguish of our disappearance. We can conclude from this that the idea of death is foreign to truth. If, to the contrary, one holds this idea to be constitutive of our consciousness, it must be admitted that reason cannot suffice to explain man. On this point, one must choose.[86]

Alquié's reduction of their dispute to an existential choice is consistent with his entire project. He says as much when he writes that "the truth of a philosophy must stand up to the truth of man, and the truth of man is that of experience. At least such is the thesis that, in all my writings, I have not ceased to defend and support."[87] For Gueroult, as we have seen, philosophical truth must remain intrinsic, unbeholden to a standard external to itself, least of all the "truth of experience." But Gueroult no less than Alquié acknowledges, inadvertently perhaps, that the foundation of Spinoza's philosophy is in itself not philosophical when he writes that "absolute rationalism, imposing the total intelligibility of God, key to the total intelligibility of things, is Spinozism's *first article of faith*."[88] For all their shared hostility to "history" and "theology" as surrogates, the agreement between Gueroult and Alquié that philosophy must speak to the eternal, that it must be the domain of "philosophical truth," appears rooted in the evident impossibility of deciding upon the meaning of truth itself.

. . .

Although Alquié and Gueroult's debate over Spinozism ended in an impasse, Gueroult's assessment of Spinoza effectively consolidated a line of Spinozist rationalism with roots in Brunschvicg's project. The virtue of Gueroult's reading lies in its abstraction. For this abstract quality will serve a heuristic purpose in helping to tease out the fundamentally rationalist philosophical elements of Althusser's Spinozism. Again, with Deleuze, we will see how his assent to Gueroult's reading at once provides a foundation for his own assessment of Spinozism but also serves as a source of tension with his commitment to the virtual—arguably an *arrière-monde*—that was in part stimulated by Alquié's early influence on his thought.

In the next chapter, however, we return to the conflict between Husserlian phenomenology and Spinozist rationalism in a singular case. Alongside Granger or Vuillemin, Jean-Toussaint Desanti can be put forward as one of the main inheritors of Cavaillès's project. In his major philosophical statement, *Les Idéalités mathématiques*, Desanti produced his own version of Cavaillès's aborted *L'Expérience mathématique*. But this project evinced less of a complete break with Husserl than a recalibration of Husserl's method into something that might allow it to speak to the experience of rationalist necessity at the heart of mathematical discourse. Desanti's historical significance has several facets. First, in his vacillation between Spinozist rationalism and Husserlian phenomenology, we see something like the Gueroult/Alquié differend *en acte*. The fact that this vacillation remains unresolved in Desanti's case (that is, Husserl and Spinoza are in fact not reconciled) further evinces the incommensurability of the Spinozist and phenomenological positions in the French context. Second, before now, apart from our discussion of Cavaillès's Resistance activity, politics has been absent from this account. In the decade following the Second World War, Desanti was one of the most hard-line Stalinists in the French Communist Party. Putting his career as an epistemologist and philosopher of science on hold, Desanti devoted pages to Stalinist apologetics from 1945 to 1956. Near the end of this period, he produced his first book, a Marxist study of the history of philosophy that read Spinoza as a privileged case. Several years later, Desanti would attempt something similar with Husserl in a short book titled *Phénoménologie et praxis*. In each of these studies, Desanti's effort to reckon with his political judgment is discernible. Moreover, the tension between these accounts helps illuminate the tension of Desanti's philosophical thought more generally. One student of Desanti's would effectively come to link his complicity with Stalinism to his indulgence toward phenomenology. As a result, Louis Althusser would attempt what his erstwhile teacher, and the philosopher who helped recruit him into the Communist Party, deemed impossible, politically and philosophically: a wholesale commitment to Spinozist rationalism.

3

From Stalinism to Asceticism
Jean-Toussaint Desanti between Spinoza and Husserl

> Spinoza still held me in his grip back then. And even now he has not ceased to hold me. So much so that when I read Husserl, I told myself: "This is a different reform of the intellect that I'm going to have to learn."
>
> Jean-Toussaint Desanti, *Introduction à la phénoménologie*, 1994[1]

Born in 1914 in Ajaccio, Corsica, Jean-Toussaint Desanti came to Paris in the early 1930s fortified by an education in classical subjects such as mathematics, Latin, and Greek. By his own admission, he also brought along an "icy disdain" for the frivolities of modern life.[2] His first formative influence at the ENS was Jean Cavaillès, Desanti's mathematical background having predisposed him to Cavaillès's teaching. And since Desanti was uneasy with the tendency among his classmates to identify with one hero along the "royal way" of philosophy being offered by Brunschvicg at the time[3]— be it Plato, Descartes, Spinoza, or, most popularly, Kant—Cavaillès's more narrow and technical focus on "logistics" allowed Desanti to remain uncommitted even as he developed an early expertise in a field otherwise marginalized in the French context.[4]

We have seen how integral Spinozism was to Cavaillès's philosophical outlook. Desanti recognized this at the time.[5] It is thus no accident that Desanti's first serious philosophical engagement with a major philosopher was with Spinoza. Again, Desanti's mathematical mind predisposed him toward a fascination with Spinoza's philosophy, which attempted to present philosophical thought in as secure a manner as that of a geometrical proof. The effect of this initial encounter with the *Ethics* was so intoxicating for Desanti that he imagined being able to perform "Spinozist exercises" along lines similar to "Euclidean exercises."[6] What he quickly discovered, however, was that Spinoza's philosophy was marked by the "silence of the already said."[7] In other words, Desanti found that Spinoza had already taken each and every step the only way it could be taken in his unique philosophical system. Unlike mathematical reasoning, which affords a plurality of routes and ways to achieve the same rational conclusions, Spinoza's strictness was in extremis and eliminated any wandering from the set path.[8] Nevertheless, Spinoza's commitment to rationalism would mark Desanti indelibly; this commitment remained a clear feature of Desanti's thought for the rest of his career.

In 1935, Maurice Merleau-Ponty replaced Cavaillès as *caïman*, the instructor charged with preparing students at the ENS for the *agrégation* in philosophy. Shortly after his arrival, he charged Desanti with the task of preparing a presentation on the subject of the "immediate." The result of this experience was decisive for Desanti's own intellectual development. He shared the following anecdote often:

> I was a total novice at the time, but since I'd read a lot of Spinoza, I thought I was pretty well prepared. Having repudiated the standard and vulgar notions of the immediate, I'd concluded with an imprudent phrase: "Such that I myself think as *Deus quatenus* I coincide with the connection and intrinsic productivity of ideas in me." Merleau-Ponty raised his eyebrows in astonishment. "Desanti," he said, "it seems impossible to me that you could seriously grant any sense whatsoever to this phrase you've just uttered. For my part, I can't make out anything that I could possibly think as I'm hearing it." At the time I was totally unaware of phenomenology, and I didn't understand the scope of what Merleau was trying to tell me. I put his negative reaction up to a doctrinal incompatibility between Spinoza and himself.
>
> I only began to understand much later, at the moment when I ran into the difficulty of fully coming to terms with the sense of mathematical expressions designating "Cantorian" objects. For example, how do you carry out the signification of the written expression, "$2^{\aleph_\alpha}$" (2 to the power of aleph α), "α" designating any ordinal whatsoever? It's impossible to behold the "object" thus named in a full and adequate intuition in your mind. I then understood how Merleau-Ponty must have found himself in a similar situation with regard to the expression *Deus quatenus*: the impossibility of effectuating the "filling out" ["*remplissement*"] of "the intention of signification" that the expression in question required.[9]

This text comes from a talk titled "Spinoza and Phenomenology" that Desanti delivered in 1990 at a Sorbonne symposium on Spinoza and the twentieth century. The talk's contents are a protracted "thought experiment" in which Desanti seeks to account for the silence over Spinoza in evidence among the "Masters of Phenomenology." Playing the role of an "impenitent phenomenologist," Desanti tries to "effectuate the sense" of Spinoza's key phrase from the *Treatise on the Emendation of the Intellect*: *habemus enim ideam verum* (roughly, for we have true ideas). Desanti's contention is that it is integral to the phenomenological method that this expression be nonsensical, for the method itself demands that every experience of purportedly having a true idea be subjected to the eidetic reduction in order to reveal this experience's own subtending structures. Desanti recognizes that this process leads *either* to the proposition of a transcendental ego or structure, in any event a putative "zero point" at which the methodological process stops, *or* to an infinite regress. Desanti, taking Spinoza as his guide on this score, opts for the latter option, because, in his view, the infinite regress also portends an infinite progress. This process—be it regress or progress—is for Desanti the essential temporality of thinking. In a provocative twist, Desanti suggests that it is this process of thinking itself, so well described by the phenomenological method, that in fact displays the validity of Spinoza's remark. In each phenomenological reduction, a "true idea" is produced. Spinoza's contempt for the concept of "zero point" means that the phenomenologist is constitutionally unable to understand what Spinoza could possibly mean by "true idea." A true idea for Spinoza is an adequate idea; moving beyond it to the next true idea in no way compromises the truth of the true idea that is the condition for the next one. Desanti's claim is that it is the phenomenologist's own rational methodology, moving from one "immediate" idea to the next without mediation, that develops Spinoza's proposition despite the phenomenologist's intentions.

Cavaillès and Merleau-Ponty, Spinozist and phenomenologist. Time and again Desanti indicated these two thinkers as the most formative for his own "philosophical destiny."[10] The tension between these two poles—and Desanti's attentiveness to it—accounts for the emblematic quality of his thought. This tension is in evidence throughout Desanti's writings, from his earliest books on Spinoza and phenomenology to his later works on epistemology and mathematics, to his ethical reflections in the years before his death in 2002.[11] In the case of Cavaillès, we saw an effort to mobilize Spinozist rationalism against the tendencies toward irrationalism he saw in phenomenology. In the case of Gueroult and Alquié, we saw the tension between rationalist Spinozism and phenomenological Cartesianism in stark form. The Gueroult/Alquié differend in fact provides a point of entry into the tensions in Desanti's philosophical thought. For what Desanti liked about Spinozism is what Gueroult lauded in it; what disquieted him were the same elements that troubled Alquié. Yet rather than see the conflict between these two modes of thinking as evidence of the need for a philosophical decision, Desanti saw the irresoluble conflict between these perspectives as constitutive not only of Spinoza's philosophy but also of the philosophical enterprise as he understood it. This sense of permanent tension at work in Desanti's own philosophical efforts of the 1960s and 1970s accounts for the effect they have of being at once stimulating and frustrating in their constant deferral of any sense of resolution.[12] Desanti himself, in his later years, had no qualms admitting the modesty of his philosophical aims, a modesty he saw as largely conditioned by the philosophical travesties of his political youth.[13] Finally, to gesture forward a bit, if in Althusser we find an unequivocal decision for Spinozism against phenomenology, and in Deleuze we find a synthesis of the positions, what we see in Desanti is a career of theoretical activity operating as it were in feverish tension between these two theoretical poles, like a pinball ricocheting at top speed between two targets.

Unpacking this polar tension further is one of the chief tasks of the present chapter. But the case for Desanti's importance to the history of French Spinozism rests on two other components of equal importance and of a more concrete nature. The first is institutional; the second, related to the first, is political. One of Cavaillès's last students, Desanti was one of Althusser's last teachers. In the second half of the 1940s, Desanti held a series of unofficial seminars at the ENS designed to reacclimatize students, such as Althusser, whose educations had been brutally interrupted by the Second World War.[14] Althusser's archive contains his notes from these lectures, which range in content from ancient philosophy, to "logistics," to phenomenology, to Spinoza's philosophy.[15] Desanti's archive contains his notes on Spinoza from this same period, some appearing as course materials and others like drafts for potential publication.[16] Cross-referencing these archival materials gives us a sense of the Spinoza Althusser heard from Desanti's lips in these years. There is a thread of continuity that links the rationalist Spinoza of Cavaillès via Desanti to Althusser.

This archival record naturally raises the question: If Desanti was an important philosophical influence on Althusser, why did the latter not acknowledge him as such? The few words that Althusser devotes to Desanti in his autobiographical writings are not kind ones. Here the history of one institution, the ENS, must be elucidated with reference to another, that of the French Communist Party (PCF).

Along with his wife, the journalist and writer Dominique Desanti (née Persky), Jean-Toussaint Desanti was one of the most vociferous apologists for Stalinism in France in the early postwar years. With Laurent Casanova and Jean Kanapa, Desanti served as an ideological mouthpiece for the PCF, lending his scientific and philosophical imprimatur to numerous articles.[17] The titles and subheadings of his contributions to *La Nouvelle Critique*, established in 1948, say as much (one gem: "Stalin, a new kind of scientist").[18] The most notorious of Desanti's contributions was his contorted defense of Lysenkoism, the set of agricultural sciences and policies indebted to the Soviet alternative to genetics developed by Ivan Michurin, in an article and subsequent pamphlet titled "Bourgeois Science, Proletarian Science."[19] The title was not Desanti's own choosing, and the content of his contribution was sophisticated enough to avoid brokering any real distinction in the biological sciences between bourgeois and proletarian results in the laboratory. But there was certainly an emphasis on ideological motives, reading scientific goals in terms of social goals. The chief authority on this score was of course Stalin himself.

Dominique, who quit the party abruptly in 1956 after the events in Hungary, would later take her husband to task for an instance of intellectual shame that was, in her view, much more egregious than the science question. At the party's behest, Jean-Toussaint prepared some "reflections on the 20th Party Congress," the site of Khrushchev's "secret speech," in which he deliberately feigned ignorance of the reality of Soviet crimes. The details had been relayed to the Desantis by one of Dominique's journalist contacts in Poland.[20] Her recollection of these years concludes with an appendix in which Dominique interrogates her husband about this period in his intellectual life.[21] His comments cast light on the modesty of his later philosophical aims.[22] Desanti indicts the intellectual's desire to have an impact where, by his very trade, he is typically impotent: the domain of action. He also suggests the ways in which a desire to perform a "service" to humanity—a desire that he sees as pervasive in the history of philosophy, citing Husserl as one example—contains the seeds of its own perversion into a desire to make an impact on the material world. What does the party give to the intellectual? Desanti responds: "the simulacrum of power."[23]

Desanti's textual self-indictment, pursued at length in *Un Destin philosophique*, invites comparison with Czeslow Milosz's classic *The Captive Mind* as a meditation on the relationship between intellectual activity and illusory notions of service to humankind produced by the Communist experience of the twentieth century.[24] It also points to the decisiveness of a personal break that helps account for the distance between Althusser and his erstwhile teacher. Unlike Desanti, Althusser remained a member of the PCF throughout his intellectual career. Also unlike Desanti, Althusser was too young to be fully compromised by the Stalinism of the PCF. When Althusser's project gained an audience in the early 1960s, it was understood as an effort to infuse the Marxist enterprise with an intellectual rigor and philosophical acuity that had been lacking in previous French readings. For many, Althusser's effort was both catalytic and cathartic, in that it proffered a renunciation of Stalinism that would not be a renunciation of communism *tout court*. What was needed was a reassertion of philosophy that would no longer be tarnished by the ideological servitude of PCF "philosophy" in the Stalinist period. Althusser contributed to this narrative in the introduction to *For Marx* when he lamented the lack of any philosophical reading of Marx in France among Communists.[25] While Althusser was establishing his project, the only potential intellectual rival was Roger Garaudy, the "official" philosopher of the party who sought to marry Marxism with Christian socialism.[26] By this point, Desanti was beyond the pale of respectability for having severed his ties with the party, and thus Althusser could hardly acknowledge him as a viable predecessor. Nonetheless, it is significant that, of all the contributors to *La Nouvelle Critique*, Desanti was most emphatic about the need to argue philosophically for Marxism's scientific footing. The notion that philosophy could bestow the status of science upon Marxism was integral to Althusser's project in the 1960s, and it owes something to Desanti's early, aborted effort. More striking still is the extent to which Desanti's case for the scientificity of Marxism was largely pursued with respect to Hegel and predicated on a "break" of sorts between the Hegel of the *Phenomenology of Spirit* and that of the *Science of Logic*.[27]

The story of Althusser's relationship to Desanti also involves a more personal component. According to Althusser's biographer, the recollections of Dominique Desanti, and—begrudgingly, it seems—by Althusser's own admission, Jean-Toussaint was instrumental in recruiting Althusser to the PCF in the 1940s.[28] Althusser usually names his friend in wartime captivity, Jacques Martin, as the key figure leading him to Marxism. This may well have been the case, but as for the practical side of actually joining the party, the influence of Althusser's Communist teacher at the ENS at this key moment in his personal biography appears to have been decisive. To complicate matters further, in 1949 Dominique and Jean-Toussaint together had been instrumental in making the case for Hélène Legotien, Althusser's partner and a friend of the Desantis since the Resistance, to be permitted some sort of involvement in party activities.[29] The Desantis risked their own party reputations as a concession to Althusser's pleading, though they would eventually discontinue their efforts when it became clear that certain party men, for reasons that remain obscure, did not want Legotien around.[30] A "break" between the Althussers and the Desantis followed shortly after the latter couple conceded to pressures from above.

The family quarrels of the PCF are not a chief concern, but they are essential for establishing the complexity of these institutional links between Desanti and Althusser. Despite the personal falling out, there was real content to Althusser's misgivings over Desanti's theoretical example. These concerns turned primarily on Desanti's resurgent sympathy in the 1950s for Althusser's bête noire, phenomenology. Though they were driven by his political convictions, Althusser's efforts to excise Hegelian traces from Marx are also the manifestation of a local, philosophical dispute with phenomenology. In reaction to Desanti's *Phénoménologie et praxis*, the result of a seminar on Husserl's *Cartesian Meditations* addressed to Marxist students, Althusser remarked: "[W]hat's ridiculous about Touki [Desanti's nickname] is that he still believes in the possibility of Husserl's project. And that all he charges him with is being unable to keep his promises, as if his only vice were one of weakness!"[31]

The violence of Althusser's reaction to Desanti's phenomenological *parti pris* needs to be understood in light of the fact that five years earlier Desanti had produced the first extensive "materialist" reading of Spinoza in the French context with his *Introduction à l'histoire de la philosophie*.[32] Étienne Balibar recalls arriving at the ENS in 1961 and being intimidated by the mere existence of Desanti, the "mythic figure" who had produced this reading. He also recalls searching with his classmates for copies of the book among the bouquinistes along the Seine.³³ The book, originally published by *La Nouvelle Critique*, was out of print for many years until PUF reissued it in 2006. It is a fascinating historical document and the most natural place to continue coming to terms with the knotted imbrication of Spinozism, Marxism, and phenomenology in Desanti's historical example. Most striking of all, perhaps, is to note how, in contrast to Althusser, for whom Spinoza's philosophy would serve as the authority for his renovation of Marxism, for Desanti an extended engagement with Spinoza's thought, using the tools of a vaguely defined historical materialism, could produce an analysis that his companion described as "the turning point of his evolution and his post-Marxist return" to the epistemological concerns of his youth.³⁴

After examining Desanti's book on Spinoza, this chapter provides a reading of the short book on Husserl that followed. In both cases, one of the main goals is to show the Spinozism/phenomenology tension—or, the Cavaillès/Merleau-Ponty tension—that informs Desanti's own philosophical method. At the same time, however, in these books one can catch glimpses of Desanti's reckoning with his Stalinist complicity and the earliest foundations for the philosophical asceticism that marks his later career. The asceticism that Desanti develops is not a simple disavowal of political engagement. It is in itself a philosophical project that uses philosophy to undercut efforts to extrapolate political or ethical injunctions from philosophical activity, all the while retaining what Desanti called a "weak materialist epistemology."³⁵ This materialism was deliberately "weak" in that it sought to retain a pluralist conception of matter that would allow for a proliferation of concepts and theories for myriad domains, rather than an overarching theory of matter that might absolve philosophy of its critical tasks. In a piece titled "The Silence of J.-T. Desanti," Blandine Kriegel links Desanti's epistemological concerns with his long-standing debts to Spinoza:

> Against Plato, who had proclaimed: "The good genealogist is the one who makes Iris the daughter of Thaumas," Spinoza opposed his view that philosophy must not be the daughter of astonishment and that in order to know the truth it was useless to depart from error. On the contrary, one must establish oneself on an acquired first truth. This is the affirmation that grounds the autonomy and the normativity of the scientific statement [*énoncé*] recuperated by any epistemology, and the procedure that disqualifies the prerequisite of methodical doubt in the theory of knowledge [. . .] while at the same time excluding all moral interpretation of

error customary in the idealist tradition. In designating an eternal culprit—the body (and the sensible faculties that depend on it)—a unique path of rectification was indicated: asceticism.[36]

To be sure, Spinoza's asceticism broke with previous models in that it did not deny the body but included it in "an absolute rationalism" that stood alongside a "materialist conception of the world."[37] Desanti's ascetic engagement with mathematics might be read as the belated recognition of this unique path of rectification, one nearly foreclosed by the dalliances, and deviations, of his political youth.

The Spinoza Pole: *Introduction à l'histoire de la philosophie*

The new edition of *Introduction à l'histoire de la philosophie* (1956) contains a preface and an afterword that speak to the volume's historical significance and theoretical pertinence. The preface, by Dominique Desanti, situates the work in its historical moment.[38] Khrushchev's "secret speech" took place while the book was in press; the invasion of Hungary happened shortly after its release. Dominique reproduces the correspondence with an artist friend from the Occupation period that resulted from Desanti's efforts to procure a new, modern picture of Spinoza for his book's cover. When Pablo Picasso delivered the sketch—an austere image, devoid of shading, reproduced for the 2006 edition—he confessed he had given Spinoza his own eyes by studying them in a mirror. Desanti responded that Picasso had provided him with "Spinoza as he was: an essential Spinoza," better than Desanti's own account. He also made an ambiguous gesture of historical solidarity with Spinoza as the voice of one persecuted for his faith in reason.[39]

Dominique Desanti's aim is to locate this book in a time of unease and to read it as the product of two conflicting pressures: first, that from the party to produce a sophisticated piece of scholarship that would lend philosophical credibility to historical materialism; and second, that born of Desanti's own desire to produce a sophisticated piece of scholarship beholden to his own notions of philosophical integrity rather than the demands of the party line.[40] Dominique suggests there was an increasing disillusionment at work in the production of this volume that was the combined result of a gnawing sense of political disappointment and Desanti's first extended theoretical engagement with Marxism beyond ideological service to the PCF. Yet this sense of disillusionment is in tension with a clinging faith in society's potential to organize itself rationally, if only it has the right tools to do so. The key component of Desanti's analysis of Spinoza "in his time" is the contention, rooted in the tenets of historical materialism, that Spinoza's epoch was one of profound contradiction. The Netherlands of Spinoza's day was at once the site of an ascendant bourgeoisie, and thus a model of society structurally tethered to market forces rather than any external authority, and the site of an attempt, ideologically rooted in the theological fallout of the Reformation, to organize a rational republic that could provide both tolerance and salvation for all. According to Dominique Desanti, the homology between this three-hundred-year-old "society in contradiction with itself," whose reality did not live up to its ideology of universal inclusion, and the historical experiment in disarray to the east was not lost on those comrades still reeling from the revelations of the Twentieth Party Congress of the Communist Party of the Soviet Union when her husband's book was published.

The afterword to the volume is the philosophical complement to Dominique's efforts at contextualization. Written by Pierre-François Moreau and titled "Philosophy and Singularity," the brief text suggests that Desanti was confronted with a Marxist problematic—how to make sense of a philosophy in its historical conditions—and in the process of addressing it, produced a deeply Spinozist analysis.[41] The first point it makes, and here Marxist and Spinozist perspectives are in agreement, is that philosophy cannot occupy a space external to the historical, cultural, and scientific domain in which it takes place. It must work with what is historically presented. In Moreau's view, the novel Spinozist insight of Desanti's analysis is that rather than isolate a singular thread of determinant causality through which to explain a historically situated philosophy, it acknowledges the presence of an "excess of causality and determination" that can never be empirically disentangled,[42] but that points to the singularity of Spinoza's philosophy (or any philosophy for that matter). More important, however, this Spinozistically inspired method develops a concept of singularity as such. Citing from Desanti's own text, Moreau writes:

The recognition of "contingency" is thus not a concession to a putative irrationality in history; it is on the contrary a necessary move for understanding each element as a "*transitory* but *efficient* expression of the reciprocal relation of beings." This idea of a "reciprocal relation of beings" clearly rings Spinozist; the model that allows us to decipher the paradoxical necessity of contingency is the status of the mode in Spinoza's philosophy: irreducible in its singularity, but bearing a power that inscribes it in universal laws.[43]

As we saw in the previous chapter, disagreements over Spinoza's philosophy tend to coalesce around the status of the modes. Moreau reads in Desanti an anticipation of the French work on Spinoza descending from Althusser's and Deleuze's intervention, where the concerns were to develop a historical theory of overdetermination (Althusser) or an ontology of excess (Deleuze). Though equally attuned to the ontological remit of Spinozism, Cavaillès and Gueroult had been much more interested in developing Spinozism's epistemological implications, either for a theory of science, in Cavaillès's case, or for rationalist philosophy more generally, in Gueroult's. In other words, for these earlier figures Spinozism is above all a question of philosophical method rather than metaphysical content, even as their own efforts show that a real fidelity to Spinoza's philosophy forecloses the possibility of separating the two domains. Desanti, however, occupies a mediate position between these two moments in French Spinozism, affirming Spinoza's rationalism though hesitating to draw out the full range of its ontological implications.

The main text of *Introduction à l'histoire de la philosophie* (hereafter *IHP*) is the first half of an unfinished project. Consistent with a common trope in French philosophy, *IHP* is supposed to be the prolegomenon, the ground-clearing and methodological preparation, for a second book in which the method sketched therein will be put to work on a given philosophical system, in this case Spinoza's. Though the second volume never materialized, the republication of the first contains a "sketch of the second volume" culled from Desanti's archives. We are also assisted by other contents of the archives in the form of lectures on Spinoza dating from this period, and what is speculated to be one chapter—titled "Dieu ou Nature"—of an earlier attempt at a Marxist reading of Spinoza.[44] Nevertheless, there is still plenty of discussion of Spinoza and his philosophy in the volume that was published in 1956, and the archival materials mainly flesh out the reading present therein.

The book is divided into two parts: part I, "Philosophy and Its History," and part II, "Research Concerning Spinoza." In 1975, Desanti maintained the viability of the second part but disavowed the first; in 2001, he said the book was a preface to what he would have written about Spinoza "if he had had the time."[45] The first part reads largely as a Communist screed against "bourgeois thought." Here Bertrand Russell, "veteran of bourgeois philosophy," is reduced, along with his French counterpart Paul Valéry, to little more than an apologist for the bourgeoisie's efforts to enshrine the history of the world in its own image. "Hatred of Communists" and "fear of Marxism" are the chief principles of Russell's "doctrine." In the French context, Desanti turns his sights against the "impressionist" school in the history of philosophy, of which Ferdinand Alquié is the latest exemplar. This particular "form desires to be eternal" when, in reality, it is entirely personal and subjective. It is this brand of thinking that is, in Desanti's view, common to Brunschvicg and Bergson, and Sartre and Alain. It has only received renewed vigor and authority from Husserl's phenomenology. The root problem is the rampant subjectivism: "From now on the past has no sense in itself; this sense is constituted by the eye that sees it."[46]

Leaving aside the zealotry, Desanti's survey of the French philosophical terrain is by and large consistent with an understanding we have seen in play with Cavaillès and Gueroult and that is consolidated in a distrust of phenomenology. In Desanti's case, however, we are forced to consider how much of this disparagement was rooted in the PCF party line rather than Desanti's own philosophical convictions. According to Althusser, although Desanti led the charge against existentialism and its links to phenomenology, he never abandoned his sympathies for Husserl, even at the peak of his Marxist commitments.[47] There may be some truth to Althusser's charge, because, although Desanti's support for phenomenology appears to be at an all-time low in this book on Spinoza, Husserl remains, as we shall see, an unacknowledged influence on the analysis it contains.

Abruptly terminating his brisk dismissal of phenomenological existentialism, Desanti concludes his "glance at bourgeois historiography" with a consideration of "several respectable 'schools.'"[48] In this section, Brunschvicg's reputation is recuperated to no small degree. He is praised for his notion that there should be a homogeneity between a conceptual scientific object, for example, gravity, and the law that describes it, and that the free mind is one that coincides with the rationality of ideas.[49] What Desanti likes about Brunschvicg is what was identified as his Spinozism in Chapter 1. Brunschvicg is criticized, however, for remaining essentially ideological in Engels's sense, that is, for abstracting his own preferred form of thought—idealism—from its historical conditions to one side of a Manichean transhistorical struggle against its opposite.[50]

The "bourgeois philosopher" who emerges the least scathed in Desanti's overview is none other than Martial Gueroult. Desanti endorses Gueroult's critique of the fantastic "interpretations" of Descartes and praises the virtues of his general method, which is rooted in an "absolute fidelity to the text."[51] By and large, Desanti finds Gueroult's method valid, except that it does not "put us in possession of the whole truth,"[52] since it brackets out all consideration of the historical consciousness shaping Descartes' effort. To be sure, Desanti notes that no philosopher can ever say the whole truth. Nonetheless, it is the link "between the elaborated concepts and the form of the consciousness that made its way in them" that must be understood.[53] Desanti insists that establishing this consciousness is not a matter of subjective identification. Indeed, what is valuable about Gueroult's method is the total submission of the subjective perspective to two criteria not of the "subject's" own choosing: the materiality of the text as a singular system and a method of reasoning that operates intrinsically and without recourse to suppositions external to the "order of reasons" manifested in that textual system. In other words, Gueroult is lauded for what we have identified as his own brand of methodological Spinozism.

The following chapter in Desanti's account, titled "Marxism and the History of Philosophy," is an inventory of what is needed to salvage Gueroult's method from its relentless idealism and to expand its domain to the history of philosophy writ large. Desanti identifies the three essential "preliminary moves" that must accompany research into the history of philosophy: (1) internal analysis of the doctrine, that is, the Gueroult method; (2) genealogy of the fundamental concepts, a task linked to the examples of Alexandre Koyré and Gaston Bachelard; (3) and "analysis of the society in which the philosophy developed."[54] Although a large portion of the book's second half is devoted to a discussion of the politics and social structures of Spinoza's Holland, it becomes clear that Desanti sees the links among the items on his agenda coalescing around the *sciences* of a given historical moment. Notwithstanding their propagandistic rhetoric, Desanti's PCF writings make clear his conviction that the sciences were the domain in which a society's ideological structures were clearest. This is not to denigrate the truth content of science per se but to attempt to read science as a historical battleground. The ideal of science is not compromised;

it is not reduced to an effect of ideology. In fact, Desanti's claim is that in any given moment, there is a "true science" in play and that the most just society is the one that adheres to the "objectivity" the latest science portends.[55] Consistent with a preference for scientism in French Communist circles, a preference aggravated by the critique of scientism among intellectual fellow travelers, Desanti's praise of science as the supreme source of epistemological criteria is again a prescient anticipation of Althusser's efforts in the next decade.

Throughout Desanti's discussion in *IHP*, however, a curious slippage occurs wherein theoretical feats attributed to Marx, Engels, and Lenin appear to have much firmer foundations in the Spinozist rationalism outlined in Cavaillès's theoretical project. As one pertinent example, Desanti offers his own take on the "reversal of Hegelianism" Marx and Engels undertook to save the dialectic from idealism. Essential to this "reversal," in Desanti's reading, was a submission of speculative thought to the contemporary conditions of the sciences.[56] Desanti's argument is that the only way to avoid falling victim to the fetishization of the concept—for example, the notion that the "idea" of the apple has more reality or being than the physical apple—is to recognize the historicity of conceptual production as an interminable process. In lines that take their inspiration from Marx but would not have been out of place in Cavaillès's *Sur la logique et la théorie de la science*, Desanti writes, "For the first time thought *by* concepts *can* be, at the same time, an objective thought *of* the concept, which is to say knowledge of the process through which, in consciousness, the approximately exact reflection of the essence of things is constituted."[57]

In the afterword, Moreau suggests that Desanti's later critique of the "silent philosophy" that interrupts scientific practice to pursue ulterior ends is already present here in this manual of Marxist pedagogy.[58] Desanti's later work in many ways resumed Cavaillès's project, and it can be read as tackling some of the unresolved problems of his first teacher's attenuated efforts. Indeed, the project in *Les Idéalités mathématiques*—his belated doctoral thesis, published in 1968, and the one book to which Desanti himself attached any real lasting importance[59]—is largely an effort to unlock the mysteries of *thématisation* explored in Chapter 1, which took inspiration from the Spinozist principle of the "idea of the idea."[60] In Spinoza's view, and by extension Cavaillès's, the fact that the nominally "first" idea is the recognition of any material presentation whatsoever was immaterial to the process as such. The problems of this approach, however, would exercise Desanti later. Chief among his concerns were the evacuation of the subject from this process—Desanti made use of the obvious but no less essential fact that mathematics requires mathematicians—and the devaluation of material to the benefit of the ideal, a failing that Desanti attributed to a regressive commitment to Platonism.[61] Nevertheless, the conviction that the process of concept production has its own veracity and historicity independent of the subject who performs it was of mathematical and Spinozist inspiration for Desanti. But this conviction produced its own misgivings, which are present in the reading of Spinoza's philosophy itself in *IHP*.

Two themes dominate the remainder of this book, both of which speak to the irreducibility of thought to either the mind that produces it or the theoretical context in which it takes place. On the one hand, and of primary importance for our purposes, is the concern to disentangle "several contradictions internal to Spinoza's philosophy"; on the other is the desire to make sense of Spinoza in his time as the site of a world historical "contradiction," the one attendant to the transition from feudalism to capitalism.[62] Spinoza lived at a time and in a place in which contradiction was felt most acutely, an observation that Desanti links to the fact that, in his view, Spinoza's is the supreme example of a philosophical system whose most salient feature is the pure contradiction at its core. The previous chapter attempted to present the "Alquié/Gueroult differend" in clear terms, as comprising two irreconcilable versions of Spinozism: a rationalist pluralism (Gueroult) and a naturalist theology (Alquié). Desanti's reading grants equal weight to both interpretations in a refusal to reduce Spinozism to one tendency over the other.

In *IHP*, these two tendencies are identified as materialist and idealist. Though Gueroult found the term anathema, it is the materialist line in Spinoza, as Desanti presents it, that is in fact closest to the Gueroultian reading and the idealist elements that are the source of Alquié's critique. The materialist current in Spinoza is the one that links him to Lucretius and Epicurus; it accounts for his critique of any Christian philosophy of transcendence; it leads to his overcoming of subject/object dualism. Error, for the materialist Spinoza, is never falsehood, and as such it is not essentially distinct from truth; error is instead mere privation of knowledge.[63] A dogged emphasis on infinity against finitude is the complementary thesis to the denial of transcendence. Desanti reads this denial as the necessary result of Spinoza's emphasis on the singularity of Substance. Desanti performs a curious maneuver, however, in his presentation of this dual aspect of Spinoza's materialism, its infinite and singular qualities. He presents the concept of eternity as actuality—not to be confused with indefinite duration as potentiality—as the necessary result of Spinoza's materialist stance when pushed to its logical conclusion. But, at the same time, he uses the concept of eternity in Spinoza's philosophy as the point of departure for his inquiry into its idealist tendencies.[64] These idealist tendencies are manifest in Spinoza's gestures toward an alternative concept of immortality. Those committed to the materialist reading of Spinoza see his talk of immortality and "the intellectual love of God" in Book V more as concessions to the religiously needy than as viable positions in their own right. But Desanti commits to giving this moment the weight that its place in Spinoza's system appears to require. Spinoza's notion of immortality is linked to the beatitude that comes with the "third kind of knowledge," which is in itself constituted by a kind of intuition of eternity in an immediate present. For Desanti, the positing of this third kind of knowledge, and the putative salvation that is its result, is the site of an idealist concession at loggerheads with the preceding materialist rationalism of Spinoza's project. On this point, Desanti's critique of Spinoza is pure Alquié. This aspect of Spinozism is not only hopelessly idealist. It also points to a kind of rationalism that, by beginning with pure materiality, abandons it in an abstraction ultimately devoid of content. Desanti concludes:

Here we see a move of a rational character, which is coherent with the principles of materialism, end in its contrary. In the very process of drawing close to the object of *scientia intuitiva*, we see it vanish, and in the end, nothing remains but the emptiest abstraction. In this void, the entirety of nature disappears and is lost [*la nature tout entière se perd et s'abîme*].[65]

In this instance, Desanti levels a charge against Spinozism that he will also apply to Husserl's phenomenology: the rational procedure exhausts itself in an abstraction without purchase.

The central ambiguity of Spinozism, responsible for this abstraction, can be stated as follows: In denying the existence of an outside, Spinoza must begin with an axiomatic assertion of the infinite as an actuality. *Deus sive Nature*, the name for Spinoza's Substance, must be intrinsically infinite. But, as experience attests, finitude—the very condition for which the *in*finite is a negation—is a very real feature of human existence. The infinity of nature, which we can supposedly "access," is in contradiction with its composite moments of finitude; to deny these moments their status as finite is to be left with a concept of reality without content. Desanti for his part refuses to resolve the ambiguity that leads to this collapse. Unlike Gueroult, or Deleuze later on, he does not recuperate a Spinozistic concept of finitude through an exposition of the modes in Spinoza's metaphysics. He more or less accepts the Alquié position regarding this contradiction in Spinozism. He devotes his energies instead to an exposition of the convergence of traditions that resulted in this contradiction in Spinoza's singular case.

Making good on a methodological technique indebted to Husserl and that will reach fruition in *Les Idéalités mathématiques* in a different context, Desanti reads Spinoza's thought as conditioned by the two poles designating the theoretical space in which it takes place. In marked contrast to the most common reading of Spinoza's formula "God, or Nature," which reads the "or" as a "that is to say" or "in other words," Desanti reads the "or" as designating an impossible synthesis of an either/or relationship. In Desanti's reading, the expression does *not* render an equivalence; it instead brings into a single relationship two irreconcilable terms in polar tension. To return to Desanti's historical materialist rubric, Spinozism is the site of a confrontation of two conflicting ideologies: the *theology* of a dying feudal era and the *science* of a nascent capitalist one. In Spinozism, this historical conflict between theology and science effectively becomes the principle *Deus sive Natura*. On the theological issue, Desanti's observations are consistent with the scholarship of Leszek Kolakowski and Richard Popkin, which has emphasized Spinoza's exposure to Protestant circles in seventeenth-century Holland in order to argue for the likely influence this element had on his thought.[66]

In the section titled "Spinoza Was Not a 'Recluse,'"[67] Desanti situates Spinoza in his milieu, as a thinker who was social and conversant with radical Calvinists after his excommunication from the Amsterdam synagogue. These radical Christians were the primary supporters of the republican experiment in Holland. In their view, Calvinist piety was not inimical to state authority; it was indifferent to it. All that was desired was tolerance; with tolerance, salvation would follow in due course. The case for tolerance in such terms found its supreme expression in Spinoza's *Tractatus Theologico-Politicus*. The idea was that social peace could not be enacted by force by a legislating authority; rather, peace would be the result of the internal regulating mechanisms of a society with all included, that is, with no "outside" remaining within the totality of the social space. Where Hardt and Negri find in Spinoza's political writings the prefigurations of a communism for a global age, for a world that lacks an "outside,"[68] Desanti sees a supreme expression of bourgeois ideology. The disavowal of legislative authority is the bourgeois dream of a self-regulating market; who needs authority when the market takes care of itself? Salvation lies within the market of free exchange. The ultimately failed experiment of the Dutch Republic in fact witnessed a brief dehierarchization of authority. In the *Political Treatise*, a document that postdates the public murder of the de Witt brothers and the reestablishment of royal authority in Holland, Spinoza would come to advocate a stronger role for political authority. Yet the political arguments for tolerance in the *Theologico-Political Treatise* find metaphysical correlates in the *Ethics*. The point of Desanti's sociopolitical excursus with regard to Spinoza's philosophy is to show that the theological concerns of the feudal era were not eliminated. Salvation was still the "goal," even if it was to be immanent to this world rather than transcendent to it. Desanti suggests that Spinoza was complicit with this manipulation of an inherited theology in the creation of a new ideology, that he, too, felt the sincere need to hang on to a concept of salvation, and its immortal implications, in a new system of social relations with no outside.

This is the content of the theological or "God" pole of Spinoza's thinking: beatitude, immortality, in a word, salvation, all as a result of aligning the self with broader, rational forces. Yet in the very structure of this redemptive narrative, which is teleological insofar as it imputes to rational thought the goal of beatitude, we see the lingering traces of a medieval Aristotelian Scholasticism that the "new science" of Spinoza's era was doing so much to undermine. Here the pendulum swings to the other pole of Spinoza's thinking, the one rooted in a science of geometric abstraction, that posits infinity as actuality instead of potentiality and that as a result evacuates teleology from Substance. Aristotle's concept of teleological substance had been effectively hollowed out by Galilean science; at least this was how Descartes and Spinoza saw it.[69] Galileo's radicalization of the Copernican Revolution had a profound equalizing effect, in that it took the decentering accomplished by Copernicus further and undermined a hierarchical image of the universe. In this new Galilean worldview, "to know an object by its concept, this is now no longer solely knowing what its place in nature is, nor is it a matter of simply being capable of stating the properties this object possesses in common with those that belong in the same class as it. It is quite more: knowing its internal law of composition, the internal relation of the elements that constitute it."[70]

This principle, scientific in Galileo's project, will acquire philosophical force in Spinoza's system, and it is this rationalist aspect of Spinozism that will appeal to Brunschvicg and exercise Cavaillès. And Spinoza's wholesale privileging of this kind of knowing over others enacts an assault on a hierarchically ordered "great chain of being." This is what is revolutionary in Spinozism, and in the Marxist sense as well. Notwithstanding the invective unleashed against bourgeois philosophers in the book's opening section, Desanti, as a Marxist philosopher, does not devalue the bourgeoisie as a necessary historical reality. For, in this version of events, the bourgeoisie's historical appearance coincided with that of the market, and along with it, the scientific concept of an order with no outside and nothing to regulate it but its own internal principles. In this the bourgeoisie is historically progressive and lays the groundwork, "scientifically," for the communism that will replace capitalism. Where the class is regressive is in its inability to do away with the "religious mystification" that serves as its ideological self-justification. In Desanti's view, this historical moment required a new concept of being, and the one Spinoza provided—*Deus sive Natura*—was entirely appropriate. But this element in Spinoza's philosophy remains for Desanti the mark of its contradictory polar structure. The creator-God of a good and just cosmos has been replaced with a concept of nature whose laws are intrinsic and no longer external but that somehow still provide salvation.[71] Spinoza's keeping God as creator, even as *causa sui* (self-caused), in play is thus deemed complicit and of a piece with bourgeois ideology. Far from being "anti-modern,"[72] in Desanti's reading Spinozism emerges as the philosophy of the modern age.

Judging from the verdict in this unfinished project, one might expect Desanti to think that if only Spinoza were able to relinquish these theological vestiges (an impossibility in the context of Desanti's Marxist analysis, given the horizons of Spinoza's historical experience) and had pushed the eliminative tendencies in his project to the farthest extremes, then his thought would be the pinnacle of philosophical achievement. In *IHP*, Desanti appears to endorse the Spinozist critique of the *cogito*. The evidence for his sympathy with this aspect of Spinoza's philosophy is also discernible in those instances in his later work when he praises Cavaillès's critique of the transcendental subject, be it Kantian consciousness or the Husserlian transcendental ego.[73] In Desanti's view, and in Deleuze's as well, the transcendental subject or ego is a solipsistic category in that the foundational structures of thought are deemed to have the same structure as the lived experience of thought.[74] But the critique of the transcendental subject is not a disavowal of subjectivity *tout court* as a philosophical problem. As we have already suggested, Desanti was uneasy with the implications of Spinoza's philosophy in relation to the category of the subject and the subjective contingencies of thought attendant to its temporal development. This uneasiness is captured best in his laconic claim that Spinozism manifests the "silence of the already said." In other words, for all the strength of Cavaillès's own Spinozist critique of ego consciousness, the tendency to extract thought as a process from its temporal and material conditions afforded no way to think philosophically about thought's procedural nature. The problem with Spinozism is not that the subject position was evacuated of a discernible structure or animating principle. Such a gesture would leave the subject position merely void of content, which would make Spinozism commensurate with a range of theories from Sartre's to Lacan's. Much more drastic was the fact that the subject position, the *site* itself, was totally obliterated to the profit of an ideational process that proceeded "without a subject." The only "subject" that remained was eternal Substance itself. Desanti found this unacceptable. And it was here that phenomenology would provide solace and a necessary rejoinder to those Spinozist aspects of his own thought.

A final word, however, on *IHP* before moving on to Desanti's writings on Husserl. One gathers from Dominique and Jean-Toussaint's reflections that this extended study of Spinoza in his time was instrumental in Desanti's abandonment of Marxism on a theoretical level. In 2001, Desanti recalled that, though his break with communism and the PCF was obviously political, his abandonment of Marxism-Leninism was rooted in the realization that, for all its pretensions to the contrary, the doctrine was in no way a science and that, as a theory of history or society, it could in no way be granted scientific status.[75] Desanti's reading of Spinoza illuminates his recollection. For what he praised in Spinoza was the linking of philosophy to the exigencies of science, and in particular Galilean science. What he castigated were the vestigial theological principles of Aristotelian

Scholasticism, which manifested themselves in a teleology of salvation imposed onto an otherwise scientific philosophy of infinite historicity devoid of origins or goals. Dominique Desanti's claim that *IHP* was "the turning point" of her husband's "post-Marxist return" to an engagement with philosophy's relationship to science suggests the following conjecture: if Spinozism's failure to measure up to its own claims to scientificity was rooted in a commitment to preserve an inescapably theological and teleological concept of salvation, then by the same token, Marxism-Leninism's claims to scientificity stood no chance. What will be novel and, in the eyes of his detractors, quixotic in Althusser's intervention in the next decade, will be the decision to regard the teleological aspects of Marxism-Leninism as inessential to the question of its historical and theoretical viability. This reading will necessitate that certain blinders be kept in place, not only for Althusser's reading of Marx but also for his consideration of Spinoza.

The Husserl Pole: *Phénoménologie et praxis*

Phénoménologie et praxis (1963) was Desanti's last book to be published by a Communist press. Composed of lectures on Husserl's *Cartesian Meditations* delivered in 1961, the book was published by Éditions Sociales in 1963, three years after Desanti's own definitive departure from the PCF. Though the book is addressed to a Marxist audience, here, unlike in *IHP*, the Marxist frame is just that, a framing mechanism independent of the analysis itself.[76] In this regard, the work is also different from that of Desanti's colleague in things Marxist and phenomenological, Tran Duc Thao. Thao's *Phénoménologie et matérialisme dialectique* was an ambitious, if flawed attempt to make Husserl and Marx work together.[77] In France, Desanti's book, along with Thao's, joined the studies of Suzanne Bachelard and a young Jacques Derrida in constituting a concentrated engagement with Husserl in the late 1950s and early 1960s.[78]

The project with which Desanti's has most in common is Derrida's, especially as it was articulated in the latter's introduction to his translation of "The Origin of Geometry."[79] Like Derrida, Desanti felt a genuine sympathy for what Husserl tried to accomplish in his efforts at a kind of experiential access to, rather than an axiomatic declaration of, the absolute. Like Derrida as well, however, Desanti was frustrated by Husserl's unremitting desire to secure foundations, to lock in phenomenology as a rigorous science dedicated to the uncovering of origins per se. In the introduction to the most recent edition of *Phénoménologie et praxis*—published in 1994 by Gallimard and now titled *Introduction à la phénoménologie*—Desanti revisits the exchange with Merleau-Ponty relayed at the beginning of this chapter. Realizing that he could not spend a philosophical career rewriting the "already said" of the *Ethics*, Desanti was moved by Merleau-Ponty's suggestion that a reading of the *Cartesian Meditations* would result in a more fecund conception of thought as a productive series of acts or gestures.[80] Desanti writes, "What I took for my inherited structure of understanding [i.e., Spinoza's], what I thought I had to believe and effectuate in this mode, it seemed that I had to set all this before me and put it in motion again like an open work site [*chantier*], pending action."[81] Located in these lines is an expression that Desanti would use time and again in *Les Idéalités mathématiques* and *La Philosophie silencieuse*: "remettre en chantier." The phrase could be loosely translated as "get going again," "back to square one," or perhaps "back to the drawing board." But it is its ungainly literal translation that gets closest to what Desanti sees as the true method and activity of philosophical thought, roughly "to put something back into the state of a work site." For Desanti, the "something" in question was typically a mathematical object or concept rather than a linguistic utterance or a physical thing; in any event, this indefinite process was best expressed, though still only approximately, with the tools initially provided by Husserl. Surely the narrow specialization of Desanti's work accounts for its limited reception beyond French academe. But one cannot help speculating that if he had come up with a more economical, and more easily translatable, expression to suggest taking a given and revealing its own internal incompleteness, thus returning it to a "work site"—for instance, "deconstruction"—then perhaps his work may have had a broader impact.

A comparison of Desanti's project with Derrida's is certainly to be desired, but it is not the goal here.[82] Rather, the task now is to turn the tables and to read Desanti's engagement with Husserlian phenomenology with an eye toward its formal similarities with the narrative found in the book on Spinoza. Chief among these similarities is an initial methodological sympathy countered by an increasing reticence before the philosophy's tendency to collapse in abstraction. Though it is never articulated as such, there is a Husserlian component to the argument from *IHP* that we just presented, and it gives a modicum of credibility to Althusser's insistence that, despite protestations to the contrary, Desanti was always more faithful to Husserl than to Marx. Desanti's positing of Spinoza's thought as occupying a space between two poles is itself a decidedly Husserlian gesture. Husserl eliminated the notion of a confrontation between an isolated subject and an isolated object in favor of a concept of the two as poles of a *noetic-noematic* relationship, an "ego pole" and an "object pole." We might say, then, that Desanti interprets Spinoza in *IHP* with an application of this Husserlian structure to his reading; this polar tension accounts for the undecidability of which is the "true" Spinoza. To be sure, the theology/science dyad is not exactly homologous to a subject/object dyad. The point, however, is to see the breadth of this Husserlian principle in terms of method, to note a way of reading in terms of attentiveness to a plurality of polar tensions that are constitutive of thought itself, be it the thought taking place in the here and now or the historically produced "body of thought" of a Spinoza.

Desanti never ceased to value this methodological component of the phenomenological enterprise; it is clearly in play in *Les Idéalités mathématiques*. Yet, in reference to that work, Desanti once remarked that "the situation was paradoxical. I could speak nothing but the language of a philosophy whose fundamental principles I had deemed unrealizable."[83] The contention here is that there is a marshaling of Spinozist principles—mediated through Cavaillès—against Husserl that takes place over the course of Desanti's engagement with this later figure. Desanti's critique of Husserl is Cavaillèsian, but insofar as Cavaillès's ultimate hostility to phenomenology is grounded in Spinozist rationalism, then Desanti's critique has a Spinozist component as well. As we consider what is Spinozist in Desanti's reservations about phenomenology, it is important to keep in mind the "nature pole" over the "God pole." Spinoza's strictures against transcendence—even if Spinoza himself failed to remain true to those strictures—left a profound mark on Desanti. At the same time, however, Desanti understood the difficulties of insisting on immanence without collapsing into a philosophy devoid of content or a viable notion of historical novelty and production. On this score, Husserl is susceptible to the same charges as Spinoza, except that where it is Spinoza's commitment to immanence that leads to the "void" of abstraction, it is Husserl's excavation of the transcendental that leads to the same vacuous result. Ultimately, a key component of Desanti's critique of Husserl is that the transcendental Ego winds up playing a role similar to the Spinozist God, as a kind of alibi for a naturalist or animist principle that determines the content of all that it encounters. It is worth quoting Desanti's elaboration of this point at length:

> The philosopher (reduced to his "transcendental Ego") is thus a little like the Spinozist God, for whom "the matter has not lacked to create everything from the highest to the lowest degree of perfection." For the philosopher as well, the "matter" will not be lacking in order to make his way toward the determination of essence in all things. His reflexive field remains always immanent to himself. In this field, it is always in his power to accomplish acts (variations) likely to put him in the presence of experience's general structures as an obvious correlate. [. . .] The "philosophizing Self" has thus become for itself what, by virtue of its project, it had to be: the absolute narrator of the true, the ultimate provider of sense. [. . .] Open (and *ad infinitum*) as the place of origin, this "philosophizing Self" is, as a universal gaze, structurally closed and normed by itself.[84]

It is striking to see Desanti explicitly linking his critique of Husserl to his critique of Spinoza. The threat of solipsism compromises Husserl's transcendental phenomenology, just as Spinoza's metaphysics teeters at the brink of collapse into a meaningless tautology. What is more striking still is that when Desanti develops this critique more fully, it will rely upon rationalist resources indebted to Spinozism.

Desanti was not the first French interlocutor to subject Husserl's transcendental Ego to critique for its tendencies toward solipsism. Desanti's critique owes something to Jean-Paul Sartre's *Transcendence of the Ego*, first published in 1937. Before further addressing the Spinozist elements of Desanti's assessment of Husserl, it will be helpful to explore Desanti's relationship to Sartre in order to understand some of the idiosyncrasies of Desanti's own take. Elements of Sartre's critique certainly inform Desanti's, chief among them the stricture against the positing of consciousness as a source of personhood, or, in other words, the notion that the ego is cause rather than effect. Merleau-Ponty's personal influence on Desanti has been noted, but Sartre's should not be overlooked. The two were closest in the early years of the Occupation.[85] The Desantis, along with François Cuzin and Merleau-Ponty, joined Sartre in the formation of the group Socialisme et liberté in late 1940. In fact, Dominique served as Sartre's personal secretary during this period, typing up manuscripts for him. In outright opposition to collaborationism, the members of this short-lived group were uneasy with the dominant role of the Communists in the Resistance. The group ran out of steam by the end of 1941, however. Desanti was radicalized by two events that made taking up common cause with the Communists the more attractive option. The first was the rage provoked by his witnessing of the French police rounding up segments of the Jewish population in 1942; the second was the turning of the tide in the war between Nazi Germany and the Soviet Union. At this point, the Desantis decided that Sartre "had gotten lost in the quicksands of action, because he had neither the preparation nor the competence nor the means to realize the clandestine project he had concocted."[86] They joined the PCF in 1943, and a distance from Sartre was one result.

All the same, there was a real period of friendship with Sartre in these formative months that was not without its own philosophical importance. Sartre was feverishly composing his first philosophical masterpiece, *Being and Nothingness*, during this period. In Dominique's recollection, her husband and Sartre spent long hours at Café Flore discussing the contents of the book, Sartre having shared all his drafts with Desanti.[87] Desanti was interviewed for a commemorative piece for *Being and Nothingness* published by *Le Monde* in 1993 wherein he discussed the profound impact of the book on his generation. His general tenor is one of praise, given the occasion. But he does not fail to reiterate his criticisms of the book, which are irreducible to a political falling-out. Desanti claims that Sartre never gave him a satisfactory answer to the following question, which aimed at the heart of the book's argument: "How can we think the advent of the for-itself at the heart of the in-itself? Must we even attempt to think it?"[88] This question was also at the heart of Gueroult's study of Spinoza: How do we think the synthesis constitutive of knowledge and meaningful subjective experience in terms of its "advent" in ontogenesis? It is arguably the fundamental challenge of Spinoza's metaphysics. By Desanti's account, Sartre's response to this pressure was to say that some metaphysics would be needed to answer such a question, but the task at hand in his work was one of description, a phenomenological ontology. This merely skirted the problem in Desanti's view and was tantamount to a confession that, yes, there is a metaphysics determining this system that remains unstated. For all of its ostensible focus on mere description, *Being and Nothingness* is animated by an unspoken metaphysical presence. In Sartre's displacement of the ego as origin—on this score, Desanti read *The Transcendence of the Ego* as *Being and Nothingness* in embryo[89]—he did not transcend the limitations of Husserl's project as much as he displaced them, or rather, silenced them.[90]

In 1975, Desanti would publish a collection of articles under the title *La Philosophie silencieuse* in which his critique of the silent presence of a determinant principle informing nearly all philosophies of science would reach full force.[91] But the intimations of this critique date back to *Phénoménologie et praxis* wherein Desanti first takes Husserl to task in his quest for a fixed point. Looking back on the gestation of this critique, Desanti wrote, "Having tried my hand over a long period of time at the phenomenological method, I had, it seemed to me, experienced the futility of seeking this fixed point. In truth, I had always seen it flee at my approach, unceasingly presupposed, never reached in itself. Like the 'ground' of the empiricists, it always slipped away."[92] The *Cartesian Meditations* were the ideal place to drive to the heart of Husserl's project—which was always evolving—because it was there that the question of a "radical recommencement" was most emphatically posed.[93] This search for a radical new beginning immediately runs into problems, however, because in the effort to evacuate thought of any of its presuppositions—the gesture of the *epoché*—it is time itself that cannot be bracketed. Desanti observes, "It will be necessary to establish that the fundamental temporality of consciousness is of another dimension than the temporal framework of natural experience belonging to this same consciousness."[94]

From the outset, then, Husserl seeks to establish two different frameworks of temporality, one that feels natural and spontaneous and another that subtends it and accounts for consciousness's essential inner workings. It is the intimation that the latter temporality is somehow more "essential" than the first that is problematic for Desanti. This proposition is anathema to Spinozism because of the controversial "parallelism thesis" of EIIP7: "the order and connection of ideas is the same as the order and connection of things." There are not two orders, two temporalities; there can be only one. And it is precisely along these lines that Desanti marshals a Cavaillèsian critique of Husserl's position on this issue. Thought cannot "access" a temporality other than its own; in all instances, that of natural spontaneity or that of focused interiority, there is *one* kind of time. Recall Cavaillès's strict ripostes to Étienne Borne discussed in Chapter 1; there is no above or below to thought that it is thought's task to reach. Desanti posits the same stricture against Husserl. The question is not how do we sketch "a still silent, fundamental experience" that lies at the beginning, but "instead to seek *by what means philosophical discourse begins*, with it being well understood that the demand for such a discourse and the necessity of following it are already there, understood and reflected in the 'temporality of the concept.'"[95]

Desanti's reading helps unpack Cavaillès's call for a philosophy of the concept to replace one of consciousness. The problem with positing consciousness in the way that Husserl does is that the "donateur du sens" (roughly, the giver/conferrer of meaning/sense) is located in a site extrinsic to the experience of sense itself. The problem with nominating this "sense-giver" the transcendental ego is that "what is 'discovered' finds itself preconstituted in the immanent unity and ceaselessly reeffectuated from this same consciousness baptized 'the transcendental ego.'"[96] Desanti pushes the critique further by interrogating the relationship between horizon and potentiality as presented by Husserl in the fourth meditation. Husserl argues that "when it is a matter of the pure eidetic type, we no longer find ourselves before the empirical *ego*, but *before the eidos ego*; in other words, any constitution of a truly pure possibility, among other pure possibilities, *implies*, as a horizon, *a possible ego—in the sense of pure possibility*, a pure variant of *my* empirical *ego*, for myself."[97] But Desanti asks what the content of this "pure possibility" could possibly be.

And what could this potentiality be if not this: the Ego must always be able to rediscover itself as the closed domain of sense-giving acts? And how is it that this potentiality would be able to constitute itself if this same Ego were not also constituted as a *Self*, that is, as a pole of unity assuring the synthesis of its acts and always capable of rediscovering itself as the originary site wherein such a function is practiced?[98]

In this critique as stated, we see why Althusser could claim that Desanti charges Husserl with a simple failure to follow through rather than with an inherent incorrectness. Husserl ultimately sacrifices all the virtues of his polar analyses to opt ultimately for one pole—the "ego pole"—as the unifying and constituting pole. This collapse into solipsism is, for Althusser, the essential feature of phenomenology.

But this danger of phenomenology was also what clearly distressed Cavaillès and Gueroult and what continued to alarm Desanti. Althusser's polemical intentions prevent him from seeing just how incisive Desanti's critique of phenomenology ultimately is and, moreover, the sites of potential dialogue between Desanti's project and his own. For the gist of Desanti's critique is that phenomenology renders absolute what is in reality historical and contingent. In its dogged pursuit of access to the absolute, phenomenology, like Spinozism, seeks escape from the constraints of finitude. In the case of phenomenology, Desanti designates these two constraints as time and others (*autrui*).[99] "The truth is that *the thinker, in the reduction, has never neutralized the fact of his belonging to the world and history*. In this auto-positioning of the self that, in the *Cogito*, manifested him as the absolute thinker, he is already for himself primordial world, originary time, and bearer of universal sense."[100] Time (i.e., history) and others (i.e., the world) together produce a temporal-spatial situatedness that the phenomenologist attempts to will into the foundation for absolute knowledge, but his will finds itself "confronted with its irreducible beyond. In this field, wherein everything must be thinkable, something shows itself (genetic time and otherness) whose essence is to remain out of reach."[101]

Desanti's immanent critique is notably prescient of certain positions in contemporary French phenomenology, in particular those found in the project of Jean-Luc Marion. For Marion, the virtue of phenomenology was also the virtue of Cartesianism: to provide the means to arrive, rationally, at the philosophical articulation of a beyond that serves as the unthinkable ground for the domain of human existence and experience.[102] Except that in the case of Desanti, this unavoidable conclusion is read as the failure, not the fruition, of the phenomenological project. It is Desanti's Spinozism that accounts for his judgment of the project as a failure, for Spinoza will not countenance the proposal of a beyond that remains inaccessible to thought. For all its limitations, Spinoza's rationalism, mediated through Cavaillès, remains the ground of Desanti's own thinking. If phenomenology, at its most solipsistic, takes one contingent experience and elevates it to the status of the necessary form of the absolute, then the power of Spinozism's riposte is in its insistence that the content of the particular thought or experience not be privileged above or mistaken for the mere *fact* that the thought exists or has happened at all. This explains why for Spinoza the nominally "first" idea of philosophical thought is immaterial. Descartes' error was to posit the *cogito* as the necessary result of the process of radical doubt rather than see that the process of thinking itself was its own result.

But with Desanti there is always an "and yet," and here the pole again swings away from a flirtation with this Spinozist-Cavaillèsian rationalism to the influence of another key mentor. Maurice Merleau-Ponty's contempt for Spinozism ran deeper than the intermittent negative comments on Spinoza throughout his oeuvre attest.[103] Desanti once wrote, "Merleau-Ponty, for his part was not inclined toward what he called *'mathesis.'* And he was surprised at my taste for it, gently reproaching me in his role of benevolent mentor."[104] Evoking the aspirations of the seventeenth-century rationalists, Merleau-Ponty called *mathesis* the desire for the total explanation. It is hard to conceive of more opposed projects than Merleau-Ponty's and Spinoza's, especially if we follow Claude Lefort's assessment of the goal of Merleau-Ponty's later, and unfinished, work collected in *The Visible and the Invisible*:

> [I]n the first drafts for an introduction, he started with the observation that we cannot find an origin in God, in nature, or in man, that such attempts in fact converge in the myth of a total explication of the world, of a complete adequation between thought and being, which nowise takes into account our insertion in the being of which we speak; that, moreover, this myth no longer sustains any fruitful research in our time, and that to dissipate it is not to fall back into skepticism and irrationalism but is to know for the first time the truth of our situation.[105]

Desanti came to share this deep unease with the "myth of a total explication" that motivated the Spinozist enterprise, and what he wanted to salvage from it was its critical potential. This critical potential lay in the restrictions on thought that Spinoza's method sought to impose, among which the most important was its prohibition of recourse to an outside, figurative or not. In this way, Desanti's regard toward phenomenology was similar, geared toward a salvaging act to save the method from its own worst tendencies. Again, what is valuable in it is that which is *restrictive*. In phenomenology's case, the methodological resources to be maintained are, first, the interminable bracketing and reduction, a process that must shed its own origins in a quest for origins, and, second, the emphasis on polar indeterminacy. But it is the experience of those very concrete things that phenomenology ultimately turns us toward, the temporal and the spatial—"the truth of our situation" in Merleau-Ponty's phrase—that prevents the arrival at any stopping point where a kind of pure givenness may be contemplated. For Desanti, political and philosophical experience taught him that the path of the philosopher must be narrow and interminable; its chief aim must be precisely to help one avoid "the snares of belief."[106]

. . .

In Desanti's fluctuations between a Spinozist insistence on the absence of origins and transcendental structures, on the one hand, and a phenomenological method that aims to discern the fundamental movements of thought, on the other, we see the intellectual framework for the "thought experiment" confronting these two philosophical modes recounted at the beginning of this chapter. Playing the "impenitent phenomenologist," that is, a phenomenologist lacking all conviction that he might reach a fundamental ground of givenness or essence, Desanti showed the compelling breadth of Spinoza's unique concept of the "true idea." The "true idea" is always factic for Spinoza; it is a fundamental imposition of thought itself that is repeated in a plurality of instances. No "true idea" is ever more true than another. But due to each true idea's discrete existence, it is also the case that the "true idea" is singular, which means that it is not fully communicable and also never fungible. In other words, scientific insights are *only* scientific insights. They have no bearing beyond their own proper domain. Desanti's incessant movement between the poles of phenomenological indeterminacy and Spinozistic intermittency provides the ground for his own ascetic turn toward a philosophical investigation of the epistemology of mathematics.

In an article titled "Materialism and Epistemology," which recapitulates some of the arguments of *Les Idéalités mathématiques*, Desanti addresses the problem of the transformations of mathematical structures as a historical phenomenon. "Greek *mathesis* worked," he writes. "It doesn't work anymore. What does this 'anymore' mean? A different one works. What does this 'different' mean? How did this 'different' one come into being?"[107] For Desanti, it makes no sense from a philosophical perspective to disqualify the "truth" of Greek mathematics. However, it equally makes no sense to treat this domain as somehow "still" true. Desanti's engagement with the mathematical theory of the function of real variables—the terrain of *Les Idéalités mathématiques*—was a deliberate exercise in asceticism. The preliminary condition, in Desanti's view, for any viable philosophical or epistemological account of a given science was that the scholar "install himself in the fabric of this science itself and that he force himself to acquire its practice from within."[108] Only by fully assimilating one's thought to the scientific practice itself, through discipline and scientific work, could one hope to produce a philosophical account of its structures, terms, and temporal unfolding.

What Desanti discovers time and again throughout *Les Idéalités mathématiques* are moments of apparent indeterminacy in the development of a mathematical theory that nonetheless become fully concretized as necessary steps in the very process of their own theoretical resolution and accomplishment. Desanti designates the edifice of axiomatized discourse, that is, the formalized concepts and procedures of a given scientific enterprise, "Theory 1." The target of Desanti's analysis, however, is what he names "Theory 2," which subtends Theory 1 and is obscured by the recorded history that we have of the latter. Theory 2 refers to the contextual system subtending spontaneous "organic" discourse. In each instance, Desanti examines how this "contextual system" operates toward the systematic destruction of the transcendental field of its operation through the production of the very results it conditions. The "end" of this operation, which gets repeated ad infinitum, is the axiomatization, or concretization, of scientific results, that is, Theory 1. It is not Desanti's task to somehow recover a lost moment of contingency and to reenact it with a different outcome, thus making manifest the surplus of the "transcendental field" of Theory 2. Rather, his point is to show how the transcendental field is a heuristic name for, to borrow Cavaillès's words, a process of "deepening and erasure." If one raison d'être for the transcendental subject, from Kant to Husserl, is to determine the source of the inexhaustible productivity of human thought, Desanti finds that the true historical nature of the "transcendental field" of possibilities is, in each instance, to exhaust itself in the generation of a new "transcendental field" of possibilities. Cavaillès's critique of the "philosophy of consciousness" showed that, in trying to establish the framework for scientific innovation, transcendental philosophy in effect hamstrung it. It did this by attempting to determine transcendental structures as static forms. With Desanti's effort, we see before us the very process by which the transcendental field is exhausted and reconstituted anew *through* its own exhaustion. It is clear that Desanti sees this account of the transcendental field as working toward an answer to the problem of scientific subjectivity. While there is no transcendental subject whose qualities might be fixed, there is a phenomenon of transcendental subjectivity that operates by an incessant process of exhaustion and creation in the constitution of discrete moments of subjective determination. The transcendental Ego is not the subject, but neither is the Spinozist God. There is no reduction to pure immanence, for Desanti insists that the movement of scientific thought is itself generative of new concepts and ideas that operatively transcend their origins and thus serve as the "transcendental field"—

the subject operator or function—for new scientific developments. But once this field is exhausted, this "subject" is exhausted. The discrete subject cannot be "reactivated," nor can its operations be applied elsewhere, beyond the domain of its own theoretical and finite field of existence.

Beyond its overwhelmingly technical recapitulation of an antiquated mathematical theory, and its provocative though ultimately unresolved theory of the transcendental field as a phenomenon of operative subjectivity, *Les Idéalités mathématiques* leaves us with two lessons: (1) Scientific thought operates by way of the creation of its own objects; and (2) each scientific concept is viable only within the framework in which it was created and effectively operates. To be sure, scientific concepts provide the ground for predictive measure within their respective fields. But Desanti's point is that scientific concepts are not exchangeable beyond their own historical and theoretical context. One can never "borrow" from science to legitimize an operation extrinsic to that science.

Desanti's ascetic exercises in mathematics ultimately result in a philosophy of asceticism itself. This is a philosophy that insists on strict discipline and the impossibility of manipulating concepts to implement them beyond their original functions. One aim of the preceding account of Desanti's intellectual biography and his early philosophical efforts has been to illuminate this philosophical position. It is conditioned philosophically by Desanti's shuttling back and forth between Spinozism and phenomenology. But it is also conditioned historically by Desanti's own political experiences. Desanti's indulgence toward Stalinism was cause for regret; what added insult to injury, however, was that Desanti had thought himself a man of science and that in his ideological service to the PCF he compromised his own philosophical and scientific credentials. His later critique of the "silent philosophy" as an agenda that seeks, in some instances, to exploit science from without, and in others, to compromise it from within, was complexly overdetermined by the trajectory of Desanti's own "philosophical destiny."

4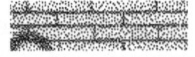

Recuperating Science
The Sources of Louis Althusser's Spinozism

[A] single phrase, a banner flapping in the void: "bourgeois science, proletarian science."

Louis Althusser, For Marx, 1965[1]

The Spinozism of Louis Althusser confounds the expectations of the intellectual historian because its development over time ultimately results more from the deductive logic of its initial premises than the influence of shifting political and cultural conditions. This claim, whose merits I will attempt to justify over the next two chapters, is in flagrant conflict with the majority of accounts of Althusser's itinerary, including not least the interpretation of events offered by Louis Althusser himself. Althusser has begun to receive a new hearing, one that is yielding a deeper appreciation for his thought and the breadth of its impact.[2] But historically most of his readers, detractors and celebrants alike, have taken Althusser at his word in his repeated insistence that his duties as a Communist and a philosopher were complementary aspects of a single theoretical project, one whose guiding thread was a rigorous adherence to the demands of an always-shifting political conjuncture. The interpretations follow from this entanglement in due course, one side emphasizing unraveling and collapse, the other discerning adjustment and refinement. The more critical line, which is common to Althusser's French Maoist detractors in the immediate post-1968 period,[3] Hegelian Marxists,[4] Trotskyists,[5] and more contemporary liberal commentators,[6] reads the systematic disintegration of the Althusserian enterprise as a result of its hopelessly rationalist qualities coupled with a pathetic commitment to a political movement whose exhaustion was increasingly evident, if it was not defunct from the outset. The laudatory line reads Althusser as a thinker who, though a committed Communist Party member, had the philosophical wherewithal to salvage Marxism as a historical science precisely by rejecting the notion that it would ever "be able to transform itself from an interpretative to a predictive form of knowledge."[7] Rather than an abrogation of Marxism's historical mandate, however, this revelation then becomes Althusser's license to reconceive Marxist political engagement along more open lines, as a shifting attentiveness to the shifting demands of shifting conjunctures.[8] The problem with this line of interpretation is that, though hewing to some of Althusser's own pronouncements, it tends to convert Althusser's project into a variant of the pragmatism castigated with compelling vigor in *For Marx* and *Reading Capital*. To salvage such a reading, in effect Althusser's own enterprise must be periodized along a series of "epistemological breaks" not unlike the one Althusser dubiously attributed to Marx. Otherwise, the basic integrity of the critique of Althusser's project as a progressive dissolution into incoherence must be given its full due.

The common element of these interpretations is the importance attributed to changing circumstances and the efforts—successful or dismal—of Althusser to adjust his views accordingly. As indicated, this notion is buttressed by Althusser's meta-narration of his own project, beginning with his qualms over a politically expedient "theoreticism" expressed in the preface to the English edition of *For Marx* and present still in the manic vacillation between apologetics and intransigence that constitutes a share of his memoir, *The Future Lasts Forever*.[9] In light of this surfeit of commentary, I point to the epigraph of what remains one of the best overviews of Althusser's project—a volume more or less situated in the laudatory camp but one that emphasizes the propaedeutic qualities of Althusser's "detour" through theory against its immediate political efficacy.[10] The line is a citation of Althusser's own professed intentions in relation to Montesquieu: "Let us do him the duty, which is the duty of every historian, of taking him not at his word, but at his work."[11] Gregory Elliott's ironic use of this remark obscures its original sense, however, for Althusser's point is that, though at his "word" Montesquieu believed himself to be wholly objective, his "work" betrayed the particularities of his class position. From my perspective, it is Althusser's qualification of this initial claim that is of the utmost importance: "But [. . .] I should not like anyone to believe that Montesquieu's enthusiastic *parti pris* in the political struggles of his time ever reduced his work to a mere commentary on his wishes."[12] In the end, not only is Althusser's commitment to Spinozism irreducible to his wishes; it will persist in spite of them.

The chief aim of this chapter is to explain the emergence of Althusser's Spinozism as conditioned at once by his hostility to phenomenology and the imperative to salvage Marxism from Stalinism. The nexus of these two radically disparate historical conditions resides in a single concept whose centrality to Althusser's way of thought has heretofore been more disparaged than illuminated: science. The knotted imbrication of phenomenology, Stalinism, science, and Spinozism will be untangled in the course of what follows. The goal of the next chapter is to flesh out the claim with which it began: that once established in the concentrated effort of *For Marx* and *Reading Capital*, the development of Althusser's Spinozism exemplified a logic intrinsic to Spinoza's philosophy itself.[13] This goal requires pursuing an argument that is at once philosophical and historical. Narrating the logical development of this Spinozism will require repeated gestures back toward Althusser's rich though idiosyncratic understanding of phenomenology, the gestation of which it is one of our first tasks to elaborate. Given that Althusser's liaison with Spinozism lasted more than thirty years, however, a brief sketch of its contours is in order before pursuing the details.

In his introduction to a collection of unpublished writings from the years 1966–67, G. M. Goshgarian suggests that the difficulty of making sense of Althusser's Spinozism draws in large part from the fact the he sought to redress the excess of Spinozistic "theoreticism" that marked his most famous writings with the application of more Spinozism.[14] Goshgarian's point is that the meaning of Althusser's Spinozism shifts in its essentials from a set of epistemological claims to those of an ontological variety. But this apparent shift is ultimately only one of three total that one can roughly identify, thus marking out four periods of Spinozism in Althusser's philosophy. During the first period, coextensive with the production of *For Marx* and *Reading Capital*, from 1960 to 1965, Althusser's project is indeed epistemological in its essentials.[15] It is a critical project determined above all to isolate what is scientific in Marx's thought, to provide a viable concept of scientificity to support these claims, and to develop a corresponding philosophy able to assist this science. Philosophy, in this period, is the "Theory of theoretical practice."

The second phase is the one that finds Althusser trying to supplement his epistemology with a historical ontology in which alternately the Marxist concept of "production" or a uniquely Althusserian understanding of the "unconscious" functions in a manner similar to Spinoza's Substance, as the ontological precondition and process that determines all that follows, manifested in two attributes, that of materiality, accessed through rational thought (science), and consciousness, as the "site" of lived experience (ideology). This move, which confronts the ontological implications of a set of epistemological positions, mimics Spinoza's own transition from the rejoinder to Descartes' theory of knowledge constitutive of the *Treatise on the Emendation of the Intellect* to the metaphysics elaborated in the *Ethics*. This second period in Althusser's trajectory witnessed an aborted effort to produce a collaborative work titled *Elements of Dialectical Materialism*, which, as Althusser described it to Étienne Balibar, would be a "true work of philosophy that can stand as our *Ethics*."[16] The events of May 1968 interrupted this collective enterprise, dispersing its participants and turning many of them against their teacher. The famous essay on ideology and "ideological state apparatuses" (ISAs), which many have read as Althusser's own reflection on those events, can also be read as the culmination of this second period.[17] What before was merely an epistemological distinction between science and ideology becomes, in this essay, tantamount to a cut across the fabric of existence, with the entire domain of the lived relegated to "ideology."

The third phase culminates in the "essays in self-criticism" of the 1970s wherein Althusser first publicly argued that what was read as structuralism in his thought, and bewailed as "theoreticism," was in reality Spinozism.[18] But even as Althusser apologizes for his Spinozism in these essays, he continues to rely on Spinoza to articulate a new concept of philosophy as 'the class struggle in theory." This slogan was the polemical expression of ideas Althusser had developed in his "Philosophy Course for Scientists" in 1967–68,[19] and in his presentation before the Société française de philosophie on "Lenin and philosophy."[20] (In this regard, what I have heuristically distinguished as the second and the third periods exhibit a historical overlap, a complication mitigated somewhat by the fact that it is not always clear when and for what purposes Althusser composed the initial versions of his texts.) The real content of the slogan lay in the abandonment of philosophy as a theoretical practice that assists science in uncovering the true content of some external reality in favor of an understanding of philosophy as the articulation of dogmatic theses designed to produce intra- and extra-philosophical effects. Here again, Spinoza is the authority. Reflecting on this period of engagement with Spinoza, Althusser wrote the following:

> I discovered in him first an astonishing contradiction: this man who reasons *more geometrico* through definitions, axioms, theorems, corollaries, lemmas, and deductions—therefore, in the most "dogmatic" way in the world—was in fact an incomparable liberator of the mind. How then could dogmatism not only result in the exaltation of freedom but also "produce" it? [. . .] I only understood it later while elaborating my personal little "theory" of philosophy as the activity of the positing of theses to be demarcated from existing theses. I noted that the truth of a philosophy lies entirely in its *effects*, while in fact it acts only at a distance from real objects, therefore, in the space of freedom that it opens up to research and action and not in its form of exposition alone.[21]

Here Althusser manages to distance himself further from his earlier theoreticism yet to radicalize it at the same time. The distancing results from the concession that philosophy does not augment the claims of science, that is, there is no need for Marx's scientific revolution to be completed by a philosophical one that will give us some firmer purchase on the reality of world history. But the radicalization lies in the embrace of a rationalism without object. In the second-phase writings, Althusser used Spinozist ontology to criticize the formalism of structuralism. But in his "dogmatic theses" period, he celebrates philosophical discourse's lack of a presupposed external referent, a referent whose existence is not contingent upon its being posited by that discourse itself. The result is a new conception of philosophy irreducible to, yet permanently dependent upon, the discursive provinces of science and ideology that serve as its inescapable terrain.

This vision will be paramount in Althusser's writings of the 1980s, discovered after their author's death. Given their underdeveloped character, it is debatable whether these efforts truly constitute a fourth phase in the development of his Spinozism. At the very least, they constitute a fascinating postscript. Though serious engagement with these writings would take us beyond the parameters of this study, their significant aspects are nevertheless worthy of note.[22] The most conspicuous among them is a belated reckoning with Heidegger, one reflective of the shifts in Heidegger's French reception brokered by Derrida and others who, like Heidegger himself, moved away from *Being and Time* as the core presentation of his philosophy. In other words, Heidegger garners Althusser's sympathy in this period precisely to the extent that he is no longer regarded as the phenomenological Heidegger who was a negative condition of his earlier project. More to the point, in these late texts Althusser pushes the logic of a philosophy without object to its ultimate conclusion, arguing that, "for Spinoza, the object of philosophy is the void."[23] Althusser's claim is that for Spinoza God qua Substance is—paradoxically, given the name of the concept—a literally *insubstantial* category and thus a "void." Spinoza's motivation in beginning with the concept of God as singular substance is purely strategic. The design is to borrow the ideological concept of God in order to hollow it out from within. Martial Gueroult once claimed that Spinoza "shelled God to the core," rendering the concept devoid of mystery or irrationality.[24] For Althusser "man" was the conceptual replacement for God, thus the need to attack this concept in similar terms, to occupy its demystified space and draw out the philosophical consequences.[25]

For all the twists and turns of this itinerary, a guiding principle runs through it, one predicated upon the progressive eradication of the contents of lived experience as a viable object of philosophical purchase or reflection. This maneuver has its roots in the science/ideology distinction that serves as the core problematic of *For Marx* and *Reading Capital*. This distinction ultimately gets "ontologized" in ensuing works. Concurrently, philosophy becomes redefined as the articulation of dogmatic theses without object; such is the case considering that any philosophy that claims to elucidate the "lived" as it is lived itself remains wedded to ideology. This moment of the third period retains an ostensibly political bearing in that it legislates for philosophy a decisional task of identifying distinctions between science and ideology in discourse more generally. Thus, what was first pursued as a distinction *in* Marx becomes broadened to the distinction *tout court* it is philosophy's task to maintain. Finally, there is the period of the "late Althusser" when his political career was unequivocally over. During this time—the Spinoza of the "void"—Althusser develops an "aleatory materialism" of the encounter and accepts a definition of the materialist philosopher as the one who gets on the train without knowing where it is going.²⁶ Regardless of its philosophical merits, the embrace of this poetically expressed position signaled nothing less than the utter exhaustion of his Spinozism as a philosophy with a political remit.

The relentlessness of Althusser's hostility to phenomenology, a mode of philosophy whose object encompasses the constitutive elements and effects of lived experience, is matched by the tenacity with which Althusser remained committed to Spinozist rationalism as an alternative. To be sure, there is something harrowing in his fidelity to a mode of philosophy whose heralding of thought's positive capacities produces a kind of pure negativity without sublimation, concluding, in Althusser's case, with an interminable confrontation with the "void." Althusser's refusal of any compromise with phenomenology is what, among other things, distinguishes Althusser from Deleuze, wherein we find a fantastic attempt at a synthesis of the phenomenological and Spinozist lines of French thought. Althusser takes the Spinozist rationalism whose development has been traced over previous chapters into and out of the domain of the political, ultimately remaining more faithful to the philosophical imperative than to any political one. If Althusser's commitments to rationalism and to science seem as peculiar as they do intransigent, it is because they were quintessentially untimely. As one of Althusser's collaborators during the science seminars, Alain Badiou, argued in a 1967 review of *For Marx* and *Reading Capital*, these works sought "to *take the measure* of Marx, and, consequently, to assign him his fair place, his double function—scientific and scientifico-philosophical—in the complex intellectual conjuncture in which we are witnessing the break-up of the dominant ideology of the postwar moment: phenomenological idealism."²⁷ In order to make sense of the genesis of Althusser's project within this moment, we would do well to return to his unresolved conflicts with the subject of the previous chapter.

Stalinism and Phenomenology

Stalinism in politics and phenomenology in philosophy were the chief conditions that precipitated Althusser's Spinozist rethinking of Marxist philosophy in the 1960s as the "Theory of theoretical practice." The historical convergence of these two enterprises in the figure of Jean-Toussaint Desanti accounts for the intensity of Althusser's distaste for the instructor who taught him Spinoza at the ENS in the 1940s and the Communist who first inducted him into the French Communist Party (PCF) around the same time. As we saw in the previous chapter, many commentators, including Althusser's biographer and Desanti's widow, have attributed Althusser's hostility largely to personal grievances. Whatever the contents of Althusser's misgivings, it is of greater importance that Desanti incarnated, however temporarily, the two chief tendencies Althusser deemed it his philosophical task to redress.

As a member of the PCF at the height of its Stalinism, Desanti represented all that had become pitiful in Marxist politics. Toeing the Soviet line in France meant bowing to an "economism" that read the advent of emancipation in the bureaucratic organization of human labor power. It would come to be one of Althusser's most provocative claims that this economism was cut from the same ideological cloth as the post-Stalinist humanism that replaced it—captured in the slogan "everything for Man." Economism, most often manifested as "technocracy," was a formula that read history as the mechanical unfolding of a single, determinant essence in lockstep logic.[28] "Humanism" replaced a generic, and reductive, concept of the economic with a generic, and reductive, concept of man whose referent was an essence, not unlike an ideal economy, that would flourish under the right conditions. Humanism thus remained formally indistinguishable from its economistic predecessor, which explains why despite their ostensible opposition the two outlooks were of a piece; the "ethical idealism" of humanism was the subjectivist complement to the neopositivism of technocracy.[29] In Althusser's view, it was misguided meditation on the abstract (and ostensibly fictional) essence of man that distracted from the reality of determinant social and historical, in a word, *structural* conditions. Althusser's flair for polemic was rarely lacking: "It is impossible to *know* anything about men," he wrote in 1964, "except on the absolute precondition that the philosophical (theoretical) myth of man is reduced to ashes."[30]

The shared myth at the core of these ideological "-isms"—economism and humanism—was, in Althusser's view, given its supreme philosophical expression and imprimatur in phenomenology. In its French manifestation especially, this tradition identified "lived experience" (*l'expérience vécu*) as at once the object of philosophical investigation and the adjudicative standard of its results.[31] But as we saw in Desanti's reading of Husserl in the previous chapter, phenomenology's insistence on the mediatory relation between consciousness and the lived encounter with the world had a fundamental tendency to enshrine human consciousness, the "Ego," as the source of meaning, value, and, ultimately, philosophical truth. A mechanistic phenomenology seems almost a contradiction in terms, but the common component resides in this image of the world as the efflorescence of an original, essential source. Desanti was thus in error twice over, not only for his politics but also for his failure to see that phenomenology was unsalvageable. His support of Stalinism amounted to complicity with an egregious historical error. To be sure, Althusser himself was a member of the thoroughly Stalinized PCF from 1948 onward, and he shared the blinkered enthusiasm for Stalin's Soviet Union that marked this generation of French intellectuals.[32] Nonetheless, a generational divide separated Desanti and Althusser, in that the former, along with Jean Kanapa and Laurent Casanova, operated primarily as an ideological mouthpiece for the party, subordinating any potential philosophical misgivings to the demands of the party line. Althusser's philosophical interventions of the post-Stalinist era were genuine as philosophical efforts, whatever the conjunctural political demands subtending them and whatever the motives to redress a deflated zeal.[33] Althusser's fidelity to philosophy accounts for what truly added insult to injury in Desanti's example. His Stalinist propaganda appeared buttressed by his main philosophical inclination.

Notwithstanding the convergent threads in the figure of Desanti, the notion that Joseph Stalin and Edmund Husserl have anything to with each other, theoretical or otherwise, is prima facie comical. To understand how Althusser could forge such a link, we must turn to the sources of Althusser's hostility to phenomenology. It is hard to locate the exact moment at which phenomenology became philosophical enemy number one, but his distaste appears to have coalesced at the end of the 1940s, shortly after he submitted his master's thesis on Hegel in 1948. Althusser's time as a student at the ENS was interrupted by the Second World War, which he spent in a prisoner-of-war camp in Germany. In the 1930s, Althusser's main teachers had been Jean Guitton, a spiritualist philosopher who would become implicated with Pétainism, and Jean Lacroix, a personalist close to Emmanuel Mounier of *Esprit* and with links to Gabriel Marcel and other Christian existentialists. In 1949, shortly after his formal adherence to the PCF, Althusser wrote a letter to Lacroix in response to a draft the latter had shared of his soon-to-be-published book, *Marxisme, existentialisme, personnalisme.* The long letter bears the marks of intellectual growing pains and achieves Althusser's own break with Mounier and Christian democracy. It contains the following charge against Lacroix: "with your good conscience, we fall back into a subjectivism which is the counter-theory of *what we actually do*."[34] The bulk of the letter consists of a critique of Lacroix's interpretation of alienation as a kind of spiritual crisis to be resolved at the "end of history." Recent scholarship has pointed to the intricate liaison between phenomenology and Christianity in France, historically and intellectually.[35] There is certainly something both evocative and ultimately plausible in reading Althusser's abandonment of Catholicism for Marxism as itself entailing a concomitant critique of phenomenology more generally, and phenomenological existentialism more specifically. But to leave it at that neglects the contents of Althusser's intellectual efforts at this time, as well as the more proximate influences at the ENS, which included, among professors, Maurice Merleau-Ponty and Desanti, and, among friends, Michel Foucault and the enigmatic Jacques Martin.

Though Merleau-Ponty found strong promise in Althusser, it appears the high regard was not mutual at the time.[36] Evidently Althusser was a brilliant but also somewhat petulant student. According to Étienne Balibar's recollection, Althusser, Foucault, and Martin thought of themselves in the late 1940s as the triumvirate of Hegel, Hölderlin, and Schelling for twentieth-century France.[37] On the one hand, this meant seriously engaging with the writings of Hegel and German Idealism. On the other, it meant a self-aggrandizing ambition to shift the terms of philosophical discourse. Merleau-Ponty was impressed enough with Althusser's thesis on Hegel, "On Content in the Thought of G. W. F. Hegel,"[38] that he encouraged its publication alongside Martin's, "Remarks on the Notion of the Individual in Hegel's Philosophy." In 1963, shortly after Martin's suicide, Althusser wrote his friend Franca Madonia reflecting on this shared engagement with Hegel and Merleau-Ponty's support:

We put up fierce resistance, saying that these texts had merely provided an opportunity to rid ourselves of our youthful errors. "One doesn't publish one's youthful errors." Merleau was very annoyed, we fought him off as best we could, though to tell you the truth we weren't so much fighting him off as his line of thinking: we didn't want to give him any sort of support or approval.[39]

The "line of thinking" Althusser and Martin were fighting was phenomenology, of which Merleau-Ponty was a chief purveyor. But Althusser's pugnacity raises the question, what were the contents of these youthful errors?

Althusser's study naturally speaks as much to his perspective on the vicissitudes of French Hegelianism as it does to Hegel's philosophy itself. The content of his thesis is an extremely technical assessment of the circularity that inheres in the Hegelian concept of content, a circularity whose own theoretical exhaustion was saved by Marx's introduction of those "concrete" elements of history that had remained impervious to the machinations of the dialectic of form and content. Althusser's emphasis on this aspect of Marx's debt to Hegel—a debt that is really more of a correction, or perhaps even a "break"—is in marked contrast to a reading that emphasizes Marx's debts to the Hegelian conception of subjectivity. Ultimately, the question of how much Hegel already anticipated Marx's amendments is held in provocative abeyance. One thing is clear, however. Althusser does not yet seem to hold humanism in particularly low regard, nor does it appear to be a crucial aspect of Marx's thought.

Further insight into Althusser's understanding of Hegelianism comes from a short piece titled "Man, That Night,"[40] published in the *Cahiers du Sud* in 1947, the same period during which Althusser was preparing his thesis. The text is a review of Alexandre Kojève's recently published *Introduction à la lecture de Hegel*.[41] Looking back, Althusser would claim that he and Martin wrote their theses as deliberate rebukes of Kojève.[42] The review, a masterful display of backhanded praise, supports this assessment. Althusser lauds Kojève for rescuing Hegel from a decades-long (French) misreading that sees in him an apologist for (German) totality qua Substance. But Althusser notes that Kojève is only partially right in his insistence that "Substance is a Subject." For the real import of Hegelian philosophy, in Althusser's reading, resides in the fact that "Substance is *also* a Subject." In other words, a tireless emphasis on subjectivity—Kojève's modus operandi—obfuscates the material, concrete underpinnings of nature as something that is not historical in a linear, teleological sense. Althusser writes, "The animal kingdom reabsorbs its monsters, the economy its crises: man alone is a triumphant error who makes his aberration the law of the world."[43] In 1968, Althusser suggested that although concurrent with his political maturation, and ultimately compatible with its goals, his philosophical option for materialism was not purely political.[44] In the 1980s, he wrote that "from the beginning I felt my attitude towards philosophy as such was irreversibly and profoundly critical, destructive even. [. . .] My involvement in politics reinforced this attitude."[45] Judging from his writings, "philosophy as such" seems to have been largely equated with subjectivism, idealism, and anything sympathetic to Husserl or Heidegger. Judging from the specific passage cited previously, in which "man" gets coded as an error, it would seem his alternative materialism had a philosophical depth beyond its political utility for Marxism.

"Man, That Night" concludes with the judgment that "Kojève's existentialist Marx is a travesty in which Marxists will not recognize their own. It is difficult to understand Marx, if we neglect, as Kojève does, the objective (or substantialist) aspect of Hegelian negativity."[46] Kojève is subjected to the same charge as Lacroix, an excess of subjectivism. If Althusser's hostility to this mode of philosophy is clear from the textual record, what is not so evident is how and where Althusser developed such a firm and rationalist proclivity for science, or a philosophical appropriation of science, as an alternative to this subjectivism.[47] Indeed, the name "Cavaillès," as well as "Canguilhem" and "Bachelard," is nowhere to be found in these writings. If anything, Althusser's attitude toward Bachelard, from whom the concept of the "epistemological break" was borrowed (and modified), seems dismissive during this period.[48] Also absent is any sense of Spinoza's value as anything more than a precursor to Hegel.

In *The Facts*, his first attempt at autobiography, written in the late 1970s, Althusser commented on the subject of influences: "[O]ne can no more choose one's influences than the age in which one lives. As well as Marx, who was not much of a philosopher, there was someone else who influenced me: Spinoza. Unfortunately, he was not teaching anywhere."[49] Spinoza was on the *agrégation* the year Althusser took this exam in 1948.[50] But the fact is that Spinoza was ubiquitous in French philosophical culture, most high school students having read the *Treatise on the Emendation of the Intellect* for the *concours*. So the question of Spinoza's influence is not one of *if* but *which*, that is, to which aspects of Spinoza's philosophy did Althusser take? The archival record is of some help in this regard. As discussed in the previous chapter, Althusser's notes from Desanti's lectures present a Spinoza with a firmly rationalist emphasis.[51] Spinoza's virtue was his recognition that philosophy had to be conceived along scientific lines. Not only was it necessary for philosophy to pay heed to the developments of science; philosophy itself should aspire to the same rationalist integrity. These lessons must have seemed alluring in a period during which phenomenological existentialism was so clearly in ascendance.

More perplexing is the subject of Cavaillès specifically, who is repeatedly praised throughout Althusser's oeuvre but who receives in it even less theoretical attention than Spinoza himself. Desanti's lectures on logical positivism and modern physics show Cavaillès's theoretical influence.[52] And Althusser's archive contains notebooks that show he was familiar with Cavaillès's doctoral works at a relatively young age.[53] The martyred Resistant's mythic status must have played a further role in his appeal. He was the most highly regarded *normalien* of his generation, philosophically, and his heroism was legendary. His antipathy toward the existentialist variant of phenomenology was well known, and his more technical grievances with Husserl's project were legible in his published texts. Canguilhem never made a secret of his high regard for Cavaillès. When his edited version of *Sur la logique et la théorie de la science* appeared in 1946, the slogan that pitted a philosophy of the concept against a philosophy of consciousness quickly became common currency in the Latin Quarter.[54]

Althusser's relationship with Martin may provide further light. In his memoir, Althusser attributes his discovery of Cavaillès and Canguilhem, "two thinkers to whom I practically owe everything," to Martin.[55] We referred to Martin earlier as enigmatic because very little is known about him beyond the details recorded by Althusser himself and those discovered by Althusser's biographer. We know that they were very good friends in the years at the ENS following the war. We also know that Althusser considered his friend's suicide in 1963 to be a central event in his own life. Althusser's major autobiography is highly suspect in terms of details and interpretation. But Moulier Boutang has suggested that there is some cause for Althusser's insistence that he had in effect pursued Martin's own intellectual itinerary for him, that is, in lieu of him. The evidence for this lies, according to Moulier Boutang, in Martin's thesis on Hegel, which remains unpublished and unavailable to the public. In it we apparently find a whole set of issues mobilized, chief among them a reading of Hegel that emphasized the individual as an effect of a conglomeration of forces, a concept of overdetermination clearly anticipatory of Althusser's, and the imperative above all to drive to the heart of Hegel's "problematic" (*problèmatique*).[56] This term, like "overdetermination," would come to be a keyword for Althusser. Althusser's debt to Martin was poignantly captured in the dedication to *For Marx*: "These pages are dedicated to the memory of Jacques Martin, the friend who, in the most terrible ordeal, alone discovered the road to Marx's philosophy—and guided me on to it." One presumes the ordeal referred to here is the depression that culminated in his friend's suicide.[57] We will never know the exact nature of Martin's "discovery." Althusser claimed Martin "taught [him] how to think [. . .]. Without [Martin], [he] would never have put two thoughts together."[58] It would be tendentious to suggest that Martin's discovery was Cavaillès's philosophy, but we can at least garner from the details we do know, which included a shared admiration for Cavaillès and a disregard for Merleau-Ponty, what kind of thinker Martin was and what his influence on Althusser may have been.

If Cavaillès's fondness for Spinoza was generally recognized, we can surmise that Merleau-Ponty's distaste for the latter was as well. What we find then, in Althusser's example, is a general conglomeration of influences and revulsions, which pitted a certain scientism and rationalism against his more proximate *maîtres*. To this we could add a final point adduced by Pierre Bourdieu. The sociologist argues that French philosophy of science, in its institutional forms, possessed a strong class character and that this partially accounted for much of its appeal.[59] In particular, those distrustful of the "total intellectual" incarnated by Sartre, whose institutional clout seemed to provide the authority to speak in totalizing terms, deliberately pursued a more self-consciously rigorous approach to philosophy, which sutured it to the history of science in an effort to undercut philosophy's aspirations to speak to the totality. Bachelard was a former postman who came to philosophy late in life; Cavaillès was a descendant of Calvinists from the west of France and felt isolated in Paris; Koyré was a Russian émigré. Bourdieu suggests that Canguilhem was separated from his classmates Aron and Sartre "by his popular and provincial origins."[60] All were cultural outsiders living at the heart of France's metropolitan institutions. Althusser read the renown of Sartre and the success of Merleau-Ponty as a resurgence of spiritualism, the most institutionally dominant mode of French philosophy of the nineteenth century, and precisely that aspect of French thought that, in Althusser's view, accounted for its congenital backwardness.[61] Auguste Comte—called out for praise by Althusser,[62] and certainly a precursor to French philosophy of science—was a renegade in this context where figures like Victor Cousin and later Félix Ravaisson ruled the roost. In the twentieth century, Brunschvicg occupied a peculiar position in that the spiritualist vestiges of his republican idealism were mitigated, if not supplanted, by his rationalism. Bergson, who like

Brunschvicg was Jewish, notably conceived his project as the ultimate fruition of the spiritualist line, and his sympathies with Catholicism, which almost amounted to conversion, were well known. Insofar as phenomenology was heralded in France as the coming of "True Bergsonianism,"[63] the class and cultural alignments coagulated further. For all the excitement the latest German import generated in Paris, there is a sense in which phenomenology stands at the cumulative point of an aristocratic and Catholic trajectory in France, which certain "rigorous" provincials sought to hollow out from within. Althusser was a *pied noir* from Algeria, of Alsatian stock, who, after time in Marseille and Lyon, arrived in Paris in 1939 to begin his schooling at the ENS before his mobilization for war as a foot soldier deferred his education. Althusser *dixit*: we don't choose our influences.

If Althusser's philosophical sensibilities were thus "overdetermined," this state of affairs still does not explain how he was able to link the "dominant" philosophy he distrusted with the fallout from Stalinism. For Althusser, phenomenology privileged the "lived" in philosophy in a manner homologous to the way Stalinist economism and post-Stalinist humanism each did with "history" or "humanity" in political practice. In all cases, a singular and determinant essence was deemed available to a privileged few (the party, in the case of Stalinism; initiates into philosophy, in the case of phenomenology) able to discern and guide the manifestation of that essence in the "lived" world. Althusser's insistence in his memoir that "though he claimed he was a Marxist, [Desanti] never entirely disowned Husserl"[64] is at once evidence of Althusser's fidelity to Marxism and a suggestive indicator of the virulence Althusser attributed to phenomenology and its complicity with a regressive Marxist politics. When Balibar, cognizant of Husserl's growing importance in his philosophical culture, approached his teacher for guidance on which texts to consult first, Althusser told him he would find nothing in Husserl that was not already present in Hegel and Feuerbach.[65] It was precisely the traces of these latter thinkers that Althusser sought to expurgate from Marxist philosophy. As Kojève reduced Hegel to subjectivity, so Althusser came to reduce Hegel to Kojève, and in turn all the "subjectivism" that Kojève's impact entailed for French philosophy. It would be tempting to attribute the effort to read links between this loose philosophical configuration and Stalinist ideology to the idiosyncrasies of Althusser's intellect and a Manichean tendency to see complicity among all his enemies. But there was a nexus in which the two modes of thought had a convergent historical bearing, a domain of knowledge and theoretical activity that Althusser saw as betrayed twice over, by phenomenology on the level of philosophy, and Stalinism at the level of politics. This nexus, in a word, was *science*.

In his blistering critique of his former mentor and collaborator, Jacques Rancière turned the critique of privilege against Althusser, describing the atmosphere at the ENS in the early 1960s thus: "Our privileged situation allowed us to make science the only important thing and to push everything else—the petty academic, financial, or sexual grievances of students—into that realm of illusion known in our discourse by the term *lived experience* [*le vécu*]."[66] Science was opposed to the lived, opposed to experience. This was the ethos of the period of high Althusserianism in the 1960s. By and large, Althusser's scientism accounts for his uneasy status in the canon of Western Marxism. The criticisms of Althusserian Marxism for its elitism, its vanguardism, its Leninism, and its resultant defeatism, are legion. All of these critiques find their primary target in the privileging of theory as an autonomous practice and the effort to make that practice rigorously coherent. In a discussion of Kant in his *Negative Dialectics*, Theodor Adorno wrote, "A thought that is purely consistent will irresistibly turn into an absolute for itself."[67] To be sure, Adorno had nary an interest in Althusser's project, but this phrase can serve as a fitting distillation of the hostility to Althusser within Western Marxism.

In its efforts for pure consistency, with the concomitant appeal to scientificity, Althusser's rethinking of Marxism appeared to be a betrayal of all that had been novel in Marxist theory in the first place.[68] Perry Anderson offered one of the more generous versions of this critique when he suggested that, in comparison to the version of Marxism on offer by his interlocutor E. P. Thompson, "Althusser's unilateral and remorseless stress on the overpowering weight of structural necessity in history corresponds more faithfully to the central tenets of historical materialism, and to the actual lessons of scientific study of the past—but at the price of obscuring the novelty of the modern labor movement and attenuating the vocation of revolutionary socialism."[69] The implication of Anderson's assessment is consistent with the core paradox of Althusserianism, that the privileging of true knowledge above all—and, on this score, Anderson conceded more to Althusser than most—results in a corresponding diminution in the capacity to intervene in the world through the medium of confident political action.

Nevertheless, to approach Althusser's Spinozism as one more or less isolated philosophical ingredient among many would be misleading. Rather, Spinozist rationalism, mediated through Cavaillès, was itself the means through which Althusser sought philosophically to recuperate science from what he viewed as its twice-over degradation in the hands of Stalinist ideology and phenomenological philosophy. In effect, one cannot understand Althusser's philosophical reliance on Spinozism if one does not understand his historical relationship to science, and vice versa. Althusser's repeated insistence that Marxism was a science, or more specifically, that Marx created the science of historical materialism, may be called into question. It certainly has been. But what gets lost in the condemnations of Althusser's failure to succeed in his own project—not least Althusser's own self-recriminations in his later years—is the countervailing success with which Althusser redeemed science as a concept, shorn of its positivist naïveté, that philosophy and politics both could ignore only to their common peril. In either case, the peril in wait was a collapse into ideology. Althusser's efforts in 1967–68 to philosophically siphon the "spontaneous philosophy of the scientists" from their scientific practice were designed to articulate the distinction between scientific practice, on the one hand, and the ideologically driven interests of the scientists as members of society, on the other. But this was no mere abstract enterprise resulting from Althusser's own fanatical embrace of scientificity. We can trace its roots to particular historical developments. In the events typically listed to explain Althusser's sudden intervention on the world stage, the collapse of Stalinism and the "right-wing" turn that followed in the Soviet Union number alongside the emergence of a nascent humanism within Marxist philosophical circles. These developments certainly set the stage for Althusser's appearance on the scene of Marxist thought. But in the opening essay of *For Marx*, where he identifies these broader factors, Althusser points as well to more specific conditions of a decidedly local character: the contents of his own "philosophical memory [. . .] the period summed up in caricature by a single phrase, a banner flapping in the void: 'bourgeois science, proletarian science.'"[70]

Althusser ascribes a metonymic function to the defense of Lysenkoism Desanti produced under that title.[71] It acquired importance as the exemplar of a bastardization that made science the manipulated preserve of an ideological agenda rather than a discursive aggregate of knowledge able to act as a check on ideological "interest," whether its manifestation be chiefly philosophical or political.[72] Indeed, this resounding critique of manipulated science is of a piece with Althusser's more explicit political criticism expressed most starkly in his heretical rejoinder to Thesis Eleven on Feuerbach in the same essay. Recognizing that the putative "end of philosophy" involved an abrogation of science and opened the floodgates to ideology, Althusser admitted to his own culpability in the enterprise for which Desanti served as a figurehead:

> Those of us who were the most militant and the most generous tended towards an interpretation of the "end of philosophy" as its "realization" and celebrated the death of philosophy in action, in its political realization and proletarian consummation, unreservedly endorsing the famous Thesis on Feuerbach which, in theoretically ambiguous words, counterposes the transformation of the world to its interpretation. It was, *and always will be*, only a short step from here to theoretical pragmatism.[73]

Pragmatism in politics was thus understood to be a correlate to pragmatism in theory, the latter of which involved a subordination of rational method to an "end" prefigured in a design determined by an extra-scientific interest. The legibility of the goal in the origin was for Althusser the universal marker of teleology. His critique of teleology as a formal and existential fixture is among the more resilient of Althusser's theoretical legacies; it is arguably the linchpin of his political and philosophical aims. Yet a Marxist politics hostile to the concept of telos hardly seems to be a Marxist politics at all. While surely opposed to religiosity in his affect, Althusser's own commitments to Marxism at the political level, distinct from the "scientific," betrayed a sort of despondent messianism, a messianism maintained in full knowledge that "the lonely hour of the 'last instance' never comes."[74] It is generally recognized that Althusser's intransigent commitment to Marxism operated like a transfiguration of the Catholic faith of his youth. Balibar has conceded the validity of this point, remarking that whereas Sartre most likely intended to provoke with his comment that Marxism was "the unsurpassable horizon of our time," for Althusser this was absolutely, literally, true.[75] Ultimately Althusser presents us with an inversion of the Gramscian formula: pessimism of the will, optimism of the intellect.

Though he repeatedly insisted on the inseparability of his philosophical and Communist commitments, Althusser remained something of a schizophrenic along these very lines. If Althusser's political commitment to Marxism evinced a theological component, this was matched if not exceed by his philosophical commitment to Spinozism. For notwithstanding his own talk of radical "breaks," Althusser stands at the cumulative point of a trajectory of French Spinozism that has its roots in Cavaillès, if not Brunschvicg himself. Althusser castigated Brunschvicg repeatedly for his concessions to spiritualism and for what was viewed in his thought and example as mere bourgeois apologetics.[76] In this dismissal, Althusser simply rehearsed the polemics against this "watchdog of the established order" launched by Paul Nizan in the 1930s.[77] At a philosophical level, Brunschvicg's own assessment of Spinozism would reach its supreme expression in Althusser's project. Althusser's decision to place the Spinozist conception of the true—*verum index sui et falsi* (the true is its own sign, and that of the false)—at the heart of his contribution to *Reading Capital* was a veritable rebuttal of a conception of Marxist philosophy indebted to a renovated Hegelian dialectical philosophy of history and inspired by Giambattista Vico's *verum-factum* principle, the latter of which claimed that man can know his history precisely because he has made it. In this reading, history is man's creation. But to posit man as creator was simply to beg the question and to ascribe to the concept "man" an essence that was structurally indistinguishable from the theological concept of God as creator.[78] Such was the gravamen of Althusser's critique of Feuerbach, and the young Marx still indebted to Feuerbach.[79] In supplanting one epistemic principle, *verum-factum*, with another, *verum index sui et falsi*, Althusser fastened on to an aspect of Spinoza's philosophy identified as "the Spinozist conception of truth" in Brunschvicg's masterwork, *Les Étapes de la philosophie mathématique*: "[Spinoza] alone was capable of going all the way with the exclusion of the scholastic notion of *faculty*. Intelligence is an activity coextensive with the life of man; it is *judgment* and *will*. Every idea affirms itself and produces from itself its consequences."[80] To exclude the notion of faculty, and to argue that every idea affirms itself, is to short-circuit a representational model of truth and to insist on the factic nature of truth itself as an undeniable and imposing force. This aspect of Spinoza's conception is also captured in another line of his Althusser liked to cite: *habemus enim ideam verum* (roughly, for we have true ideas). Richard Popkin argued that for Spinoza there were no true skeptics, only ignoramuses.[81] The point is that it is impossible not to know whether or not one knows. For Spinoza, you either know you know, or you know you don't know. To say that you don't know if you don't know is not simply redundant; it is delusional self-deception.

In Brunschvicg's particular case, the praise of the union of judgment and will under the banner of intelligence owes something to his own optimistic faith in the putatively rational structure of the Third Republic. Be it the Third Republic or the class antagonisms of history writ large, the point remains the same: there is no "faculty" extrinsic to the manifestations of human history. The only adjudicative standard, and the only determinant is intelligence itself, that is, the idea in its own development. This position cannot but appear idealist. But whereas Brunschvicg's "critical idealism" reads the history of science as the consequence of ideas, and thus reintroduces an idealist temporality that makes that world and its history the "effect" of preceding ideas, Althusser wants to pursue the Spinozist logic further in the recognition that the world and history are *nothing but effects*, that is, there is no antecedent essence—God, or man—that "has" the ideas that produce effects. As to the question of will, it remained unconsidered in Althusser's thought, largely because as a (theologically committed) Marxist, the will was taken for granted. Thus philosophy, conceived along intrinsically rationalist, Spinozist lines, could proceed autonomously.

If Althusser's will was pessimistic at a theologically Marxist level, we can nonetheless see more clearly why he was able to commit himself so unreservedly to Spinozism. In Spinozist rationalism, as Brunschvicg's interpretation suggests, the question of will becomes fully sutured to that of the rational. For Spinoza, "desire" may or may not be rational, and thus it can be errant, but the will, or *conatus* in Spinoza's vernacular, that subtends desire is not. As a result, what requires philosophical elaboration is the concept of rational qua rational, and nothing else. Again, here Althusser's Spinozism and his commitments to post-positivist science are two sides of the same coin. In an essay on Althusser's relationship to French epistemology, Peter Dews makes specific reference to Althusser's "Spinozist view of science [. . .] according to which all knowledge of necessity must be logico-deductive in form."[82] In other words, science is not an empirical quest for the putative "causes" of "events" but instead an effort to articulate conceptually the coherence of a given scientific object in its rational integrity.[83] Dews goes on to contrast Althusser with Bachelard, the inspiration behind the concept of the "epistemological break" thought to separate the young from the mature Marx. Unlike Bachelard, for whom the *coupure* marked the moment for the scientist when chaotic nature coalesced into coherence, Althusser "argues that the epistemological break does not consist in a leap from the spontaneous to the organized, from nature to culture, but rather in a shift from one system of concepts to another: from an 'ideological problematic' to the problematic of a science."[84] In either case, ideology or science, the system of concepts can be coherent. As a result of this problem, the bulk of Althusser's effort in *Reading Capital* is devoted to defining what distinguishes a science from ideology; ultimately, the distinction lies in the relationship of concepts to their objects. Ideology receives its objects, whereas science generates them. Dews's assessment, by noting the polyvalence of the concept "epistemological break," also points to a confusion in the science/ideology dyad sown by Althusser himself. In one sense, Althusser sees science as emerging from the stuff of ideology, an emergence that is coextensive with the moment of the "break." The model for this process is Spinoza's own account of the transition from the first level of ideas, the realm of *vaga experientia* (the received notions of lived experience), to the properly scientific level on the second order, where things are grasped by their concept, and finally on to the third level, where singular things are understood in their singularity, that is, without analogy or borrowed concepts. This transition in Spinoza's philosophy is presented in the form of a prescriptive personal narrative, one that each person seeking true knowledge should follow, hence the title *Treatise on the Emendation of the Intellect*.

But Althusser wants to extrapolate from this general form the narrative of Marx's specific intellectual itinerary, and that only after a detour through a speculative master narrative of Western intellectual history where we see Spinoza's tripartite distinction in play. The universality of Spinoza's schema resides in the fact that it is purely formal. But Althusser finds it in particular instances, specifically the various creations of science that have marked human history, and the philosophical systems that have resulted from these "discoveries." For example, the creation of geometrical mathematics by Thales is a case of moving from the first kind of knowledge to the second; Platonist philosophy gives us the achievement of the third. Another case is the science of Newtonian physics, whose ultimate philosophical result will be Kant. What was a universal narrative in Spinoza becomes a world historical one, with different actors at different points, before ultimately becoming a *biographical* process in the singular case of Marx. It is immediately apparent, however, that this set of claims about Marx's personal "epistemological break" is more philological than philosophical. The "break" occurs when Marx, perhaps unbeknownst to himself, moves from one kind of knowledge to the second, the realm of lived ideology to that of conceptual science. He never broke through to the third level, which is precisely why Althusser deems it his task to do so "for Marx."

Althusser claimed that the Marxist revolution in thought resulted in a dual creation, the science of historical materialism and the philosophy of dialectical materialism. The problem, however, was that although the science of historical materialism was legible in *Capital*—that is, Marx achieved the second kind of knowledge—the philosophical complement (the ostensible third kind of knowledge) was not. Althusser's task, then, was to elaborate the philosophy by hewing closely to the science as it was presented in *Capital*, thus remaining committed to the Spinozist imperative to produce the third kind of knowledge out of the second. This philosophy would be tantamount to a singular grasp of Marxist science in its singular essence, that is, an understanding of the science in its pure essentials, without concepts borrowed from ideology. In the mere idea for this project we find the real nub of the confusion, obscured by Althusser's obsession with Marx's intellectual biography. Althusser's broader theoretical agenda, which remains wedded to the initial Spinozist conviction that any intellect can and must make this move from the first kind of knowledge to the second, and ultimately the third, is to articulate the philosophy that can and will be the propaedeutic that instigates this transition for whoever should encounter it. The "problem" with this project—which, to be precise, is only a problem for doctrinaire Marxists—is that, aside from its general bearing on the Marxist concept of ideology, which remained untheorized by Marx himself, in its philosophical essentials it has virtually nothing to do with Marx and almost everything to do with Spinoza.[85]

5

Redefining Philosophy

The Development of Louis Althusser's Spinozism

One cannot be both a Marxist and coherent.

          Louis Althusser, "Conversation with Richard Hyland," 1982[1]

  Althusser eventually pled mea culpa to Raymond Aron's charge that he had concocted an "imaginary Marxism."[2] In 1978, he sent a letter to the Georgian philosopher Merab Mardashvili in which he shared some reflections on this theme:

I see clear as day that what I did fifteen years ago was to fabricate a little, typically French justification, in a neat little rationalism bolstered with a few references (Cavaillès, Bachelard, Canguilhem, and behind them, a bit of the Spinoza-Hegel tradition), for Marxism's (historical materialism's) pretension to being a science. Ultimately, this is (or, rather, was, because I've changed a little since) in the good old tradition of any philosophical enterprise conceived as a guarantee or a warrant. I also see that, things being what they were, the claims and counter-claims being what they were, and I being what I was, it couldn't have happened any differently; my counterattack was, as it were, natural, as natural as Spinoza's storms and hail.[3]

Althusser's continued commitment to the figure of necessity in history, up to and including his own thought, was an aspect of his Spinozism inextricable from the science and ideology distinction operative in his work. "Natural," in the context of this letter, has no other meaning than necessary. Regarding his effort in general, he continued, "I only half believed in it, like anyone of 'sound mind,' but the doubtful half had to be there so that the other half could write."

Though his account bears the trappings of ex post facto justification, it at least has the virtue of being consistent with his earlier Spinozist conviction that ideas produce themselves. French is a language that lends itself to the philosophical logic of immanent necessity because the distinction between the passive and the reflexive is often collapsed into one grammatical structure. Where an Anglophone must choose between "ideas are produced" and "ideas produce themselves," the Francophone simply writes, *les idées se produisent*. This maneuver always raises the specter of evasion, not unlike the *es* in Heidegger's *es gibt*, or the *il* of Levinas's *il y a*. The question becomes: *what* is giving/doing/having the idea? The provocation of Spinozism, as we elaborated in our discussion of Gueroult in Chapter 2, is to short-circuit this question altogether or, more precisely, to render it irrelevant by insisting on the factic nature of thought. The first evidence is the thought itself, irrespective of any gesture that then sutures that thought to a *cogito* or *Ego* or *Dasein* where the thought can be "located." For the rationalist Spinoza the effort to excavate this "location" is a misguided lost cause. "Reason" is the imperative to follow through on the concatenation of thought's own constitutive ideas and to realize their integral necessity. Or, to hew more closely to Spinoza's point, "reason" *is* the concatenation of thought's own constitutive ideas. Althusser was no stranger to evasive rhetoric in his own writing, but in his letter to Mardashvili he affirms that the skeptical, critical half never completely won the day against this necessity:

I've become certain of another thing: that one text follows another by a logic such that, if you simply recognize, in a general way, the necessity of it because you have at least a modicum of the philosopher about you, it can't be "rectified" all that easily. Rectify as much as you like; something of it will *always* remain.[4]

That which remains to the end in Althusser's project is the commitment to Spinozist rationalism, and it is the task of this chapter to trace the logic of this commitment's development. We can accept Althusser's word on this matter only if the record of his philosophical output bears it out. In the latter half of the preceding chapter, we provided an overview of how Althusser's newfangled understanding of philosophy and its relationship to science was conceived with recourse to Spinozist rationalism. Now the aim is to make sense of this project's development in the three main phases of Althusser's itinerary identified at the outset. Along the way, we will see how Althusser's tenacity becomes fortified by the constant threat of phenomenology, which manifests under the recurrent guise of a potential collapse into ideology. Althusser professed to abhor pragmatism in all its forms. And while he was not immune to the tendency toward opportunism that afflicts every politically engaged intellectual, Althusser's philosophical tenacity in the face of critique is striking. Repeatedly faced with the limitations of his efforts, Althusser nevertheless consistently breaks toward an ever firmer rationalism that further tempers the political purchase of his project even as it deepens its philosophical foundations.

The First Moment: Spinozist Epistemology

For Marx

Although his posthumous output now exceeds that of his lifetime, the essays in *For Marx* and his contribution to *Reading Capital* remain the core texts of Althusser's theoretical endeavor. Much of the content of the critique of humanism in *For Marx* was addressed in the preceding chapter. What remains to be clarified is how Althusser's Spinozism informs his more positive efforts, chief among them the theory of history sketched in "Contradiction and Overdetermination" and the epistemology that buttresses this theory in what is arguably the most essential essay of the volume, "On the Materialist Dialectic."

It is in this latter essay that Althusser articulates his version of the theory of knowledge presented in Spinoza's *Treatise on the Emendation of the Intellect*, codifying it along the tripartite scheme of the "Generalities." Offering an alternative to dialectical accounts of knowledge, Althusser suggests a process of knowledge production wherein Generality II, the theory of a science at a given moment, works upon Generality I, the raw materials of scientific and ideological practice (i.e., lived experience), to produce the concrete, scientific Generality III. Despite its baroque character, Althusser's scheme serves as a provocative riposte to phenomenology, for his point is to maintain the irreducibility of Generality III—the new scientific entity, singular in its essence—to Generality I, the site of the "lived." In other words, the transformation that takes place is a real one and, moreover, is not already legible or prefigured in the initial lived object (or Generality). We should contrast these claims with those contained in

Husserl's late, seminal essay "The Origin of Geometry." Husserl lamented mathematics' abandonment of its roots in the lifeworld and sought a return in order to recover a truth obscured by centuries of arithmetization.[5] Althusser has virtually no sympathy for such a project. He expresses the superiority of his method to the phenomenological enterprise as follows:

> The critique which, in the last instance, counterposes the abstraction it attributes to theory and to science and the concrete it regards as the real itself, remains an ideological critique, since it denies the reality of scientific practice, the validity of its abstractions and ultimately the reality of that theoretical "concrete" which is a knowledge.[6]

The key phrase of this passage is "remains an ideological critique," because the preceding "counterposing" is precisely the one integral to phenomenology and given supreme expression in Husserl's "Origin of Geometry." For all his valorization of science, Husserl regards it as an abstraction from a concrete that is real in and of itself and thus somehow more "real" than the scientific result. But Althusser's point is that the concrete as it immediately presents itself cannot in any way be qualified as "the real itself" because it is shot through with layers of ideological investment, layers that cannot be obviated by the gesture of the *epoché* since they traverse subjectivity itself.[7] Note, however, the distinction and reserve of the passage just cited. Althusser does not disqualify this critique of validity on its own terms. He merely names it "ideological critique" and juxtaposes it with scientific practice. It is not as if there is ideological critique on the one hand and scientific critique on the other. The implication is that the process of critique qua critique is itself inherently ideological insofar as it ultimately addresses lived experience in terms of lived experience.

Paul Ricoeur developed several acute insights into this aspect of Althusser's thought in his lectures "Ideology and Utopia" delivered at the University of Chicago in 1975. Focusing upon the hostility to lived experience inherent in the Althusserian concept of science, Ricoeur suggests that "the higher in fact that we raise the concept of science, the broader becomes the field of ideology, because each is defined in relation to the other. If we reinforce the scientific requirement of a theory, then we lose its capacity for making sense of ordinary life."[8] Althusser's famous theses on ideology, ideological interpellation, and "ideological state apparatuses" (ISAs), the main references for Ricoeur's comments, were written in the aftermath of May 1968.[9] They served as the necessary complement to the unremitting emphasis on science in the essays of *For Marx*. The argument of the ISA essay followed through on the implications of the earlier theses in that it relegated the entire world of lived experience to the domain of ideology. "The burden of ideology is to make subjects of us," Ricoeur notes. "It is a strange philosophical situation, since all of our concrete existence is put on the side of ideology."[10]

Though he intends it as a criticism, Ricoeur has identified the crux of Althusser's grasp of phenomenology as it is already evident in *For Marx*. Following Althusser's line on the relative autonomy of the superstructure, Ricoeur maintains that it is this very autonomy that suggests "ideologies have a content of their own. In turn, this requires before an understanding of these ideologies' use a phenomenology of their specific mode." "The assumption that ideologies' content is exhausted by their use is without justification," Ricoeur argues; "their use does not exhaust their meaning."[11] This is a curious formula: How could something's use ever exhaust its meaning? A household's hammer may be used to hit nails, but this fact does nothing to mitigate the web of significance the old piece of metal may possess for the family that lived there. Nowhere does Althusser assume that "ideologies' content is exhausted by their use," because nowhere does Althusser suggest that ideology is devoid of meaning. If anything, ideology is nothing but "meaning," nothing but an aggregate network of the significations of material practices that coalesce through repetition and habit into—precisely—a coherent meaning. On this score, Althusser was Pascalian: the meaning of one's existence comes from the practices and rituals that saturate our lives. So when Ricoeur says that the inexhaustible meanings of ideologies need to be subjected to a phenomenology, his critique of Althusser is wide of the mark. The point is that this phenomenology will certainly achieve a stunning proliferation of meaning and its inherent riches, all the while remaining purely within the realm of ideology, the domain of the lived, the site of meaning, par excellence.

Althusser denies nothing of the richness and the reality of ideology; if anything, he liberates the concept from the pejorative connotation of "false consciousness." But his goal is to distinguish it from science, a task that will become increasingly difficult after Althusser grants to ideology its full measure of "reality" in later essays. If we want to draw a distinction between Althusserian science and his own concept of ideology (and phenomenology as the latter's philosophical correlate), we could do worse than to identify science as a process of *discovery* and ideology/phenomenology as a process of *recognition*.¹² There is a certain poetry to Althusser's recollection in *For Marx* that "we were only too eager and happy to rediscover our own burning passions in the ideological flame of [Marx's] Early Works" (23). But there is a valuable philosophical point as well: the recognition, or rediscovery, of one's passion in an exterior source is itself the result of the dialectical logic of ideology and ideological projection. Insight into this process can be found in Althusser's earliest major work, published in 1959, wherein Montesquieu was praised as the founder of modern political science. Though Montesquieu himself never escaped the ideological *parti pris* of his aristocratic status, his insight lay in the recognition that "the necessity that governs history, in order to begin to be scientific, must stop borrowing its reasons from any order transcending history."¹³ Breaking with the dictates of theology or morality, Montesquieu sought "to produce the science not of society in general but of all the concrete societies in history."¹⁴ This contrast appears to supplant one philosophy of history with another, but Althusser's aim is to show Montesquieu breaking with any notion of a singular essence that one may nominate as the "essence" of society in moral or theological terms. Instead, through "the correction of errant consciousness by well-founded science" the "unconscious laws that govern [men]," and that change over time, become cognizable.¹⁵

Montesquieu's method, in a way similar to Marx's, is deemed scientific despite its embeddedness in a set of ideological commitments. Althusser concludes his analysis of Montesquieu with an observation of the aristocrat's return to a defense of aristocracy: "As if this traveler, having set out for distant lands, and spent many years in the unknown, believed on returning home that time had stood still."¹⁶ This return is the "return" from science to ideology, a process whose general structure is one of recognition, that is, the recognition of one's home, where one belongs. Moreover, since ideology "has no history," operating as if its contents and categories are eternal rather than historically contingent, "home" becomes the place where "time stands still," as Althusser's concluding flourish suggests.

The implication, then, is that history itself in its temporal progression appears to be ideological insofar as, looking back, "history's" goals are legible in advance of the events that constitute that very history and thus confer upon it a sense of completeness or wholeness. Since history can be viewed only with hindsight, this structure of ideological interpretation is extremely difficult to avoid. These themes are at the core of "Contradiction and Overdetermination." The essay begins with an extended exegesis of Marx's precise meaning in his claim to have stood the Hegelian dialectic back on its feet in order to "discover the rational kernel within the mystical shell." Althusser's manipulation of this metaphor is ultimately symmetrical with his argument, which destroys the logic of extraction contained in the suggestion that a rational kernel resides "within" a shell. Against a mere inversion that retains the form of the original and that would understand history as the emanation of a material rather than an ideal essence, Althusser presents a concept of history where historical events are not the phenomenal manifestation of an essence but instead the momentary and fleeting "fusion" in "unity" of disparate, concrete elements. In an oblique criticism of Lenin, otherwise a lauded figure in the essay, Althusser undercuts the logic of pregnancy in his work, the notion that the past is somehow pregnant with the future. "Because the past is never more than the internal essence (in-itself) of the future it encloses," in this logic, "this presence of the past is the presence to consciousness of consciousness itself, *and no true external determination*" (97, 102). History is not a circle of circles in which we can locate a center: "this is not the case" (102). What's rational in the "Marxist" dialectic is the notion of tense relations among disparate material and ideal elements; what's mystical in the "Hegelian" dialectic is the resolution of this disparate state of affairs through a singular core mechanism of contradiction. Althusser castigates the centrality of contradiction to Hegel's philosophy of history in emphatic terms:

> The reduction of *all* the elements that make up the concrete life of a historical epoch [. . .] to *one* principle of internal unity, is itself only possible on the *absolute condition* of taking the whole concrete life of a people for the externalization-alienation (*Entäusserung-Entfremdung*) of an *internal spiritual principle*, which can never definitely be anything but the most abstract form of that epoch's consciousness of itself; its religious or philosophical consciousness, that is, its own ideology. (103)

To refer to the epoch's consciousness of itself as ideology is not necessarily to disqualify it; it is to give it a name that distinguishes the contents of this consciousness from a putatively "scientific" account of the epoch that need not be assimilated to the epoch's consciousness of itself. Moreover, the distinction between the scientific and the ideological account of a given history is predicated upon the "relative autonomy" of the components of that epoch along these very lines.[17]

Against the reduction of one aspect to the other, Althusser posits the "relative autonomy" of the base and the superstructure, in effect the material and the ideal of the Marxist lexicon. By insisting on the relative autonomy of these domains, Althusser forecloses any notion that one of them may actually come into direct contact with the other. They are autonomous, yet they relate. This refusal of dialectical sublimation, a strict insistence on the distinction between domains, is crucially Spinozist in that it maintains the fundamental incommensurability between thought and thing, between the attributes of Thought (the ideal, the "superstructure") and Extension (the material, the "base"), which we spelled out earlier with reference to Gueroult's reading. The two "attributes" are part of the same order; they occupy a singular logic, one that Althusser will attempt to supply in later efforts through recourse to his own variation of the "unconscious." To be sure, the processes of the base and of the superstructure interact and even converge in the production of historical effects; after all, these are the sites of overdetermination. But the point is that there can never be any true *contact* between them. There is no historical pineal gland. Their processes constitute a unity in effect without a union in essence.

Overdetermination, Althusser argues, "is inevitable and thinkable as soon as the real evidence of the forms of the superstructure and of the national and international conjuncture has been recognized—an existence largely specific and autonomous, and therefore irreducible to a pure *phenomenon*" (113). In other words, the overdetermined historical event is not the phenomenal manifestation of anything; it simply *is* history. Althusser's efforts to subtract from the historical event its "phenomenal" qualities are what mark his project more as one of historical epistemology than a philosophy of history. Althusser is more concerned with how we understand history than how we experience it. The latter is left to ideology. "History 'asserts itself' through the multiform world of the superstructures, from local tradition to international circumstance" (112). The point is not to capture all of the details of history; writing history *wie es eigentlich gewesen* is a norm, not a possibility. But granting the impossibility of this goal does not entail swinging toward an abstraction and reduction that would read the superstructure in the base, or vice versa. This logic is rendered obsolete in Althusser's argument, in spite of his unelaborated claim that the economy remains determinant in the last instance. In any event, the political expediency of this qualification is immediately undercut by his rejoinder that the last instance never comes. By extirpating the telos within history, the very factor that makes it retrospectively legible in a Hegelian view, and amenable to a metaphysical philosophy of history as a result, Althusser intimates an alternative way to "read" history. The elaboration of this new method constitutes his contributions to *Reading Capital*.

Reading Capital

Though Althusser praises Spinoza in the essays of *For Marx*, there is a notable increase of affirmation in the pages of *Reading Capital*. Althusser's concept of reading in this volume is pointedly anti-hermeneutic. His critique of phenomenology at the level of epistemology gets transposed to a critique of phenomenology's methodological correlate—hermeneutics—in the reading of texts. The inspiration behind Althusser's new concept of "symptomatic reading" is Spinoza's biblical criticism in the *Tractatus Theologico-Politicus*. Spinoza was attentive to the gaps in the Bible's composite accounts, gaps that become stark when the text is read to the letter with nary a hermeneutic concern for its referents. Ostensible inconsistencies are taken at face value. By adhering to the materiality of the letter in the Bible, Spinoza claimed to "read" the structure of the society that produced the document. Claims were evaluated neither in terms of their potential true reference—for example, did the Red Sea really part?—nor in terms of their metaphorical or allegorical value but in terms of their functional role in the presentation of a certain coherent world, the indispensable ideological prerequisite for the Hebrew state. Similarly, Althusser wants to understand how *Capital* works and by extension understand something about how "capital" works. *For Marx* and *Reading Capital* are laconic titles. They are also puns. It is by reading the book *Capital* that we will learn how to "read" our history in capitalism, a history that remains contemporary. "With [Spinoza], for the first time ever, a man linked together [. . .] the essence of reading and the essence of history in a theory of the difference between the imaginary and the true."[18] Spinoza affirmed "the opacity of the immediate." Althusser speaks of the need to break "the religious complicity between Logos and Being." The "truth of history cannot be read in its manifest discourse, because the text of history is not a text in which a voice (the Logos) speaks, but the inaudible and illegible notation of the effects of a structure of structures" (17).

The opening essay of *Reading Capital*, "From 'Capital' to Marx's Philosophy," is one of Althusser's most successful documents, a seamless synthesis of rhetorical flair and argumentative rigor. The core thesis of the piece turns on the relation of the "object of knowledge" to the "real object." It is the disjuncture of the two that is the mark of any viable science, and it is the virtue of philosophy to be able to read this disjuncture. Science is limited, Althusser argues. A science can pose problems only within its definite terrain and horizon. "Any object or problem situated on the terrain and within the horizon, i.e., in the definite structured field of the theoretical problematic of a given theoretical discipline, is visible. We must take these words literally" (25). It is the core liability of both empiricism and absolute-idealism, the latter of which Althusser links with Hegel, Husserl, and Heidegger, to persist in the confusion of the object of knowledge with the real object. In the case of empiricism, this confusion resides in the mistaken belief that the essence of the object of sensory experience can be extracted from the object and then discussed in its immediacy. In the case of the phenomenological school, the same error occurs through a process of reduction that for Althusser is, in its essentials, indistinguishable from Christian recourse to "original sin." The common theme is the evocation of a lost unity. Whereas a "one-to-one correspondence" between thought and its thing is read as that which is *achieved* in empiricism, in phenomenology "the Husserlian 'pre-reflexive' world of 'life,' the passive ante-predicative synthesis," serves as the site where this "one-to-one correspondence" *used to be*, and which must be recovered. The "consistency" of this philosophy, according to Althusser, "requires support from the myth of the origin; from an original unity undivided between *subject* and *object*." The "goal to be achieved" and the "origin to be recovered," for Althusser, are mirror images of the same myth.[19]

Althusser's alternative to this "myth" is unequivocally Spinozist. More specifically, it is the Spinozism of permanent incommensurability elaborated most clearly by Gueroult. "Knowledge working on its 'object' [. . .] does not work on the *real* object but on the peculiar raw material, which constitutes, in its strict sense of the term, *its 'object' (of knowledge)*, and which, even in its most rudimentary forms of knowledge, is distinct from the *real object*" (43). As we suggested in Chapter 2, following Gueroult, the parallelism thesis in the *Ethics*—"The order and connection of ideas is the same as the order and connection of things"—is misleading and misnamed. The point, we argued, is not that there are two orders running in parallel tandem and that an occasionalist faith à la Malebranche ensures their symmetry. It is that there is only *one* order, and thus it is the "same" order. But within that order the two attributes never touch; they never coincide. For Gueroult, the radical noncoincidence between the attributes Thought and Extension was the precondition for the knowledge itself that could come to be within Thought. For Althusser, too, "the problem of the relation between these two objects (the object of knowledge and the real object), [is] a relation which constitutes the very existence of knowledge" (52). The relation must always remain a relation; it can never be "resolved" in an original or an achieved unity. Althusser reads a "vicious circle" in Western philosophy from Descartes through Hegel to Husserl in which the radical discontinuity between thought and its externality is repeatedly forsaken for a resolution that remains fictive. But Husserl at least deserves special credit in this history:

Its high point of consciousness and honesty was reached precisely with the philosophy (Husserl) which was prepared to take theoretical responsibility for the necessary existence of this *circle*, i.e., to think it as essential to its ideological undertaking; however, this did not *make it leave the circle*, did not deliver it from its ideological captivity—nor could the philosopher who has tried to think in an "openness" (which seems to be only the ideological non-closure of the closure) the absolute condition of possibility of this "closure," i.e., of the closed history of the "repetition" of this closure in Western metaphysics—Heidegger—leave this circle. (53)

For Althusser, the search for the "absolute condition" entails a kind of flight that never gets outside the circle of reasoning; it merely leads one into another circle, containing a circle within it, ad infinitum. Such is Althusser's take on the hermeneutic circle. In contradistinction to this ultimately reflective enterprise, Althusser wants to conceive theoretical activity itself as a practice that "produces" knowledge. Invoking the model of mathematics, Althusser argues that this mode of "knowledge production" requires no external justification; mathematicians do not wait for physics to "prove" their theories. Once a science is established, it operates of its own accord. The gauntlet here is clear. Althusser must establish that Marx established the science of historical materialism.

This is Althusser's task in his second contribution to the *Reading Capital* volume, "The Object of *Capital*." The title suggests the argument.

What makes historical materialism a science distinct from the political economy of Ricardo and others is that it actively constitutes its theoretical object by working through those sites in political economy where theoretical objects, in this case "given economic phenomena and the ideological anthropology of the *homo oeconomicus* which underlies it," were passively received, remaining "un-thought" and thus, in a word, ideological (165). Let it be noted that this mechanism—occupying the terrain of ideological political economy to produce the science of historical materialism—mimics the Spinozist maneuver of occupying the terrain of the religious theology to produce the rationalism of the *Ethics*. In the end, Marx's "immense theoretical revolution" is predicated upon its critical rejection of a category whose descriptive breadth is matched by its centrality to phenomenological philosophy: the *given*. "There is no *immediate* grasp of the economic, there is no raw economic 'given'" (178).[20] Marx's materialism "presupposes a materialist conception of economic production, i.e., among other conditions, a demonstration of the irreducible material conditions of the labor process" (172). In other words, "material conditions" are irreducible to the given materiality of experience. For Althusser, the "relations of production" are paramount, relations that immediate experience cannot help obscuring. The key here again resides in Althusser's peculiar notion of relationality. For the structure of relations, or combinatory, which is itself a composite of relationality, "defines the economic as such" (178). But these relations can be thought as relations only through a relation in turn, the one established in the concept as thought's relation to these relations. And it is because the concept as such is the product of a nonidentical relation that it is able itself to *think* the countervailing and incongruent relations that constitute the ever incomplete structure of the social totality. In Spinozism, the "idea of the idea" constitutive of the concept or "adequate idea" is predicated upon the radical nonidentity of the two ideas, just as the first idea of the external object becomes adequate to that object only by understanding it is *not* that object but the idea of it. The idea and its object are nonidentical. Similarly, the relation that inheres in the Spinozist or Cavaillèsian "concept" central to Althusser's assessments is precisely the incommensurable relation of thought to its object. In other words, the idea becomes "adequate," to use the Spinozist term, to its theoretical object in the moment of understanding that the object of knowledge is radically distinct from the real object that occasioned it.

If we might divide the key relations philosophy seeks to describe into four—thing to thought; thought to thought; thought to thing; thing to thing—the merit of the Althusserian enterprise is that it provides powerful accounts of the first two. We may, however, rearticulate in esoteric terms the demerit of Althusserianism charged by its political detractors and say that it provides no way to think the third relation in our series, (nor ultimately the fourth, which in any event most have deemed chimerical since Hume). Because of this, Althusser's project is "doomed" to be a historical epistemology. In terms of Marxist politics, the "cost" of overdetermination is that it cannot be orchestrated; the impossibility of its prefiguration is essential to the concept. But by recognizing that every view of history is synchronic, even if our own diachronic situatedness means one synchronic snapshot will always be replaced by another, Althusser provides a fascinating account of how things have worked and a seductive program for how we should "emend" our thinking to *see* how they worked. When Althusser writes that "the knowledge of history is no more historical than the knowledge of sugar is sweet," he is providing a concise example of these notions (106). E. P. Thompson read in this line the acme of sophistry, suggesting that, for it to make sense, "sweet" would have to be replaced with "chemical."[21] Thompson's suggestion alters nothing of Althusser's point, however, which is that in the end knowledge shares nothing with its objects, be they theoretical or sensory, that though knowledge is always and only the knowledge *of*, the result is knowledge alone. Knowledge qua knowledge is no more sweet than chemical, than historical. Althusser liked to paraphrase Spinoza often on this score: the concept "dog" does not bark.

It is not surprising that those who have read *Reading Capital* have tended to assess it by how well it reads *Capital*.[22] From our perspective, however, what is most striking when *Reading Capital* is read to the letter, not even paying attention to the symptomatic silences, but merely the *words*, is the way Althusser's engagement with Marx's thought per se ultimately seems subordinate to the critique of phenomenology that is the driving principle of the argument. Indeed, certain of Althusser's aphoristic insights have a critical bearing on "phenomenological idealism" which is totally independent of any uniquely Marxist context: for example, "The function of the concept of origin, as in original sin, is to summarize in one word what has not to be thought in order to be able to think what one wants to think" (63). This tendency is clearest near the end of "The Object of *Capital*,' where we witness a kind of shedding of the Marxist skin, however unwitting. Althusser begins by insisting that the transition from Volume One of *Capital* to Volume Three must not be understood as a move from the abstract to the concrete, which is certainly a debatable claim. The observation serves, however, to preface Althusser's insistence that "we never leave abstraction on the way from Volume One to Volume Three, i.e., we never leave knowledge, the 'product of thinking and conceiving': *we never leave the concept.*" At this point, reference to the Marxist corpus drops out and Althusser pursues his conclusion at fever pitch, his notorious fondness for italics in rare form:

We simply pass within the abstraction of knowledge from the concept of the structure and of its most general effects, to the concept of the structure's particular effects—never for an instant do we set foot beyond the absolutely impassable frontier which separates the "development" or specification of the concept from the development and particularity of things—and for a very good reason: *this frontier is impassable in principle because it cannot be a frontier, because there is no common homogeneous space (spirit or real) between the abstract of the concept of a thing and the empirical concrete of this thing which could justify the use of the concept of a frontier.* (190)

This argument is tantamount to the excision of any mediatory element—*frontier*—that might serve to connect thought and thing. Its plausibility has nothing to do with Marxism. Elaboration of this frontier element, discernment of the essential stuff of this mediation had been the central quest of French phenomenology, from Sartre's efforts to trace the advent of the *pour-soi* in the *en-soi* to Merleau-Ponty's concept of chiasmic flesh. As an intervention within the context of an international Western Marxism Althusser's effort appeared hermetic, idiosyncratic, and to many downright bizarre.[23] But as an intervention within French philosophy, it appeared as the most polemical statement yet of a Spinozist critique of phenomenology with its roots in Cavaillès's underdeveloped ripostes to Husserl. For example, Alasdair MacIntyre criticized Vincent Descombes's account for insufficiently emphasizing "the profound gratitude that we all owe to Althusser for having brought French Marxism back into dialogue with the rest of French philosophy."[24] What MacIntyre sufficiently emphasizes is the primary dialogue that conditioned Althusser's philosophical output: that of French philosophy. Althusser began *Reading Capital* with the caveat that he and his collaborators were philosophers, not economists or historians.

Philosophers produce philosophical arguments. *Reading Capital* gropes toward a certain notion of philosophy, offering various tentative definitions. At one point in the volume, Althusser defines the object of "Marxist philosophy"—not the object of *Capital*—as a "theory of scientific practice, i.e., a theory of the conditions of the process of knowledge" (86).

This definition, Althusser suggests, can be drawn from Marx's claims in the *1857 Introduction*, a text that Althusser describes as the veritable *Discourse on Method* of Marxist philosophy. The Kantian ring of Althusser's assessment, combined with the homage to Descartes, father of French rationalism, speaks to the Spinozist quality of his response. Here again, Spinoza plays a role as Descartes' inheritor, critic, and savior, the thinker who saves rationalism from obscurantism. Spinoza's philosophical output began with a systematic reconstruction of the *Cartesian Meditations*.[25] Through this rigorous effort, originally pedagogical in its purposes (not unlike a reading of *Capital* at the ENS in the early 1960s), the incompleteness and errors of Descartes' philosophy became discernible to Spinoza.[26] In effect, Descartes tempered his own rationalist conviction in order to preserve a notion of God that would ensure his system of its integrity. The deus ex machina of the Cartesian enterprise was literal, and Descartes needed to be saved from himself.

We can understand Althusser's self-conception as a latter-day Spinoza in one of two ways. On the one hand, Althusser clearly wants to "save" Marx from Marx, with the idealist concept of Man having replaced the vestigial Cartesian God. What is peculiar in this scenario is that it is not as if Marx somehow betrayed himself; he simply did not finish the task of producing his own philosophy. But in its essentials the Althusserian move with regard to Marx is very similar to the Spinozist move with regard to Descartes: rescue the rational from the theological. On the other hand, there is a way to read Althusser as trying to separate the wheat from the chaff in the liaison between Marxism and philosophy pursued in France by Sartre. In this scenario, Althusser plays the Spinoza to Sartre's Descartes. The Cartesianism of Sartre's existentialism was unmistakable. As for his engagement with Marx, Althusser concurred with Sartre on the weight attributed to praxis. What he lamented in Sartre was the reduction of various kinds of heterogeneous practice—from economic practice to theoretical practice—to a single kind of practice conceived as mediation. "Sartre is the philosopher of mediations *par excellence*: their function is precisely to ensure unity in the negation of differences" (136). Althusser's critique of Sartre's reductive concept of practice in favor of what might be termed a pluralism of practices bears echoes of Gueroult's Spinozist critique of Alquié's Descartes, which we addressed in Chapter 2. The singularity of Cartesian experience becomes discarded in favor of a pluralist, infinite repetition of conceptual maneuvers and insights.

For Marx and *Reading Capital* together constitute a tour de force of rationalist critique of phenomenological idealism. Yet very quickly after the completion of these volumes, Althusser recognized the key menace threatening to compromise their results: formalism. Throughout this preceding section we have emphasized the formalist virtues of Althusser's enterprise. This is clear in our insistence that his claims extend beyond Marxism, that as a theory of philosophy's understanding of science—that is, the understanding of the production of the scientific object—the viability of this *formal* claim is independent of whether or not we find this process fully developed *in* Marx. None of this is to suggest that the relationship to Marx is not important, or even essential to the project. Althusser's going public with his reconsideration of Marx was a combined result of political events, his own critical acumen, and the goading of students who encouraged Althusser's polemical tendencies. In the years immediately following the appearance of Althusserian Marxism on the French scene, Althusser's intellectual energies were directed to shoring up his philosophical system, primarily from the threats of formalist vacuity. However, no further engagement with Marx's writings is pursued in these texts, which rank among the most illuminating of Althusser's posthumous publications. To be sure, a reinvigoration of Marxism remains the overarching aim, but, to anticipate one of Althusser's later formulations, the aim seems to be more to develop a philosophy *for* Marxism than a philosophy *of* Marxism.[27] The problem of what his philosophy was actually intended to *do* in politics does not yet seem to have become the sticking point for Althusser that it would be toward the end of the decade, when the notion of philosophy as a discourse without an object yet that produces effects would be elaborated more fully.

The Second Moment: Spinozist Ontology

On June 26, 1966, Althusser delivered a lecture at the ENS, titled "The Philosophical Conjuncture and Marxist Theoretical Research,"[28] wherein he solidified some of the more provocative theses of *For Marx* and

Reading Capital. In addition to maintaining that the "ideologues of the creation of man by man" were latter-day spiritualists, Althusser remains intransigent on the contention "that it is possible to identify something as ideology only retrospectively, from the vantage point of non-ideological knowledge."[29] In order to achieve this vantage point, however, Althusser seeks to develop a new "theory of the knowledge-effect," a theory that "presupposes a *general theory of discourse* and a distinction between the specific types of discourses that would bring out the characteristic features of scientific discourse."[30] This agenda sounds unrepentantly structuralist, especially the call for a "general theory of discourse." But Althusser has something else in mind. For Lévi-Strauss and Lacan serve Althusser more as rivals than as allies at this stage.

This lecture is valuable for its concise presentation of Althusser's ideas when his rationalist conviction and confidence were at their peak. Also on display is Althusser's pedagogical talent, evidenced above all in the compelling way he aligned certain ideas and intellectual traditions. François Matheron, the editor of the majority of Althusser's posthumous publications, has emphasized the need to consider Althusser's role as *caïman*, the instructor charged with preparing students for the *agrégation*, in our consideration of his own philosophical work.[31] There was no sharp line dividing his intellectual abilities toward one task instead of the other. The drawback of serving as *caïman*, one we see obliquely lamented in Althusser's autobiographical writings, is that he never developed a sustained pedagogical engagement and research agenda with any one philosopher or philosophical tradition, a precondition seemingly indispensable for success in the institutions of French academia.[32] His course load was determined every year by what was on the exam, its contents decided by a committee appointed by the French state, though time permitting, he would run seminars of his own design as well, such as the one on *Capital*. The virtue of Althusser's professional position was that he developed a certain way of reading philosophy, of considering the common links and core tensions between sets of ideas. At heart a "lumper" more than a "splitter"—this is the man after all who lumped Hegel, Husserl, and Heidegger together under the banner "phenomenological idealism"—Althusser nonetheless managed to mine the heuristic value of noting sharp distinctions between traditions.

Althusser begins this particular lecture with typology, tracing the various lines of modern philosophy descendant from Descartes. The role of

Descartes in Althusser's oeuvre is ambiguous, and here we can see why. In effect, two overarching traditions have determined modern French thought, a "religious-spiritualist" element with its roots in medieval Thomism and Augustinianism, and a "rationalist-idealist" element rooted in Descartes. But the Cartesian element is itself split, Althusser insists, between a "mechanistic materialism" and a "critical idealism." The former persists in contemporary experimental psychology and empirical sociology; the latter set the terms for dualist philosophy from Kant to Husserl and remains "*the dominant element* in the theoretical conjuncture."[33]

Aside from these overarching traditions, a more subterranean component of the Cartesian legacy becomes salient in the eighteenth century. Neither theological nor mechanist, this is the oxymoronic notion of "rationalist empiricism," itself bifurcated into two lines, "materialist rationalist empiricism" and "idealist rationalist empiricism." The former line culminates in "psycho-physiology," by which Althusser means a kind of cognitive science whose rational methods confront and assort the empirical data of firing synapses and other physiological phenomena. In another instance, Althusser includes Noam Chomsky's linguistics in this category.[34] But it is "idealist rationalist materialism" that, in Althusser's view, has "produced the more interesting results." This is the post-Cartesian tradition that flourished among the *Encyclopédistes*, d'Alembert and Diderot; it persisted into the nineteenth century with Comte, "who saved the honor of French philosophy" against the spiritualists, with assistance from Cournot, Couturat, and Duhem; it culminated in the twentieth century with Cavaillès, Bachelard, Koyré, and Canguilhem.

Two things are striking about this characterization. The first is the absence of any reference to Spinoza. The second is that the line that Althusser valorizes, and in which he wants to situate his own project, is that of *idealist* rationalist empiricism and not *materialist* rationalist empiricism. As to the first quandary, Spinoza's absence need not be taken at face value. For Althusser suggests paradoxically, and without elaboration, that idealist rationalist empiricism picks up the "materialist" aspects of Descartes' work to emerge in the eighteenth century. A key thesis of Paul Vernière's *Spinoza et la pensée française avant la Révolution*, a large synthetic work published in 1954, was that the philosophes of the Enlightenment read Spinoza as developing a materialist variation on Cartesianism. Vernière characterizes this reading of Spinoza as an "erreur féconde,"[35] an error because it downplayed Spinoza's metaphysics and the theological components of his thought, fecund because of its results. Althusser, like Spinoza, was attentive to conspicuous silences. In this case, Althusser's failure to mention Spinoza smacks of a desire not to reveal his cards so fully. The extent of Althusser's debt to Spinoza, and that the latter belonged to this lauded lineage, was likely transparent to any listener.

As for the second point, how "materialist" aspects of Descartes' work produced an *idealist* rationalist empiricism superior to *materialist* rationalist empiricism, things become more complicated. Illumination on this distinction is provided by Althusser's engagement with Lévi-Strauss and Lacan during this same period, which we will explore further. But first a word about the oxymoron "rationalist empiricism." This formulation constitutes a rebuke to phenomenology. To insist on the compatibility of rationalism and empiricism in such terms is to insist on the absence of a mediatory frontier between rational thought and the objects it confronts empirically.[36] Althusser establishes this concept and then quickly moves beyond it, but its motivation is clear: to cede no ground to notions of the fundamental unity of experience that subtend the Bergsonian project and its phenomenological inheritors in France. In fact, it is the vitalist variant of materiality that one sees in a figure like Bergson and his concept of the élan vital that ends up producing an idealist result in spite of itself. Here Bergson shares something with the "psycho-physiologists" of cognitive science. Reproducing a critique intimated by Georges Bataille in the interwar years, Althusser's argument suggests that most variants of "materialism," including dialectical materialism in its orthodox guise, reproduce an idealism by imbuing material with an "ideal" spirit or essence that motivates it.[37]

The reason that Lévi-Strauss and Lacan, both of whom found phenomenology anathema, provide no respite from the lurking idealism of materialism is that they commit the same error of reduction: they nominate one particular discourse as *the* general discourse for reality itself. In other words, if there is a certain idealist tendency in the effort to reduce existence to "pure materiality," there is a considerably greater one in the attempt to nominate one discourse as *the* discourse of human existence *tout court*, be it that of structural anthropology or psychoanalysis. The relationship between a "general theory of discourse" and a "particular theory of discourse" will exercise Althusser greatly, especially as it relates to Lacan.

But Lévi-Strauss provides Althusser with a more expedient way to distinguish his own project from the structuralism of a sole general theory that explains it all. In his critique of Lévi-Strauss, written in August 1966, we can also read Althusser coming to terms with some of the problematic tendencies of *Reading Capital*. The motivating factor behind his critique remains the effort to develop a "rationalist empiricism" with explanatory power that does not collapse into formalist vacuity.

Althusser begins with a typically Marxist critique of Lévi-Strauss. Since the latter possesses no viable theory of the ideological, he is unable to draw a distinction between a social formation and an ideological one. For example, Lévi-Strauss writes of kinship relations, which, for Althusser, are the ideological correlate to relations of production.[38] Althusser criticizes Lévi-Strauss for consistently eliding the distinction between form and function, imputing to formal distinctions a function in the development of a given society. "Just as one must criticize this functionalism, which, on the theoretical plane, invariably takes the form of a subjectivism that confers upon 'society' the form of existence of a subject endowed with intentions and goals, so one must criticize and reject the concept of the *unconscious*, its indispensable correlative, of which Lévi-Strauss *is compelled* to make liberal use" (25–26). The social "unconscious" to which Lévi-Strauss takes recourse is the composite set of the binary distinctions that determine social life. Althusser's critique of this position is uncanny for its similarity to charges soon leveled against his own. He suggests that Lévi-Strauss's set of binary structures, a society's conditions of possibility, can only ever account for possibility and never necessity. In other words, Lévi-Strauss can never explain why a certain society or historical development not only *could have gone* but *did go* a certain way. At the level of historical explanation structural anthropology remains decidedly lacking.

"Lévi-Strauss takes the formalism of *possibility* for the *formalization of necessity*" (27). As a result, when he formalizes a certain myth, he imputes to it, or extracts from it, a universal remit that is unwarranted. Thus, "he is unaware that he is talking about this determinate, real, necessary instance: he thinks he is talking about the human spirit!" (29). By reading the ur-myths of "the human spirit" in the "savage mind," Lévi-Strauss effectively suggests the superiority of the "savage mind" to the modern, unscientific one. Not only does this reproduce a gesture similar to Husserl's in "The Origin of Geometry"; it also recalls Bergson, as Althusser suggests. The culmination of his critique effectively recapitulates Cavaillès:

> The one little problem (for Bergson and Lévi-Strauss) is that it is possible to think the singular and concrete only in *concepts* (which are thus "'abstract" and "'general"); but that is the very condition for *thinking* the singular, since there can be no thinking without concepts (which are, consequently, abstract and "general"). Philosophers such as Spinoza (the "singular essences") and Leibniz did not wait until our day to assign the non-savage mind the task of thinking singularity (that is, to register the *reality* of modern science in philosophy). (30)[39]

Althusser concludes by stating that this commitment to thinking singularities in their necessity is what distinguishes his project from Lévi-Strauss's and a fortiori from that of all "structuralists." Unfortunately, he says nothing about *how* his project purports to be superior. The fact that accounting for necessity poses a problem for Althusser is evidence at once of his continued adherence to Spinozism and the complications this Spinozism creates in his own project. For Spinoza, the "necessity" that inheres in history need not be proved or explained. The mere fact of happening is itself the proof of the necessity of that event. Recognition of this proof *as* proof is one of the goals of Spinoza's philosophy as a prescriptive epistemological project. Yet Althusser, no less than Cavaillès before him, becomes fixated on the problem of necessity at this stage, searching for a logical proof to supplement the historical one.

More substantive moves toward a solution are discernible in Althusser's "Three Notes on the Theory of Discourses." This set of texts was written in the autumn of 1966 and remains the most valuable remainder of the aborted effort to produce an *Elements of Dialectical Materialism* "that can stand as our *Ethics*" (34). Althusser uses a critical assessment of Lacan's rethinking of psychoanalysis as an opportunity to provide real substance to the provocative but tenuous concept of "structural causality" outlined in *For Marx* and *Reading Capital*. In fact, the real substance of the concept is precisely to be Substance conceived along Spinozist lines. The technicalities of Althusser's engagement with Lacan need not concern us here.[40] The core issue of this text for our purposes is Althusser's continued insistence on the impossibility of contact between the domains of "science" and of "ideology," here codified as two radically distinct General Theories (GTs), the General Theory of historical materialism and the General Theory of the signifier. To be clear, since the concern of the argument is precisely "discourse," Althusser's aim is to show not just the irreducibility of one level of discourse to the other but also the fact that each GT viably persists only in its "differential articulation" from the other. In other words, science is science only insofar as it is completely *not* ideology, and vice versa. Yet, returning to the problematic of "structural causality," Althusser speaks of the urgency of coming to terms with the "articulation between GTs," an esoteric way of restating the figure of causality as the "overdetermined" convergence of disparate elements. For Althusser the prospects are dire:

> If we do not think the possibility of an articulation between GTs, we will remain at the level of the *parallelism of the attributes* and of the temptation that constantly accompanies it, the *conflation* of the attributes. The parallelism of the attributes is tempered and corrected in Spinoza by the concept of substance: the different attributes are attributes *of one and the same substance*. It is the concept of *substance* which plays the role of the concept of articulation of the attributes (it plays other roles, too, but that is one of them). The *distinction* between attributes is possible only on condition that they are articulated. (65)

Althusser then translates these comments into his own language of General and Regional Theories: "the distinction between the GTs (which are our attributes) is possible only on condition that they are *differentially articulated.*" In the preceding pages, Althusser had identified historical materialism as one GT and the theory of the signifier as another, suggesting that the psychoanalytic theory of the unconscious was an RT contingent upon a co-articulation of these two otherwise distinct GTs, which in this context occupy the roles of "science" and "ideology," respectively.

Althusser's point is that historical materialism is the discourse that articulates the behavior of the material, physical world, the attribute of Extension in Spinoza's lexicon. The "theory of the signifier," in this particular text of Althusser's, is loaded with being the discourse that articulates the goings-on of the mental world as it is experienced, Spinoza's attribute of Thought and the domain of ideology. The singularity of the "unconscious" as a concept, and its value for Althusser, is a result of its being nothing more than a name for the site of the convergent effects of these two "attributes." In other words, it is insubstantial in and of itself (70–72). The "unconscious" does not *produce* effects in a mechanistic way. When Althusser writes "what is designated by the concept of *discourse* applied to the unconscious cannot account for the specific *reality* of the unconscious," he is attempting to distinguish his nascent version of the "unconscious" from

Lacan's. Whereas Lacan's notion that the "unconscious is structured like a language" turns the unconscious into a discourse that produces effects, Althusser wants to replace the latent mechanism of Lacan's vision with the claim that "the effect is nothing other than the discourse itself" (72).

Twenty years before calling Spinoza the philosopher of the void, Althusser is already struggling with a conception of philosophy predicated upon the insubstantiality of existence.[41] In effect, "unconscious" sometimes works as a surrogate for Spinozist Substance in this document. What matters in this scenario is not matter per se—this is the "error" of base materialism—but precisely the effort to produce a theory of "effects" that does not call upon an external principle, a deus ex machina, that absolves the philosopher of explanation for material events rather than accounts for them. To argue, as Althusser does near the end of the second note, that ideological discourse is the *main articulation* of unconscious discourse is to witness both the increasing strain of the term "discourse" and the accomplishment of an underdeveloped line of thinking in *For Marx* and *Reading Capital*. Ideology, the "lived," is the "main articulation" of "unconscious discourse," meaning that our lives are where we witness the manifestation of the convergence of determinants that constitute the fundament of existence. It is uncertain what is more striking about this theoretical conclusion, the dizzying level of philosophical thought needed to arrive at it or the simplicity of its implications. For what Althusser has shown at this stage is simply that what we experience as our lives is nothing more than an "effect" of something else that is not in reality a some*thing* else at all but the contingent accumulation of all the preceding "effects" convergent in a temporal moment or spatial point.

At this stage a philosophical recourse awaits to save Althusser from what appears to be a vacuous tautology. But whatever its guise—the will, agency, the human, the mind—Althusser absolutely refuses to endorse any notion of subjectivity as a determining phenomenon that might account for the concatenation of "effects." Such a move would be a concession to the idealism he is intent to avoid. But if the problematic of the "subject" was consistently elided in *For Marx* and *Reading Capital*, it is confronted directly near the conclusion of the "Three Notes on the Theory of Discourses." "Increasingly," Althusser writes, "the notion of subject seems to me to pertain to *ideological* discourse alone, of which it is constitutive" (77). This confession immediately puts a very fine point on the core weakness of the Althusserian edifice: *how* Althusser can then account for his own discursive pronouncements as anything other than ideological. Here the theoretical utility of calling "ideological discourse" the *main articulation* of "unconscious discourse" becomes obvious. The unconscious (read: insubstantial Substance, a surrogate concept for existence itself) manifests itself in other ways as well, because mutatis mutandis, all manifestation is manifestation of the singular Substance of which the other "attributes" are attributes. The other attribute besides the ideological is, naturally, the scientific, the discourse of the material.[42] And ultimately what makes science scientific is its disavowal of the subject, the supreme ideological category. "There is no such thing as a *subject* of science as far as scientific discourse, scientific statements, are concerned—which, precisely, are sustained by the fact that they can do without any kind of subject—any more than there are individuals 'who make history,' in the ideological sense of the proposition" (77).

Althusser's Spinozism at this stage is maximal, in the sense that the essentially heuristic distinction between science and ideology in the earlier works is acquiring a broader purchase. What Althusser is calling for in this document is nothing less than a wholesale commitment to a scientific discourse whose integral result will be the transgression of the limited purview of first-person experience. The paradoxes of this project are isomorphic to those of the *Ethics*. The goal of Spinoza's masterpiece was to bring the intellect in line with that intellect of which it was a part without knowing it: "God's intellect," or the "infinite intellect," terms for which "the rational" would serve Spinoza as a functional equivalent. This procedure involves a disavowal of the particularities of one's subjectivity in the commitment of thought to a rational discourse initially extrinsic to the thought that comes upon it, for example, the formalization of mathematics that so appealed to Cavaillès. To his credit, Althusser recognizes near the end of the third note that he is at a loss to connect his burgeoning "theory of discourse" with *practice*. In this instance, contemporary readers benefit from the fact that this was never intended to be a document for public consumption. Althusser gestures toward a distinction between discourse and practice that threatens to bring the preceding argumentation crashing down: "a discourse produces only *effects* of, let us say, meaning, whereas practices produce *real* modifications-transformations in existing objects, and, at the limit, new real *objects* (economic practice, political practice, theoretical practice, etc.)." The question of how discourses have effects on real objects is "an entire field waiting to be explored" (79). That a nominal Marxist would say such a thing in good faith shows the extent to which Althusser held Thesis Eleven in contempt. Althusser's preferred slogan was always Lenin's "without revolutionary theory, no revolutionary practice." But the private comments in the third note reveal Althusser at a loss to understand precisely how the first part of the formula implied the latter.

The public face of Althusser at this moment was another matter. Here is a supreme instance where we see a hardening of Althusser's rationalist intransigence against the demands of political expediency.[43] The crux of *Elements of Dialectical Materialism* was to be a new thinking of the relationship between theory and practice in Spinozist terms. Clearly, if "Three Notes on the Theory of Discourses" is any indicator, this was no easy task. What is also clear, however, is that Althusser at this stage sought to accentuate the positive aspects of his work rather than quibble with the shortcomings. Chief among the remaining problems was the relation of "practice" as a concept to the science/ideology dyad. If our mental grasp of our lived experience was inextricable from ideology, was all practice itself ideological? Was merely our cognition of that practice ideological? Was there to be a material component of practice independent of our ideological grasp of it but available to a scientific one? More fearful of pragmatism than formalism, Althusser committed himself to the epistemological merits of his project, going so far as to present them to Mark Borisovich Mitin, the "pillar of the Soviet philosophical establishment" who had made a name for himself in the 1930s condemning Trotskyists and ingratiating himself as "Stalin's philosopher" (155). Althusser prepared the article "The Historical Task of Marxist Philosophy" in April 1967 at Mitin's request, but the result was never published in the Soviet Union. The arguments presented in the document's conclusion leave no mystery as to why an official Soviet audience would find it unpalatable. Temporarily bracketing the science/ideology distinction, Althusser discusses the relationship among three terms: "science," "philosophy," and "politics." "What radically distinguishes philosophy from the sciences," Althusser writes, "the science of history included, is the internal, intimate, organic relation that it maintains with politics" (209). He distinguishes this claim from pragmatism by suggesting that "*the object* of philosophy is not politics, but philosophy is *political by nature*" (217). In other words, philosophy is a practice that is neither ideological nor scientific. It is neither because it is without object—this fact, for Althusser, is also what makes it quintessentially political.

This peculiar understanding of philosophy and the political with regard to science will be addressed in the next section, when we consider Althusser's "Philosophy Course for Scientists," which took place around this same time. But the key issue at hand is what must have been the real site of scandal for the "old fox" Mitin, who had been one of the primary promoters of Lysenkoism. Althusser contends that science is not, and can never be, political:

> Spinoza observed that the concept of a dog does not bark; similarly, we might say that the concept of sugar is not sweet, that the knowledge of atoms is not atomic, that the knowledge of life is not "a living thing," that the science of history is not "historical," and so on. *In the same way, it may be said that the science of politics is not political.* This is a way of expressing the fact that the qualitative nature of the object of a science does not affect—internally, intimately, organically—the intrinsic nature of a science, which is its scientificity. Politics or "ideology" is therefore not the determining principle of the Marxist history of science *qua* science. (210–11, emphasis added)

The logic and the implications here are essential. Althusser had spent the past several years arguing for Marxism's scientificity. More emphatically, historical materialism's world historical significance was a result of its being a science of history. Yet now it is revealed that being a science does nothing in terms of politics, that it has no bearing in the political; that neither is it determined by the political nor does it have an effect on the political. Science qua science is simply knowledge conceived as Althusser has been elaborating it in preceding texts. This remarkable admission is a logical result of the arguments proceeding from Althusser's own Spinozist rationalism; the fact that his concession is stated most clearly *in a text to a Soviet philosopher* is a testament both to Althusser's confidence and his delusions. But the philosophical point remains that scientific knowledge itself accomplishes nothing in practical terms. This maneuver has a liberating effect on Althusser and finally permits him to develop a concept of philosophy taking "as its object what is traditionally, and improperly, called the 'totality' of the real" (212). "Improperly" is the key word here. Philosophy's "object" is now registered as the fleeting, infinitely repeating "convergence" of the two attributes whose "differential articulation" Althusser has been trying to express. What makes "philosophy" and "politics" isomorphic in this regard, or in other words, what permits Althusser to claim that "when philosophy takes politics into account in posing its own problems, it truly takes its own object into account," is that both philosophy and politics become a matter of an insubstantial object, a non-object, a pure happening as such, the moments of convergent "effects," what Deleuze will later name "events." This is what Althusser's repeated insistence that there is no object of philosophy nor an object of politics is trying to communicate.[44] Science and ideology deal with materiality, with practices, with objects, with matters of substance, with the artifacts of lived experience. By dealing exclusively with "effects," philosophy and politics each recognize a fundamental insubstantiality to their "objects."

Far from rescinding it, this move constitutes a further radicalization of Althusser's Spinozism. More to the point, it accomplishes the articulation of Spinozism against a structuralist formalism whose resemblances to Althusser's project were too close for comfort. By nominating philosophy and politics together as the nexus point of the "attributes" discursively articulated by science and ideology, Althusser shirks a synchronic formalism whose account of causality can in the end only be regarded as mechanistic, and thus of a piece with humanism and economism, the original bugbears of the Althusserian enterprise. For Lévi-Strauss and Lacan both, in Althusser's view, the form *is* the function, and the result is an insufficient account of causality and the differential relation between thought and material. In a way, this is the same problem as Brunschvicg's "critical idealism," in the sense that the integrity and coherence of ideas alone are deemed sufficient to "determine" the world. Althusser held philosophy as ontology in contempt as a result of the travesties of "Diamat,"[45] but these efforts show his own recognition of the urgency of furnishing his cognitive project with an ontological grounding that could distinguish it from the formalism of structuralism.

What is most striking about this ontological ground, however, is its resolutely apolitical nature in and of itself. It is as if Althusser works out an ontology only to discover that ontology alone cannot and will not produce his politics. Yet rather than abandon the philosophical essentials, Althusser stays committed to them. Though this ontology will provide the ground on which Althusser will develop his imbricated notions of philosophy and politics, nothing in these conceptual developments compromises the fundamental lessons of that ontology, precisely those that turn on a vision of causality as necessity and the impossibility of prefiguration. Indeed, Althusser's

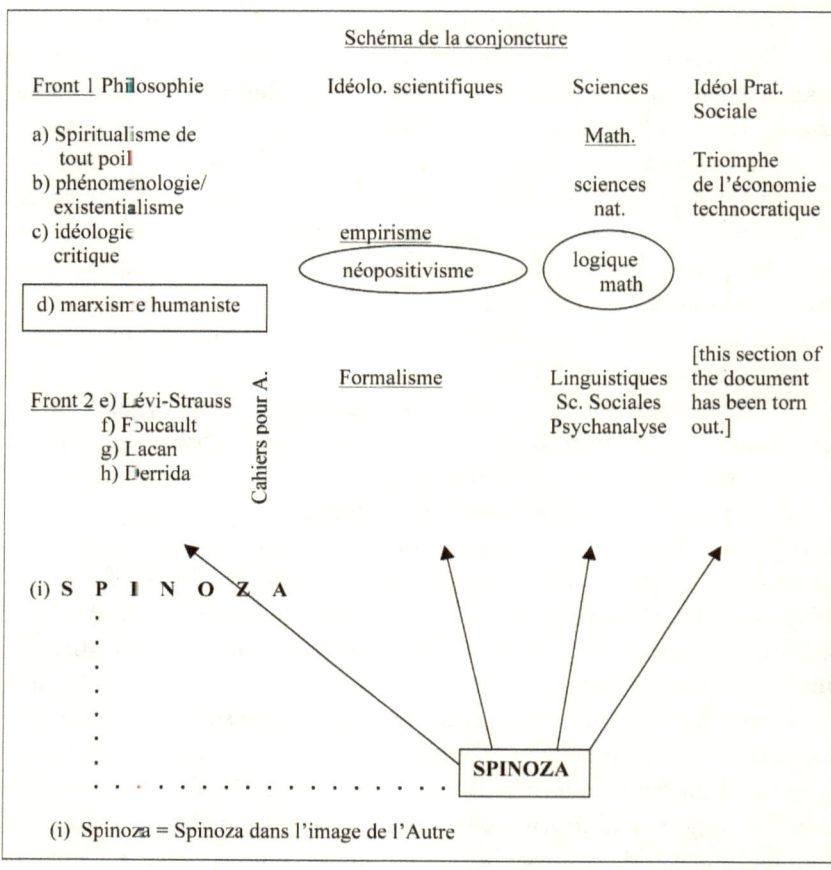

Figure 1. Michel Tort's sketch of the "Groupe Spinoza" strategy. Source: ALT2.A11-03.11, Fonds Althusser. Tort prepared this drawing in December 1967 to schematize the discussions of the Groupe Spinoza, a "clandestine" meeting of intellectuals spearheaded by Althusser, which lasted from the middle of 1967 until the spring of 1969. In January 1969, Althusser prepared a code sheet of the participants' pseudonyms (Louis became "Pierre"; Alain [Badiou], "Gérard"; Étienne [Balibar], "René"; Pierre [Macherey], "Jean"; etc.), the total list of entries numbering sixteen. In the splits among student Marxist groups following the events of May 1968, pseudonyms were deemed necessary to maintain maximum secrecy and minimum culpability as the group reconsidered the foundations of Marxism and the strategy of attack on a two-front war. Althusser's comments in the correspondence surrounding the Groupe Spinoza suggest a tactical maneuver of temporary alignment with partisans of "Front 2," associated with the journal *Cahiers pour l'Analyse*, in order to battle the more dominant "Front 1." For example, Tort addressed the need "to use critiques to force Derrida to maximize his critique against phenomenology" (ALT2.A11-03.11). The idea was ultimately to mobilize the secret weapon of "SPINOZA" against both fronts.

thought remains unrepentant in its rationalism, and whatever its plausibility, his project is now irreducible to an uncritical or vacuous formalism.

Two things are remarkable here. The first is the *extent* of Althusser's debt to Spinoza. We are no longer talking about borrowed concepts but instead a wholesale reconfiguration of Spinoza's metaphysics in the context of twentieth-century philosophy and politics. Second, there is the incredible earnestness of Althusser's conception of his project. This historical moment immediately precedes May 1968, an event that disqualified Althusser in the eyes of many. But in the months surrounding May 1968, Althusser had organized a "Groupe Spinoza" whose mandate was nothing less than to develop a new philosophy. Such a development would take strategy and time. The schematic diagram reproduced here was prepared by Michel Tort, one of Althusser's student collaborators, which gives a sense of how the participants understood their task.

What are we to make of this "schematic of the conjuncture?" Its contents are largely consistent with Althusser's project thus far. Of note is the addition of the Critical Theory of the Frankfurt School, under the name "ideology critique," to a list including phenomenology/existentialism, "spiritualism of all kinds," and humanist Marxism. Whereas in *Reading Capital* phenomenological idealism and empiricism were presented as inversions of one another, now we see empiricism and neopositivism together codified as a scientific ideology buttressed by all components of the dominant philosophical front, including phenomenology. The Frankfurt School's hostility to empiricism, positivism, and technocracy makes Althusser's inclusion of their project in "Front 1" a curiosity. Presumably the charge is one of complicity with the "triumph of the technocratic economy" rather than endorsement. "Front 2" consists of Althusser's formalist "allies," all writers associated with the *Cahiers pour l'Analyse*. The *Cahiers* were published between 1966 and 1969 by the Cercle d'Épistémologie, a group of *normaliens* influenced by Althusser and Lacan, the latter of whom had been associated with the ENS at Althusser's behest, since 1964. Jacques-Alain Miller was at the helm of the collective effort, but Badiou came to play a large role as well. Many key texts of French structuralism were first published in the *Cahiers*. In addition to Althusser's own exposition of Rousseau,[46] the *Cahiers* published Lacan's "Science and Truth," eventually the capstone essay of his *Écrits*.[47] A key section of *Of Grammatology* first saw light of day in Derrida's contribution, "Nature, culture, écriture (de Lévi-Strauss à Rousseau)."[48] One issue began with an exchange with Michel Foucault, wherein he further developed his arguments concerning "the archaeology of knowledge," producing a draft introduction to the work that would appear under that name.⁴⁹ A quotation from Canguilhem served as the epigraph for every volume: "To work on a concept [. . .] is to confer upon it, through a regulated series of transformations, the function of a form."⁵⁰

Unfortunately, there is no supplementary material in this particular dossier to suggest what might be meant by "Spinoza in the image of the Other" and the line connecting this Spinoza with the boxed-in one. It seems plausible that Tort intended to convey that there is a certain prevalent image of Spinoza at work in French philosophy, and that the two fronts are not suspecting the "SPINOZA" that is about to be unleashed upon them. Speculation aside, the point is clear enough. Spinoza offers an alternative model, a new mode of philosophy. This seems to be the message: Spinoza's time is now. Yet, as the historical record makes clear, this time did *not* come. The *Elements of Dialectical Materialism*, Althusser's *Ethics*, was never produced. The project was aborted. Why?

The answer is obvious, in one sense. The May events of 1968 rendered the Althusserian project null and void. As the graffiti read: Althusser is worthless (*Althu sert à rien*). Structures do not occupy the streets. Althusser's absence from May 1968 was duly noted by many observers. His radio silence until April 1970, with the publication of the ISA essay in *La Pensée* was also palpable. His *Eléments d'autocritique* was not published until 1974. In truth, Althusser "missed" the May events because he was in the hospital undergoing treatment for the latest bout of his recurring depression. Given the rancor against Althusser concurrent with and following May 1968, and the number of former collaborators who turned on him in the 1970s, Rancière and Badiou chief among them,⁵¹ one would expect a revision of Althusser's fundamental principles, a kind of "abort mission" for the program pursued by the Groupe Spinoza. But, concerning the essentials of Althusser's own philosophical thought, this is not what happens at all.

As I have already suggested, the ISA essay, undoubtedly Althusser's most famous post-1968 piece of writing, is not to be read as a cynical take on the misguided delusions of the students of the Latin Quarter but instead as a consolidation of the implications of Althusser's work until that point.⁵² The twin key theses of the essay—"Ideology is a 'representation' of the imaginary relationship of individuals to their real conditions of existence" and "Ideology interpellates individuals as subjects"—are concise restatements of the ideas developed in 1966–67. To be sure, with the concept of interpellation Althusser introduces the evocative metaphor of "hailing," the "hey you!" from the policeman that instigates one's subjectivity. But this is merely to add siding to the frame of "the theory of discourse." Though uncertain on some essentials, Althusser understood that ideological discourse required a subject in order to function, and thus its effect was equally discursive and practical.[53] The subject effect of ideological discourse was a site where discourse was also practical, but the knowledge effect of science was one where scientific practice was also discursive.

If we pare down Althusser's most famous slogan to its essentials, what we find is that ideology is a representation of a relation. It is not the relation itself but the way that relation is represented. In other words, ideology is the discursive correlate, on the level of thought and lived experience, that "represents" the relational goings-on of the material substrata, the "real conditions of existence." But lest this be read as a disavowal of the version of Spinozism outlined previously, and a return to an unsanctioned parallelism, Althusser's point remains that the aspiration to science takes place initially within that realm of ideological experience, and the only way to discover "scientifically" the material reality that helps generate ideology but does not mechanistically determine it, is through a rational mode of thought predicated upon the incommensurability of thought to its object. For Spinoza, access to the rational still begins within the domain of *vaga experientia*, in which the attribute of Thought encounters the attribute of Extension. Closure, wholeness, and identity, specifically the identity of the concept with its object, are the mark of ideology and our experience of ideology. Science emerges from this scenario, and it is philosophy's task to register it. Philosophy is the effect of a disjuncture, not a parallelism. In 1967, Althusser wrote, "The sciences are sciences: they are not philosophy. Theoretical ideologies are theoretical ideologies: they are not reducible to philosophy. But 'the scientific' and 'the ideological' are *philosophical* categories and the contradictory couple they form is brought to light by philosophy: it is philosophical."[54]

The Third Moment: Spinozist Philosophy

The period immediately following *For Marx* and *Reading Capital* witnessed a private effort on Althusser's part to develop a Spinozist ontology able to support the Spinozist epistemology laid out in those volumes.

Concurrent with this attempt, and more publicly, Althusser focused his attention on distinguishing philosophy from "science" and "ideology" and coming to grips with its status as a practice. George Lichtheim once remarked that the essence of Leninism was the conviction that certain theoretical problems can only be resolved in practice.[55] Althusser's Leninism was unorthodox then, because although he, too, believed in this formula, the practice portending the resolution remained "theoretical practice." Althusser's "Philosophy Course for Scientists" was a course given in 1967 whose popularity, judging from the attendance record, exceeded that of the *Capital* seminars.[56] These lectures show a move away from the definition of philosophy as the "Theory of theoretical practice," toward, but not yet reaching, the slogan of philosophy as the "class struggle in theory." Avoided is the explicit linkage of philosophy to politics as sharing the same (non-)object pronounced several months earlier in "The Historical Task of Marxist Philosophy." In this context, the relation is read as largely analogical, the problems of which we will address later. What is most important about these lectures for our purposes is that in them Althusser moves toward a concept of philosophy that is strangely evocative of the arguments produced toward the end of Spinoza's *Ethics*, in the fifth book, "On the Power of the Understanding, or On Human Freedom." If we pursue to its conclusion our claim that the development of Althusser's thought follows a logic similar to Spinoza's, then it makes sense that the effort to distinguish science and ideology, first epistemologically (at the "first level") and then ontologically (at the "second level"), would ultimately entail a philosophical purchase on this distinction relatable to Spinoza's "third kind of knowledge," the latter of which purports to know things in their "singular essence."[57]

Naturally, this suggestion provokes many objections. In Book V of the *Ethics*, the third kind of knowledge is the culmination of what Spinoza calls "the intellectual love of God," a formula that has caused no small amount of chagrin among Spinoza's materialist epigones. How, then, could Althusser's understanding of philosophy in *Philosophy and the Spontaneous Philosophy of the Scientists* (hereafter *PSPS*) have anything to do with this metaphysical hubris? To make our case requires reconstructing the arguments of this seminar in a careful way, in order to show how the development of philosophy as something that produces theses that are never evaluated for their "truthfulness" but only their possible "correctness" (*justesse*), is contingent upon Althusser's concomitant Spinozist thinking, detailed in the preceding section, which considers singularities as necessary effects of the momentary convergence between attributes. The insubstantiality of "effects," their irreducibility to a material or ideal cause, was something we insisted upon earlier because only science, in Althusser's view, is able to say whether or not something is true, because science is the domain of knowledge that has access to, and articulates, the reality of material being. All science is science of materials, so science can then evaluate claims about material as being true or false. Ideology, too, has its own version of truth distinct from scientific truth. These are the truths of morality or religion. Philosophy, Althusser avers, has nothing to do with truth as such because its only task is to register the relation between the domain articulated by science and that articulated by ideology. Its task is one of demarcation, registering effects and then identifying the convergent ideological and scientific components that "produced" said effect. But if every "effect" is singularly unpredictable and singularly unrepeatable, then it is a "singular thing," or since it is an "effect," and thus insubstantial in its existence, we can go one better and call it a "singular essence." And to "know" this singular essence in its necessity is to understand its immanent cause expressed through its irreducible components. This is Spinoza's "third kind of knowledge," the pinnacle of his philosophy. Althusser invests philosophy with nothing less.

One of the peculiar aspects of *PSPS* is again the paucity of reference to Marx and his texts. Althusser's Marxist credentials and convictions are not in doubt, but the task of the lectures seems to be to develop a materialist conception of philosophy that can have a productive, rather than derivative or derisive, relationship with science, and that as a result will produce the extra-philosophical "effect" of distinguishing science from ideology more generally. Althusser will ultimately insist, with assistance from Lenin,[58] that this extra-philosophical effect cannot but be political because the effect of philosophy is to draw a division within society itself. Because of this emphasis on demarcation and sides Althusser's relationship to ideology is not one of immanent critique, even if all thought begins with the raw materials presented by ideology. Over the course of the lectures, the concept of the "spontaneous philosophy of the sciences" (SPS) comes to play the role of ideology in Althusser's argument. The SPS is in effect the scientist's ideology, an ideology formally indistinguishable in its essentials from any individual's ideology in civil society. Like the latter, it is inescapable: "scientific ideology (or the ideology of scientists) is inseparable from scientific practice: it is the 'spontaneous' ideology of scientific practice."[59] Yet "the balance of power within an SPS cannot be changed through an immanent critique: there must be a counterforce, and that counterforce can only be philosophical and materialist" (139). "Materialist" here is largely defined negatively as "not idealist." The mark of idealism at this stage is, oddly enough, a belief in the "omnipotence of scientific truth," that science alone can accomplish social or political goals. Althusser criticizes the philosophes of the Enlightenment for compromising their own materialism, mobilized in the critique of religion, for an idealist philosophy of history that sees history driven by scientific truth (138). What distinguishes Althusser's position, what makes it "not idealist" and thus "materialist," is its recognition that there will be no end to the struggle. The "[theses of materialist philosophy] do not constitute a 'system' as in the idealist philosophies: the system of a totally and closed Truth" (143).

If philosophy is a struggle, and if, in this struggle, it is idealist philosophy that is dominant, this inevitably means that *dialectical materialist philosophy must itself be constituted in the struggle*, and that in the course of this struggle it must gradually win its own positions against the enemy simply in order to exist, to acquire the existence of a historical force. (143, emphasis added)

The allegory and metaphor of this passage are unmistakable. Althusser wants to claim for "materialist philosophy" a function not unlike that ascribed to the proletariat as a class in Marxist theory. "Constituted in the struggle," materialist philosophy's task appears to be one of pure negation, a relentless hostility to the dominant idealist element, but with no thought of victory, only vigilance.

It is not least of the ironies of Althusser's thought that the same thinker who berated phenomenological idealism for its refusal to admit its analogical debt to Christian theology is here perfectly transparent in his own use of analogy to link his philosophical project to the history of class struggle. It is ironic yet ultimately fitting, for in Althusser's evocation here of philosophy as a permanent struggle with an eye toward a victory that can never be achieved, we see most clearly why Althusser is the representative figure in recent French thought for the latest resurgence of Spinozism. Spinozism's function in Western intellectual history seems to be one of permanent negation with the impossibility of instantiation. Its recurrence always seems to take place at times of political or cultural crisis as a "threat" to be neutralized before history and philosophy can progress. Spinozism threatens the "dominant ideology," to use Althusser's language, or the philosophical complacency that appears to buttress the "dominant" power in such a political crisis. What accounts for Althusser's fidelity in spite of himself to this legacy of Spinozism is that his own thinking—notwithstanding his attempts to insist otherwise—is ultimately a pure theoretical negation void of a positive political program.

This fidelity is most clearly at work in the provocative theses of *PSPS*, which we must continue to explore in order to see how the peak of Althusser's Spinozism as philosophy also portends its inutility as a positive political theory. Though the main aim of the seminar is to articulate a new relationship between philosophy and science, Althusser remains concerned to distinguish his position from pragmatism. Recall that already in *For Marx* pragmatism served Althusser as a threat common to science and politics; in either domain, the pragmatic error was the same. In *PSPS*, Althusser returns to this theme suggesting that pragmatism rears its head whenever there is an emphasis on practice (104). The mechanic works on the part to make the motor run; the surgeon intervenes to make the body function. Evidently, Lenin was not a pragmatist because, unlike the mechanic or the surgeon, each of whom has an external perspective on the whole he wishes to make function with his intervention, Lenin merely affirmed what was "correct" without illusory notions about his grasp of the totality (105). There are many who would fail to see what distinguishes the pragmatic Lenin from the practical one; arguably Lenin's greatest attribute, however vexed the results, was his sheer political cunning as a realist more than any refined sense of distinction between practice and pragmatism. But Althusser's point is to introduce an analogy, to say that philosophy operates like Lenin's politics. It traces lines of demarcation that reveal the totality itself to be an illusion obscuring a rift. All of these lines "are ultimately modalities of a fundamental line: the line between the scientific and the ideological" (106).

The important argument here is the one more pointedly stated in "The Historical Task of Marxist Philosophy": philosophy and politics are similar domains because in each there is a rejection of totality, and thus a final perspective from which to adjudicate, and also an absence of objects per se on which to work. The disavowal of "pragmatism" in such terms is intimately related to another critical line at the heart of *PSPS*, the critique of the juridical subject. For Althusser, the "juridical" serves as a nexus for his philosophical and political arguments regarding bourgeois ideology. Pursuing an argument that will be more fully developed by Étienne Balibar and Antonio Negri, with explicit reference to Spinoza, Althusser links the bourgeois subject to the critical subject of Kantian philosophy and "critical idealism" more generally.[60] "In all its variants, philosophy appears to be the discipline that *establishes the rights* of the sciences, for it *poses the question of rights* and answers it by defining *legal rights* to scientific knowledge" (127). The juridical and the pragmatic are linked because each decides the outcome in advance, from a blinkered "total" perspective. In Althusser's estimation, it is not the task of philosophy to decide what science can and cannot produce as true. Kant's privileging of "experience" over "experiential data" results in the expulsion of "a materially existing external object" from consideration (135). Juridical ideology is a supreme example, Althusser argues, of a "practical ideology" that has infected modern science, in the sense that it has provided scientists with their "spontaneous philosophy." If anything, this juridical figure is the ideological figure of modern philosophy:

> It is not by chance that in response to the "question of right," the classical theory of knowledge puts into play a category like that of the "subject" (from the Cartesian *ego cogito* to the Kantian transcendental Subject to the "concrete," transcendental subjects of Husserl). This category is simply a reproduction within the field of philosophy of the ideological notion of "subject," itself taken from the juridical category of the "legal subject." And the "subject-object" couple, the "subject" and its "object," is merely a reflection within the philosophical field, and within a properly philosophical mode, of the juridical categories of the "legal subject," "owner" *of itself and* of its goods (things). So with consciousness: it is owner of itself (*self-consciousness*) and of its goods (consciousness *of its* object, of *its* objects). (128)

The Husserlian concept of intentionality is read as the consolidation of this line in the twentieth century. The function of this mode of philosophy is to provide a guarantee in advance not only of what can be thought but of what science can discover. In contrast, Althusser says to the scientists in attendance, "In all honesty [. . .] we cannot offer you an absolute *guarantee*" (129). He concludes his fourth lecture with an offer of an alliance, in which philosophy will never intervene in science itself, but only in the "spontaneous philosophy of the sciences," that is, in ideology. "Through this Alliance, materialist philosophy is authorized to intervene in the SPS and *only in the SPS*. Which means that philosophy intervenes *only* in philosophy. It refrains from making any intervention in science proper, in its problems, in its practice" (141–42). Philosophy will never adjudicate the results of science, but the concurrent implication seems inescapable: philosophy will indeed still adjudicate what is science and what is not science.

In the end, Althusser calls for a relationship between science and philosophy in which the latter serves the former, rather than exploits it. It is remarkable to see the lesson of Lysenkoism still so central to Althusser's philosophical project. Be it the orchestrations of Stalin or the machinations of capital, exploitation of science is still exploitation of science. What is equally remarkable is that, notwithstanding his critique of the philosophes' idealism, Althusser evokes here a quintessentially Enlightenment faith in the power of rational thought to produce political effects. For Althusser's critique of the bourgeois juridical subject is really an effort to show that what goes on in the world of the bourgeoisie is not politics at all but juridical ideology, a question of management and bureaucratic organization. In other words, the "politics" of the bourgeoisie is not truly politics. The allegation is that this politics is not truly political because it is ideological. Because what Althusser is offering is a way to discern true science as nonideological, the implication is that a "true," rather than a deluded, politics will emerge as a result. Althusser's effort to develop a version of philosophy that is not juridical, not modeled on Kantian critique, is thus concurrently an effort to develop the political corollary that would accompany this resurgence of rational philosophy, just as phenomenological idealism accompanied the enshrinement of the bourgeois juridical subject at the heart of postwar French philosophy.

The problem, however, is that this version of politics is nowhere developed at all *as politics*. The philosophy alone is deemed sufficient to entail the politics. If phenomenological idealism is insufficient as philosophy because its concepts are all borrowed from bourgeois "politics," then by the same token, can one say that Althusser's "politics" is ineffective because all its concepts are borrowed from his rationalist materialist philosophy? Althusser's retort would be that phenomenological idealism is not incorrect because its concepts are borrowed but because they are borrowed from arguments rooted in false premises, those of Christian theology. What makes Althusser's materialist alternative "correct" is that its premises are those of materialist science, a field of knowledge that disregards the theological concepts of "origins" and "goals" as they relate to existence in the broadest sense of the term. The suturing of philosophy to politics as two domains "without object" is a deft theoretical maneuver, one that remains committed to this materialist conviction. But it presents no positive figure of the political in that it introduces no agent or mechanism for change. It is as if demarcating material science and registering the implications will somehow induce change the way one induces labor, a metaphor Althusser surely would not countenance. On a related note, in its analogical linkage of material philosophy, which basically calls upon a materialism on a cosmic scale, to the materialism of working laborers, Althusser relies upon an ideological image of the proletariat wholly incongruous with the rest of his project, an image more Lukácsian than Althusserian. In the end, Althusser vacillates between gesturing toward the political implications of his philosophy (e.g., this model of philosophy is *like* politics) and declaring them by fiat (e.g., this philosophy *is* politics). In no sense are these implications ever really developed. Althusser's political detractors, of all stripes, are largely justified on this score. The political seems to be the philosophical pursued by other means, and not the other way around, which is what one would expect from a concept of philosophy that purports to call itself "the class struggle in theory."[61]

In a recollection of his time as Althusser's student at the ENS, Clément Rosset reflected on the extremes of Althusserian earnestness, captured in Badiou's notion that Communist revolution in France would really be possible only once French laborers came to grips with Lacan's *Écrits*, which entailed, in Rosset's view, "some serious overtime for our workers."[62] All the same, Rosset averred that Althusser's definition of materialist philosophy—to no longer tell oneself stories (*ne plus se raconter d'histoires*)—continued to ring true for him.[63] One does not need to subscribe to a concept of politics as mainly a matter of narratives to recognize that Althusser's own understanding of materialist philosophy as a disavowal of stories seriously compromises its bearing on political questions. This is so because, no matter its material underpinnings, which may or may not be available to science, politics is something that happens in the domain of lived experience and, as a goal-oriented phenomenon, requires at least a modicum of narrative in order to take place. When Althusser himself says that the science of politics is not political, he is affirming that scientific knowledge, even when highlighted by the philosopher who assists the scientist, cannot in and of itself produce a political effect. To be sure, it will produce an effect just as any discourse will, but being discursive in its essentials the effect will either be "ideological" or "scientific." How can it be political? More to the point, it is not even clear what it would mean for it to be political.

The core of Althusser's philosophical effort was the development of a Spinozist rationalism able to act as a powerful critical weapon against phenomenological philosophy. His critique of "origins," and the illusions produced by recourse to origins, was one component of a philosophical effort that viewed the insights of modern science not as problems for philosophy to circumvent but as conditions themselves for philosophical activity. In general, Althusser avoided the vocabulary of ontology. But the key legacy of his thought can best be presented as the claim that any philosophy that wants to invoke ontological principles or claims must do so without borrowing its arguments from theology. Or, if it does "borrow" concepts from theology, it must render them nontheological in the transformation, which effectively means sapping them of their transcendental norms. This is the quintessentially Spinozist maneuver of Althusser's effort. Althusser remained committed to the implications of his own philosophical *parti pris*, which had to maintain, in Spinozist terms, that the subject was not an agent but an effect, or better that the subject was best understood as a site of convergence. In the best of all possible worlds, the one called for at the end of Spinoza's *Ethics*, the subject-effect of ideology and the knowledge-effect of science would coincide in a singular, unique site. In his memoir, Althusser recalled a phrase of Jacques Martin's on the subject of communism that remained with him and that makes sense only in light of Althusser's subsequent Spinozism. The future is a time "in which there are no longer human beings, only individuals."[64]

Whatever its philosophical value, Althusser himself recognized the inadequacy of his baseline Spinozism as political theory. The evidence for this can be found in his later turn to Machiavelli as a thinker whose insights might supplement his already-established Spinozism. Among the discoveries in Althusser's personal archive following his death was a manuscript devoted to Machiavelli, whom Althusser had identified alongside Spinoza as the second key figure in the "materialist tradition."[65] This text was the result of a course given in 1972, and it possessed a polish consistent with much that Althusser published during his lifetime.[66] A good portion of the study concerns elaborating a theory of political *duration*: How can the state, once founded through a revolutionary act, not devolve into corruption and tyranny? The examples of the USSR and Mao's China hover in the background of this discussion. In addition to dealing with this political exigency, however, the manuscript evinces an urgent need to develop a theory of political subjectivity that would be consistent with Althusser's broader philosophical convictions. In an apparent effort to avoid contradiction with the concept of subjectivity outlined in the ISA essay, Althusser cautions that it would be advisable to replace the "ambiguous term *subject*" with *agent*.[67] Nominal concerns aside, the point remains the same: Althusser's study of Machiavelli is an effort to think through the problematic of radical beginnings, innovation—*change*—in a world ostensibly governed by necessity. "Aleatory materialism" is adumbrated in this discussion, which focuses on the political content and effect of a philosophy that views political subjectivity as the result of unforeseen encounters and the constitutive seizures of opportunity unfolding within those encounters. One could plausibly read in Althusser's turn to Machiavelli a decision to find a new Lenin whose philosophical prowess, and political purchase, might prove more compelling than the actual Lenin. It was also consistent with Althusser's long-standing aversion to political ontologies and anthropologies. Yet for all of its provocation, and for all of its celebration of the political subject as the one who seizes unforeseen opportunities, this set of arguments did nothing to mitigate Althusser's essential Spinozism, grounded as it was in a conception of rationalist philosophy as the recognition of necessity. On the level of philosophy, Althusser's Machiavellian subject bears fascinating comparison with the subject of "rationalist empiricism" hinted at in 1966, the subject born of the nonmediated, nonphenomenological "encounter." But the political implications of this vision remain obscure. In a way, however, this was Althusser's point. The virtue of Machiavelli was precisely that he was not a philosopher, which meant he was not concerned to justify or ground political actions in philosophical problematics. But it is precisely his indifference to philosophy that accounts for why political philosophers ought to take him seriously, in Althusser's view.

In the end, the philosopher who helps us to best understand the political minimalism of Althusser's thought is Althusser himself. What Althusser accomplished in his critique of phenomenology was at root a striking critique of analogical thinking. Phenomenology's weakness as philosophy lay in its blindness to its own metaphorical nature. Althusser's Spinozism meant above all a critique of the identity of the concept. Subtending subject/object dualism in its idealist or its empiricist guises was a *will* or *desire* to collapse the one into the other, either at the site of putative origin or at the site of prefigured goal. As a result, both philosophical programs are motivated by a desire that sees truth in likeness rather than in distinction. Forsaking an evaluation of ideas as true or false in favor of a measure of adequate or inadequate, the Spinozist model of knowledge that Althusser followed so closely was predicated upon the radical discontinuity of thought and its object. The task of philosophy was a kind of vigilance that maintained the impossibility of a frontier between them and recognized events as effects irreducible to an immediate, and by implication clearly discernible, cause. The "opacity of the immediate," far from being a barrier to science, ensured it.

So when Althusser develops a new notion of philosophy as a practice without object, as a recognition of effects in their nonfungible singularity and contingent basis, he remains faithful to a generally Spinozist imperative. But when he analogizes from this new model of philosophy via the figure of Lenin to a new thinking of politics, it looks as if his own politics will betray his philosophy. Rhetorically, this is what appears to happen. Althusser sutures materialist philosophy to "materialist" politics. But in so doing, he saps the political of anything that makes it recognizably political and ultimately remains committed to the Spinozist lessons of his philosophy. Registering effects, pronouncing dogmatic theses, demarcating the line between science and ideology, this is Althusser's Spinozist philosophy: Spinozism is an attack on illusions. Althusser's definition of materialist philosophy as a disavowal of stories implies a disavowal of illusions, the stuff of ideology. But the disavowal of ideology results, in Althusser's thought, in a disavowal of the lived.

Peter Hallward once described Spinozism as "the disarming of politics."[68] For Hallward, Deleuze is the chief culprit of latter-day Spinozism because he advocates what amounts to a monist metaphysics that reduces all specificity to singularity, thus making an impossibility of change or novelty.[69] We will see what distinguishes Deleuze's Spinozism from Althusser's in the next chapter. But there is a certain "disarming of politics" at work in Althusser's project, too, albeit of a different sort. Althusser's metaphysics, by hewing to the permanent incommensurability of attributes in Spinoza's project, is anything but reductive. Rather, the problem with Althusserianism is essentially the complete inversion of Hallward's problem with Deleuze. By insisting on radical novelty and the impossibility of any kind of prefigurative telos in history, Althusser, too, produces a philosophy that, because it can accomplish nothing *purposefully* other than its own refinement, is ultimately ascetic in its implications.

But to call it ascetic is not to call it incorrect. For the judgment of asceticism is only definitively a negative one to a philosopher who remains committed to Thesis Eleven as the core commandment of modern philosophical effort. We know Althusser's thought on this score. He was a Communist and a philosopher, as he always maintained, and I have argued that his philosophical inclinations were ultimately in conflict with his political convictions and that the former won the day. In his unflagging commitment to a philosophy predicated upon the infinite against the totality, and the incommensurability of thought to its objects, Althusser produced a manner of thought that could know no possible closure. Toward the end of his life Althusser continued to adhere to the Spinozist formula—*verum index sui et falsi*—with the caveat that for Spinoza there was no Truth per se, only the "true," a true produced ad infinitum "as the result of a labor of a process that discovers it, and [. . .] as proving itself in its very production."[70] A philosophy pursued in such terms knows neither origin nor goal. Which means it also knows no exhaustion.

6

Toward a Science of the Singular
Gilles Deleuze between Heidegger and Spinoza

> All that Spinozism needed to make the univocal an object of pure affirmation was to make substance turn around the modes.
>
> Gilles Deleuze, *Difference and* Repetition, 1968[1]

Among the major thinkers of twentieth-century French philosophy, few had as wide a field of interest as Gilles Deleuze. The diversity of objects that garnered Deleuze's attention—from the writings of Leopold von Sacher-Masoch to the paintings of Francis Bacon[2]—is exceeded only by the diversity of intellectual resources called upon to develop his thinking in the first place. Aside from the canonical thinkers covered in his monographs of the 1950s and 1960s, Deleuze's philosophical writings refer to a set of themes and writers that can seem affected in its eclecticism and willful in its obscurantism.[3] For example, his major philosophical statement *Difference and Repetition* (1968) takes us from the occultism of József Maria Hoene-Wronski's post-Kantian consideration of differential calculus to the biophysical gnosticism of one of Deleuze's contemporaries, Raymond Ruyer.[4] These figures are joined by a cast of characters that is alternately ancient, medieval, and modern; the preface to *The Logic of Sense* is titled "From Lewis Carroll to the Stoics."[5] Deleuze's idiosyncrasy is often taken for granted in general assessments of recent French thought.[6] In order to acquire some purchase on the sources of his complex project, as well as its fundamental arguments and concerns, let us begin by considering the impact of two proximate influences on Deleuze who are familiar faces from our account: Ferdinand Alquié and Martial Gueroult.

On January 28, 1967, Deleuze delivered a lecture to the Société française de philosophie titled "The Method of Dramatization."[7] Keeping with a long-standing tradition in French academia, the event provided him the opportunity to publicly share a condensed version of his doctoral work with his peers. Alquié was in the audience, along with Maurice de Gandillac, Jean Beaufret, and Alexis Philonenko, among others. Most of the material Deleuze presented was culled from the fourth and fifth chapters of *Difference and Repetition*, the work to be submitted as his major doctoral thesis several months later. Beginning as an excursus on philosophical methodology—arguing for questions of *who* and *how* to replace those of *what*—the bulk of the talk explicated his conception of the relation of the virtual to the actual as an equally ontological and epistemological phenomenon. Deleuze emphasized the role of spatiotemporal dynamic processes in generating both new concepts and new physical entities. Revising Kant's account of the relation of ideas to concepts, Deleuze insisted that the play of ideas takes place on a virtual plane and that concepts serve as their actualization. In themselves, ideas qua ideas are virtual multiplicities analogous to the multiplicity inherent in all being; like sensations, they are virtual, since they evade empirical verification, and multiple, since they express change. The common denominator is intensity: "Though experience always puts us in the presence of intensities already developed [*développées*] in extensions, already covered over with qualities, we must conceive, precisely as a condition of experience, pure intensities veiled [*enveloppées*] in a depth, in an intensive *spatium* that preexists all quality and all extension."[8] In this instance, Deleuze's *spatium* plays a role not unlike Kant's *sensorium*, as the domain in which all intellection and sensation take place, thereby serving as a common frame for the material and the ideal.[9]

Shortly after the conclusion of Deleuze's talk, Alquié pressed his student on a number of key points. Alquié was the main reader for Deleuze's minor thesis, *Spinoza and the Problem of Expression*,[10] and the two had a relationship that went back to Deleuze's days as a student at the Sorbonne in the late 1940s. Alquié effectively charged Deleuze with not doing philosophy, with evading its most fundamental questions. Though he expressed sympathy for Deleuze's contention that philosophy needed to concern itself with problems, he was chagrined that none of Deleuze's examples were themselves philosophical:

He has spoken to us about the straight line, which is a mathematical example, about the egg, which is a physiological example, about genes, which are a biological example. When he got to truth, I said: finally, here is a philosophical example! But this example quickly went astray, for Deleuze told us we must ask ourselves: who wants truth? why does one want truth? is the one who wants truth jealous?, etc. No doubt very interesting questions, but they don't touch on the very essence of truth, so perhaps they are not strictly philosophical questions.[11]

Deleuze's response to Alquié is illuminating, even if we make allowances for the element of academic propriety that is in play. After clarifying the way questions of *what* can often mask more urgent questions of *how*, for example, Kant's question "*what* is an object?" is secondary to *how* is an object possible?, Deleuze tells Alquié: "Your other criticism concerns me even more. For I believe entirely in philosophy's specificity, and, in fact, I get this conviction from you."[12] To elaborate his point, Deleuze reaffirms the irreducibility of the Idea to any of its actualizations, making the case for philosophy as a practice ultimately concerned with a specific object: the Idea, conceived as a virtual multiplicity inexhaustible in its riches.[13]

As we saw in Chapter 2, for Alquié philosophy was a practice that, while unable to grant unmediated access, nonetheless provided the intuition of an ineffable beyond or excess of being irreducible to the here and now of the world as it is presented to us. The titles of Alquié's books tell this story: *La Nostalgie de l'être, Le Désir de l'éternité*. For Alquié, any philosophy that sought to capture or fully express this excess was a philosophy in bad faith. On this score, Deleuze was not speaking in bad faith himself when he averred that he got this notion from Alquié. Indeed, he had concluded his talk with the following pronouncement: "The clear and distinct is the claim [*prétention*] of the concept in the Apollonian world of representation; but beneath representation there is always the Idea and its distinct-obscure ground [*fond*], a 'drama' beneath all logos."[14] Employing Nietzschean terms, Deleuze put forward a thesis nonetheless consistent with Alquié's own in *La Découverte métaphysique de l'homme chez Descartes*. Subtending the clear and distinct idea is an obscure ground, a "drama" that is never concluded or exhausted by its fleeting capture in the clear and distinct. This seems to be the sense of the virtual/actual relation as it is presented in this talk. The realm of the virtual is always in excess of its actualization.

Yet this notion of ideas as in excess of their conceptual expression squares awkwardly with arguments Deleuze put forward the next year in one of the most glowing reviews of his career: "Spinoza and the General Method of M. Gueroult."[15] Gueroult's book, Deleuze argued, "found[ed] the truly scientific study of Spinozism."[16] It possessed a double importance, as at once a study of Spinoza's *Ethics* and the culmination of Gueroult's own rationalist methodology in the history of philosophy. The engagement with Spinozism was not simply "one application [of this method] among others," following upon previous studies of Descartes, Malebranche, and Leibniz. Spinozism was where Gueroult's method found "its most adequate, most saturated, most exhaustive object."[17] By all appearances, Deleuze endorsed Gueroult's insistence on the nature of understanding in Spinozism, and "Spinozism's most radical thesis: absolute rationalism, founded on the adequation of our understanding to absolute knowledge [*savoir*]."[18] "Absolute rationalism, imposing the total intelligibility of God, the key of the total intelligibility of things, is thus for Spinozism the first article of faith."[19]

The similarities between Gueroult's account of Spinoza's philosophy and the one Deleuze published the same year are striking and illuminating. The most important of these shared positions is the insistence that the first eight propositions of the *Ethics*, which make the case for the substantiality of the attributes, do not serve as a mere heuristic to affirm the logical impossibility of more than one substance but are instead to be read as genetic components integral to the construction of a metaphysics in which the attributes Thought and Extension are really distinct. The point is technical, but important. What Deleuze and Gueroult agree on is the real substantial distinction of Thought and Extension, meaning that these two attributes are not mere categories of the understanding in a Kantian sense; they are and must be ontologically distinct.[20] It is their distinction that then allows them to relate without being reducible to, or subsumed within, one another. This distinction is the linchpin of Gueroult's own effort to read the process common to Spinoza's concept of substance, and the philosophical method that results, as one that is "genetic, in other words synthetic."[21] We can translate this formula into "ontological, in other words epistemological" and lose little of its sense, for the claim is that the ontological process of genesis and the epistemological process of synthesis are, from a philosophical point of view, always formally the *same* process. There is no transcendental subject or operator that enacts the synthesis needed to constitute discrete beings. Deleuze's problem with Kant is the same as Gueroult's; the synthetic components of the transcendental unity of apperception are posited without being ontologically explained, that is, without having their own genesis accounted for. Spinoza gives us "*absolute* rationalism" because he unifies epistemology and ontology, synthesis and genesis. The principle of sufficient reason knows no limits, including its own genesis as a principle within the immanent terms of Spinoza's philosophy.[22]

If anything, this system, with its insistence upon absolute intelligibility, countenances no notion of excess. The impossibility of excess in Being is the flip side of Spinoza's insistence that substance knows no privation. How does this square with Deleuze's claims in "The Method of Dramatization" for the Idea as a virtual multiplicity that is forever distinct-*obscure*, inexhaustible in its actualization? At this stage, it seems that Deleuze was sincere in his claim that the purpose of philosophy is to produce problems, and insoluble ones at that.

The point of revisiting the Gueroult/Alquié differend that was mapped in Chapter 2 is to emphasize its constitutive presence in Deleuze's own thought and to use it as a point of entry into what is arguably the guiding tension, in a historical and philosophical sense, of his enterprise: that between a Spinozist rationalism that affirms absolute intelligibility and a Heideggerian phenomenological existentialism that emphasizes movement and disjuncture, and imputes a philosophical value to the obscure. On this score, Deleuze's affirmation of Gueroult's project is no isolated incident. Peers have indicated how much Deleuze's thinking about method in the history of philosophy was shaped by Gueroult's example.[23] As we will see further on, Gueroult's study of Salomon Maimon was one of Deleuze's key references throughout his works, as was Jules Vuillemin's study of *The Kantian Legacy*, a book dedicated to Gueroult and that anticipates many of Deleuze's own concerns.[24] This influence of Gueroult, or a Gueroultian school, on Deleuze's thinking manifests itself in an uncompromising commitment to rationalism and an affinity for Spinozism.

But if Gueroult's role in Deleuze's thought provides us a way into the latter's Spinozism, what of Alquié's influence? Though it was presented as a comical aside, we should recall Jacques Derrida's comment in his interview with Dominique Janicaud that Alquié always felt that Heidegger had stolen his philosophical idea.[25] As a Sorbonne professor, Alquié served as something of an institutionally domesticated surrogate for Heidegger's influence in France, in that his readings of the metaphysicians of early modern philosophy by and large squared with the existential pathos of Heidegger's critique of metaphysics. As noted, Alquié was a formative influence on the generation of French thinkers that Janicaud deemed illustrative of the "theological turn" in French phenomenology, chief among them Michel Henry and Jean-Luc Marion.[26] One of Deleuze's most assiduous students and readers, Éric Alliez, has suggested that Deleuzean philosophy is itself a critical reflection of the "impossibility of phenomenology," that is, the conviction that phenomenology cannot but lead to a negative theology in its interminable displacement of the sources of givenness.[27] Against accounts of the phenomenological given, Deleuze proffers a philosophy of "transcendental empiricism," a "hyperrationalism" that yields a philosophical account in which everything is *produced* within an immanent conception of being, and nothing is ever *given* from an inaccessible exteriority.[28] Despite the recurrent presentation of this agenda as a rejection of phenomenology, Heidegger's philosophy, with its critical destruction of consciousness as an effect of more primordial modalities of being, was a fundamental condition of Deleuze's thought and not merely in a negative sense.

In recent years, philosophers have recognized the utility of considering Deleuze in relation to Heidegger. Shortly after Deleuze's death in 1995, Giorgio Agamben and Alain Badiou each published assessments that emphasized the unexpected commonalities between the two thinkers.[29] A sense of their related projects can be gained from the excerpts from "The Method of Dramatization" cited previously. Deleuze's emphasis on the question of "who" over "what" is one example. More suggestive still is Deleuze's claim that the existence of qualities in extension masks the intensive processes that generate them, a position that can be usefully compared with Heidegger's account of the present-at-hand as grounded in a more primordial readiness-to-hand.[30]

There is much to be gained through speculative comparisons of Deleuze and Heidegger on a philosophical level.[31] But the first aim here is historical: to account for the genesis of Deleuze's own thought and to argue for the underappreciated role of Heidegger's philosophy in it. Given the emphasis in the preceding chapters on Spinozism's resurgence as a critical response to phenomenology in France, it may seem odd that an assessment of Deleuze's Spinozism would be so concerned with his Heideggerianism. But this is precisely the point. For I intend to show the way in which Deleuze's engagement with Spinoza was initially shaped by a set of Heideggerian concerns, and how Deleuze's own thinking came to render each thinker unrecognizable in his refraction through the other, giving us a philosophy that could be alternately described as a rationalist Heideggerianism and an existentialist Spinozism. Deleuze's importance is clear from his placement at the terminal point of this inquiry. In terms of its broader aims, the argument is that French Spinozism is fundamentally transformed by Deleuze's work, and that the variant of this Spinozism that continues to inform much contemporary political thought often draws more on the Heideggerian elements that Deleuze brings to Spinozism than on the formal, subtractive, in a word *rationalist*, elements of Spinozism whose critical relation to phenomenology has been explored in the preceding chapters.

The structure of the presentation is as follows. In this first chapter, I attempt to reconstruct the genesis of Deleuze's own thinking by showing how and why the desire to move beyond Heidegger resulted in recourse to Spinoza. This involves first showing the generally underappreciated importance of Heideggerian philosophy, and its French variants, in the gestation of Deleuze's project. Second, I argue that Deleuze's turn to Spinoza as a way to move beyond Heidegger's problematic was in fact stimulated by the hostility to Heidegger's project evinced in the studies of post-Kantian philosophy produced by Gueroult and his student Jules Vuillemin, both of whom figure as prominent references throughout the first half of Deleuze's career.[32] Finally, I attempt to show that Deleuze's doctoral work on Spinoza in effect reads Spinoza not simply as a post-Kantian but as a post-Heideggerian. This effort results in an involution of Heidegger's and Spinoza's philosophies that produces a kind of hybrid Heidegger-Spinoza that would have been unthinkable for Jean Cavaillès, Martial Gueroult, or indeed Louis Althusser.

It is this very involution of Heidegger and Spinoza whose consequences will be charted throughout the following chapter, which is a reading of Deleuze's most significant philosophical works, *Difference and Repetition* and *The Logic of Sense*. The aim is to illuminate the way Deleuze's thinking moves between Heidegger and Spinoza in its own argumentative procedures. Deleuze is a notoriously slippery thinker; his fondness for the figures of folds and smooth spaces is of a piece with his most basic philosophical methodology. The sense of conceptual movement that results is one of a repetitive vacillation between Heideggerian and Spinozist positions that nonetheless moves forward in an increasingly robust critique of the predominant category of Heideggerian ontology in Deleuze's understanding: possibility. Moving through the figures of time, death, origins, negation, in each instance Deleuze attempts to undermine these concepts' ontological remit by showing them to be grounded in the category of "the possible," a concept that is, in Deleuze's rationalist view, inapplicable to ontology. What Deleuze offers in place of the possible's relation to the real is the putatively more primordial relation of the virtual to the actual. A guiding concern will be how well Deleuze's renewed understanding of the virtual and the actual, mediated through Spinoza's rationalism, manages to "transcend" the Heideggerian problematic that is its ostensible target of critique.

Following this reading of Deleuze's major works, I briefly consider Deleuze's post-1960s development to suggest that, even as he evinces an ever stronger commitment to Spinozism, his philosophy will not shake the constitutive dualism of the virtual/actual relation and its early debts to a selective appropriation of Heidegger's ontological difference between Being and beings. Yet I also submit that it is only in his later writings that Deleuze's most fundamental conviction, which is also his most fundamental debt to Spinoza, will acquire its greatest clarity: the primacy accorded to thought itself over any other mode of existence.

An Ubuesque Heidegger

In 1996, Agamben described Deleuze's commitment to "liquidating the values of consciousness" in the following terms: "Deleuze carries out the gesture of a philosopher who, despite Deleuze's lack of fondness for him, is certainly closer to Deleuze than any other representative of phenomenology in the twentieth century: Heidegger, the 'pataphysical' Heidegger of the wonderful article on Alfred Jarry, the Heidegger whom Deleuze, through this incomparable Ubuesque caricature, can finally reconcile himself."[33] Agamben is referring to one of Deleuze's very last writings, a short piece titled "An Unrecognized Precursor to Heidegger: Alfred Jarry."[34] Deleuze contends that the French absurdist's conception of 'pataphysics as standing in the same relation to metaphysics as the latter does to physics is an adumbration of Heidegger's project. Promising to take us beyond metaphysics, 'pataphysics will give us the science of the singular, the contingent, or the particular. In a similar vein, Badiou identified "the real question" for Deleuze as being "that of singularity: where and how does the singular meet up with the concept?"[35] Omitting references to Jarry,

Badiou nonetheless also recognized Deleuze's critical relation to Heidegger on this subject.[36]

Though Agamben treats Deleuze's ubuesque caricature of Heidegger as a late development, the unlikely comparison appears to have been part of Deleuze's thinking for a long time. In the late 1940s, Deleuze attended Jean Beaufret's courses on Heidegger at the lycée Henri-IV, where it was impressed upon students that the only way they would ever understand Heidegger was if they thought in German themselves.[37] Deleuze would have none of it, suggesting that the French Jarry not only understood Heidegger's thought but anticipated it. Deleuze took this impudent comparison public in a review of Kostas Axelos's *Vers un pensée planétaire*, first published in 1964 bearing the title "By Creating Pataphysics Jarry Opened the Way for Phenomenology."[38] Deleuze cited Jarry himself to justify the claim:

Pataphysics must be defined: "An epiphenomenon is what is added on [*se surajoute*] to a phenomenon. Pataphysics [...] is the science of what is added on to metaphysics, whether in it, or out of it, extending as far beyond metaphysics as metaphysics extends beyond physics. E.g.: the epiphenomenon often being the accident, pataphysics will be above all the science of the particular, even though it is said that science only deals with the general." Let us be clear for the specialists: Being [*l'Être*] is the epiphenomenon of all the beings [*étants*] which must be thought by the new thinker, who is an epiphenomenon of man.[39]

Though he intends it to capture, in a sardonic sense to be sure, the nature of Heidegger's project and the attempted synthesis of Heidegger and Marx being undertaken by Axelos, there are in fact few other passages in Deleuze's corpus that describe his own efforts as well as Jarry's definition does. Deleuze's attitude to phenomenology was thus by no means wholly derisive; he was impressed by the method but not by its objects, which all too often amounted to generic structures—of cognition, being, or comportment—rather than discrete singularities or events.[40] For Deleuze humor had a serious philosophical purpose. Years later, Deleuze described Foucault's relation to Heidegger in terms similar to his own: "It is not a question of taking away Heidegger's seriousness, but of rediscovering the imperturbable seriousness of Rousset (or Jarry). Ontological seriousness needs a diabolical or phenomenological humor."[41]

Deleuze's diabolical engagement with serious ontology had early roots. His very first publication in 1945 was a pastiche of Sartrean existentialism titled "Description of a Woman: For a Philosophy of the Sexed Other."[42] The text pursues a critique of the Sartrean model of love to be found in *Being and Nothingness*, a model in which love is not only unsexed but also decidedly not concrete, a battle over the possession of souls instead of an encounter between bodies. Deleuze offers an engagement with the concrete that evolves into a disquisition on the intercalated relation between interiority and exteriority. So what makes it diabolical, if not necessarily humorous? The article is primarily about women's cosmetics. "*Make-up* is the formation of [woman's] interiority. [. . .] Sometimes the exterior is internalized: the black mascara that surrounds the eye ensconces the look and renders it internal to itself. Sometimes the internal is externalized, while retaining, beyond its externalization, its internal being: reddened lips are the opening out of a thick interiority."[43] From here Deleuze moves on to fingernails, eyebrows, and even addresses the "mysterious and perfect *élan*" of freckles.[44]

Deleuze's Sartrean "moment"—if it can even be called that—was fleeting. Much more extensive was his consideration of Heidegger. The strongest evidence that Deleuze took Heidegger more seriously than his flippant allusions suggest is to be found in the surviving notes for a course taught in the 1956–57 school year at the lycée Louis-le-Grand in Paris, bearing the name "What Is Grounding?" (*Qu'est-ce que fonder?*).[45] An extensive interrogation of the problem of commencement in philosophy, that is, how one begins to think philosophically, and concurrently a historical exploration of the principle of sufficient reason, the course bears the traces of a very evident textual inspiration: Henry Corbin's translation and presentation of Heidegger in the collection titled *Qu'est-ce que la métaphysique?*[46] Scholars have recognized the important function of this volume, first published in 1938, in shaping the reception of Heidegger in France. In addition to the full translation of Heidegger's inaugural Freiburg lecture "Was ist Metaphysik?" and excerpts from division two of *Being and Time*, Corbin's volume contained a complete translation of the essay "Vom Wesen des Grundes" ("The Essence of Ground," translated into French as "Ce qui fait l'etre-essentiel d'un fondement ou 'raison'") and the fourth and final section of *Kant and the Problem of Metaphysics*. These latter two texts especially were clearly significant for Deleuze's course and his own thinking on the problem of grounding or *fondement*, as would become manifest in *Difference and Repetition* in the next decade.

As Christian Kerslake rightly remarks, "[T]he discussions of Heidegger in *What Is Grounding?* have no equivalent elsewhere in Deleuze's writings."⁴⁷ Kerslake identifies the following key passage:

With Heidegger the transcendental becomes a structure of empirical subjectivity itself. The transcendental is reduced to transcendence, to going beyond. Perhaps in that case transcendental subjectivity might seem to lose its importance. With Kant, it made knowledge possible because it submitted sensible objects to human knowledge. But the transcendental subject is what makes transcendence possible by submitting phenomena to this very operation of transcending. The transcendental subject ends up being simply that to which transcendence itself is immanent. With Heidegger, on the contrary, the distinction between transcendence and the transcendental finally disappears. With him they are identified to the point that one can no longer distinguish that which grounds from that which is grounded. Which is why the root of every grounding is freedom.⁴⁸

Heidegger no less than Kant before him identifies human freedom with transcendence, but the putative superiority of Heidegger's account is to make transcendence itself a component of lived experience, an instance that is temporal in its essence, grounding and being grounded at once. Kant had sought to develop an account of freedom reconcilable with the world of Newtonian necessity, but he accomplished this at a cost, making freedom unknowable by locating it in the noumenal sphere.

In his persistent attention to the Kant/Heidegger relation throughout this course, Deleuze depends not only on the contents of Corbin's volume but also on Corbin's own editorial presentation of the texts. As Ethan Kleinberg has noted, certain of Corbin's translation decisions helped contribute to the initial, anthropocentric account of Heidegger's thought that informed the earliest readings in France.⁴⁹ Rendering Dasein as "réalité-humain" sapped Heidegger's concept of much of its spatial connotation, though Heidegger approved the translation himself. Likewise the notion of a reality unique to the human subject helped contribute to a perceived consonance between Heideggerian Dasein and the Cartesian *cogito* in France. Stefanos Geroulanos's emphasis on the suitability of "réalité humain" as an expression that named the essential vacuity of that reality, effectively serving as a conceptual placeholder for other determinant processes, helps us understand how the *ego cogito*, too, could increasingly become a vacuous placeholder in a variety of projects.⁵⁰ Evincing a disregard for questions of subjectivity, Deleuze nonetheless participates in the reception of Heidegger elaborated in Geroulanos's account, deploying the German philosopher not as a celebrant of existential angst but as a conceptual way station to a more primordial ontology. Following Corbin, Deleuze expresses the need to reconceive the Kantian problem of transcendental conditions in terms of *structures* of existence indifferent to any presupposed categories of human subjectivity.

Deleuze's own revisionist attitude to Heideggerian ontology against any nominally humanist reading is adumbrated in Corbin's *avant-propos* to the collection. First, Corbin observes with regard to the study of Kant: "As a *repetition* of Kant's question, the research releases the Idea of a Metaphysics of *réalité-humaine* in a way that shows the worthlessness of the occasional charges of anthropologism or anthropocentrism thoughtlessly leveled at Heidegger."[51] Significantly, the emphasis on "repetition" in this passage is Corbin's. More important still is the way that Corbin's assessment reads Heidegger's repetition of Kant's question as geared toward producing something different from Kant's answer, though still conditioned by it. In other words, difference results from repetition, or, as Deleuze will argue, repetition is the temporal form that difference takes. Finally, there is Corbin's gloss on Heidegger's *ekstasis*: "Ex-sistance is ek-statique: the triple *ekstasis* of Time's temporality is the very structure of its transcendence."[52] A major portion of *Difference and Repetition* will be devoted precisely to an account of what Deleuze terms the "three syntheses of time."[53] The first synthesis is that of habit, the "living present" of passive experience. The second synthesis is that grounded in memory; in this instance each present is merely the most contracted moment of a virtual past. The third synthesis is what Deleuze terms "the pure and empty form of time." It is the site of Nietzsche's eternal return, the abyss that grounds time as lived present and as retained past while keeping it open to the future. The eternal return as the pure and empty form of time is what makes possible a gesture that inscribes itself in a future created by the gesture itself.

These themes will be fleshed out in the next chapter when we return to the contents of *Difference and Repetition*. But the most urgent issue for the moment is simply to highlight the importance of Heidegger for this component of Deleuze's thought. To be sure, Nietzsche is Deleuze's major reference, and Kierkegaard is given a significant amount of attention as well. But each of these engagements is mediated through Heidegger's problematic. In this sense, Deleuze's project is as much a result of the arrival of Heidegger in France as the thinkers covered in Kleinberg's account of the "generation existential" and Geroulanos's assessment of French antihumanism. Rather than being indebted to those thinkers most often associated with the first reading of Heidegger, chiefly Sartre and Kojève, for whom the problematic of subjectivity, if not humanism, was the primary concern, Deleuze has much more in common with the readings pursued by Emmanuel Levinas and Maurice Blanchot. Though Levinas is conspicuously absent from virtually all of Deleuze's work, Blanchot is a guiding reference whenever Deleuze considers the relationship between death and possibility.[54] The common link between Levinas, Blanchot, and Deleuze is an emphasis on the structural components of time as entailing an inescapable opening toward a future. The signal difference between Levinas and Deleuze on this score would be that whereas Levinas reads this structure as an ontological condition to which one passively submits, for Deleuze the opening to the future is always the result of creative forces that are in excess of their subjective representation.

A short detour through one of Deleuze's richest texts will help make this contrast clearer. In one of his early writings, *Time and the Other*, Levinas laid the groundwork for his later reversal of Heidegger's concept of Dasein's authentic appropriation of time by emphasizing the opening toward otherness as an intrinsic feature of time itself. The openness toward otherness was a result of the fact that the infinite was ontologically anterior to the finite, providing the basic structures of finite existence as grounded in a constitutive openness. In 1967, Deleuze published an article in *Critique*, "Michel Tournier and the World without Others,"[55] devoted to Tournier's retelling of *Robinson Crusoe* in his novel *Vendredi; ou Les Limbes de la Pacifique*.[56] Deleuze's assessment, which references Sartre but makes no explicit mention of Levinas despite its evocation of the positions of *Time and the Other*, maintains that otherness is a structural and ontological condition of existence but that in the end it is a second-order one. Tournier's fiction complicates Levinasian ontology by showing that beneath the phenomenon of structured otherness, a phenomenon as endemic to existence as the effects of representation, there is a more fundamental "world without others" generating these effects. The core of Deleuze's perversion of Levinas—and it is fitting that Deleuze's account of Tournier's Robinson begins with a discussion of perversion—is a kind of flattening, or spatialization of Levinas's account of temporality, into a world devoid of distinction and the discrete. The "world without others" is a structural impossibility for Levinas, since one could never occupy a temporal existence that is not constitutively open to the otherness inherent in temporal unfolding. But Deleuze insists upon the value of Tournier's "fiction," which, by taking place on a desert island completely removed from the world, provides the lineaments of an existence lacking the "other-structure" of the perceptive field, allowing us to "penetrate into a particular informal realm."[57] Deleuze readily admits that Tournier has given us a "necessary fiction."[58] He cites and endorses William James's contention that a priori otherness is "the oxygen of possibility."[59] Nonetheless, Tournier's fiction is necessary in two senses. It is necessarily fictional in that it could never take place in the world of lived experience. But it is also a fiction that serves as the only viable base of rationalist philosophy in that it presents a world in which precisely there is no longer the human artifact of possibility, a world that Deleuze significantly describes as one lacking the "laws which structure the order of the real in general and the succession of time."[60] He concludes his account ambiguously:

> The world of the pervert is a world without others, and thus a world without the possible. The Other is that which renders possible [*Autrui, c'est ce qui possibilise*]. The perverse world is a world in which the category of the necessary has completely replaced that of the possible: a *strange Spinozism* where the oxygen lacks to the benefit of a more elementary energy and a rarefied air (Sky-Necessity).[61]

This detour through Deleuze's reading of Tournier has served to illustrate two points. First, it shows the extent to which Deleuze's own engagements were conditioned by a Heidegger mediated through Corbin's reading, along with Sartre's, Levinas's, and Blanchot's. But it also shows how these problems dovetail with Deleuze's engagement with Spinozism, positing the latter as the philosophy best suited to the ontological field that Deleuze believes is anterior to the one described in Heideggerian philosophy. What is most striking about this conclusion is the way that Deleuze imbues Spinozism, however "strange," with an ethical ambiguity. Who could breathe this rarefied air? Deleuze does not will or call for a "world without others," even as he indirectly questions the philosophical utility of a project that posits the existential phenomena of otherness and lived temporality as its primary concerns.

One final key text from the earliest years of Deleuze's career shows the centrality of this critical motive to his effort: his review of Jean Hyppolite's account of Hegel's *Logic, Logic and Existence*.⁶² Deleuze assents to most of Hyppolite's reading, especially its critique of the primacy accorded to subjectivity in Kojève's influential account. For his part, Hyppolite sought to return the focus to the account of substance in Hegel's philosophy, arguing that contradiction was an intrinsic component of existence and that the contradiction constitutive of subjectivity was merely an epiphenomenon of this more foundational movement. Nonetheless, Deleuze concludes his review by questioning whether Hyppolite's positing of contradiction as the pinnacle of difference, difference taken to its limit, is itself not reflective of an anthropocentric bias in Hyppolite's Hegel. Deleuze asks, "[C]an we not make an ontology of difference that does not go all the way to contradiction, because contradiction would be less than difference and not more?" Deleuze's questions then take a more pointed cast: "[I]s it the same thing to say that Being expresses itself and that it contradicts itself? [. . .] Does Hyppolite not ground a theory of expression wherein difference is expression itself, and contradiction is only its phenomenal aspect?"⁶³

The title of Deleuze's thesis on Spinoza, whose composition was begun in the years following the publication of this review in 1954, is *Spinoza and the Problem of Expression*.⁶⁴ It is thus via a return to Spinoza that Deleuze seeks a nonanthropocentric and nonphenomenal account of difference as expression itself. In his critique of Deleuze's thought, Badiou suggests that Deleuze's ambivalent relationship to Heidegger's philosophy is a result of his recognition that Heidegger had gone only "half-way" in his account of ontological difference, limiting it to the intentional structures of the human experience of the world that had been its own point of departure.⁶⁵ What Deleuze shared with Heidegger was the concern to show that that which grounds and that which is grounded must be considered in their inseparability as a fundamental structure of existence. But Heidegger's shortcoming was similar to that of Hyppolite's Hegel. In seeking to move beyond Kant, Heidegger accepted as unimpeachable certain elements nominally intrinsic to human experience, most important, the thematic of finitude. When Deleuze says that Alfred Jarry has anticipated Heidegger with 'pataphysics, there is no doubt that his tongue is firmly in cheek. But the point remains a serious one. In effect, Deleuze mobilizes Jarry's absurdist example to promote his own rationalist project, which aims to be a philosophy not of generic forms or structures but of singular instances or events. The apparent tendencies toward irrationalism in Heidegger's project are to be recuperated as tendencies toward an even more foundational rationalism subtending the irrationality of existence.

A Post-Kantian Spinoza

Admittedly, a return to rationalism in Heidegger's wake seems an unlikely project. Here some bibliographic reconstruction helps make sense of why Deleuze sought the antidote to the impasses of Heideggerianism in rationalism itself rather than in ethics, as Levinas would do, or in historical epistemes, as in the case of Foucault's project. Concurrent with his engagement with Heidegger, Deleuze was working through the writings of some of Heidegger's fiercest critics in the French context. These writings were those of the "Gueroult school," which included, in addition to Gueroult's own texts, those of his student Jules Vuillemin. For Gueroult and Vuillemin both, the rehabilitation of rationalism first involved an interrogation of post-Kantianism. The arguments pursued by these two scholars would be foundational for Deleuze's own study of Spinoza, where the desires of Salomon Maimon and J. G. Fichte in particular to reunite the domains of epistemology and ontology (or metaphysics) torn asunder by Kant would be read as answered *avant la lettre* by the seventeenth-century post-Cartesian, Spinoza.

Heidegger's primary virtue for Deleuze was his resumption of the Kantian project. Deleuze's words from his course on Heidegger emphasize this point: "The renewed encounter with the post-Kantians in Heidegger's book on Kant invites us to enact a repetition of the Kantian enterprise."[66] In Deleuze's renewed encounter with post-Kantian philosophy, Maimon and Fichte loom large. These thinkers are key references both in *Nietzsche and Philosophy*, a book concerned to develop a post-Kantian notion of critical philosophy, and in *Difference and Repetition*.[67] Moreover, whenever Maimon and Fichte are cited in Deleuze's work, it is almost always with reference to Gueroult and Vuillemin. The books in question are Gueroult's two doctoral works, *L'Évolution et la structure de la doctrine de la science chez Fichte* and *La Philosophie transcendantale de Salomon Maimon*, and Vuillemin's *L'Héritage kantien et la copernicienne révolution: Fichte—Cohen—Heidegger*.

The central arguments of Vuillemin's account will be striking to any reader familiar with Deleuze's project.[68] It is likely that Vuillemin's book, published the year prior to Deleuze's "What Is Grounding?," was as much of an influence on that course as the Corbin volume was. Vuillemin's project is to interrogate the "success" of Kant's Copernican Revolution in philosophy by tracing three successive post-Kantian efforts to render Kant more coherent than his own system appears to allow. Hegel had criticized Kant for the fundamental tension in his philosophy between the determinate quality of nature and the fact that human freedom, though ostensibly grounded in nature, was itself somehow exempt from determinism. Vuillemin's claim is that post-Kantian, neo-Kantian, and existentialist philosophies—exemplified by Fichte, Hermann Cohen, and Heidegger, respectively—each tried to render transcendental philosophy consistent by taking it upon themselves to complete the Copernican Revolution through a renewed philosophical account of constitutive finitude that would avoid recourse to the *arrière-monde* of an ungraspable metaphysical infinite in which this finitude might be grounded.

Part of the appeal of Vuillemin's critical account is the way he reads each stage of this post-Kantian effort as drawing upon a different component of the *Critique of Pure Reason*. For Fichte, the resolution to Kant's problems is to be found in the account of the transcendental *dialectic* of ideas; for Cohen, the logic of the *analytic* is paramount; for Heidegger, it will be the intuition of the *aesthetic*. Vuillemin's claim is that in each instance the philosopher in question tries to show that grounding philosophy in one of the other components cannot avoid invoking some metaphysical infinite in which to ground its own pronouncements. Yet in each instance the result is simply an ongoing displacement of the problem. There is a persistent failure to "achieve" the Copernican Revolution in that a metaphysical principle, a principle that is not itself explained but that does the explaining, always remains determinant in the last instance; the ego for Fichte, logic for Cohen, time for Heidegger—all are *explanans* and never *explananda*. In effect, Vuillemin reads Heidegger as a reductio ad absurdum of Kantian philosophy. "It is totally natural that the history of interpretations and the descent toward intuition are sustained as the deepening of the concept of finitude."[69] Vuillemin's conclusion is a powerful indictment of any philosophy that takes this finitude as its point of departure:

Since time must become originary and constituent, since we have been unable to find it in departing from the *Cogito*, neither in morality, nor nature, nor existence, then perhaps we must seriously consider coming back on this side of

Copernicus. Perhaps what philosophy needs is not a Copernican, but a Ptolemaic Revolution! Maybe then the displacements will cease, and philosophy will no longer need to replace knowledge with faith, for it will have effectively begun when it substitutes for the human *Cogito* in a universe of gods, human work in the world of men.[70]

But for the humanism that remains, it would be hard to overstate the resonance of this critical conclusion with Deleuze's own efforts, as well as the similarities between Vuillemin's reading of Kant, which pits various components of his project against the others, and Deleuze's own. Indeed, in Deleuze's short book on Kant, the guiding thread is the way that each faculty must be grasped in its playful rapport with the other two. The conclusion to be drawn from Kant is that this play is itself interminable, the fundamental movement of a thought irreducible to any of its components.[71] But Vuillemin's chief concern is to reassert the claims of rationalist philosophy and science, the latter of which is understood, notwithstanding the Marxist connotations, as the site of "human work in the world of men" against the strictures of Kantian critique. The irony of Kant's strictures is that they leave the door open to theological accounts of the infinite that fill the void left by the abrogation of a philosophical one.

It is this desire to bring concerns usually left to theology wholly within the remit of philosophy that Vuillemin owes to Gueroult, the mentor to whom Vuillemin's volume is dedicated. Along with Vuillemin's book, Gueroult's engagements with Fichte, and above all with Maimon, were a vital resource for Deleuze's thought. It was noted at the outset of this chapter that Deleuze's sympathy with Gueroult could best be described as a philosophical commitment to insisting upon synthesis and genesis as coextensive processes. A guiding concern of Gueroult's study of Maimon is the effort to rethink the category of the sensible *given* in Kantian philosophy in terms of determinate *production*. In other words, that which is given to the understanding must not be understood as simply given without cause but must be grasped as something that is produced in itself. On this score, Maimon's Spinozism—that is, his effort to read the facts of epistemic synthesis and ontic genesis as coextensive processes—is striking.[72] In Maimon's own words, "The understanding cannot think any object [. . .] except as a process. In effect, since the task of the understanding is nothing other than *thinking*, which is to say, to produce unity in diversity, it can think only inasmuch as it indicates the rule or mode of genesis."[73] The differentials inherent in all sensibility were in Maimon's view the very sites of Kant's noumena:

> These noumena are Ideas of reason, which act as principles of explication of the genesis of objects according to certain rules of the understanding. When I say, for example, *red* is different from *green*, the pure concept of the understanding, difference, must not be considered as the relation of sensible qualities (for otherwise the Kantian question *quid juris* would remain hanging), but must be considered either, according to Kant's theory, as the relation of their spaces as *a priori* forms, or, according to my theory, as the relation of their differentials, which are Ideas of *a priori* reason.[74]

For Gueroult it is this element of Maimon's thinking that accounts for its coherence as an absolute idealism, the forerunner to the absolute rationalism Gueroult will present via Spinoza several decades later.

This absolute idealism is clearly manifested in Maimon's claim that "the understanding does not simply have the power to *think* general relations between determined objects of the intuition, but the power to *determine* objects by relations."[75] Gueroult's sympathy with Maimon is clear, even if he questions the efficacy of Maimon's solution, which seems to end in panpsychism. Yet *Difference and Repetition* and *The Logic of Sense* can be read together as an extensive endorsement and elaboration of this post-Kantian thesis. A similar thesis will be in play in Gueroult's reading of Fichte, wherein Maimon's influence on the latter is stressed. When Deleuze speaks of Fichte's "profound Spinozism,"[76] it is this line of argument that he has in mind. It is this striking commonality of concern between post-Kantian philosophy and Spinozism that leads Deleuze back to Spinoza as the ideal source for confronting these philosophical problems. Though its first volume was not published until 1968, Gueroult's mammoth study of Spinoza was in effect produced over a series of lectures at the Collège de France beginning in the late 1950s and early 1960s, the moment Deleuze was producing the first draft of his own study of Spinoza and thinking through the fundamental issues of *Difference and Repetition*. In Deleuze's reading, the post-Kantian "self" for Maimon and Fichte plays the same role as "Substance" in Spinoza's philosophy, as a relational *site* of genesis. In his attempt to progress beyond Kantianism, Deleuze deliberately regresses to a metaphysics prior to Kantianism, with the result that what was simply a site of epistemological synthesis in Kant's philosophy becomes formally transformed into a site of ontological genesis. In *The Logic of Sense*, Deleuze writes, "Kant's genius lies in his showing that the self is the Idea which corresponds to the category of substance. Indeed, the self conditions not only the attribution of this category to the phenomena of internal sense, but to those of outer sense as well, in virtue of their no less great immediacy."[77] While it is unlikely that Deleuze was very familiar with the contents of Kant's *Opus Postumum*, we can nonetheless be struck by the similarity of Deleuze's own words to those of the aging Kant:

> We cannot know any objects, neither in us nor as found outside of us, except in so far as we place in ourselves the act of knowing according to certain laws. The mind (*Geist*) of man is Spinoza's God (which concerns the formal element of all sensible objects). And transcendental idealism is realism in the absolute sense.[78]

In Fichte's absolute idealism, the I is self-positing and distinguishes itself from the world, the domain of the not-I. But it is nonetheless this primary positing that accounts for intelligibility as such. Substance performs a similar function in Spinoza's philosophy as an inaugural idea.[79] What's important about the category of substance in this reading is that, like Fichte's absolute ego or that of the later Kant, the category is one without content in itself. Rather, its role is as an auto-positional function that grounds the auto-genesis of rational thought. If the Kantian self and the concept of substance traditionally associated with rationalist metaphysics are each compromised by their status as conceptual "black boxes," then Deleuze's philosophy is an attempt to render the "black box" superfluous, to take leave of inputs and outputs in favor of pure process as such.[80]

It is the convergence of these concerns, a Heidegger-inspired desire to develop an *ontology* that conceives of being as a verb, as a process irreducible to its concrete instantiations, on the one hand, and, on the other, an uncompromising commitment to a *rationalism* that refuses to let the integrity of our theoretical grasp of being be compromised by these processes but instead sustained by them, that accounts for the idiosyncratic reading of Spinoza that Deleuze develops in his doctoral work. By taking the "problem of expression" as his central concern, Deleuze announces the ingenuity of his approach. Nowhere in the myriad definitions that the *Ethics* comprises is "expression" defined. Yet the verb form of the concept appears on the very first page in the definition of "God": "By God I mean an absolutely infinite being; that is, a substance consisting of infinite attributes, each of which *expresses* eternal and infinite essence."[81] The analysis that follows from

Deleuze's opening gambit verges on the scholastic, and a comprehensive explication of it would be beyond the parameters of this study. But, to conclude this genealogy of Deleuze's strange Spinozism, his minor doctoral thesis requires an assessment that illuminates its fundamental motivations and accounts for the peculiar "post-Heideggerian" Spinoza that results.

Spinoza and the Problem of Expression

As soon as it is introduced in Deleuze's argument, the concept "expression" is immediately bifurcated into two senses. The virtue of this concept for Deleuze is that it provides a single name for two heterogeneous processes, *explication* and *implication*.[82] Deleuze argues that in Spinozism the modes, as affections of substance, effectively explicate substance. But it is equally true that each modal modification implicates substance in turn. The usual connotations of these two words are fully in force in Deleuze's reading; substance is effectively elaborated through, that is, explicated *by*, the modes. But the modes implicate substance, in that they impinge on its putative autonomy, never leaving it unchanged. Existence itself is implicated by every discrete modal act. But the common center of these Latinate expressions—*pli*, or "fold"—is equally essential for Deleuze's ontological argument. Deleuze's point is that in Spinoza substance is in an incessant state of unfolding (*explication*) via the modes, and folding back in on itself (*implication*) as a result of these modal affectations. Expression captures both of these senses in one concept and thus serves as the term for the two-way relation between substance and its modes.[83] But how then do the attributes—the middle term of Spinoza's tripartite metaphysics—serve to mediate this relation?

As indicated earlier, Deleuze follows Gueroult in reading the key attributes in Spinoza's system, Thought and Extension, as formal categories indistinguishable from substance itself except in a purely heuristic sense. In other words, Thought and Extension are substantial in themselves, whereas the technical category of "Substance" is simply the *idea* of their substantiality registered as the necessity of their coexistence in a single, unitary frame. The attributes are the substantial forms through which this unitary frame, equivalent to the totality of existence, "expresses itself."[84] Deleuze's Spinoza is thus marked by two constitutive dualisms. There is the dualism of Thought and Extension, two "substances" that in themselves are formally, and thus really, distinct from one another. But there is also the dualism between substance/attributes, on the one hand, taken as a unitary category, and modes, on the other. Regarding the first dualism, Deleuze is at pains to put forth two claims constituting a single argument. First, Thought and Extension are not only wholly distinct but also wholly infinite, in their kind. Second, any distinction that takes place uniquely within one of these attributes, that is, a distinction that is not registered in the other, can be understood only as a purely quantitative, and in no way a qualitative, distinction.[85] The argument is that the attributes of substance, as ontologically infinite and impervious to real distinction within themselves, are intrinsically *common*. They are the ontological ground for the commonality of existence. Anything that happens in matter is common with all matter, and anything that happens in thought is common with all thought. But for anything to effectively "happen" at all—in the sense of an event registered in thought or inscribed in matter—thought and matter must relate to one another. As we will see later when Deleuze addresses the relation of the quantitative to the qualitative in *Difference and Repetition*, the move from merely quantitative distinction to a qualitative distinction *must* involve *both* attributes in order to take place. In other words, it is the ontologically grounded relation between the autonomous attributes Thought and Extension that serves as the mechanism of qualitative change as such.

The second dualism, between substance/attributes and modes, is best grasped as the two "kinds" of nature in play in Spinoza's philosophy, *natura naturans* and *natura naturata*, that is, nature as a *verb* (nature *naturing*) and nature as a *noun* (nature *natured*). In his critique of Deleuze's philosophy as a theophany that aims to dissolve creaturely existence in favor of the act of creating itself, Peter Hallward has emphasized the significance of this distinction for making sense of Deleuze's appropriation of Bergson's distinction between the virtual and the actual. Hallward writes, "Much of the essential difference between virtual and actual (along with the key to Deleuze's understanding of *essence* and its homophonic cognate *sens*, or sense) follows directly from Spinoza's celebrated distinction of an active or creative *naturans* from a passive or created *naturata*."[86] Hallward's claim is that for Deleuze's Spinoza it is always substance itself that is functionally *active* and that its modal manifestations—which, to be clear, include the category of the human being, a "finite mode" in Spinoza's system—can thus be regarded only as passive effects of the cause on which they depend. While capturing its explicative nature, Hallward underplays the other meaning of expression in Deleuze's account of Spinoza, the *implicative* nature of modes and the changes they implement in substance itself.

Nonetheless, the value of Hallward's assessment is that it highlights the similarity between an operative dualism of Deleuze's Spinozism and the key dualism of Heidegger's philosophy, the "ontological difference" between Being and beings (*Sein/l'Être* and *die Seiendes/les étants*). On the one hand, the distinction between substance and its modal affections in Spinozism could be read as an example of the relation of essence to existence that is the target of so much of Heidegger's thinking. The way Hallward presents this relation leaves Deleuze open to precisely this charge. Modes *exist*, but only as expressions of the essence of substance. On the other hand, what we find in Deleuze's Spinoza is something strangely similar to Heidegger's ontological difference, with Being as a verb, that is, the domain of ontology, read in terms of Spinoza's *natura naturans*, and *natura naturata* referring to the realm of the ontic. In effect, Deleuze reads Spinoza to develop a recuperated concept of substance that evades the Heideggerian critique and that as a result can complete or "go beyond" Heidegger's own philosophical project while retaining its insights concerning the nature of difference. To understand how the version of Spinozist substance on offer from Deleuze might evade Heidegger's critique, we must first grasp how this critique works in Heidegger's thought.

In his assessment of Descartes in *Being and Time* Heidegger showed the error of any philosophy that sought to ground itself in substance. Recourse to substance for Heidegger was one example of a metaphysics of presence, of *ousia*, that committed the signal error of mistaking the merely *ontic* for the *ontological*. Heidegger focuses his critique of Descartes on the equivocal nature of Being in the latter's philosophy. "Because 'Being' is not in fact accessible *as an entity*, it is expressed through attributes—definite characteristics of the entities under consideration, characteristics which themselves are."[87] But the substance subtending these expressions remains unclear; "the idea of substantiality [. . .] gets passed off as something incapable of clarification." In a riposte that appears to apply as well to Spinoza as it does to Descartes, Heidegger argues:

Because something ontical is made to underlie the ontological, the expression "*substantia*" functions sometimes with a signification which is ontological, sometimes with one which is ontical, but mostly with one which is hazily ontico-ontological.

Behind this slight difference of signification, however, there lies hidden a failure to master the basic problem of Being.[88]

Several pages later, Heidegger will develop the implications of this judgment in his account of the "who" of Dasein:

[I]f the Self is conceived 'only' as a way of Being of this entity, this seems tantamount to volatilizing the real 'core' of Dasein. Any apprehensiveness however which one may have about this gets its nourishment from the perverse assumption that the entity in question has at bottom the kind of Being which belongs to something present-at-hand, even if one is far from attributing it to the solidity of an occurrent corporal Thing. Yet man's *'substance'* is not spirit as a synthesis of soul and body; it is rather *existence*.[89]

In effect, then, for Heidegger "substance"—however qualified in scare quotes—becomes a process; it is the temporal phenomenon of *existence*. As the development of Heidegger's own thinking will make clear, being effectively *is* time, lacking any kind of content or substance in-itself of which it might be the expression.

What does any of this have to do with Deleuze's study of Spinoza? There, too, substance is paradoxically evacuated of substantiality. The theoretical payoff for understanding the attributes to be substantial in themselves is that it means that substance per se, as an operative, grounding concept in Spinoza's system, is purely *ideational*. It is formal, without content in itself, the singular concept that allows for the articulation of a plurality of substantial attributes and the modal variations that supply their contents. If for Heidegger, substance is ultimately a process, for Spinoza, substance is first an idea. On the very first page of his book, Deleuze signals the bearing of his reading on the concerns of post-Kantian philosophy by suggesting that "the idea of expression contains within it all the difficulties relating to the unity of substance and the diversity of the attributes."[90] As becomes clear over the course of his study, "the idea of expression" is synonymous with three other interchangeable terms of Spinoza's *Ethics*: God, Nature, and, indeed, substance. That these terms are qualified together as an "idea" seems to fly in the face of Spinoza's ostensible materialism. Yet it is precisely Deleuze's point to emphasize that the principle *Deus sive Natura* (God, that is Nature) is to be read above all as an idea, one that allows us to *think* unity in the substantial diversity of the attributes without recourse to an outside or an extrinsic phenomenological ground.

As such, substance's status as a "hazily ontico-ontological" category becomes a virtue in Deleuze's reading in that it mediates the ontic and the ontological domains. Substance in its ideal character is a bridge between the formal categories of the attributes, which Deleuze reads as *active* forms, expressing the "essence" of substance as an idea (*natura naturans*), and the modes as the material instantiations or concrete concepts that exist as expressions of this essence (*natura naturata*). The twist in Deleuze's conception is that the modes, as the "content" of the attributes' "forms," retrojectively "activate" or implicate the very forms that were deemed to serve as the ontological condition of modal existence. This conceptual maneuver abjures—is in fact logically inconsistent with—any linear conception of temporality, and the result is a willful embrace of the Spinozist injunction to view things "under the aspect of eternity." In the recuperation of substance as the concept correlative to the process expressed in this "Idea," what we find is a deliberate rejoinder to Heidegger's project, the latter of which seeks to do away with substance altogether as one variant of a misleading metaphysics of presence. If we might describe Heidegger as giving us a philosophy of modality all the way down, an account of *modes* or *ways* of being as anterior to and supervening upon substantial incarnation, with Deleuze's Spinoza we have an account that conceives modality precisely in its interminable rapport with the substantial attributes of Thought and Extension. It is as if Heidegger has given us an untenable philosophy because it seeks to present a world of pure modality, wherein *that which is modified* is forever held in conceptual abeyance. But for Deleuze, the notion that there is nothing for the modes to effectively modify is as nonsensical as Spinoza's proposition that "Substance is by nature anterior to its affections" would be for Heidegger.[91] It is the auto-positional idea of substance, thinking the relation of these attributes "under the aspect of eternity," that prevents the infinite displacement of ground that Vuillemin saw in Heidegger's project as leaving the door open to negative theology. Deleuze uses Spinoza to reassert the primacy of the rational idea as the antecedent ground necessary to make sense of modal existence, human or otherwise. At the same time, he wants to retain for modality the vibrancy and philosophical importance that Heidegger has granted it. This explains why he is at such pains to maintain the *implicative*, or active, nature of the modes alongside their *explicative*, or passive, nature as mediums of expression.

But the question remains: Does refracting Spinoza through this Heideggerian lens produce an honest reading of the *Ethics*? In the conclusion of *Difference and Repetition*, Deleuze writes that "all that Spinozism needed to make univocity an object of pure affirmation"—that is, to make his ontology operative—"was to *make substance turn around the modes*."[92] This line is telling, for it suggests that Deleuze is perfectly aware of the primacy accorded to substance in Spinoza's system and the consequent diminution of modalities of existence that results. In other words, Deleuze implicitly admits that Spinozism needs to be complemented by the Heideggerian understanding of modality in order to reach its own fruition. This proposition also casts an illuminating light on the structure of *Spinoza and the Problem of Expression*, making clear that Deleuze himself has effectively performed the much-needed operation—"making substance turn around the modes"—that was lacking in Spinoza's *Ethics*. This explains why the third and final part of Deleuze's study is devoted to the "Theory of the Finite Mode."[93] Here the "finite mode" is read as a reinvigorated, substantially grounded reformulation of Heideggerian Dasein, except for one vital difference, one that reveals equally that Spinozism entails for Deleuze a modification of Heidegger's project, just as Heidegger modified Spinoza.

Where for Heidegger Dasein is ultimately a discrete and personal phenomenon, characterized by its essential "mineness," Deleuze-Spinoza's "finite mode" exists as such only through its participation in the foundational "common notions" of Thought and Extension.[94] The point of Deleuze's baroque discussion of the difference between the purely quantitative distinction within each attribute, and the qualitative distinction that occurs through their relation, acquires its full bearing only in this third section of his study. Modal existence, insofar as it evinces a qualitative development, that is, things do really change, has as its most primordial condition the repeatedly iterated two-way relation between the infinite attributes of Thought and Extension. In other words, each discrete, qualitative event—what Deleuze calls singularities—owes its uniqueness not to a *rupture* with what is common to all being but precisely to its status as an individuated *expression* of what is common to all being, the formal attributes Thought and Extension. This is the utmost sense of the "science of the singular" that Deleuze heralded in Jarry's anticipation of Heidegger's effort. Spinoza, more than any other thinker, gives Deleuze the theoretical resources to effectively "have it both ways," that is, to have a philosophy that sacrifices nothing of the discrete quality of singularities as such but that also grasps each singularity in its effective relation to the radically expansive, and consistent, continuity of substance qua Thought and Extension in which it is situated. The result is a philosophy that decouples singularity from the anthropomorphic (and -centric) essence of Dasein. Singularities are infinitely plural in their manifestation, and there is no philosophical reason to privilege the unique singularity of one human being—Dasein—over singularities infinitely larger and infinitely smaller than this one discrete instance among infinite others.

The radical involution of Heideggerian Dasein that Deleuze undertakes via Spinoza is best captured in a formula that Deleuze uses at a key moment in *The Logic of Sense*: "the splendor of the '*on*'" (*on* = the French impersonal pronoun).[95] For Heidegger, Dasein's utmost imperative is to distinguish itself from the impersonality of *das Man*. For Deleuze, it is this primordial impersonality that is the occluded condition of Dasein's or the "finite mode's" very existence as a phenomenally discrete singularity. Rediscovery of this essential commonality, through the rationally discovered *common* forms of Thought and Extension, is the fundamental aim of Deleuze's rationalist reading of Spinozism. The ethical implications of this position are by and large underdeveloped in *Spinoza and the Problem of Expression*. But the contours of Deleuze's ontological project are clear. In order to produce a Spinozism that is truly "post-Heideggerian," Deleuze must recuperate a notion of the infinite as anterior to the finite temporality regnant in Heidegger's exquisite account of modal existence. This task, tantamount to a fundamental reversal of Heideggerianism, is the project of *Difference and Repetition* and *The Logic of Sense*. To accomplish this task, however, Deleuze must in a perverse way follow Heidegger's own methodological lead. The vital difference is that where Heidegger pursued his goal through a wholesale destruction of the metaphysics of presence, Deleuze devotes his energy to the destruction of another metaphysical category, one deemed to be much more tenacious in its grip on the human intellect: possibility as such.

7

Nothing Is Possible

The Strange Spinozism of Gilles Deleuze

> There is no longer any possible: a relentless Spinozism.
>
> Deleuze, "The Exhausted," 1992[1]

Althusser's intransigent refusal to compromise with the methods and insights of phenomenology resulted in a Spinozist rationalism that tended toward increasing abstraction and the development of a "philosophy without object" designed to distinguish science from ideology. In this, the remit of Althusser's philosophy was primarily discursive. Philosophy never determined its own objects, but it was a mode of thought that allowed one to determine if a discourse was "ideological"—manipulating its terms to coordinate with the dictates of transcendental criteria—or "scientific"—developing its terms as a consequence of immanent rational criteria. In this regard, it recused itself of the ontological problematic that had become the predominant theme of French phenomenology, focusing instead on the implications, political and otherwise, of various discursive arrangements. Where Althusser rejected the ontological turn that dominated postwar French thought, Deleuze embraced it and made it his own in a quite literal sense.

The crucial difference between Althusser and Deleuze was that, for the latter, Spinozism was not a philosophical mode that could function independently of phenomenology, as if it were able to demarcate and occupy a philosophical space extrinsic to its fundamental concerns. For Deleuze, Spinozism was the means for working through the phenomenological tradition in order to produce philosophical conclusions that could not be reached with either Spinozism or phenomenology alone. Like others before him, Deleuze surmised that the phenomenological method, left to its own devices, had a tendency to become stuck in solipsism. For Deleuze, the persistent desire to determine the conditions of *possible* experience, from Kant to Heidegger, resulted in the occlusion of a philosophical account of the conditions of *real* experience.[2] Previous Spinozists criticized recourse to transcendental structures whose reason for existence remained obscure but that were nevertheless charged with accounting for the possibility of possibility itself. Deleuze instead sought to develop a philosophy destructive of the concept of possibility as such. His method appropriated Heidegger's account of primordial temporal differentiation and expanded its remit beyond the experiences of Dasein, in effect transforming it into the grounding principle for a renovated Spinozist rationalism designed to articulate an ontology anterior to the limited purview of the existential or humanist subject.

Ultimately seeking to displace the "possible," a central category of Heidegger's ontology, Deleuze developed his own concept of the "virtual." Deleuze argued that the relation of the virtual to the actual could never be confused with that between the possible and the real.[3] With this rubric, developed in Bergsonian terms, Deleuze believed he was remaining true to a Spinozist philosophy of pure immanence that recognized no transcendental beyond, or *arrière-monde*, that might serve as the condition for actualization in the here and now. But in seeking to make Spinozism function as a philosophy that might have some purchase on our lived experiences of the world, Deleuze arguably took leave of the essentials of the rationalist Spinozism presented in the preceding chapters. The philosophical primacy that Deleuze accorded the virtual is equivocal, in that the concept appears to function sometimes as an ontological antechamber for the actualization of existence and, in others, as the name for a thinking unencumbered by material constraints. This is in fact the peculiar paradox of Deleuze's Spinozism: by working through phenomenology with Spinoza, and thus ostensibly bringing Spinozism to bear on the material morass of existence and its constitutive processes, Deleuze manages nonetheless to reaffirm the ontological primacy of thinking itself.

The first section of this chapter begins with a brief overview of *Difference and Repetition*, Deleuze's most substantial philosophical statement. Moving between this volume and *The Logic of Sense*, which was published the year after *Difference and Repetition*, and situating these books in the context of Deleuze's broader oeuvre, I then attempt to establish how Deleuze's ontological destruction of the category of the possible works. Here we witness an incessant vacillation between the Heideggerian and Spinozist impulses in Deleuze's thought. Deleuze follows Heidegger in developing an account of the subject as fractured by time. But he persistently seeks to move beyond Heidegger in discerning within this fracture a primordial, though no less rational, process anterior to the phenomenon of subjectivity. Deleuze's formalist account of these ontological processes of differentiation and individuation is deeply indebted to his Spinozism. Not only do we see the account of qualitative and quantitative distinction in *Spinoza and the Problem of Expression* brought to bear on other matters; we also see how the account of the relation of the attributes Thought and Extension in Martial Gueroult's reading of Spinoza sheds light on Deleuze's goals and argumentative procedures. Yet in the concluding sections of the reading, I argue that Deleuze's concept of the virtual, especially as it is presented in *Difference and Repetition*, does not transcend the Heideggerian problematic that was its initial condition. It is clear that Deleuze wants his "virtual" to function as a surrogate concept for Spinoza's Substance. But as I hope to show through an exploration of Deleuze's debts to Albert Lautman, the concept of the virtual in play is conceptually homologous to Heideggerian possibility.

Taken together *Difference and Repetition* and *The Logic of Sense* do not resolve the formative tension between Heideggerianism and Spinozism in Deleuze's thought. They exacerbate it. The two concluding sections of this chapter trace the effects of this irreconcilable tension in Deleuze's later works. The virtual continues to function in Deleuze's thought as an *arrière-monde* that is conceptually complicit with currents of negative theology emanating from Heidegger's philosophy. But for several exceptional moments, the actual is increasingly denigrated in Deleuze's thought to the profit of an inexhaustible virtual in excess of the world itself. This element of Deleuze's project runs counter to the Spinozism elaborated in previous chapters and accounts for the peculiar, and transformative, nature of the version one finds in Deleuze.

The final section concludes with an assessment of a Spinozist element of Deleuze's philosophy that persists in tension with his theory of the virtual: the power accorded to thought's formal capacities. For Spinoza, the idea comes first. Thought is ontologically primary over its location in discrete subjects or consciousnesses. Deleuze remains true to this fundamental ontological precept. Yet for Deleuze the virtue of thought is its incessant movement, the fact that it can never resolve into a set of meaningful claims before its own formal power disrupts any fleeting docility. With his commitment to thinking in such terms, Deleuze proffers a variant of Spinozist philosophy capable of dislodging a thought that has become stuck in the "blockage of the concept," to borrow one of Deleuze's own phrases.[4] But by this very same commitment to accelerating the formal proliferation of "true ideas," Deleuze restricts philosophy's capacity—for better or for worse—to determine the contents of anything one might aim to implement in the world and have remain there.

Difference and Repetition and *The Logic of Sense*

Much of Deleuze's study of Spinoza was devoted to showing the mutual implication of the modes and substance in Spinoza's ontology. The virtue of the term "expression" for Deleuze was its equivocal ability to refer to two different processes: explication and implication. The modes *explicate* being (substance)—it is via the modes that substance unfolds into an expressive openness. The modes *implicate* being in that they modify substance in turn. There is a dialectical movement here, an involuted process in which all that remains is difference itself—nothing is static except the process of change. This intertwining structure is put to work in *Difference and Repetition*, a work of philosophy whose structural integrity testifies to the degree of care that went into its construction. The book itself is structured like a mirror, signaled by the fact that the introduction is titled "Repetition and Difference" and the conclusion is "Difference and Repetition." The middle chapter of five, "The Image of Thought," is the one section completely devoted to a critique of representational thought and serves as a hinge linking the book's two halves. The first two chapters, "Difference in Itself" and "Repetition for Itself," provide philosophical accounts of these two concepts through explorations of various thinkers of modern philosophy. The final two chapters, "The Ideal Synthesis of Difference" and "The Asymmetric Synthesis of the Sensible," provide rarefied accounts of the two concepts in a deliberately nonrepresentational manner.

One of the primary aims of this book is to show how synthesis, far from being a purely epistemological principle as it is in Kant's critical philosophy, is itself an ontological principle. Because there is no origin in which to ground the synthetic act that bestows unity on objects and the coherence of their appearance, it is Deleuze's ontological thesis that this synthesis occurs in Being itself. By implication, "the Ideal synthesis of difference," that is, the synthetic production of knowledge at the level of the Idea, is an illustrative variant of a broader process that is equally synthetic and genetic. Deleuze affirms this point in a discussion of Nietzsche's eternal return:

> The eternal return has no other sense but this: the absence of assignable origin—in other words, the assignation of origin as being difference, which then relates different to different in order to make it (or them) return as such. In this sense, the eternal return is indeed the consequence of an originary difference, pure, synthetic, and in-itself (what Nietzsche called will to power). If difference is the in-itself, then repetition in the eternal return is the for-itself of difference. (*DR*, 164/125tm)

If difference *is* in-itself, only becoming for-itself through repetition, then difference would be the Deleuzean correlate for Kant's noumenal realm, and repetition would be the mechanism and condition for the phenomenal manifestation of difference in the world of appearances.

The previous chapter sought to show that Deleuze is indebted to Heidegger, directly and indirectly, for his grasp of difference as a constitutive element of being-in-the-world, of existence in time and space. Thus it is no surprise that, in *Difference and Repetition*, Deleuze follows Heidegger in a rereading of Kant that aims to show that primordial difference is manifested in the fractured, intrinsically unequal nature of subjectivity itself. This "return to Kant" takes place in the chapter "Repetition for Itself," where Deleuze addresses the "pure and empty form of time" in the third synthesis. The third synthesis is the catchall category that includes previously defined concepts of the first synthesis of habit, that is, the experience of "the living present," and the second synthesis of memory, which is read as the contraction of the "pure past" coextensive with the lived experience of the first synthesis. But these temporal syntheses are possible only because they are grounded in the pure and empty form of time of the third synthesis.[5] The "long inexhaustible history [of] I is an other [*JE est un autre*]" properly began with Kant, Deleuze argues, when he established that "the form under which undetermined existence is determinable by the 'I think' is the form of time" (116/86tm). To the Cartesian categories of the "I think" and the "I am," Kant adds the "self" (*moi*), the passive position of the "receptivity of intuition" (117/86). But in Deleuze's reading this "self" is little more than the attempted interiorization of difference in-itself. In other words, the "self" is the name of the permanently unbridgeable difference between the "I think" and the "I am," the impossibility that these would, or could, ever be the same "I."

"From one end to the other, it is as though a fracture runs through the I: it is fractured by the pure and empty form of time" (117/86tm). Kant himself will recoil from the implications of this schism:

> If the greatest initiative of transcendental philosophy was to introduce the form of time into thought as such, then this pure and empty form in turn signifies indissolubly the death of God, the fractured I and the passive self. It is true that Kant did not pursue this initiative: both God and the I underwent a practical resurrection. Even in the speculative domain, the fracture is quickly filled by a new form of identity—namely, active synthetic identity; whereas the passive self is defined only by receptivity and, as such, endowed with no power of synthesis. (117/87)[6]

In Deleuze's view, Kant's reluctance does nothing to compromise the philosophical importance of his own discovery. "Just as the ground [*fondement*] is in a sense 'bent' and must lead us towards a beyond, so the second synthesis of time points beyond itself in the direction of a third which denounces the illusion of the in-itself as still a correlate of representation" (119/88). In this move, the "in-itself" is a category revealed to be without content by time itself, the "pure form" of incessant differentiation.

Deleuze's account of temporal differentiation evokes Heidegger's account of the same. But we know that Deleuze's primary reference for thinking about time was in fact one of Heidegger's targets of critique on this subject: Henri Bergson.[7] In Heidegger's reading, Bergson was, despite his own professed intentions, the latest instantiation of an error as old as Aristotle that thought of time in terms assimilable to space. For Heidegger, the finite comes first. "Primordial time is finite."[8] "Only because primordial time is *finite* can the 'derived' time temporalize itself as *infinite*."[9] From Aristotle to Bergson, the error has been to try to derive the finite from the posited infinite. But the source of the error is that the concept of the infinite is itself derived from the encounter with ontically finite entities. Thus the concept of the infinite is grounded in the finite without knowing it. Heidegger writes,

> The kind of "time" which is first found ontically in within-time-ness, becomes the basis on which the ordinary traditional conception of time takes form. But time,

as within-time-ness, arises from an essential kind of temporalizing of primordial temporality. The fact that this is its source, tells us that the time "in which" what is present-at-hand arises and passes away, is a genuine phenomenon of time; it is not an externalization of a "qualitative time" into space, as Bergson's interpretation of time—which is ontologically quite indefinite and inadequate—would have us believe.[10]

Just as Descartes' substance was "hazily ontico-ontological," the time one finds in Bergson is "quite indefinite and inadequate." But if Heidegger's move is to show us how the traditional grasp of the infinite is itself primordially rooted in a more proximate experience of the finite, then Deleuze attempts to show that our proximate experience of the finite is rooted in an even more primordial infinity that is so radically expansive and inclusive that it can in fact never be *experienced* as temporality but only *thought* as the "pure and empty form of time." In other words, the spatialization of time that Heidegger castigated in Bergson is precisely what accounts for the latter's value in Deleuze's philosophy. For Deleuze's Bergson, the *virtual* qua "pure past," the ideal totality of existence, was the condition for any actualization within that virtual totality. Here the irreal connotations of the word "virtual" help make Deleuze's point. Deleuze cites Proust's assessment of states of resonance to define the virtual: "real without being actual; ideal without being abstract" (269/208). Insofar as the virtual qua infinite past is thought of as a totality, it is ideal since it is never fully actualized. But Deleuze's provocative claim is that this virtual is no less real as a result.

The notion that the virtual might refer at once to the totality of the pure past and the pure and empty form of time is problematic insofar as it seems to sap time of its essentially temporal quality. What qualifies time as time if it is equivalent to the totality of existence all at once? In *The Logic of Sense*, Deleuze reconsiders this problem in his discussion of the Stoic distinction between two kinds of time, Aiôn and Chronos.[11] According to Deleuze, Chronos describes the time of the living present, whereas Aiôn describes the essentially unlimited past and future. Chronos has thickness and depth; it is limited in that it pertains only to the lived present, but it is also infinite in its chronological procession and expansiveness. "Whereas Chronos [is] limited and infinite, Aiôn is unlimited, the way that future and past are unlimited, and finite like the instant" (*LS*, 194/165). Chronos is a temporalized corporeal process, Heidegger's primordial finite temporality. With Aiôn, however, "only the past and the future insist or subsist in time" (192/164tm). What is the relation between these two kinds of time? Deleuze introduces two dualisms to make his point, a dualism of depths and surfaces and another of the corporeal and the incorporeal. Chronos is associated with depth and corporeality, and the image is precisely that of a primordial finitude of movement and material existing in time (190/162). Aiôn is the time of fleeting surfaces and incorporeal *events*. The Deleuzean concept of the event is radically idiosyncratic. For Deleuze, an event, what *happens*, is always qua event incorporeal in itself, much in the way that Heidegger's concept of being effectively *as* time can never be correlated to a discrete corporeal entity. Deleuze's claim is that the irreducibility of *sense* in language to the materiality of its component parts is homologous to the irreducibility of an *event* in existence to the corporeal substance in which it occurs. Deleuze maps this dualism, between sense and events as *occurrences* and materiality or corporeality as *substance*, onto his conceptual distinction between Aiôn and Chronos.

"Whereas Chronos expressed the action of bodies and the creation of corporeal qualities, Aiôn is the locus of incorporeal events and of attributes that are distinct from qualities" (193/165). Though it receives only a cursory mention in *The Logic of Sense*, one of the examples Deleuze invokes to clarify his distinction is Zeno's paradox of Achilles and the tortoise (27/15).[12] If the tortoise gets a head start on Achilles, and Achilles is only ever able to close the distance between himself and the tortoise by increments, how is it possible that he ever catches the tortoise? Experience shows that he will, but Zeno's point was to show that, according to our mathematical reasoning of this event, Achilles never catches up because with each distance closed, the tortoise still moves forward. This paradox can be expressed in Deleuze's terms of Chronos and Aiôn. In the purely corporeal time of Chronos, the time of mechanical cause and effect and of succession, Achilles can never catch up, for reasons that the mathematics of this corporeal process make perfectly clear. But there is a "present"—a moment, an instant—that shatters this corporeal succession, the moment when Achilles overtakes the tortoise despite the impossibility of doing so according to constraints of time as Chronos. "It is no longer the future and past that subvert the existing present; it is the instant that perverts the present into an insistent past and future" (193/165tm). The introduced cut of this "instant" is what divides past from future in an otherwise indivisible time—it is a "sense-event" incorporeal in itself, precisely because it can never be fully localized in corporeality.

Always already past and eternally yet to come, Aiôn is the eternal truth of time: *pure empty form of time* which has freed itself from its present corporeal content and has thereby unwound its own circle, stretching itself out in a straight line. It is perhaps all the more dangerous, more labyrinthine, more tortuous for this reason. (194/165)

For this reason. Strange as it seems, Deleuze's baroque account of Aiôn is not intended as an abrogation of a rationalist account of time. It is instead designed to function as a kind of hyperrationalist ground for the finite time of Chronos as succession. The "pure empty form of time" is itself a purely formal rationalist concept that refers not to the content of corporeal existence but to a virtual domain that is "ideal without being abstract and real without being actual." Lacking actuality—that is, lacking any spatial point *or* temporal moment that might be discretely identified—the essence of the sense-event lacks material content in turn. The "sense-event" cannot be wholly accounted for by its material referents.

A comparison of *Difference and Repetition* and *The Logic of Sense* makes clear that there is a relation between the virtual and the actual as it is developed in the former volume and the Aiôn and Chronos borrowed from the Stoics.[13] But it must be admitted that the nature of this relation is not entirely evident. In *Difference and Repetition*, the virtual is coded as a site of expansive excess that is the condition itself for actualization. Aiôn, as "the pure empty form of time" that "contains" the entire past and the entire future, seems to play a similar role in *The Logic of Sense*. Yet Deleuze insists that the time peculiar to Aiôn makes itself felt each time sense is made or an event occurs. Sapping "event" of any sense of rarity or exceptionality, Deleuze writes, "The event refers to states of things, but only as the logical attribute of these states. It is entirely different from their physical qualities, despite the fact that it may happen to them, or be embodied or actualized in them" (195/167tm). What are Deleuze's motives in developing this formulation?

Just as Deleuze is opposed to reduction in terms of events or sense, so, too, is he committed to developing a logic of causality that avoids all tendencies to read effects as reducible to, or contained within, their causes. Deleuzean ontology pursues a wholesale attack against the related concepts of potentiality and possibility. The arcane formulations of *The Logic of Sense* are an attempt to develop an account of causality, how things happen, that makes no recourse to a possible that becomes real or a potential that becomes actual. In this, they are the crucial supplement to the theory of the virtual in *Difference and Repetition*. Time and again throughout his project, Deleuze reiterates that the "virtual" is never to be confused with the possible.[14]

The primary source for Deleuze's case that the virtual is not the same as the possible is indeed Bergson. But many of the arguments Deleuze pulls from Bergson can in fact also be expressed in the terms of Deleuze's Spinoza in *Spinoza and the Problem of Expression*. Together, the projects of Bergson and Spinoza serve Deleuze as sources of critical claims against Hegel, Kant, and Heidegger as well. In one of his earliest writings on Bergson, "Bergson's Conception of Difference" from 1956, Deleuze argued for Bergson's critical relation to Hegel:

In Bergson, thanks to the notion of the virtual, the thing differs with itself, *first, immediately*. According to Hegel, the thing differs with itself because it differs first with everything that it is not, so much so that difference goes all the way to contradiction. The distinction between the contrary and contradiction matters little here, since contradiction is but the presentation of a whole as the contrary. [. . .] It is our ignorance of the virtual that makes us believe in contradiction and negation. The opposition of two terms is only the actualization of the virtuality that contained them both: which is to say that difference is more profound than negation or contradiction.[15]

Here the virtual plays the role later occupied by Aiôn, the pure and empty form of time that contains all dualistic cause/effect relations within it. As we saw in the previous chapter, Spinozist substance is yet another name for this all-inclusive idea that allows us to think difference in-itself as an always immediate, unconditioned expression.

In a course on Bergson given in 1960, Deleuze articulated how Bergson was not only the anti-Hegel but also the anti-Kant. Here again, however, Deleuze articulates via Bergson a thesis that was also central to his study of Spinoza. "For Kant—Bergson says—one sees things in forms that come from us. Bergson says: you see yourselves under forms that come from things."[16] If the forms of the understanding are *produced* in being itself, then it is incoherent to speak of these forms as anything but adequate to their objects, which inhere in being in the same way as the forms of the understanding. In effect, Bergson and Spinoza are assimilated to one another to produce the same argument for the union of ontological and epistemological processes. In the Spinozist universe, a true idea can never be predicated upon a negation, because there can be no lack, or negation, that inheres in being itself. Much as Deleuze suggested that Hegelian contradiction was but the "epiphenomenon" of a more primordial difference, so, too, does Deleuze view lack and negation, not as ontological occurrences but as phenomena unique to the human perspective. The crucial problem, however, is how something that does not lack in itself manifests itself as such.

Heidegger's answer to this question, crucial for the development of twentieth-century philosophy, was the fundamental provocation that motivated Deleuze's effort. For Heidegger, it is finite temporality that is both the medium and cause of negation. And finite temporality as an ontological category is completely inseparable from the way it is existentially experienced by Dasein as possibility: "As a modal category of presence-at-hand, possibility signifies what is *not yet* actual and what is *not at any time* necessary. It characterizes the *merely* possible. Ontologically it is on a lower level than actuality and necessity. On the other hand, possibility as an *existentiale* is the most primordial and ultimate positive way in which Dasein is characterized ontologically."[17] Heidegger proposes an ontological sense for possibility that will distinguish it from its "merely" modal and flawed use in philosophies such as Aristotle's and Bergson's. The ontological assessment of death as Dasein's ultimate possibility will occupy later chapters of his magnum opus: "The certain possibility of death, however, discloses Dasein as a possibility, but does so only in such a way that, in anticipating this possibility, Dasein *makes* this possibility *possible* for itself as its ownmost potentiality-for-Being."[18] In Heidegger's account, it is intrinsic to Dasein's existence that it experience itself as possibility, and it is the horizon of death as the ultimate possibility that one must appropriate in order to achieve authenticity as a living possibility transformed into actuality. Thus, what we witness is a move from the *possible* to the *authentic* wherein Dasein serves as the mediate term for this transformation.

Deleuze's goal, however, is to show that, ontologically, *nothing is possible*. The problem with possibility as an ontological principle is that it calls upon a set, an antechamber, of potential acts that can then be executed in the here and now when there is no way to account philosophically for what the content of that original set might be. Much as Deleuze accepts that contradiction is an idea that can be conceived by the human intellect, he also accepts that we often experience our lives as a set of possibilities motivated by desires and various other demands and imperatives. What he does not accept is the transposition of these concepts from their human or existential context to the domain of fundamental ontology. To do so is to read being-in-itself as somehow dependent upon the limited purview of human subjectivity, which is conceptualized as Dasein in Heidegger's philosophy. Heidegger's claims to Dasein's essential "thrownness" do nothing to compromise the conceptual nature of Dasein in his own philosophical argument. Based on the contents of *Difference and Repetition*, it is as if Deleuze recognizes that Dasein is but the conceptual name for the *existentiale* of possibility. For Deleuze, it is the error of thinking of ontology in terms of possibility that leads to conceiving of being as comprehensible solely in terms of origins and goals, never in-itself. In this regard, Deleuze expands Althusser's critique of phenomenological accounts of history to phenomenological ontology *tout court*.

Heidegger's vision makes recourse to a profound concept of origin. That Heidegger spent much of the rest of his career excavating the origins of words is testament to the fetish for the original in his thought. But the "origin" in play throughout *Being and Time* is finite temporality, which, as the development of that work makes clear, is another name for death. The sole "necessary possibility" that conditions all the others is death itself. What Deleuze attempts via Spinoza is a perverse involution of this problematic. Spinoza said that "a free man thinks of death least of all things."[19] What this means for Deleuze is that, although death is indeed the ur-possibility of human experience in the Heideggerian framework, there is no philosophically tenable reason for granting death a predominant role in fundamental ontology. The commitment to thought's own insights against all the evidence of one's lived experience, wherein the death of others and the fate of oneself are inescapable facts, is radical in the extreme, and it is also a position that is truly the inverse of Heidegger's.

Another of Spinoza's pronouncements that has perplexed many interpreters evokes this same position: "we feel and experience that we are eternal."[20] For Spinoza it is the arguably childlike sentiment that one has always been and always will be that is primordial and that is anterior to any sort of anxiety before the finitude and death that Heidegger reads as Dasein's most fundamental intuition. Deleuze's repeated affirmations of "life" throughout his philosophical oeuvre are to be read in these terms, not so much as the rehabilitation of a Bergsonian vitalism—he in fact criticized Bergson on this score—but as evidence of the unshakable conviction that ontology cannot "begin" with death. Deleuze was aware of the naïveté of this position. When asked what he thought of Michel Foucault's claim that "perhaps one day the century will be seen as Deleuzean," Deleuze suggested that Foucault was pointing out that he was "the most naïve philosopher of our generation, [. . .] I wasn't better than others, but more naïve, producing a kind of *art brut*, so to speak; not the most profound but the most innocent."[21]

Deleuze's philosophical effort is more cunning than innocent. What is striking about *Difference and Repetition* is that it takes Heidegger's critique of the metaphysics of presence and pushes it to such an extreme that it undermines Heidegger's own commitment to constitutive finitude as the primordial ontological phenomenon. Spinoza is indispensable to Deleuze's effort to present an ontology of infinite necessity that is anterior to the human experience of finite possibility. Recall the comment Deleuze made at the end of his review of Tournier's *Vendredi*. Tournier has given us a "world without any possible [. . .] a *strange Spinozism* wherein the oxygen is lacking." This metaphor would resurface again in one of Deleuze's very last writings, "The Exhausted," an account of several of Samuel Beckett's theatrical pieces. Deleuze praises Beckett's "relentless Spinozism," his aesthetic achievement of an exhaustion of the possible.[22] These figures—of exhaustion, the "rarefied air of Sky-Necessity"—that posit the lack of breath as a positive ontological condition acquire a strong pathos in light of the respiratory ailments that affected Deleuze for most of his adult life. At the time of writing *Difference and Repetition*, in the summer of 1968, Deleuze was suffering from a giant sore in one of his lungs, the belated symptom of the tuberculosis he had contracted in his youth.[23] His private doctoral defense of this work—an event distinct from his presentation before the Société française de philosophie—in January 1969 was shortened due to his exhaustion. In the days following its conclusion he was taken to the hospital to have his lung removed, an operation that required a year of convalescence.[24] By the 1990s, when "The Exhausted" was written, Deleuze was nearly fully reliant on oxygen tanks. In the months leading up to his suicide in November 1995, an event many of his friends feared and expected, Deleuze had all but lost the ability to speak without suffering severe, suffocating respiratory attacks.[25]

It would be contrary to the spirit of Deleuze's philosophy to reduce it to a symptom of this physical ailment. But insofar as Deleuze followed Pierre Klossowski in understanding thought to be inseparable from its bodily conditions, his philosophical commitment to exploring a world lacking oxygen,[26] and by extension possibility—the foundational element of constitutive finitude—cannot but seem revelatory. One of the most striking things about Deleuze is that his entire philosophical effort seems to be geared toward undercutting any foundations that might serve to bestow a meaning or a purpose for existence, human or otherwise. The methodical nihilism of Deleuze's approach was perhaps expressed best by his friend, and fellow reader of Nietzsche, Clément Rosset. Commenting on the dizzying arcana of *Difference and Repetition*, Rosset observed that Deleuze's philosophical method was one of "precision for nothing."[27] Elsewhere, in a study of Schopenhauer, Rosset himself observed that "one must not count on the philosopher to find reasons to live."[28] At times *Difference and Repetition* seems designed to exhaust itself of any purchase on lived experience or purposeful existence, which raises the question of a philosophy's relationship to its motives.

Like Spinoza, the Deleuze of *Difference and Repetition* was committed to the philosophical imperative of developing true ideas. Also like Spinoza, Deleuze was committed to conceiving of the true idea as something that is wholly singular, fleeting in its determinate relation to the next true idea and ultimately indifferent to its moral implications. Deleuze took for granted the Spinozist affirmation that the true was its own sign and that of the false, and that determining the proliferation of true ideas was a philosophical value in itself. To speak of privation or negativity as inhering in being itself was a falsehood that could be demonstrated by the rational procedures of Spinoza's philosophy. For Deleuze, negativity, whether it was presented as contradiction or temporality, was an epiphenomenon of a process about which it was incoherent to say that it lacked anything. It is again Rosset, who, in his work *L'Objet singulier* made this point more succinctly than Deleuze ever did: "The absence of lack means that there is no 'not': which is to say that what exists exhausts the whole possibility of existence, and is thus at once perfect—since it lacks nothing—and essentially 'suitable' [*convenable*] in that it leaves nothing to desire, or to complain about [*redire*]."[29] For Rosset, the only honest philosophy is one that acknowledges the idiocy of the real in the literal sense of the term: idiotic as in idiosyncratic, wholly singular, lacking all double, and as a result signifying nothing.[30] Spinoza himself made this very point with the laconic definition "[b]y reality and perfection I mean the same thing."[31]

What makes affirmation of this position, which cannot but evoke Leibniz's theodicy, scandalous in the French context is that it seems unconscionable in the wake of the defining events for thinkers of Deleuze's generation: the Second World War and the Holocaust. Deleuze's elder brother, his only sibling, fought in the Resistance and died in transit shortly after the Germans arrested him, though one would be unable to deduce this from any of Deleuze's writings.[32] How might Deleuze be situated in the litany of post-Heideggerian thinkers in France, for whom these experiences were formative? In his study of the "Generation Existential," Ethan Kleinberg has shown how for the main purveyors of what he terms the "third reading"—Blanchot and Levinas—death on a world historical scale, the Shoah, was an impossibility become actuality.[33] The involution of the impossible and the possible was the guiding concern of Blanchot's meditations on writing. For Levinas, Heidegger's error was to approach death in terms of a wholly subjective possibility, one that forsook the existence of the other as a condition of subjectivity itself and, as a result, produced a philosophy indifferent to the possibility of the other's suffering. For Deleuze, possibility could only ever be the projected result of a subjective, limited, and irrational perspective. Thus, the most egregious error of Heidegger's thinking, ontologically and in terms of its ethical implications, was its predication on the anterior and obscure category of the possible. If for Blanchot, the concern of modern thinking is to show how the impossible becomes possible, for Deleuze the task is to show that possibility itself is *ontologically impossible*.[34]

Deleuze's philosophical commitment to the "exhaustion of the possible" as a category of existence is deeply rooted in a Spinozism that prohibits recourse to any figurative elsewhere in its account of existence. Even the idea of substance, which, as Gueroult noted, implies that Spinozist immanence "does not go without a certain transcendence,"[35] is not coded as an elsewhere insofar as its status as an idea is deemed to be fully present to the understanding in the here and now. Deleuze's study of Spinoza is, among other things, an attempt to elaborate the thesis of ontological univocity, with which *Difference and Repetition* concludes. For Deleuze, the primordial difference that is constitutive of being entails a univocal differentiation in which all that is differentiated is granted the same measure of being. Deleuze's arguments for the univocal nature of primordial differentiation are designed to prevent the positing of any transcendental standard or site extrinsic to the site of differentiation itself—existence—that might then provide a ground from which to judge the discrete singularities that inhere in it. The "elsewhere" under fire in Spinoza's system is the God of negative theology; for the Deleuze of *Difference and Repetition* it is the inaccessible interiority of the noumenal self in Kantian philosophy. The signal error of Kant's philosophy is to preserve this mystified space of an elsewhere that is no less of an elsewhere for being relegated to the structures of the human mind. Deleuze emphasizes the commonality of the Kantian "self" and Spinozist Substance in order to demystify the Kantian self and to recuperate what he deems of value in Kant's irreversible effort.[36] Self and substance are simply two different names for the site wherein *synthesis* takes place or occurs, except in the latter instance this process is fully out in the open, not locked away in a figurative interiority. Yet it is Deleuze's contention that the imbricated processes of ideational synthesis and ontological genesis are no less rational for not being grounded in a transcendental subject or a creator-God.

We are approaching here the central paradox of Deleuze's project and what accounts for its paradoxical status as a rationalist irrationalism. For Deleuze, irrationalism was not the name for arbitrary impulse or rampant subjectivism. In *Nietzsche and Philosophy* he writes, "It is a serious mistake to think that irrationalism opposes anything but thought to reason—whether it be by the rights of the given, of the heart, of feeling, caprice or passions. In irrationalism we are concerned only with thought, only with thinking. What is opposed to reason is thought itself; what is opposed to the reasonable being is the thinker himself."[37] The "reason" in question is that of the allied powers of "good sense" and "common sense" that Deleuze criticizes throughout *Difference and Repetition*'s pivotal chapter, "The Image of Thought." In the traditional "image of thought," for which Kant serves as the epitome, thought is always subjected to a "tribunal of reason" whose criteria are not its own. These criteria are not intrinsic to thought itself but are those of an externally given "common sense" that attempts to legislate what thought can and cannot accomplish. Husserl is subjected to a similar charge in *The Logic of Sense*:

We can clearly see this in the Husserlian theory of *doxa*, wherein the different kinds of belief are engendered with reference to an *Urdoxa*, which acts as a faculty of common sense in reference to the specified faculties. The powerlessness of this philosophy to break with the form of common sense, which was clearly present in Kant, is present again in Husserl. (119/97–98)

The error here is to take the form of empirical experience and to suggest that the "originary" form of manifestation itself must be isomorphic to this empirical form, even though this slippage is not rationally grounded in itself. "It is the entire dimension of manifestation, in the position of a transcendental subject, which retains the form of the person, of personal consciousness, and of subjective identity, and which is satisfied with tracing [*décalquer*] the transcendental from the characteristics of the empirical" (119/98tm). In Deleuze's view, "The foundation [*fondement*] can never resemble what it founds" (120/99).[38] Deleuze's commitment to exploring this ground that does not resemble its manifestations should not be read as a disavowal of rationalism, however. The peculiar rationalism of this effort was later given a pointed expression when Deleuze and Guattari wrote, "It is not the slumber of reason which engenders monsters, but vigilant and insomniac rationality."[39] It is clear that for Deleuze thought is capable of putting us in touch with a rationality that is more fundamental than the commonsense dictates of "merely" human reason.

A serious problem remains, however. Deleuze claims that Kant and Husserl's presumption that the form of the transcendental ground of experience must be the same as that of empirical experience is philosophically untenable. But what makes his assumption that they are *not* the same any more persuasive? To support his case, Deleuze refers us back to singularities, which he argues are anterior to consciousness:

A consciousness is nothing without a synthesis of unification, but there is no synthesis of unification of consciousness without the form of the I, or the point of view of the Self. What is neither individual nor personal are, on the contrary, emissions of singularities insofar as they occur on an unconscious surface and possess a mobile, immanent principle of auto-unification through a *nomadic distribution*, radically distinct from fixed and sedentary distributions as conditions of the syntheses of consciousness. Singularities are the true transcendental events. (*LS*, 124–25/102–3)

Taken on its own, the claim that the singularity is anterior to the subject is not very compelling. It seems to be a variation of the homunculus problem, merely displacing the animus of the sequence to a "deeper" level.

But the key phrase here is "immanent principle of auto-unification." This is a formula that is thoroughly rationalist. It is Deleuze's conviction that philosophy should be able to provide a formal account of this principle, grounded in differentiation as nonresemblance, that has purchase on a primordial rationality subtending the apparent circularity of Kant's and Husserl's accounts of subjectivity.

The Idea of the Virtual

The excavation of primordial rationality is the guiding thread of the final chapters of *Difference and Repetition*, to which we now return. This half of the book begins with Kant before turning to the "esoteric history" of differential calculus in which figures a motley assortment of thinkers: Salomon Maimon, Jean Bordas-Demoulin, Hoene-Wronski, and ultimately Albert Lautman. Deleuze explores (or indeed exploits) this history to make his own argument for a non-Kantian "Ideal Synthesis of Difference." In the chapter that follows, "The Asymmetric Synthesis of the Sensible," Deleuze will provide the material complement to the preceding idealist section through reference to the biophysical accounts of differentiation and individuation produced by Raymond Ruyer and others, above all, Gilbert Simondon. Simondon provides Deleuze an account of individuation in the sensible domain that does not rely upon a Kantian transcendental subject to bestow coherence on distinct, individuated objects.[40] Deleuze argues that it is quantitative intensity as an intrinsic component of matter itself that is "the determinant in the process of actualization. It is intensity which *dramatizes*" (*DR*, 316/245). "Intensity is individuating, and intensive quantities are individuating factors" (317/246). It is not that the results of intensive individuation are somehow rational in themselves. Rather, it is Deleuze's claim that we can conceive of the process as a rational one at the level of formal ontology.

The celebration of *quantitative* intensity has its most fundamental support in the account of quantitative distinction in *Spinoza and the Problem of Expression*. The argument was that there could be no "real distinction" within a singular attribute, be it Thought or Extension. Any distinction that occurred within either of these attributes was merely quantitative insofar as it remained undetermined. Individuation—which certainly seems to connote real distinction—is the name for this process in

Difference and Repetition. The actualization of an individual is best understood as an accumulation of quantitative intensity that manifests itself at a threshold point as qualitative change. This point is not localizable purely within the realm of quantitative intensity, even as quantitative intensity is its condition. What makes this position Spinozist is that for qualitative change to occur, somehow *both* attributes must be involved. Fluctuations in quantitative intensity take place in nature all the time, but a qualitative change takes place only at a moment of registration or discernment in an attribute other than the one in which the quantitative intensity occurs.[41]

But this paradigm raises an obvious question: What motivates, or better yet, stimulates, this quantitative intensity? Deleuze writes,

> Every body, every thing, thinks and is a thought to the extent that, reduced to its intensive reasons, it expresses an Idea the actualization of which it determines. However, the thinker himself makes his individual differences from all manner of things: it is in this sense that he is laden with stones and diamonds, plants "and even animals." The thinker, undoubtedly the thinker of eternal return, is the individual, the universal individual. [. . .] The indivisibility of the individual pertains solely to the property of intensive quantities not to divide without changing nature. [. . .] Individuality is not a characteristic of the Self but, on the contrary, forms and sustains the system of the dissolved Self. (327/254)

In other words, qualitative change results precisely from the discrete moment of *nonresemblance* registered as such. To invert the terms in a way to illuminate Deleuze's earlier critique of Kant and Husserl, nonresemblance is the necessary condition in order for something to *happen*, to qualitatively take place as a *real* change in the world. What appears fleetingly in the passage just cited as Kant's revenge on Deleuze's system—"the thinker himself makes his individual differences from all manner of things"—is avoided by relegating "the thinker" back to an anterior process subtending the Self. What "forms and nourishes" this Self are the "larval subjects" that Deleuze introduced earlier in this volume (278/215). This is the name for the discrete singularities whose intensive concatenation results in each qualitative change manifested as a new idea or entity. It is hard to see how Deleuze avoids an infinite regress with this line of reasoning, dissolving in a "bad infinity" lacking all theoretical purchase on any actual process. Harder still to decipher is how his brazen valorization of the Idea and its expression as the constitutive motor of this process results in anything other than an idealist philosophy.

Just as the "Idea of expression" is valorized as the nodal point of Spinoza's theoretical effort, so, too, is the Idea as a self-differentiating synthetic process absolutely central to *Difference and Repetition*. If "The Image of Thought" is the pivot of this work of philosophy, "The Ideal Synthesis of Difference" is its linchpin. In this chapter, Deleuze follows Kant in affirming that ideas are essentially problematic. Reason is capable of posing "false problems" only because it is inherent in its nature to pose problems as such. In its essence, the Idea is indeterminate, which is not to say that it is without object. "The problem qua problem is the object of the Idea" (219/169tm). "The undetermined is not a simple imperfection in our knowledge or a lack in the object: it is a perfectly positive, object structure which acts as a focus or horizon within perception" (220/169). The absence of lack is a sine qua non of Deleuze's system. This conviction is fully in force in the analysis of the differential calculus that follows. Deleuze's recourse to differential calculus is not simply metaphorical. Like Lautman, as we will see, Deleuze reads mathematical thought as paradigmatic for thinking as such. His point is that here we have a thought, a thinking, wherein the Idea itself is "defined as a structure" (237/183). Moreover, this structure is a multiplicity in itself:

> In all cases the multiplicity is intrinsically defined, without external reference or recourse to a uniform space in which it would be submerged. Spatio-temporal relations no doubt retain multiplicity, but lose interiority; concepts of the understanding retain interiority, but lose multiplicity, which they replace by the identity of an "I think" or something thought. Internal multiplicity, by contrast, is characteristic of the Idea alone. (237/183)

That this concept of multiplicity is connected to Deleuze's understanding of Spinoza is clear from the following statements: "'Multiplicity,' which replaces the one no less than the multiple, is the true substantive, substance itself." And, "The variable multiplicity is the how many, the how and each of the cases. Each thing is a multiplicity in so far as it incarnates an Idea" (236/182tm). The notion of substance as an insubstantial category in itself, as a site for the play of multiplicity, is a common element in both Deleuze's Spinozism and Althusser's. In fact, Althusser is cited affirmatively throughout *Difference and Repetition* for recognizing "structure" to be, like "substance," a name for a process and not an entity (241/186).

It is this Spinozist concept of multiplicity that informs Deleuze's reading of differential calculus. Differential calculus is a mode of thought exclusively focused on the *relation* of wholly autonomous fields, expressed as the variables *x* and *y*. Usually the variables in question are space and time; most high school calculus courses do not move beyond the two-dimensional *x/y* graph that is used to plot any manner of physical process. The signal problem of calculus as a development in modern mathematics was to provide a way to think continuity with tools that seemed best suited for thinking the discrete. For example, at what "point" does the infinitesimal simply become continuity? How do we think and express the line as an assemblage of points? Here the notion of the *limit* as that toward which the plotted mathematical function tends is absolutely essential. The most important thing to realize about this limit, however, is that, in terms of thought, it is purely *ideal*. Deleuze writes that "it is the notion of *limit* that grounds a new, static and purely ideal definition of continuity, and whose definition implies nothing other than number, or rather the universal in number" (223/172tm, emphasis added).

The problem for any viable theory of number is determinability, that is, how to determine the "cut" between one irrational number and the next?[42] Differential calculus avoids this problem by eliminating the need to locate the precise determined point, in fact making a virtue of its very insubstantiality as a point. "*Dx* is totally undetermined in relation to *x*, as is *dy* in relation to *y*, but they are perfectly determinable in relation to each other" (223/172tm). The point on the *x*-axis cannot be localized, nor can that on the *y*-axis; but the functional relation of the two axes can be expressed as a line of continuity. For Deleuze, this mathematical "conundrum" is expressive of a philosophical truth; the points can never be localized, fully determined solely with reference to their own genre (or axis) because their very existence is one of mutual implication:

> The relation *dy/dx* is not like a fraction which is established between particular quanta in intuition, but neither is it a general relation between variable algebraic magnitudes or quantities. *Each term exists absolutely only in its relation with the other*; it is no longer necessary, or even possible to indicate an independent variable. This is why a principle of reciprocal determination now corresponds as such to the determinability of the relation. It is in a reciprocal synthesis that the Idea presents and develops its effectively synthetic function. (223–24/172tm, emphasis added)

The unnecessary and impossible "independent variable" Deleuze has in mind is Kant's transcendental subject. Deleuze's point is to show that the synthetic function is possible only due to the indeterminable quality of either term, or field, in itself. The terms in question here—the relation that calculus was designed to access—are space and time. The result, the "lesson" of calculus discernible to Maimon and others, was that, regardless of reference to a transcendental subject, *space* was not only unthinkable but impossible in itself, as was time. It is only through their differential relation to one another that either makes sense, or indeed exists.

But is this the only relation expressed by the differential calculus? When *Difference and Repetition* is considered alongside its accompanying thesis, *Spinoza and the Problem of Expression*, it is clear that the variables x and y can also serve as functional equivalents to the attributes Thought and Extension in Spinoza's system. Consider the parallels. Thought taken as a variable field x cannot stand alone to determine dx, which would be all the affections of Thought, such as ideas and sentiments. Similarly, the qualitative changes that inhere in matter cannot be determined simply through reference to the attribute of Extension alone. Instead, it is only the attributes' modal relation *to one another* that allows us to determine their common existence as a continuous intercalated process. But how do we "think" their relation, if they are wholly autonomous in themselves? Through the *idea* of Substance itself, regardless of whatever name we give it (God, or Nature). Deleuze's preferred name for this "process" is "expression." "The idea of expression contains within it all the difficulties relating to the unity of substance and the diversity of the attributes."[43] It is the *idea* of the limit—the limit is "purely ideal"—that allows us to think the relation between space and time, just as it is the *idea* of Substance that allows us to think the relation between Thought and Extension. In both instances, it is clear, a primacy is accorded to the Idea. Thus, it is perfectly admissible to charge, as Ray Brassier has done, that *Difference and Repetition* is a work of either idealist philosophy or panpsychist mysticism.[44] For if it is not controversial to claim that space and time have only ever existed in their relation to one another, it is quite another matter to consider Thought and Extension in the same terms. If Spinoza is followed to the letter on this score, and this is what Deleuze does, then the claim is that there *has been* and *will be* Thought as long as there is Extension. In this case, we are forced to consider what kind of Thought "existed" before the historical advent of consciousness or at the time of the Big Bang, or before it.

Deleuze's response to this dilemma is to translate the Spinozist categories of Thought and Extension into his own paradigm of the virtual and the actual. In the preceding chapter, we noted Hallward's suggestion that we are best served considering the virtual/actual distinction in Deleuze's philosophy as a translation of Spinoza's distinction between two "kinds" of nature, *natura naturans* (nature naturing, i.e., nature as a verb) and *natura naturata* (nature natured, i.e., nature as a noun). The latter is but the concrete, "actual" instantiation of the anterior "virtual" activity. Yet, in *Difference and Repetition* at least, the "virtual" is coded totally in terms of the Idea, which seems to make it assimilable to Thought, whereas the actual would be its concrete instantiation in Extension. Although Spinoza maintains in the *Ethics* that the two kinds of nature are equally applicable to both attributes, Deleuze nonetheless accords a certain primacy to Thought, which draws from the fact that it is the unique site wherein the discovery of two kinds of nature is itself located.[45]

But this is not the only reason for thought's superiority in *Difference and Repetition*. For Deleuze effectively locates "the Idea" in the virtual, a domain that is always in excess of its actualization in concepts. This is a move that runs counter to the more general Spinozism of Deleuze's effort, which prohibits recourse to an *arrière-monde* that serves as the condition for actualization. In this regard, it is significant that Deleuze's primary resource for describing this process is Albert Lautman, and not, as we might expect given his professed Spinozism, Lautman's close friend and colleague Jean Cavaillès. Lautman provides Deleuze with a way to think the relation between "problems" and "solutions" in a manner that contributes to his own nascent account of the virtual and the actual. For Lautman, solutions never exhaust the problems that have led to them. In the operations of differential calculus, the "solutions" are manifested as graphical or algorithmic representations of isolated "singular points." In one stroke, this solution concretizes the process that was its own initial condition as a problem. Summarizing Lautman's position, Deleuze writes,

If the differentials disappear in the result, this is to the extent that the problem-instance differs in kind from the solution-instance; it is in the movement by which the solutions necessarily come to conceal the problem; it is in the sense that the conditions of the problem are the object of a synthesis in the Idea which cannot be expressed in the analysis of the propositional concepts constituting cases of solution. As a result, the first alternative—real or fictive?—collapses.

Neither real, nor fictive, the differential expresses the nature of the problematic as such, its objective consistency along with its subjective autonomy. (*DR*, 230–31/177–78tm)[46]

To describe this process, Deleuze introduces an unlikely term that was in fact essential to Lautman's effort: "we must speak of a *dialectic* of calculus instead of a metaphysics." The "dialectic" is "the element of the problem, as it is distinguished from the properly mathematical element of solutions" (231/178tm). Lautman defines the "problem" in terms of three components: "its difference in kind from solutions; its transcendence in relation to the solutions that it engenders on the basis of its own determinant conditions; and its immanence in the solutions which cover it, the problem *being* the better resolved the more *it is* determined" (232/178–79). Insofar as they are transcendent to their solutions, problems are virtual; as they are actualized, they become immanent to their solutions. None of this changes the fact, however, that "*problems are always dialectical*: the dialectic has no other sense, nor do problems have any other sense. What is mathematical (or physical, or biological, or psychical, or sociological . . .) are the solutions" (232/179tm). The point is that solutions always have a concrete quality, even if they are mathematical and ostensibly located purely within thought.

Lautman was briefly introduced in the discussion of Cavaillès, but we must return to his project here to clarify the stakes of Deleuze's recourse to his example. The final line of Cavaillès's *Sur la logique et la théorie de la science* is but one sign of the extent to which Cavaillès's dialogue with Lautman was instrumental in his own thinking: "the generative necessity [of scientific progress] is not one of activity, but of a dialectic."[47] In contrast to Cavaillès's commitment to Spinozism, Lautman remained a committed Platonist throughout his attenuated career. For both thinkers, nevertheless, the truths of mathematics were in no way compromised by the historical contingency of their manifestation. In point of fact, their manifestation in rational thought was a sign of their truth content. Lautman himself was unequivocal on this subject: "The participation of the sensible in the intelligible in Plato permits the identification, behind the changing appearances, of the intelligible relations of ideas. If the first contacts with the sensible are only sensations and emotions, the constitution of mathematical physics gives us access to the real through the knowledge of the structure with which it is endowed."[48] Deleuze would doubtless endorse this claim; it seems to express the element that he found so compelling in Maimon's project as well. Deleuze's call for a "reversal of Platonism" was not a call to do away with Plato but to "reverse" his denigration of the simulacrum to the benefit of the model/copy structure. Here again Lautman anticipates (or inspires) Deleuze's call: "We do not understand by Ideas the models whose mathematical entities would be merely copies, but rather, in the true Platonic sense of the term, the structural schemas according to which the effective theories are organized."[49] The Idea as "structural schema" adumbrates Deleuze's characterization of Ideas as "structures" or "multiplicities." But the resonance of Lautman's next proposition, concerning the relation of ideas to matter, with Deleuze's effort in *Difference and Repetition* is more remarkable still:

The Ideas are then like the laws according to which this matter is organized to constitute a World, but it isn't necessary that this world exist to realize in a concrete way the perfection of the Ideas. [. . .] [A]n effort of understanding adequate to the dialectical Ideas, by the very fact that it applies to knowing the internal connections of this dialectic, is creative of systems of more concrete notions in which these connections are asserted. The genesis is then no longer conceived as the material creation of the concrete from the Idea, but as the advent of notions relative to the concrete within an analysis of the Idea.[50]

If "the Idea" was clearly the keyword of Lautman's theoretical effort, it should be recalled that Cavaillès was more concerned to develop a "philosophy of the concept" and not "of the Idea." It is thus striking to find that "concept" as a concept comes under fire later in Deleuze's chapter. "It is the Idea's excess that explains the failing [*défaut*] of the concept. [. . .] In the Idea and its actualization, we find at once both the natural reason for the blockage of the concept and the supernatural reason for a repetition superior to that which the blocked concept subsumes. What remains outside the concept refers more profoundly to what is inside the Idea" (*DR*, 284/220tm). With this conclusion, Deleuze effectively recapitulates an argument Lautman and Cavaillès *actually had* concerning the relation between the Idea and the concept, and he takes Lautman's side. Spinoza was not as dear to Lautman as he was to Cavaillès. For Cavaillès, thought could not call upon an extrinsic resource or reserve of ideas in order to pursue its own execution. What was expressed in the concept was simply all that there was, with no remainder. For Lautman, the Idea's excessive relation to the concept, or solution, was fundamental. In a letter to the mathematician Maurice Fréchet, Lautman expressed his own understanding of his and Cavaillès's differences as follows:

> It is the spectacle of the constitution of these structural schemas that seemed to me to found the philosophical interest in mathematical thought. In sum, while Cavaillès searches in mathematics itself for the philosophical sense of mathematical thought, this sense appears to me rather in the connection of mathematics to a metaphysics (or Dialectic) of which it is the necessary extension. It constitutes the matter closest to Ideas. It seems to me that this is not a diminution for mathematics. It confers on it, on the contrary, an exemplary role.[51]

In an exchange of letters in 1938–39 concerning Lautman's forthcoming contribution to Cavaillès and Aron's publication venture, Cavaillès voiced his grievances with Lautman's approach. It appears that he could not countenance Lautman's recourse to a kind of *arrière-monde* for which mathematics itself served as the expression. "As for myself," Cavaillès wrote, "I would insist upon the impossibility of defining from the outside what are the internal necessities of a singular becoming."[52] A month earlier, Cavaillès sought to identify the main problem of Lautman's approach by citing Heidegger's influence on his thought. His comments on a first reading of "New Research on the Dialectical Structure of Mathematics" acquire a broader historical meaning in light of Deleuze's subsequent effort and are worth revisiting here:

> Heidegger vigorously rejects the opposition between essence and existence and wouldn't like that you even seem to be comparing him with Plato. I'd thought before that you allowed an immanence of ideas to their mathematical actualization. This doesn't seem to be the case now, at least if you go with Heidegger. Too bad—but you might be right in the end. For my part, I am so stuck in the similar problem (at root the same) of mathematical experience that I cannot see the link with any other way of posing it. But perhaps we'll wind up agreeing in the end—I'd like that very much.[53]

Cavaillès and Lautman would never have the chance to reconcile their differences. The Second World War intervened, leading to both of their premature deaths. But the great virtue of this surviving correspondence is to illuminate the core of their differences: Lautman's appropriation of Heidegger. Whereas Cavaillès evinced a growing distrust of Heidegger following the Davos encounter between the latter and Ernst Cassirer, for Lautman, Heidegger was an absolutely vital resource. Nowhere does Deleuze mention Lautman's debts to Heidegger, but they are perfectly manifest in the texts from Lautman that Deleuze cites, chief among them

"New Research." The Corbin volume *Qu'est-ce que la métaphysique?*, the source text for Deleuze's "What Is Grounding?" course in 1955–56, was Lautman's sole reference. In Lautman's short text, he insists upon the utility of applying Heidegger's distinction between ontological truth as the truth of being, and ontic truth as the truth of *existants*, to the domain of mathematics itself. The key point for Lautman is that access to these ontological truths nonetheless begins with an examination of the ontic realm: "[T]his for us is the fundamental point [. . .], that this disclosure of the ontological truth of being cannot be done without the concrete aspects of ontic existence taking shape at the same time."⁵⁴ Appreciation of this ontic/ontological relation is essential for coming to terms with the history of mathematics, in Lautman's reading, because it helps to recover the essential nature of mathematics' own historical becoming. This recovery is accomplished via a consideration of the structure of motivation subtending mathematics as a "rational activity of founding (*Begründung*)."⁵⁵ Clearly, for Lautman, consideration of the history of mathematics *tout court* is also what provides insight into the operations of mathematical thought in each discrete instance wherein it occurs. "The passage from this disclosure of the essence to the different possible forms of existence appears as soon as it is realized that the inquiry into the *why* is inseparable from a consideration of the possibles implied in *rather than* (*why* something exists *rather than* another thing, or *rather than* nothing)."⁵⁶ Whereas the implications of Heidegger's thinking for anthropological questions remain, in Lautman's estimation, "despite everything, very brief, one can, in regards to the relations between the Dialectic and Mathematics, follow the mechanism of this operation closely in which the analysis of Ideas is extended in effective creation, in which the *virtual* is transformed into the real."⁵⁷

It is striking to see how closely Deleuze's own thinking is anticipated here, notwithstanding the use of "real" for what will be thought of as "actual" in Deleuze's project. But the most surprising element of all is the extent to which this model of relation between the virtual and the actual/real—and the philosophical imperative, common to Lautman and Deleuze, to achieve a kind of "counter-actualization" that puts us back in touch with the virtual—remains tethered to a model that is neither Spinozist nor Bergsonian, but emphatically Heideggerian.

We have already defined, in our thesis, the priority of the Dialectic as that of "concern" or the "question" with respect to the response. It is a matter of an "ontological" anteriority, to use the words of Heidegger, exactly comparable to the status of the "intention" in regards to that "for the sake of." Just as the notion of "for the sake of" necessarily refers to an intention oriented toward this purpose, it is of the nature of the response to be an answer to a question already posed, and this, even if the idea of the question comes to the mind only after having seen the response. The existence of mathematical relations therefore necessarily refers back to the positive Idea of the search of similar relations in general."[58]

Combining Heideggerianism with Platonism—the very move, marrying irrationalism with rationalism, which Cavaillès deemed to be impossible—Lautman claims to be working toward a theory of genesis, not simply of mathematics but of genesis *as such*. "An intimate link thus exists between the transcendence of Ideas and the immanence of the logical structure of the solution to a dialectical problem, within mathematics. This link is the notion of genesis which we give it, at least as we have tried to grasp it, by describing the genesis of mathematics from the Dialectic."[59]

In the first chapter of *Difference and Repetition*, when Deleuze addresses Heidegger's thought directly, it is in terms of "the problem or the question" as that which is beyond the negative, or non-being, just as difference is beyond contradiction (89/54). But it is clear over the course of Deleuze's analysis in the second half of the book, where he returns to these issues, that the "question" remains too anthropocentric a formulation, much like "possibility" or "contradiction." This move is foreshadowed early on, however: "The oracle is questioned, but the oracle's response is itself a problem" (88/63). By focusing ultimately on the problem instead of the question, Deleuze aims to develop a model of problem/solution rather than question/answer. This theme then permits Deleuze to produce a philosophy that ostensibly stands in relation to Heidegger in the same way that Darwin's evolutionary biology stands in relation to anthropology.[60] It is no longer a question of "man" and his self-interrogation that is in play for philosophy but a broader issue of "life," understood to be an interminable series of broad problems and narrow solutions, expansive Ideas and "blocked concepts." But, as Lautman's formative effort shows, the form of this relation, however transformed, pushed back from man to life, is in fact conspicuously similar to Heidegger's.

In moving beyond Heidegger's ontological difference, Deleuze believes he has moved beyond man as a philosophical category and, by extension, man's constitutive essence as possibility. He is at pains to insist that the virtual not be confused with the possible: "The sole danger in all this would be to confuse the virtual with the possible. For the possible is opposed to the real; the process that belongs to the possible is thus a 'realization.' The virtual is not opposed to the real; it possesses a full reality in itself. Its process is actualization. It would be wrong to see only a verbal dispute here: it is a question of existence itself" (272–73/211tm). That Deleuze has the negative theology made possible by Heidegger's project in his sights is clear from the following passage. The possible is always retroactively imposed:

> Such is the defect of the possible: a defect that serves to condemn it as produced after the fact, as retroactively fabricated in the image of what resembles it. The actualization of the virtual, on the contrary, always takes place by difference, divergence or differenciation. Actualization breaks with resemblance as a process no less than it does with identity as a principle. Actual terms never resemble the singularities they incarnate: qualities and species never resemble the differential relations they incarnate. In this sense, actualization or differenciation is always a *genuine creation*. (273/212tm, emphasis added)[61]

No longer located at an origin, creation is deemed coextensive with existence itself. In this move, Heideggerian temporality is effectively flattened into a total, infinite space wherein everything happens *at the same time*. The peculiar time in question here is the time of Aiôn, the "pure and empty form of time." But what possible referent could the "pure and empty form of time" as a formula have, if not, quite simply, *space*?

In this instance, it would appear that Heidegger's project is folded back into Spinozism. Earlier, Deleuze followed Heidegger's lead in returning to the fractured "I" of Kant's philosophy. But where Heidegger read that fracture as constituted by time, Deleuze took the gap discerned between the "I think" and the "I am," and the spatial connotations of the figures "gap" and "fracture," literally. The gap is pure space—an *abyss*—the *empty* form of time. For time to be thought as "empty" it must be spatialized.

But if in this earlier instance we see Spinozism supervening on Heideggerian temporality, here we see, in the commitment to the causal model of the virtual and the actual, something like Heidegger supervening on Spinoza. For as the recourse to Lautman, and not Cavaillès, makes clear, Deleuze needs the concept of virtuality as an excess beyond actualization in order for his system to operate, that is, in order for anything to happen at all. Otherwise, Deleuze's Spinozism remains simply tautological.

Deleuze's Spinozism is one wherein "[n]othing is lost, each series existing only through the return of others. All has become simulacra" (*DR*, 95/69tm). But if nothing is lost, then, by the same measure, nothing is gained. Nonetheless, Deleuze affirms: "It is in this direction that we must look for the conditions, not of possible experience, but of real experience (selection, repetition, etc.). It is here that we find the lived reality of a sub-representative domain" (95/69). Throughout *Difference and Repetition*, Deleuze will not give up the conviction that this "lived reality" of a "sub-representative domain" is somehow more expansive, richer, than this world. Deleuze's response to Alquié—"I learned the specificity of philosophy from you"—acquires its full resonance here. This lived reality that Deleuze seeks is the site of the virtual, an inexhaustible resource. Given this inexhaustibile, though no less "real" element, how are we not simply returned to a vitalism, wherein life is the surplus over matter, or indeed a negative theology of the virtual?

The imperative of Gueroult's Spinozism, which Deleuze endorsed, was that nothing would remain obscure to the light of an intellect that followed the "absolute rationalism" proffered in the *Ethics*. But in *Difference and Repetition* Deleuze develops at length the notion of the Idea as the "distinct-*obscure*." The obscure in question here is the plenitude of the virtual. It would seem, then, that Spinozism is ultimately submitted to a Heideggerian structure in Deleuze's work from the 1960s. Though it is mapped onto a Spinozist notion of the two natures, the primacy of the virtual over the actual functions like that of Being to being in the readings of Heidegger developed by Corbin and Lautman. In the attempt to make Spinoza's substance "turn around the modes," Deleuze develops a post-Heideggerian antihumanism that extinguishes the category of the possible by transforming it into the virtual. But what is the real difference between these categories? Insofar as the virtual functions as Lautman's dialectic of problems, it appears there is not much difference. The moments where Deleuze comes closest to escaping Heidegger's one-way street from the possible to the real, from the ontological to the ontic, are those wherein he affirms the two-way nature of the relation between Thought and Extension, sometimes read as the virtual and the actual, and sometimes not. Nonetheless, there remains an equivocation between Heideggerianism and Spinozism that is not resolved in this pivotal moment of Deleuze's philosophical output.

The Persistence of the Virtual: Heidegger

The triumvirate of works that appeared in 1968–69—*Difference and Repetition*, *Spinoza and the Problem of Expression*, and *The Logic of Sense*—were not Deleuze's last words, on Spinoza or any other subject. In 1970, he published a short book, *Spinoza: Practical Philosophy*, that would be augmented in another edition in 1981. The aim of this work, which abandoned the technical scholasticism of his minor doctoral thesis, was the articulation of an intrinsically relational ethics of knowledge to be opposed to a hierarchical morality of law. In his 1977 dialogue with the journalist Claire Parnet, Deleuze would profess that "we have not even begun to understand Spinoza, and I no more than anyone else."[62] There is a way in which, following his encounter with Félix Guattari, Deleuze will become more Spinozist, insofar as he attempts to rethink, if not eliminate, the gap between the virtual and the actual that operated as a translation of Heidegger's ontological difference in his own system. Alberto Toscano has in fact identified a precise moment in *Anti-Oedipus* where he finds an "apparent attempt to affirm a thoroughgoing Spinozist materialism, *purged of any constitutive or genetic concept of virtuality*."[63] In the passage in question, "desiring-production," a core concept of this work, is the name for the material processes coextensive with the time of Chronos as presented in *The Logic of Sense*. Moreover, desiring-production is

> the actual factor. [. . .] On the contrary, it is Oedipus that depends on desiring-production. [. . .] [I]t is the Oedipus complex that is virtual, either inasmuch as it must be actualized in a neurotic formation as a derived effect of the actual factor, or inasmuch as it is dismembered and dissolved in a psychotic formation as the direct effect of this same factor. [. . .] Undecidable, *virtual*, reactive or reactional [*réactionnel*], such is Oedipus.[64]

As Toscano further notes, this relegation of the virtual to an *effect*, however retroactive, of the actual is anticipated in *The Logic of Sense* in the section on "Double Causality." There Deleuze writes, "There is no reason to repeat that sense is essentially *produced*. It is never originary but is always caused and derived" (116/95). As we will learn later in this book, sense, like the event, occurs in the time of Aiôn, the level or element that seems to be the site of the virtual in *Difference and Repetition*. If Chronos is the site of mechanical causality, then this would suggest it is the site of the "actual" in the terms of *Difference and Repetition*. But in this work, the actual clearly has the virtual as its condition. So how could "sense"—Aiôn's effects—be "caused" or "derived"? Part of the confusion here is that in *Difference and Repetition*, Deleuze is thinking of the relation of virtual to actual as a continuous process, a flow of accumulating and dissipating intensities. In *The Logic of Sense* the radical distinction between Aiôn and Chronos as distinct kinds of time is of paramount importance—hence the expression "double causality." To be sure, the image of depth and surfaces that accompanies this problematic would suggest continuity as well. But Deleuze's point is that surfaces themselves—like the "moment" Achilles overtakes the tortoise—are unlocalizable points that mark the disjuncture between these two causal series. In other words, Deleuze's fundamental argument remains the same in both books. Whereas in *Difference and Repetition* the wholly "ideal" nature of the limit point, as virtual and indiscernible in itself, is emphasized to the detriment of a fictive "cut" that separates instances, in *Logic of Sense* this notion of "cut" is rehabilitated in a heuristic sense to describe the moment when the events of Aiôn "divide" time into past and future.

If Alain Beaulieu is correct that much of *The Logic of Sense* was conceived to deal with the problems concerning time that remained unresolved in *Difference and Repetition*, then it seems that Deleuze himself may not have been entirely satisfied with the results.[65] When pressed on how his work with Guattari was to be understood in relation to the play of surfaces and depths in *The Logic of Sense*, Deleuze said that this relation no longer concerned him.[66] The progressive diminution of this dualism in Deleuze's thought seems to be borne out by the increasing references to a singular "plane of immanence" in his later works. In a 1978 text, "Spinoza and Us," this concept is directly attributed to Spinoza, as it will be again in *What Is Philosophy?*[67]

But the diminution of the virtual/actual dualism in favor of a singular plane of immanence is in many ways more apparent than real. The virtual itself is subjected to extensive rethinking in Deleuze's engagement with cinema in the 1980s. In these volumes the image as such, subjected to scrutiny throughout "The Image of Thought," is now read as the medium of the virtual's expression. In cinema's own progressive development, from the "movement-image" to the "time-image," the image acquires its full expressive power of counter-actualization, expressing a time that "ruptures with empirical succession."[68] Shortly after Deleuze's death in 1995, some working notes titled "The Actual and the Virtual" were found that were published as an appendix to the second edition of Deleuze's *Dialogues* with Parnet in 1996. In this compacted text, the virtual resurfaces in all its glory. "There is no purely actual object. [. . .] Any actual is surrounded by circles of constantly renewed virtualities."[69] The plane of immanence is the medium that takes us from the merely actual to the virtual that is its condition: "Here object and image are both virtual, and they constitute the plane of immanence wherein the actual object dissolves."[70] Deleuze wants to maintain the play of explication and implication between Spinozist substance and its modes; thus he writes, "The virtual is never independent of the singularities that cut and divide it."[71] It is this total lack of independence, or autonomy, on the part of the virtual that allows Deleuze to collapse this apparent dualism back into monism: "But all the planes make but one, following the path that leads to the virtual. The plane of immanence includes at once the virtual and its actualization without there being an assignable limit between the two. [. . .] The actualization of the virtual is the singularity, whereas the actual itself is constituted individuality."[72] The "actualization of the virtual" is Spinoza's *natura naturans*, whereas the actual itself is "constituted individuality," *natura naturata*. Deleuze concludes in a manner that seeks to maintain the interplay of the virtual and the actual (be it understood as that between Thought and Extension, substance and its modes, or *natura naturans* and *natura naturata*) but that makes clear the predominance of the virtual in his ontology: "The actual falls from the plane like fruit whereas actualization refers back to the plane as that which restructures the object as subject."[73]

Via Spinoza's "plane of immanence," Deleuze presents a model for how the object becomes subject through the mechanism of "counter-actualization" itself.[74] In this process, the mere "actual" object becomes aware of the "virtual" that is its vital, subjective source. Though it is presented as consistent with his Spinozism, it is precisely this aspect of Deleuze's thinking that is most indebted to the Heideggerian mode of thought developed most usefully for Deleuze by Lautman.[75] It is a testament to the power of involution, of the effort of folding ideas back in on themselves, which is the major constant of Deleuze's philosophical methodology, that we can no longer tell whether Deleuze has made Heidegger a Spinozist, or Spinoza a Heideggerian. Yet it is incumbent upon us to try to reach some sort of conclusion about the nature of this involution. One of Deleuze's own "monstrous" comparisons is of great assistance on this score.

In his later piece on Jarry and Heidegger, Deleuze describes Jarry's absurdist manipulation of language in the following terms: "The affect (A) produces in the current language (B) a kind of footstomping, a stammering, an obsessional tom-tom, like a repetition that never ceases to create something new (C)."[76] This compact formula is a fitting distillation of Deleuze's own project. The affect (A) is Spinozism, manifested as an unerring motivational commitment to absolute rationalism. The "current language" (B) is Heideggerian philosophy in France. The formative milieu of Deleuze's development was complexly overdetermined by the effort to develop all the implications of the ontological problematic that Heidegger introduced into French philosophy. The "something new" (C) is Deleuze's philosophy itself. Its mechanism is incessant repetition, reiteration of the same problem, a "footstomping" and an "obsessional tom-tom" that nonetheless results in the creation of the new in each instance. But even this "new" is bound in a sense by its own conditions. Heidegger's project remains the horizon in which Deleuze's thought is located, even as it beats the Spinozist tom-tom in an effort to transcend the very notion of horizonality itself, the sign of finitude that functions as a condition of all possibility. The virtual and the actual are a translation of Heidegger's thinking into Bergsonian terms through the operative medium of Spinozist rationalism. But if the excess of the virtual seems to countenance a kind of positive theology that is hardly distinguishable from Heidegger's negative theology, this is because reading Spinoza "after" Heidegger has meant subjecting Spinoza to Heidegger as a condition, whether Deleuze is cognizant of this fact or not.

The Power of Thought: Spinoza

If the post-1960s development of Deleuze's effort witnesses a fleeting commitment to "thoroughgoing Spinozist materialism," that is, a denigration of the virtual as an effect of the actual, which is quickly abandoned in favor of a rehabilitation of the virtual, there is another aspect of Deleuze's thought that witnesses a radicalization of the Spinozism informing his major works of the 1960s. This is the power attributed to thought, in its formal capacities, over all other aspects of existence. Already in *Spinoza and the Problem of Expression*, Deleuze recognized thought's overweening power in Spinoza's system as a problem. If being is univocal, how is it that

Thought appears to supervene on Extension, accessing not only its own domain of ideas and sentiments but the domain of material matters as well? Thought appears to possess a greater power of being, as Spinoza's interlocutor Tschirnhaus noted, because if every modal affection of an attribute requires the idea of it in order to qualify as such, then Thought seems to be greater than its Extensional counterpart.[77] Spinoza maintains that the relation of an idea to another idea, that is, when an idea takes another idea as its object, is absolutely homologous to the relation that occurs when an idea takes an object in Extension as its object. So if each attribute is infinite in its kind, there still seems to be *more going on* in the attribute of Thought than in Extension, in light of the incessant proliferation of ideas within the intellect.

Deleuze's answer to this dilemma is to introduce a distinction between powers (*puissances*) and attributes. Within each attribute there exists a dualism of powers, a power to think and to know in the case of Thought, and a power to exist and to act in the case both of Extension and the totality of existence in the most general sense. But it quickly becomes clear that Deleuze introduces this baroque distinction in order to validate the charge against Spinoza leveled by Tschirnhaus—that Thought seems privileged above Extension—and even to welcome it:

For one only finds inconsistency by confusing two very different principles of equality in Spinoza. On the one hand, all attributes are equal; but this must be understood in relation to the power of existing and acting. On the other hand, this power of existing is only one half of the absolute, the other half being a power of thinking equal to it; it is in relation to this second power that the attribute of Thought enjoys certain privileges.[78]

But this privilege ultimately plays a metonymic role for Deleuze as the formal model for *power* as such: "It is the equality of powers that confers special capacities in a domain which is no longer that of the equality of attributes. *The attribute of Thought is to the power of thinking what all attributes (including Thought) are to the power of existing and acting.*"[79] In other words, we first discover the nature of power as such through the experience of the power of thinking. For Spinoza, philosophy begins with the factic immediacy of the true idea—"for we have true ideas."[80] The reason the first idea is simply factic is that it is without content. It is the *fact* of thinking itself, experienced as an idea. In place of the temporalizing formula of Descartes—"I think *therefore* I am"—which set the rubric for modern subjectivity and which posits a movement from thinking to being, Spinoza affirms the axiom "Man thinks."[81] Period, full stop. Deleuze, no less than Spinoza, remains committed to this ontological primacy accorded to thinking throughout his work. In this regard, it is not surprising that the work in which thought appears to cede ground to another essential component of human existence—desire—is precisely that undertaken in collaboration with Guattari, for whom the task of thinking a truly interpersonal conception of desire was of the utmost urgency. Spinoza himself wrote, "Desire is the essence of man."[82] But Deleuze sought to develop a philosophy that went beyond "man," which meant remaining focused on what was ontologically primary in Spinoza's system when all was said and done: thought itself.

In *Difference and Repetition*, Deleuze explored the full riches of thought, of the Idea, on the virtual plane that was its home. But this effort squared the circle of his Spinozism by retaining the notion that thought was a domain, which qua virtual, was in a way close to the "excess" posited by Alquié as that toward which thought always moves. "Philosophers," Alquié wrote, "by showing that the world does not contain its own conditions, go toward a Being which is not a world."[83] More emphatically, "[N]othing disorients us more than philosophy precisely because it takes us out of the world to something that is not a world."[84] This is the sense of Deleuze's denigration of the concept to the profit of the Idea in this book. Though Deleuze equivocated on his abandonment of the relation between surfaces and depths (and, on a lesser scale, the virtual and the actual), his later work displayed a fundamental revision of the Idea/concept problematic. This revision appears to reconcile him more closely with Gueroult's absolute rationalism than Alquié's descriptions of philosophical transcendence. Indeed, Deleuze's final major book of philosophy, *What Is Philosophy?*, published in 1990, is best read as the valediction of a life's work.[85] Here the formal category of the concept qua concept is completely rehabilitated. Philosophy, as distinct from science and art, is defined as "the creation of concepts." Though Cavaillès's name is nowhere mentioned, Deleuze returns to the essence of the project with which our story began, affirming the power of thought itself, impervious to mitigating limits The virtual Idea is no longer privileged over the blocked, merely actualized concept. *Concepts* are now deemed to be the medium of thought itself, unblocking themselves in their own proliferation.[86]

Deleuze, more than any other thinker of contemporary philosophy, has attempted to take Spinoza's injunction to think "under the aspect of eternity" to its ultimate conclusion.[87] Spinozist "immortality" begins and ends with an Idea, and as such it is purely ideal and formal. The idea of immortality is born from the inaugural idea coterminous with thinking itself. Spinozist beatitude, or blessedness, occurs when the idea is no longer conceived as an underwhelming realization of a possibility greater than itself but as the formal expression of everything all at once in a discrete singularity. With Deleuze's Spinoza, the negative theology of Heidegger's philosophy has been turned inside out, involuted, to produce a positive theology in which nothing is ever lost and redemption does not await. In *What Is Philosophy?* Spinoza receives the appellation "Christ of philosophers."[88] The peculiar salvation on offer in this philosophy is "pure and empty," a form that is without content and thus indiscriminate as a result.

In effect, what Deleuze's Spinozism offers is an ontological *syntax* that serves as a critical riposte to all theories of ontological *semantics*. This is the full sense of Deleuze's hostility to hermeneutics. For Deleuze, to ask, "[W]hat is the *meaning* of being?" is to ask a poorly posed question because it cannot but presuppose the content of its own response. The meaning "disclosed" in the response will always be read as having come from without, yet it will be the result of a retroactively posited possibility; the question itself is an appeal to authority that seeks a secure content that might halt, however momentarily, the infinite play of formal differentiation. In a late essay, "He Stuttered," a seemingly innocuous subject serves as a medium for Deleuze to develop this specific point. Through various literary references, Deleuze shows how the stutter is evocative of language as a pure repetitive syntax that is anterior to the semantic content of full speech: "It is no longer the formal or superficial syntax that governs the equilibriums of language, but a syntax in the process of becoming, a creation of syntax that gives birth to a foreign language within language, a grammar of disequilibrium."[89]

In becoming active, however, and ceasing to "govern," syntax is no less formal as a result, just as Spinoza's attributes Thought and Extension become "active forms" in Deleuze's reading. Deleuze links the pure form of the stutter to the notion of the minor in music. For Deleuze, the concept of the minor was always to be understood in this musical sense, as the mode of expression that refuses resolution, that never accomplishes itself in the cadence of a final resolve that might retroactively impose musical "sense" on the preceding aural series. In these same terms, when asked about what the political notion of leftism meant to him, Deleuze responded that "a government of the left does not exist. [. . .] The left is never a majority qua left."[90] For him, to be on the left meant nothing other than always "becoming *minoritaire*." The paradox is that this was the only tenable position precisely because the minor is that which is untenable, always changing, and never resolving. What is most striking about this injunction is that it is again *purely* formal; there is no content to a Deleuzean "politics." For Deleuze, this abrogation of content for an embrace of constant formal displacement was the supreme virtue, and to partake of this virtue in the most maximal sense was "the supreme act of philosophy."[91] Deleuze recognized that the Spinozist universe was one wherein oxygen lacked, which explains why this participation could take place only in the incorporeal events of thought. But it was the power of thought itself that revealed the ontological primacy of form over content.

Spinoza is stuttering for all eternity in Deleuze's universe. His ethics never resolves into a content-based morality that might be followed or implemented. Spinozism does not stand as a possibility that might become a reality. There is never a meaningful answer to the "question" in Spinozism, only an interminable series of problems and incessantly revised solutions. "The world 'gets made' as [the Spinozist] God calculates; there would be no world if the calculation were correct [*juste*]" (*DR*, 286/222tm). In light of his rejection of possibility, a fundamental category of phenomenological ontology, Deleuze's insistence on the impossibility of a final reward, of a final exact answer that may absolve our efforts, yields new meaning to the proposition with which the *Ethics* ends, and with which we began: "Beatitude is not the reward of virtue, but virtue itself."[92]

Conclusion

The Sense of Spinozism

The Spinozism of Gilles Deleuze ends with neither a bang nor a whimper but a stutter. In this, it accomplishes a goal not unlike Althusser's evacuation of any fixed meaning or predetermined content for philosophy in favor of a "philosophy without object" that operates through punctual, divisive interventions in a field not of its making. There is ultimately no resolution of the Heideggerian and Spinozist elements in Deleuze's philosophy. Yet Deleuze's philosophical aim was to produce a mode of thinking that knew no resolution. His ornate account of the stutter as a primordial syntax that is anterior to the semantics of meaning is consistent with his arguments for Spinozism as a philosophy of pure forms that never coalesce into fixed entities. As a result, a politics drawn from Deleuze's philosophy cannot be said to be "meaningful" in any familiar sense of the term. This much is clear from Deleuze's own definition of leftism as always being on the side of the minor, a category formally defined as that which never resolves into a resonant or cohesive whole. But what of those situations where the "major" position might be deemed superior, or indeed, more just? By taking leave of morality in favor of a formalist Spinozist "ethics," Deleuze makes it difficult for his philosophy to illuminate such a situation. His philosophy articulates an ontological inequality anterior to human experience that is expressed in terms of the infinite differentiations of the cosmos. The ambition of his philosophical insight results in the modesty of its political bearing.

This political modesty is ambivalent in its implications. To be sure, a stuttering king can never order an execution. But a stuttering legislator also passes no law. Nevertheless, a danger in these scenarios is that, unable to discern or grasp a meaning in the authority's phrases, invested listeners will create this meaning for themselves and then attribute their directives to an order from on high that remains obscure in itself. It is easy to see how an unbridled enthusiasm might become the arbiter in this milieu. If claims to authority cannot be adjudicated with recourse to meaningful extrinsic criteria, then authority becomes the result of the maximal expression of intrinsic relations—Deleuze's favored "intensities"—devoid of decipherable content. Power becomes coextensive with right, as it does in Spinoza's *Theological-Political Treatise* and his unfinished *Political Treatise*.

The ambiguities of this position, and the political ambiguities of Spinozism more generally, are evident in Michael Hardt and Antonio Negri's attempt in the first decade of the twenty-first century to develop a neo-Marxist theory of emancipation for a global age of saturated interconnectivity. The ambition of Hardt and Negri's project naturally provoked a series of reactions, much of it targeting the Spinozism at the core of their thinking. In the words of one ungenerous critic, the Spinozism of Hardt and Negri is "a last-ditch Salvationist movement, aimed at redeeming the status of -isms. It stands for 'ismhood,' a necessarily total secular faith fusing conceptual satisfaction and moral-political guidance."[1] Tom Nairn was right to identify the redemptive element of their project, but the hyphenated linkage of "moral-political" does a disservice to the particular agenda that Hardt and Negri have in mind. Keenly aware of the disastrous consequences of the party form in its most authoritarian and programmatic historical instances, the authors have been dedicated to a thinking of politics that would itself provide no political directives yet remain emancipatory. On the first page of *Commonwealth*, the final book of their trilogy, they claim to "articulate an ethical project, an ethics of democratic political action within and against Empire."[2] Far from being a sleight of hand that would subsume the political under the ethical, Hardt and Negri's remarks here point to the most valuable element of the Deleuzean legacy in its hybrid Heideggerian/Spinozistic form. This is the notion that the best a philosophical ontology can do is to seek to induce alternate and hopefully more beneficent ways of perceiving and conceiving the world. A deductive politics is out of the question. And in case there is any ambiguity regarding the dual filiation at play in Hardt and Negri's thinking on this score, their preface to *Commonwealth* concludes as follows:

> Jean-Luc-Nancy, setting out from premises analogous to ours, wonders if "one can suggest a 'Spinozan' reading, or rewriting, of [Heidegger's] *Being and Time*." We hope that our work points in that direction, overturning the phenomenology of nihilism and opening up the multitude's processes of productivity and creativity that can revolutionize our world and institute a shared common wealth.[3]

This formulation is striking, but no doubt one of the implications of the preceding account, and its last two chapters in particular, is that Hardt and Negri need not orient themselves in the direction of a Spinozan rewriting of *Being and Time* because their work is already inscribed in a trajectory marked by that disjunctive synthesis. This synthesis is also evident in the poetic figure of their preface's closing line: "We want not only to define an event but also to grasp the spark that will set the prairie ablaze."[4] Whereas "defining an event" may fit within the terms of a Spinozistic rationalism that seeks to form an adequate idea of things, the desire to "grasp the spark that will set the prairie ablaze" suggests an ontology of excess and expression that squares awkwardly with the critical Spinozism of thinkers prior to Deleuze, including Althusser.

Notwithstanding the breadth of engagement with a variety of political thinkers and contemporary political movements, a rather singular ontological conception of power lies at the heart of Hardt and Negri's theoretical vision. In this vision, power supervenes on authority, conceptually and ontologically, which does not mean that authority disappears as a political problem or an ethical conundrum. It is merely displaced into more foundational and in the end arguably more obscure ontological processes. This is one of the troubling elements of Hardt and Negri's concept of the "multitude," the centerpiece of their thought and the vanishing mediator who will transform the trappings of "Empire" into the democratic forms of "Commonwealth." The multitude is a category that grows through the extension of common notions. But the content of this category is only ever presented as an inchoate power that results from sheer volume. This assemblage is deemed impervious to external adjudication simply as a consequence of its refusal to recognize an outside. The multitude claims authority for itself and justifies its acts as the expressed meaning of its own purely formal constitution. The excision of a procedurally conceived politics in favor of a democratic ethics figures here as a kind of return of the repressed. In the last instance, the disavowal of the juridical is a consequence of a justice that is ontologically taken for granted, and political right seems founded on the abjuration of mere politics in favor of a conception of the political as a site of more primordial or authentic relations. Spinozism is deemed revolutionary and thereby good precisely because it gives "productivity" and "creativity" ontological grounds. The question of whether certain products or creations are good or bad is rendered deliberately unintelligible in Spinoza's system. Yet one is still left with the impression that productivity and creativity are somehow goods in themselves for Hardt and Negri. This is one meaning of Spinozism in their work.

Despite Hardt and Negri's own grounding of these claims in Spinozism, there remains a peculiar paradox at the center of all of this. Notwithstanding the intercalated thematics of power and right in Spinoza's own political writings, the investment in what the fundamental relations of Spinoza's formal ontology might "mean" in any given situation, political or otherwise, is a gesture that is arguably contrary to the critical essence of Spinoza's rationalism. The appendix to Book I of the *Ethics* contains one of philosophy's most famous critiques of the "first cause," a cause conceived as a source of meaning or an explanatory principle. Spinoza narrates a fictional conversation that tends toward an infinite regress. Why did the rock fall on the man's head? Because of the wind. Why did the wind blow? Because of the sea. Why was the man walking by at that time? He was going to see a friend. "And so they will go on and on asking the causes of causes, until you take refuge in the will of God—that is, the asylum of ignorance." Spinoza develops his philosophy as a critique of the attempt to discern the "meaning" or "reason" for a discrete event in a site extrinsic to the event itself. In its disavowal of the quest for anything other than an immanent cause—which cannot be assimilated to a phenomenologically conceived giver or *donateur* of sense—Spinoza's philosophy forecloses the extrapolation of meaning. What this means, however, is that there is no way, within the terms of Spinoza's philosophy, to determine what Spinozism itself *means*.

If Spinozism does have a meaning, then, it comes from its history. For in the "rarefied air" of the Spinozist universe, nothing means anything. Things simply are; relations happen. And as soon as they happen, we can always establish that they happened of necessity because there is no other perspective or counter-factual world from which we might assess them. Ideas unfold by the same necessity that inheres in the material world, which means that they cannot be qualified from without. The only qualification that takes place in Spinozism is the qualitative change accomplished in the infinitely repeated modal relation of the substantial attributes Thought and Extension. Every idea or act is a discrete mode that is in itself and thus impervious to evaluation. As Deleuze himself says, in homage to Godard, in philosophy there are "no just ideas, just ideas" (*pas d'idées justes, juste des idées*).[5]

Kant's concern was that Spinozism, as a philosophical disposition and worldview, leads directly to enthusiasm. But perhaps it is the effort to inscribe some kind of fixed meaning in or for Spinozism that leads to enthusiasm, whether it be as the harbinger of emancipatory Enlightenment or the blueprint for a radical democracy. In light of its varied history, however, this effort at inscription can appear more as a betrayal of Spinozism than an allegiance to it.

On this score, if Hardt and Negri's project is exemplary of the ambiguities of the Spinozist rationalist legacy, Alain Badiou's philosophy is arguably all the more so for being avowedly anti-Spinozist in some of its most basic positions, especially those concerning meaning and inscription. And if Badiou does not consider himself a Spinozist, this is because he recognizes that Spinozist metaphysics leaves no space for politics as he conceives it. There is no space in the Spinozist universe, no *void*, in which meaning or sense, or, in Badiou's rubric, a truth, might be inscribed.[6] Yet Badiou's ontology, the fundamental framework for his philosophical thought, is consistent with Spinozism in that it affirms that meaning is not a matter of ontology. As Ray Brassier writes, for Badiou, being qua being "is insignificant; it means, quite literally, nothing."[7] If Badiou's theory of the Event is a betrayal of Spinozist rationalism, it is a deliberate one, for it is the impossibility of the Event, and consequently the impossibility of a meaningful category of the "subject," that accounts for Badiou's critical attitude to Spinozism.

By the very same measure, however, one can produce a Spinozist critique of Badiou. If Badiou renounces an ontology of meaning, he nevertheless retains a metaphysics of sense. For in Badiou's system, the Event, as a discrete singularity that is metaphysically transcendent to the situations described by his ontology, is what structures the existential sequences that unfold from it and imbues them with value and purpose. In this way, it plays the role of a first cause not unlike Spinoza's "will of God—the asylum of ignorance." The opacity of the Event's "truth" functions like the opacity of God's will, which is to say that its meaning is developed only in the here and now by the enthusiastic subjects who recognize it as conditioning their activity and investments. In seeking to develop a Spinozistic critique of Badiou, we come upon the paradoxical sense of Althusser's conviction that following Spinoza's dogmatism results in a liberation of the mind, for it is a dogmatism that recuses all pathos of the "Event." Indeed, the supreme virtue of Spinozism in this instance is its foreclosure of *Schwärmerei*, a foreclosure that results from its abnegation of recourse to any discrete, extrinsic instance that might serve to obviate the responsibilities of thought and action left to their own devices. By the same stroke, however, there is nothing in Spinozism to say what these responsibilities are or ought to be. The paradox is precise: it is by not entailing a politics that Spinozism allows for politics. It allows for a politics untethered to metaphysical determination and independent from speculative rumination.

Althusser and Deleuze each figure as Spinozists because their rationalist commitments at once exemplify and exhaust the political purchase of their efforts, regardless of intent. As a result their works achieve—in effect, if not necessarily in principle—a critique of the attempt, widespread in the phenomenological tradition and beyond, to make politics a derivative specimen of a more foundational ontology. Politics is not derivative from more basic ways of Being for the same reason that it cannot be derived from Substance. The whole point of Spinoza's metaphysics is to think of human affairs, political or otherwise, not as manifestations of substance but simply *as* substance. A Heideggerian might argue something similar. Politics is not derivative of Being; rather, an ontological discourse of "the political" merely describes those existential modalities that form the ontic realm of politics. But the differential valuation implicit in the Heideggerian frame is unmistakable, especially when viewed next to the Spinozist one. Such a brute comparison no doubt loses much nuance. The point nevertheless remains: in Spinoza, there is no "ontological difference." The difference between *natura naturans* and *natura naturata* is not an ontological difference. It is the difference between two ways of describing the same nature in a lateral, temporal way; the register of the distinction is epistemological. Likewise, the distinction between Thought and Extension is not an ontological difference in the Heideggerian sense of the ontological and the ontic but in a uniquely Spinozist sense of two completely equal but radically distinct attributes of Substance. The paradox is that this distinction that is thought absolutely is always experienced relatively, as the distinction between two manifestations of the same event in the realm of perception. The brain does not generate the mind for the same reason that the mind does not shape the brain. Neither is greater than or supervenient on the other as a matter of rationalist principle.

The vicissitudes of the "virtual" in Deleuze's project notwithstanding, the critical imperatives inherent in Spinoza's rationalism prohibit the identification of a realm of existence in excess of or somehow more fulsome than the world as it presents itself to thought. Thus, complications arise when Althusser and Deleuze seek to derive political lessons from Spinoza's metaphysics. The irony is that what they are really showing is that neither metaphysics nor ontology can determine the content, or the agenda, of political life. This is also why, notwithstanding the shift of register to political and ethical domains, Althusser and Deleuze remain the inheritors of the Spinozism of Cavaillès and Gueroult. Cavaillès and Gueroult held to the principles of Spinozist rationalism in order to show that any recourse to fixed transcendental structures could not but serve as refuge in an "asylum of ignorance" threatening to compromise science and rational thought.

When Deleuze writes that Spinoza, "the most philosophic of all philosophers [. . .], teaches the philosopher how to become a non-philosopher,"[8] he is affirming the consequences of a philosophical exit from philosophy's own ambitions for the world. The irony is manifold, in that arguably the most ambitious philosophical system in the history of philosophy teaches the insufficiency of philosophy. Nonetheless, its historical effect is at once salutary and corrosive, or salutary because it is corrosive. It corrodes philosophical efforts to ground morality or justification in principles that philosophy would deem a priori and thus unimpeachable. The result is a healthy skepticism toward the rights philosophy often arrogates for itself. In the end, *Deus sive Natura* is not a norm but a fact, one that undermines appeals to authority that are deemed off-limits to contestation, be they in a transcendental beyond or an affective interiority or set of relations.[9] There are many historical lessons on the insufficiency of philosophy, but the specificity of the Spinozist lesson is this: this insufficiency ought not to turn us toward other otherworldly experiences beyond philosophy's reach—for nothing is beyond philosophy's reach in Spinoza's "absolute rationalism"—but toward the world, this world, the only world there is.

In the end, perhaps F. H. Jacobi was right in targeting Spinozism's immorality and thereby launching the pantheism controversy that provoked Kant's ire. To be a Spinozist means employing the full resources of rational thought to evacuate the truth content of religious, moral, or political claims. It means recognizing what is true as something that is indifferent to its moral consequences because it is independent of the domain of morality. For Spinoza, recognition of this fact was the path to beatitude. In 2008, Jean-Luc Marion asked, "Are we really happier when we know more and better, and are we better at willing the good the better we know the true?"[10] Much as the true was its own sign for Spinoza, it was also its own value. But the rational process of abstraction required to develop an adequate understanding of the "true idea" leads to a concept of the "true idea" as one that is not commensurable with other ideas and not applicable to anything other than itself. The true is completely indifferent to opinion, which means it is also indifferent to the agonism of politics. The true is in fact not the foundation for "willing the good" in Spinoza's rationalism, but, then again, neither is the establishment of the good the pathway to truth. Spinozism helps us recognize that we cannot defend what we deem to be good by claiming it to be true, be it as a matter of rational faith or of rational thought.

In 1968, François Regnault published an essay in the *Cahiers pour l'Analyse*, "Dialectic of Epistemologies," whose method made use of a play on the French word *sens*, as signifying both meaning or sense, on the one hand, and direction or trajectory, on the other. Regnault's attempt to develop some of Cavaillès's remarks on Plato's *Parmenides* is instructive here. For the sense of a philosophical perspective, or indeed a set of philosophical claims, is intimately bound with the direction it takes, in history and in the trajectory of singular philosophical efforts. The *sens* of Regnault's dialectic ended where it began, and here, too, one thread in the history of Spinozism seems to lead us back to Spinoza's point of departure and the professed intent of his philosophical effort. As Brunschvicg remarked, "Spinoza devoted himself to philosophy because he asked himself how he ought to live."[11] For Spinoza, living according to reason did not mean establishing the limits of reason in advance. It meant recognizing that the limits to reason were not intrinsic to reason itself. If the equanimity that forms part of the popular image of Spinoza seems antithetical to the enthusiasm that has troubled others, from Kant to Marion, perhaps this has something to do with the fact that, in committing himself to reason, Spinoza did not consider himself to be committing a transgression. This explains why his confidence in reason is not to be confused with some kind of faith in its powers. Those who would insist that at root this confidence is indistinguishable from faith and thereby a subordinate species of it—rationalism as a kind of religion—do so because they are fearful of the unpredictable and untold shifts in our understanding that will continue to result from reason's interminable concatenation, locally and historically. "An evil doctrine, a forlorn philosophy—said his enemies. I know not whether good or evil—replied Spinoza; it is enough that it is true."[12] Spinoza's equanimity is intimately linked to the sense of this "enough," which need not be seen as either a cipher for irrationalism or a recipe for quietism. In fact, when read in light of the history of Spinozism, it begins to look like an antidote to both.

Notes

INTRODUCTION

1. Marion and Birnbaum, "Spinoza."
2. Badiou and Birnbaum, "Aristote." Birnbaum begins the interview by asking Badiou what place Aristotle occupies in his philosophical itinerary, to which Badiou responds: "A very important place: that of the Adversary." Glucksmann and Birnbaum, "Platon." For other examples, see Kristeva and Birnbaum, "Rousseau"; Milner and Birnbaum, "Marx"; and Nancy and Birnbaum, "Nietzsche."
3. On Descartes, see Marion, *Sur l'ontologie grise de Descartes, Sur la théologie blanche de Descartes, Sur la prisme métaphysique de Descartes*. His major works in phenomenology also form a triptych: *Reduction and Givenness, Being Given, In Excess*.
4. Kant, "What Does It Mean to Orient Oneself in Thinking?," 14–15. On the pantheism controversy that provoked Kant's response, see Beiser, *The Fate of Reason*, 44–118; and Goetschel, *Spinoza's Modernity*, 11–17.
5. For an assessment of Kant's complex relationship to fanaticism and enthusiasm, see Toscano, *Fanaticism*, 120–48.
6. Baring, *The Young Derrida*; Hammerschlag, *The Figural Jew*; Geroulanos, *An Atheism That Is Not Humanist*; Kleinberg, *Generation Existential*; Moyn, *Origins of the Other*. Vincent Descombes's classic *Modern French Philosophy* set the paradigm for postwar French intellectual history as a shift from the influence of the "three H's"—Hegel, Husserl, and Heidegger—to that of the thinkers Paul Ricoeur deemed the "masters of suspicion"—Marx, Freud, and Nietzsche (3–5). Descombes's heuristic remains useful, but this more recent historiography has shown the extent to which this transition was not so much a shift of concern as a deepening of issues first introduced by the "three H's," now pursued under a different set of proper names.
7. Israel, *Radical Enlightenment, Enlightenment Contested, Democratic Enlightenment*. The most important case for an emancipatory Spinozism in contemporary political theory also forms a triptych: Michael Hardt and Antonio Negri's *Empire, Multitude*, and *Commonwealth*. Spinoza's role in "the affective turn," in which Hardt and Negri's project can be situated, is ubiquitous, due largely to Deleuze's seminal work for this body of thought. A pioneering book in the field

was Massumi, *Parables of the Virtual*. For an extensive engagement with Spinoza from a broadly affective and materialist perspective, see Sharp, *Spinoza and the Politics of Renaturalization*. See as well the essays in Vardoulakis, *Spinoza Now*. A more explicitly structuralist engagement with Spinoza's theory of affect, one tied to an economic analysis of contemporary capitalism, has emerged in the work of Frédéric Lordon. See Lordon, *La Société des affects*.

8. The key work is Cusset, *French Theory*.

9. This phenomenon is notable in the title and conception of the two volumes that compose Dosse, *History of Structuralism*.

10. See Macksey and Donato, *The Structuralist Controversy*.

11. Cusset, *French Theory*, 28–32. Derrida's essay "Structure, Sign, and Play in the Discourse of the Human Sciences" appears in Derrida, *Writing and Difference*.

12. Despite their divergent methods and conclusions, Edward Baring and Martin Hägglund agree on this point. See Baring, *The Young Derrida*; and Hägglund, *Radical Atheism*.

13. On the peak of this formalism, see the two volumes of Hallward and Peden, *Concept and Form*.

14. Ricoeur, *Husserl*, 98.

15. In addition to Hallward and Peden, *Concept and Form*, see Eyers, *Post-Rationalism*.

16. Cited in Dosse, *The Rising Sign*, 237.

17. Zac, *La Morale de Spinoza, L'Idée de la vie dans la philosophie de Spinoza, Spinoza et l'interprétation de l'écriture*. After helping to edit the Pléaide edition of Spinoza's writings in 1954, Misrahi later prepared a doctoral thesis titled *Le Désir et la réflexion dans la philosophie de Spinoza*. Spinoza's relationship to Judaism would be a guiding theme of much of Misrahi's work. For an alternative assessment, see Brykman, *La Judéité de Spinoza*.

18. Delbos, *Le Problème morale dans la philosophie de Spinoza, Le Spinozisme*.

19. See Warren Montag's remarks in Balibar, *Spinoza and Politics*, xii–xiii; and Duffy, "French and Italian Spinozism," 149–68.

20. See Balibar, *Spinoza and Politics*; Macherey, *Hegel or Spinoza, Avec Spinoza, Introduction à l'Ethique de Spinoza*; Negri, *The Savage Anomaly*.

21. In addition to the authors cited is Pierre-François Moreau, arguably the current doyen of Spinoza studies in France. See his major study, *Spinoza: L'Éxpérience et l'éternité*. Moreau's focus on experience speaks to the extent to which post-1968 engagements with Spinoza reflected a departure from the earlier reception. Moreau's focus on experience is productive precisely to the extent the concept was previously regarded as anathema to Spinozism.

22. A brief discussion of Desanti's work and its relationship to other French readers interested in the mathematical Husserl, from Cavaillès to Derrida, can be found in Baring, *The Young Derrida*, 152–61. See as well Sebbah, *Testing the Limit*, 88–103.

23. Althusser, *Philosophy and the Spontaneous Philosophy of the Scientists*, 210.

24. On the theme of post-Marxism, see Breckman, *Adventures of the Symbolic*. For accounts of the impact of May 1968 and internal political developments in the 1970s on the development of French political thought, see, respectively, Bourg, *From Revolution to Ethics*; and Christofferson, *French Intellectuals against the Left*.

25. The three most significant current theoretico-political projects that remain indebted to Althusser are no doubt those of Alain Badiou, Étienne Balibar, and Jacques Rancière. To be sure, in Rancière's case, the populist theme of his life's work is intelligible largely as a rejection of Althusser's thought. See Rancière, *Althusser's Lesson*. The fact that Badiou and Balibar pursue such divergent projects is a testament to the fact that Althusserianism, far from being irredeemably doctrinaire, opened up a variety of paths of inquiry, not all of which are wholly reconcilable with one another (an apt description for Spinozism, too, one might add). Still, what distinguishes this work from the "post-Marxisms" of Claude Lefort and related thinkers is the continued allegiance to the Marxist inheritance. The result is a mode of critique that presents itself as self-consciously internal to Marxism rather than geared toward salvaging what is valuable from Marxism as it seeks to exit the paradigm.

26. Foucault, "Life: Experience and Science," 466; Roudinesco, *Philosophy in Turbulent Times*, 31.

27. Foucault, "Theatrum Philosophicum," 346.

28. Contemporary Spinozism in this instance refers to the materialist or vitalist Spinozism—what we might regrettably designate as a "continental Spinozism"—that squares awkwardly with the proto-liberal Spinoza described in Jonathan Israel's project. As an encyclopedia of references to Spinozism and an inventory of the dissemination of Spinoza's ideas in the early modern period, Israel's three-volume work (thus far) is an invaluable resource. But in its increasingly programmatic aims—the recovery of a "package logic" of democratic modernity deducible from Spinoza's metaphysics (*Democratic Enlightenment*, 12)—his project has begun to seem symptomatic, if not exemplary, of the kind of impervious fanaticism that troubled Kant. Endorsing D'Holbach's contention that Enlightenment "means universal re-education since it is only by teaching men the truth that they will learn their true interests" doesn't help matters on this score (ibid., 27). An impressive feat by any measure, Israel's work has nevertheless accumulated a number of critical responses. For a sustained critique that focuses on the equivocations between Spinoza's ideas and texts and the various uses of "Spinozism" as a term of opprobrium or praise, see Lilti, "Comment écrit-on l'histoire intellectuelle des Lumières?"

29. Deleuze, *Negotiations*, 5.

30. See Montag, *Althusser and His Contemporaries*, 1–4, for a survey of hostile reactions. For relatively judicious overviews of Althusser's project at a time when his reputation was at its nadir, see Anderson, *Arguments within English Marxism*; and Jay, *Marxism and Totality*, 385–422. Perry Anderson and Martin Jay were largely responsible for bringing Althusser into the heuristic fold of Western Marxism against strident resistance from authors associated with the American journal

Telos, which was largely oriented toward the Frankfurt School and, in the British context, a Marxist historiography paradigmatically represented by E. P. Thompson. Cf. Thompson, *The Poverty of Theory*.

31. On the PCF, see Lewis, *Louis Althusser and the Traditions of French Marxism*. The diligence of Althusser's French editors, François Matheron and Olivier Corpet, has been matched by his English translators, especially G. M. Goshgarian. See Goshgarian's introductions to Althusser, *The Humanist Controversy* and *Philosophy of the Encounter*.

32. The classic statement of the need for contextualism in the history of political thought is Skinner, "Meaning and Understanding in the History of Ideas" (1969), reprinted in his *Visions of Politics*, 57–89.

33. Strauss, *Spinoza's Critique of Religion*. Recently, Spinoza has been rehabilitated by other scholars in the Straussian tradition. See in particular, Smith, *Spinoza, Liberalism, and Jewish Identity*, and *Spinoza's Book of Life*. In the French context, see Lévy, *Le Meurtre du pasteur*.

34. The troubling allegorization of Heidegger's thought is a key theme of Gordon, *Continental Divide*. In a different register, Hägglund's radically atheistic Derrida can be read as an attempt to recuperate Derrida's thought from its instrumentalization in various negative theologies and the attitude to politics they imply. See Hägglund, *Radical Atheism*.

35. See, among many other works, James, *Spinoza on Philosophy, Religion, and Politics*.

36. Spinoza, EVP42. Throughout this book, I follow this convention for citing Spinoza's *Ethics*. Here, e.g., EVP42 = *Ethics*, Book V, Proposition 42. The following abbreviations will also be used: Sch signals a Scholium; A is an Axiom; Def is a Definition; and Cor is a Corollary. When citing from the *Treatise on the Emendation of the Intellect*, I will follow the convention of citing by paragraph number, e.g., *TEI* § 9 for paragraph nine, or *TEI* §§ 1–13 for the first thirteen paragraphs. When citing Spinoza's Letters, I will give the letter number (e.g., Letter 12) and, when the citation identifies a specific passage, the page number in the *Complete Works*, edited by Michael Morgan and translated by Samuel Shirley. I use Shirley's translation throughout, although in this instance I have opted for "beatitude" over "blessedness" to translate the Latin *beatitudo*. Of the many French translations of Spinoza's *Ethics*, Bernard Pautrat's bilingual edition, first published with Seuil in 1988, is guided by translation decisions that are, in many respects, representative of the rationalist Spinoza discussed in this book.

CHAPTER 1

1. G. Bachelard, "Physique et métaphysique," 84. This text is a reproduction of Bachelard's contribution to the three hundredth birthday celebration of Spinoza at The Hague, which took place in 1932. Bachelard was a member of the French

delegation, which also included Léon Brunschvicg, Albert Rivaud, and Charles Appuhn.

2. Cavaillès, *Sur la logique et la théorie de la science* (hereafter *LTS*), 78, reprinted with original pagination in Cavaillès, *Oeuvres complètes de philosophie des sciences* (hereafter *OC*). There exist two monographs devoted to Cavaillès's thought: Sinaceur, *Jean Cavaillès: Philosophie mathématique*, and Cassou-Noguès, *De l'expérience mathématique*. For a succinct exploration of Cavaillès's philosophical debts to Spinoza, see Huisman, "Cavaillès et Spinoza."

3. The essential resource for biographical material, which also reproduces many of Cavaillès's letters and diary entries, is the volume written by his sister, Gabrielle Ferrières, *Jean Cavaillès*. See as well the essays in Aglan and Azéma, *Jean Cavaillès Résistant*. On Libération-Nord and Cavaillès's participation, see Aglan, *La Résistance sacrifiée*.

4. Cavaillès, *Philosophie mathématique* (hereafter *PM*), 14. This 1962 volume, which contains the complete text of Cavaillès's secondary doctoral thesis, *Remarques sur la formation de la théorie abstraite des ensembles*; the Cantor-Dedekind correspondence that Cavaillès edited with the German mathematician Emmy Noether; and a short posthumously published article, "Transfini et continu," has been reproduced in its entirety, with its original pagination, in the *OC*.

5. Allocution de Raymond Aron, in the folder "Ceremonie du 1er décembre 1945 à la Sorbonne," 3, in the Fonds Cavaillès. Aron's recollection in these terms is cited as well by Canguilhem in the latter's inaugural speech at the Cavaillès Amphitheatre in Strasbourg. See Canguilhem, *Vie et mort de Jean Cavaillès* (hereafter *VM*), 28.

6. Cavaillès, *PM*, 14.

7. See Althusser and Balibar, *Reading Capital*, 16, 44; Althusser, *The Humanist Controversy*, 7; Althusser, *Philosophy of the Encounter*, 291. Cf. Badiou, *Metapolitics*, 1–8. On Foucault and Cavaillès, see Thompson, "Historicity and Transcendentality."

8. Cf. Cassou-Noguès, "The Philosophy of the Concept."

9. Canguilhem, *VM*, 27. The words are Cavaillès's own, taken from a letter he wrote to Léon Brunschvicg in 1941 after reading Husserl's *Krisis*. See Ferrières, *Jean Cavaillès*, 182.

10. Canguilhem, *VM*, 27, 34, 16, 44, 35–36, 35, 36.

11. Ibid., 35, 34, 18–19, 34.

12. Canguilhem, "Hegel en France," 282–97.

13. Ibid., 297.

14. Canguilhem, *VM*, 25–26.

15. Spinoza, EVP42Sch.

16. See Benoist, "Husserl et la fascination du 'formel,'" 679–711.

17. Though it was first published in the *Revue de métaphysique et de morale* in 1911, the article, "Husserl: Sa critique du psychologisme et sa conception d'une logique pure," was reprinted in Andler, *La Philosophie allemande au XIXe siècle*,

25–42. On the threat of psychologism in the gestation of phenomenology, see Kusch, *Psychologism*.

18. See Janicaud, *La Phénoménologie dans tous ses états*. Cf. Moyn, *Origins of the Other*, 38–40.

19. See Kleinberg, *Generation Existential*, 49–110, for an account of how Kojève's seminar introduced Hegel by way of a "domesticated," i.e., Cartesian, version of Heidegger that paved the way for a rapprochement between phenomenology and Marxism. Cf. Roth, *Knowing and History*, 81–146.

20. Cited in Schrift, "Is There Such a Thing as 'French Philosophy'?," 27–28. See Schrift's extended version of this essay in his *Twentieth-Century French Philosophy*, 1–81.

21. See Gordon, *Continental Divide*, esp. 87–113.

22. The French publication of these lectures in 1931, translated by Gabriel Pfeffer and a young Emmanuel Levinas, was a key resource for the reception of phenomenology in France. See Husserl, *Méditations cartésiennes*. Dorion Cairns's English translation first appeared in 1960.

23. See Geroulanos, *An Atheism That Is Not Humanist*, 40–48.

24. See Jean-Toussaint Desanti's comments about how skillfully Brunschvicg reconciled the philosophy of his spiritualist rival Henri Bergson with his own in Desanti's preface to the 1993 reissue of Brunschvicg, *Les Étapes de la philosophie mathématique*, ii.

25. Kleinberg, *Generation Existential*, 59. On Koyré's role as a mediator of rationalism and phenomenology, see Geroulanos, *An Atheism That Is Not Humanist*, 49–100.

26. Spiegelberg, *The Phenomenological Movement*, 432–35.

27. Kleinberg, *Generation Existential*, 101. See also Gutting, *French Philosophy in the Twentieth Century*, 104.

28. See Geroulanos, *An Atheism That Is Not Humanist*, 100–129.

29. Ferrières, *Jean Cavaillès*, 73.

30. This helpful formulation is Leonard Lawlor's, from his *Derrida and Husserl*, 57–58.

31. See part III of Cavaillès, *LTS*, 44–78, and the discussion later in the chapter.

32. Celestin Bouglé was a professor at the Sorbonne, sometime director of the ENS, and the foremost Durkheimian in France at this time. In the 1920s, his social thought had an impact on Cavaillès, who had worked closely with him at the Centre de documentation sociale affiliated with the ENS. According to Nicole Racine, Cavaillès was more sympathetic to the "idealist rationalism" of Bouglé than other classmates were, given their skepticism toward Bouglé's Durkheimian faith in "collective consciousness [*conscience*]." See Aglan and Azéma, *Jean Cavaillès Résistant*, 24, 44–45. For more on Bouglé, see Marcel, *Le Durkheimisme dans l'entre-deux-guerres*.

33. Heinzmann, "Jean Cavaillès und seine Beziehungen zu Deutschland," 407–8.

34. Cavaillès, "Les deuxièmes Cours," 65–81. This document is preserved in the Fonds Cavaillès. "The spirit of Locarno," a reference to the set of treaties negotiated between France, Germany, and Britain in 1925 to revise Germany's western borders, is noted on page 65.
35. Ibid., 78–79.
36. Letter to his sister, Davos, March 30, 1929 (AN), cited by Racine, "Les Années d'apprentissage," 31.
37. Ferrières, *Jean Cavaillès*, 75.
38. Ibid.
39. Moyn, *Origins of the Other*, 89.
40. Lautman's writings were collected in one French volume in 2006, which was translated into English in 2011. See Lautman, *Mathematics, Ideas, and the Physical Real*. For Lautman's engagement with Heidegger, see in particular, "New Research on the Dialectical Structure of Mathematics," 195–225. Lautman was also arrested and ultimately executed by the Germans on August 1, 1944, roughly six months after Cavaillès. On Lautman's biography and his activities in the Resistance, see the introduction by his son Jacques Lautman in ibid., xii–xix.
41. Letter from Cavaillès to Lautman, November 7, 1938, in Benis-Sinaceur, "Lettres inédites de Jean Cavaillès à Albert Lautman," 123–24.
42. Ferrières, *Jean Cavaillès*, 182.
43. Ibid., 104–5.
44. Ibid., 105.
45. Cited by Sinaceur, "Philosophie et histoire," 285. The "problem" in question is the one explored in Cavaillès's doctoral works, the relation between mathematics' history and its foundations, particularly in the wake of Cantor's set theory. See the following discussion.
46. Racine, "Les Années des apprentissage," 73. Cavaillès's Calvinism and his engagement in Protestant movements throughout the 1920s and 1930s remain subjects for future research. Cavaillès spent considerable time in Germany as a result of his studies, and he was particularly moved by Karl Barth's example in the German context. See Heinzmann, "Jean Cavaillès und seine Beziehungen zu Deutschland," 405–16. Nicole Racine has observed that Cavaillès's enthusiasm for Barth was mitigated by the latter's anti-intellectualism. See Racine, "Les Années des apprentissage," 72. On Barth in the French context, see Moyn, *Origins of the Other*, 134–41. Cavaillès's writings on German Protestantism are preserved in the Fonds Cavaillès. These include "Protestantisme et Hitlérisme: Crise du protestantisme allemand," *Le Christianisme social*, no. 7, October 1933; "Le conflit à l'intérieur du protestantisme allemand," *Politique*, 8e année, no. 2, February 1934; and "La Crise de l'église protestante allemande," *Politique*, 8e année, no. 12, December 1934. In addition to being of interest for the political history of European Protestantism in the interwar years, there is also the possibility that Cavaillès's militant Protestantism might shed some light on his inclination for Spinozism. Though on the

surface Barthian Protestantism and Spinozist rationalism seem like polar opposites—Barth's God is wholly absent; Spinoza's God is fully present—the theoretical effect of these positions is the same: God is nonanthropomorphic and, more important, *noninterventionist* in the world of human affairs. On the historical connection between Spinoza and Protestantism, see Kolakowski, *Chrétiens sans église*; and Popkin, *Spinoza*, esp. 39–44.

47. Cf. Moyn, *Origins of the Other*, 21–56.

48. Schrift, *Twentieth-Century French Philosophy*, 164.

49. Cited by Racine, "Les Années des apprentissage," 37.

50. Ibid , 38

51. Sinaceur, "Philosophie et histoire," 216–18. Sinaceur writes, "An intelligible connection is neither legitimated a priori, nor a posteriori, but by the very fact of its realization."

52. Cited by Racine, "Les Années des apprentissage," 37.

53. Letter from October 7, 1930, cited by both Racine, "Les Années des apprentissage,' 37–38; and Sinaceur, "Philosophie et histoire," 220.

54. Ferrières, *Jean Cavaillès*, 141.

55. This is not to suggest that Brunschvicg was the only important reader of Spinoza at the time. There was also Victor Delbos, who focused on the moral lessons of Spinozism before turning to his metaphysics in later work. Cf. Delbos, *Le Problème morale dans la philosophie de Spinoza*, and *Le Spinozisme*. Delbos shared with Brunschvicg an antipathy to post-Kantian German thought, and his own reading of Spinoza effectively denigrated Spinoza's reception among the German Romantics. Note the original publication date of *Le Spinozisme* is 1916.

56. Beyond his *La Modalité du jugement* (1897), a foundational work for French neo-Kantianism, Brunschvicg also authored *Les Étapes de la philosophie mathématique* (1912), *L'Expérience humaine et la causalité physique* (1922), and *Le Progrès de la conscience dans la philosophie occidentale* (1928). Brunschvicg taught at the Sorbonne from 1909 until 1940. Along with Elie Halévy and Xavier Léon, Brunschvicg was a founding editor of the *Revue de la métaphysique et de morale*, the leading journal of French philosophy in the period; he was also a frequent member of the *jury d'agrégation* and its presiding member from 1936 to 1938. The *agrégation* was the examination all prospective high school philosophy instructors had to pass and thus effectively a gateway to a philosophical career in France. On the important role of the *agrégation* in the recent history of French philosophy, see Schrift, "Effects of the *agrégation de philosophie*."

57. In a schematic overview of twentieth-century French philosophy, Badiou places Brunschvicg at the origin of a tradition that runs through Bachelard, Althusser, and Lacan on up to himself and that is opposed to the vitalism descendant from Brunschvicg's contemporary, Bergson. Badiou, *Logics of Worlds*, 6. See Luft and Capeillères, "Neo-Kantianism in Germany and France," 70–82; and Revill, "Taking France to the School of the Sciences," esp. chaps. 2 and 3.

58. Gordon, *Continental Divide*, 52. Also see Gordon's illuminating discussion of neo-Kantianism more generally, 52–69. Gordon points to the links between Cohen's neo-Kantianism and his radical politics, in particular his commitment to socialism. It is interesting to note how Brunschvicg's similar neo-Kantianism fed into this republicanism. Whether this is more reflective of the absence of a strong republican tradition in the Kaiserreich or an underappreciated element of radicalism of the Third Republic is difficult to say. Perhaps it is a bit of both.

59. Brunschvicg, *Spinoza et ses contemporaines*, 308, emphasis in original.

60. Revill, "Taking France to the School of the Sciences," 32.

61. Gutting, *French Philosophy in the Twentieth Century*, 45.

62. Althusser, *Philosophy and the Spontaneous Philosophy of the Scientists*, 124.

63. Ferrières, *Jean Cavaillès*, 79. See Friedmann, *Leibniz et Spinoza*. In his letter to Friedmann, Cavaillès cites from Spinoza's letter to Henry Oldenberg (Letter 78) in Latin: "He who will not control his desires . . . although he is to be excused for his weakness, nevertheless he cannot enjoy tranquility of mind and the knowledge and love of God, but of necessity he is lost." Cavaillès then offers the following gloss: "This is more admissible than a God placing the wicked here and there to better show the beauty of the whole." Cavaillès's estimation of Spinoza as the "true Christian," endowed with greater *caritas* than Leibniz, is but a further indication of the complex relationship between Cavaillès's Protestantism and his Spinozism.

64. Fonds Cavaillès, Box A—manuscripts and correspondence, item 19, Brunschvicg à Cavaillès, October 14, 1939.

65. Cavaillès's isolation stretched back to his teenage days, when he forswore the camaraderie of the Paris lycées for a continuing closeness to his family. He in fact withdrew from Louis-le-Grand, despite protestations from his father, to prepare for the *concours* alone. See Racine, "Les Années d'apprentissage," 15–21. Cf. Aron, *Mémoires*, 192.

66. Ferrières, *Jean Cavaillès*, 51.

67. Ibid., 140.

68. Desanti, "Souvenir de Jean Cavaillès," preface to *Méthode axiomatique et formalisme*, in *OC*, 5.

69. Ferrières, *Jean Cavaillès*, 69.

70. Ibid., 141.

71. Brunschvicg, *Les Étapes de la philosophie mathématique*, 367–426.

72. Ibid., 405, emphasis—as well as the English words "totally irrelevant"—in the original.

73. Ibid., 141–43. The section dedicated to Spinoza more generally is called "La Philosophie mathématique de Spinoza" (139–51) and is the conclusion of a larger chapter titled "La Philosophe mathématique des cartésiens" (124–51).

74. Ibid., 141.

75. Ibid., emphasis in original.

76. Ibid., 148–51. See the following discussion, however, for how Brunschvicg's own reading of Spinoza is perhaps limited in this regard.

77. Ibid., 146.

78. Ibid., 142. In *Spinoza et ses contemporains* Brunschvicg describes this "accord" or "convenance" as follows: "Accord implies, not the anteriority of the object with regard to the subject but the correspondence between the subject who understands and the object that is extended [*étendu*]. It implies the parallelism between orders of existence that are sufficient unto themselves, that never interfere with one another" (169).

79. Cf. Cavaillès, *LTS*, 15–16.

80. Ferrières, *Jean Cavaillès*, 141.

81. Pierre Cassou-Noguès has also observed that, although Cavaillès in fact composed the "thèse principale" before the "thèse complémentaire," readers should follow Cavaillès's intentions and read the two works in their order of publication, *Remarques* having appeared first in the Hermann series Actualités scientifiques et industrielles, numbers 606 and 607, with *Méthode* following in installments 608, 609, and 610 (Paris: Hermann, 1938). See Cassou-Noguès, *De l'expérience mathématique*, 19. Both works are reproduced in full in the *OC*.

82. For accessible accounts of set theory, see Grattan-Guinness, *The Search for Mathematical Roots*; and Tiles, *Philosophy of Set Theory*. See also Wallace, *Everything and More*. For a generous, though informatively critical assessment of this book by a mathematician, see Harris, "A Sometimes Funny Book Supposedly about Infinity."

83. The classic examples of this problematic are the two irrational numbers expressed algorithmically as $\sqrt{2}$ (the square root of two) and π. In both cases, geometry can "represent" them, e.g., the hypotenuse of a right triangle whose two sides equal 1, or the work involved in determining the area of a circle. But because both numbers are irrational when calculated, i.e., their decimal spaces trail off indefinitely, both geometric and algorithmic expression are purchased at the cost of arithmetical precision.

84. For a helpful account of this historical development, see chap. 3, "Georg Cantor, Richard Dedekind, and Gottlob Frege: What Is a Number, 1872–1883," in Everdell, *The First Moderns*, 30–46. Cf. chap. 12, "Bertrand Russell and Edmund Husserl: Phenomenology, Number, and the Fall of Logic, 1901," 177–92. On Cantor specifically, see Dauben, *Georg Cantor*.

85. Benoist, "Bolzano et l'idée de Wissenschaftslehre," 670. Bolzano's works are collected in English translation in *The Mathematical Works of Bernard Bolzano*. See also Sebestik, *Logique et mathématique chez Bernard Bolzano*.

86. Tiles, *Philosophy of Set Theory*, 102–3.

87. First published as *Briefwechsel Cantor-Dedekind*, ed. Jean Cavaillès and Emmy Noether (Paris: Hermann, 1937). A French translation of these letters exists in Cavaillès, *PM*, 171–251. The quotation, dating from June 29, 1877, is on page 211.

88. See Letter 12, "On the Nature of the Infinite," 267–71, in Spinoza, *Complete Works*, 787–91.
89. Ibid., 788.
90. Ibid., 789.
91. Ibid., emphasis added.
92. Gueroult, *Spinoza I: Dieu*, appendix 9, "La letter sur l'infini (Lettre XII, à Louis Meyer)," 500–528. This essay appears in English translation in Grene, *Spinoza: A Collection of Critical Essays*, 182–212. Gueroult's contrast of Spinoza's position to Bergson's is presented as follows in Kathleen McLaughlin's translation: "This notion of *the lived*, which today, particularly in Bergson, is opposed to the intellectual, in Spinoza is experienced by the understanding [*entendement*] alone. It is the imagination, and not the intellect, which substitutes the discontinuous for the continuous, cutting duration into fragments; it is the intelligence, on the contrary, which 'experiences' continuity and duration through the intuitive idea it has of the procession of all things, and of myself, starting from eternal substance, infinite and indivisible" (186; 504 in the French edition). Gueroult's recourse to the adjective "intuitive" should not obscure the broader point that our understanding of the infinite is a product of genetic, intellectual labor and not the imagination. One final note: Gueroult's use of the verb "experience"—here in scare quotes—bears affinities with Cavaillès's effort to articulate an "expérience mathématique," which will be addressed later.
93. Gueroult, *Spinoza I: Dieu*, appendix 17, "L'observation de Frege sur la critique spinoziste de l'unique dans la *Lettre L*," 578–84. The quotation comes from page 584. According to Gueroult, Frege recognized an affinity with Spinoza in that both thinkers conceived of number as properly pertaining to concepts and not things, but Spinoza erred in seeing numbers as purely imaginary representations lacking epistemic certainty. Gueroult's aim in this short piece is to reveal the intertextual ambiguity that results from comparing their two projects, and to argue that Frege's concept of number applies well to Spinoza's concept of "attributes" but that it cannot account for the singular infinite Substance essential to Spinoza's broader philosophy.
94. Like Cavaillès, Gueroult was shaped by Brunschvicg's teaching, although his exposure to Brunschvicg dated from before the First World War (Gueroult was ten years older than Cavaillès). Cavaillès and Gueroult were colleagues briefly during the Second World War at the Université de Strasbourg's temporary campus at Clermont-Ferrand, but there is no evidence that either thinker left an impression on the other. For accounts of the affinity between Cavaillès and Gueroult concerning a geneticism to be distinguished from constructivism, see Dosse, *The Rising Sign*, 78–84; and Granger, "Jean Cavaillès et l'histoire," 569–82.
95. "Extension" is capitalized in this context because it refers to one of the two attributes of substance in Spinoza's system, Thought and Extension. When used

96. On "the idea of the idea," see Spinoza, *TEI*, §§ 33–73. For Brunschvicg's assessment in such terms, see Alexandre Koyré's introduction to his 1937 bilingual edition: Spinoza, *Traité de la réforme de l'entendement*, ix.

97. Koyré, introduction to Spinoza, *Traité de la réforme de l'entendement*, ix. Koyré observes that the text's unfinished quality makes it an exceptional pedagogical tool for philosophy students.

98. Cavaillès and Lautman, "La pensée mathématique," in *OC*, 593–630. This quotation comes from page 594. Excerpts from this text have been translated by Arthur Goldhammer and published as "Mathematical Thought," in Balibar and Rajchman, *French Philosophy since 1945*, 65–70. Where Goldhammer's translation has been used, pagination from this volume will be cited following that of the *OC*.

99. Ibid., 594–95, emphasis in the original. Cf. Sinaceur, *Jean Cavaillès*, 116.

100. Sinaceur, *Jean Cavaillès*, 15.

101. Cavaillès and Lautman, "La pensée mathématique," 601/66.

102. Ibid., 601/66–67. Goldhammer translates "constaté dans son accomplissement" as "determined only after the fact," which is idiomatically justified but loses something of the immanent quality of the process that Cavaillès is attempting to describe. The achieved independence is internal to the process, not the result of a retrospective determination—even if it is discerned only retrospectively. The bracketed reminders of the French *l'expérience* are my interpolations.

103. Spinoza, *TEI*, § 37.

104. Ibid., § 38.

105. See the discussion following Desanti's talk on "Spinoza et la phénoménologie," recorded in Bloch, *Spinoza au XXe siècle*, 127–28, over the status of the article in this phrase. Note Pierre Macherey's wry suggestion that Spinoza composed the *TEI* and *Ethics* in Latin so that he could remain ambiguous on this point.

106. Spinoza, *TEI*, § 33.

107. Ibid., § 36.

108. Cavaillès had a supporter in the audience in Jean Hyppolite. Hyppolite agreed with Cavaillès's claim that mathematics possessed "an autonomous essential life." But he questioned Cavaillès's refusal of the contingent: "one might think that the necessity of mathematics' development and historical contingency should be reconciled in this 'life of mathematics.'" "La pensée mathématique," in *OC*, 621.

109. Ibid., 627.

110. Cassou-Noguès, *De l'éxpérience mathématique*, 36–37.

111. Cited in ibid., 261. For Brunschvicg the dual referent of the French word *conscience* to both "consciousness" and the English meaning of "conscience" was integral to his reading of Spinoza as an ethical touchstone.

112. See Sinaceur, "Philosophie et histoire," 216.

113. Ibid.
114. Brunschvicg, quoted in ibid., 211.
115. On Thao, see Baring, *The Young Derrida*, 113–41.
116. Ferrières, *Jean Cavaillès*, 182. The reference is to Eugen Fink, who was Husserl's research assistant and who exerted a strong influence on the late Husserl's thought. Thao's Husserl was most likely "Fink-ized" in Cavaillès's view due to the emphasis on the temporal in Thao's reading of Husserl.
117. Ibid.
118. Allocution de Maurice Leenhardt, item 55, fond D, Fonds Cavaillès.
119. Cassou-Noguès has observed that the title is somewhat misleading in that it downplays Cavaillès's conviction, following Husserl, that any viable theory of science must ultimately be an ontology as well as an epistemology. See Cassou-Noguès, *De l'expérience mathématique*, 286. Further references to *LTS* will be in the main text.
120. Granger, "Jean Cavaillès," 271–79.
121. Ibid., 277–78.
122. Ibid., 278.
123. According to Béatrice Longuenesse, Cavaillès misunderstands the Kantian distinction between general and transcendental logic and, as a result, discounts the ongoing process of transcendental critique in the establishment of logical categories. For Longuenesse it is this Kantian move that is constitutive of transcendental logic, which produces synthetic knowledge, as distinct from general logic, which produces analytic statements. See Longuenesse, *Kant et le pouvoir de juger*, 79–83.
124. Cassou-Noguès, *De l'expérience mathématique*, 318.
125. Bruno Huisman suggests that for Cavaillès "it is essentially the Bolzanian idea of science that is Spinozist." See Huisman, "Cavaillès et Spinoza," 85.
126. A helpful text for coming to terms with this, the most conceptually dense section of *LTS*, is the chapter titled "La rigueur des mathématiques," in Granger, *Pour la connaissance philosophique*, 67–92.
127. On this score, it is of crucial importance that Spinoza maintains that when an idea takes another idea as its object, this process is completely homologous to when idea takes an "object" in Extension as its object. Cavaillès pursues this same homology in *LTS*; it is in fact vital to his argument. For his claim is that the "material" of mathematical physics is already thoroughly conceptual. In other words, in its "essence" an atom is a concept, not a discrete item intuited in sensibility; this is the case even with the mediate role played by instruments in atomic physics. But being a concept makes the atom no less an "object." It is simply an "object" that a philosophy of consciousness cannot account for.
128. Cf. Cassou-Noguès, *De l'expérience mathématique*, 280–312. See S. Bachelard, *La conscience de rationalité*, 1–12. For a helpful assessment of Bachelard's misgivings, and Cavaillès's reading of Husserl more generally, see Webb, "Cavaillès, Husserl, and the Historicity of Science," 59–72.

129. The request for this volume, along with a copy of the New Testament, was made to Jean Cadier, the local minister in Montpellier, during Cavaillès's time in prison in the autumn of 1942 when *LTS* was written. See Fond E, Folder 75, *L'Agent de liaison des Forces françaises combattantes*, September 1969, in the Fonds Cavaillès. See as well Aglan and Azéma, *Jean Cavaillès Résistant*, 74.

130. Hyppolite, *Logic and Existence*. See the long footnote where Hyppolite notes the profound resonance of many of Cavaillès's claims in *LTS* with those of Hegelian logic. Hyppolite comments on the concluding lines of *LTS* as follows:

> If a dialectic proper to mathematics exists in this way, where would it fit in a Logic of being like that of Hegel? Perhaps however, in Hegel, the self is more immanent to the content than in Cavaillès; on this point, the rapprochement of Cavaillès with Spinoza would be more precise than the rapprochement of Cavaillès with Hegel. Cavaillès makes us think less of the unity of subject and object resulting in sense than of God's infinite understanding in Spinoza and of the passage from true idea to true idea. It is important to consider, however, that we could describe the development of mathematics in dialectical terms, but the question would still concern the relation of this dialectic of *mathemata* (the intermediaries in Plato) with that of the *logoi*. Nevertheless, it is remarkable to note that Cavaillès speaks of a dialectic of *mathemata* in such Hegelian terms. (52–53)

131. Desanti, "Souvenir de Jean Cavaillès," in *OC*, 8. Despite Cavaillès's mistrust of Hegelian idealism, it might prove worthwhile to explore the striking similarities, and subtle differences, between his project in *LTS* and the neo-Hegelian philosophy of the mathematical sciences developed by Imre Lakatos. On Lakatos's neo-Hegelianism, mediated through the influence of Georg Lukàcs, see Kadvany, *Imre Lakatos and the Guises of Reason*.

132. Canguilhem, *VM*, 26.

CHAPTER 2

1. Alquié, *Le Rationalisme de Spinoza* (hereafter *Rationalisme*).
2. Alquié, *Leçons sur Spinoza*, 207.
3. Giolito, *Histoires de la philosophie avec Martial Gueroult*, 82. See as well Deleuze's glowing review of Gueroult's first volume on Spinoza wherein he notes that, with Spinoza, Gueroult's method has found its "most adequate, most saturated, and most exhaustive object" (216). Deleuze, "Spinoza et la méthode générale de M. Gueroult," in his *L'Île déserte*, 202–16. The quotation comes from page 216.
4. Foucault, "Life: Experience and Science," 465–78; Roudinesco, *Philosophy in Turbulent Times*, 31.
5. See the chapters on Spinoza in Badiou, *Being and Event*, 112–20, and *Court traité de l'ontologie transitoire*, 73–93.
6. Alquié, *La Découverte métaphysique de l'homme chez Descartes* (hereafter *Découverte*). See Marion's trilogy on Descartes: *Sur l'ontologie grise de Descartes*, *Sur la théologie blanche de Descartes*, and *Sur le prisme métaphysique de Descartes*.

Note the dedication to Alquié in *Ontologie grise* and the citation of Alquié's lessons on the creation of the eternal truths as the inspiration for Marion's project in *Théologie blanche* (6). In addition to Marion, Alquié was an important influence on Michel Henry, whose post-Heideggerian reading of Descartes owes much to Alquié. See Henry, *Généalogie de la psychanalyse* 17–52, as well as Henry's contribution, "Sur l'*ego* du *cogito*," in a *Festschrift* for Alquié, Marion, *La Passion de la raison*. Finally, note Levinas's contribution to this same volume, "Sur l'idée de l'infini en nous," 49–52. In effect, then, Alquié stands at the origin of the phenomenological recuperation of Cartesianism in the French context following its critique in Heidegger's philosophy. But it is also of interest to see Alquié's pedagogical influence over the thinkers associated with what Dominique Janicaud has deemed a "theological turn" in French philosophy. In this regard, it is of historical interest that, although Alquié also exercised an early influence on Deleuze, ultimately serving as the main reader for the latter's thesis on Spinoza, Deleuze did not figure in the *Festschrift* for Alquié, which included contributions from virtually all the leading lights of French phenomenology. Deleuze's relationship to Alquié will be addressed in later chapters. For more on Alquié's biography and influence, see Guitton, *Notice sur la vie et les travaux de Ferdinand Alquié*. Note in particular Jean Guitton's observation that Marion, along with Jean-Robert Armogathe, was Alquié's most "assiduous disciple" at the Sorbonne (11).

7. The key work for Spinoza's early modern reception in France is Vernière, *Spinoza et la pensée française*. See in particular his remark, "With the collapse of the grand rational systems from Descartes to Leibniz, the *Ethics* offered the sole metaphysics capable of liquidating religious obstacles and accommodating the ambitions of science without impeding its expansion" (699).

8. Gueroult, *Spinoza I: Dieu*, and *Spinoza II: L'Âme*. Much as Alquié's project can be situated in the trajectory of French phenomenology, Gueroult occupies a crucial position in twentieth-century French rationalism. As noted in the previous chapter, there are minimal, if any, personal links between Cavaillès and Gueroult. Yet their legacies largely coalesced, chiefly in the efforts of Gilles-Gaston Granger and, above all, Jules Vuillemin, both of whom would later occupy positions at the Collège de France themselves. Note Granger's observation of the proximity of Cavaillès's and Gueroult's projects in his "Jean Cavaillès et l'histoire," 572. Regarding Vuillemin, see his *L'Héritage kantien et la révolution copernicienne*. This book, which was dedicated to Gueroult, will be vital in the development of Deleuze's thought. Jules Vuillemin's 1955 volume *Physique et métaphysique kantiennes* is dedicated to two Resistance casualties, François Cuzin and Cavaillès. Vuillemin notes that the idea for this book in fact came from a course titled "Causality, Necessity, Probability," which Cavaillès taught at the Sorbonne in the early 1940s. See Granger's and Vuillemin's contributions to Vuillemin, *Hommage à Martial Gueroult*, 43–58, 139–54. See as well Dosse, *The Rising Sign*, 78–84, which emphasizes the influence of Gueroult's methodology on structuralism more generally and its similarities to Cavaillès's project. Finally,

Althusser cites the importance of Gueroult's method, and the fact that he was a "great hit" among his students at the ENS, in his memoir, *The Future Lasts Forever*, 182. Other testimony suggests Althusser's impatience with the resolutely apolitical quality of Gueroult's Spinozism—"between Gueroult and Spinoza, nothing happens." This was Pierre-François Moreau's recollection in his and Laurent Bove's interview with Alexandre Matheron, "A propos de Spinoza."

9. On Spinoza's reception in Weimar Germany, see Lazier, *God Interrupted*, 67–132. See also Leo Strauss's autobiographical reflections in Strauss, *Spinoza's Critique of Religion*, 1–31.

10. Gueroult, *Spinoza I: Dieu*, 9.

11. Fabiani, "Sociologie et histoire des idées," 124–25.

12. Koyré, *Études galiléenes*. See as well Koyré's essays collected in *Études de l'histoire de la pensée philosophique* and *Études de l'histoire de la pensée scientifique*.

13. Gueroult, *L'Évolution et la structure de la doctrine de la science chez Fichte*.

14. Cf. Giolito, *Histoires de la philosophie avec Martial Gueroult*, 46–49.

15. Stoetzel, *Notice sur la vie et les travaux de M. Gueroult*, 14–15.

16. Gueroult, *La Philosophie transcendantale de Salomon Maimon*.

17. Gueroult, *Dianoématique, Livre I*, vols. 1–3, and *Dianoématique, Livre II*. Ginette Dreyfus, one of Gueroult's most devoted students and the editor of book I of the *Dianoématique*, describes Gueroult's radical idealism as follows: "With regard to the goal of philosophizing thought [*la pensée philosophante*], dogmatic idealism, or the idealism of thought in general, leaves unresolved the gratuitous realism of 'the thing' to be understood and explained. But when philosophizing thought reflects on itself, a new idealism springs forth, the idealism of philosophizing thought, or radical idealism, which reverses [*renverse*] this realism to the profit of the superior realism of history" (10).

18. Gueroult, *Leçon inaugurale*, 5.

19. Ibid., 18–29, 33, 22–23, 16–17.

20. See especially, *Dianoématique, Livre I*, vol. 2.

21. Gueroult, *Dianoématique, Livre II*, 180.

22. This estimate is a result of Christophe Giolito's labor (*Histoires de la philosophie avec Martial Gueroult*, 167n1). Giolito's monograph is the point of departure for any engagement with Gueroult's voluminous output.

23. Gueroult, *Dianoématique, Livre II*, 224.

24. Ibid., 59, 68.

25. Ibid., 178.

26. Cf. Cavaillès's critique of the "abdication of thought" in the preceding chapter.

27. Gueroult, *Dianoématique, Livre II*, 224. Gueroult is discussing Husserl's efforts in the *Ideen, I*:

What Husserl successfully arrives at over the course of his second phenomenological reduction is the discovery of a sole essence bearing in itself the mark of *inseity* [in-itselfness]. This is to know pure consciousness, because it is alone in giving itself to itself, positing itself for itself, revealing the inseparability of essence and existence. [. . .] But it is acknowledged, nevertheless, that the Being before which consciousness opens itself can only come to manifest an autosufficiency that remains the latter's privilege. Yet, as this autosufficiency is the sole ontologically definitive criterion, nothing proves that such a being is not simply the product of an unconscious objectivation. (178)

28. Gueroult, *Leçon inaugurale*, 30–32.

29. In this regard, Gueroult's project might be instructively compared with François Laruelle's effort to develop a method of "non-philosophy" that can serve as a "science" of philosophy. See Laruelle, *Principles of Non-Philosophy*. Laruelle has in fact noted the proximity of his project to Gueroult's. See Laruelle, *En tant qu'un*, 17.

30. Cf. Giolito, *Histoires de la philosophie avec Martial Gueroult*, 218–19. See Daniel Parrochia's comment in his *La Raison systématique* concerning what he calls the Gueroult paradox: "[T]he unacceptable character of this doctrine comes essentially from the fact that it posits itself both as a 'system of all the systems' and as one system 'like the others'" (29).

31. Alquié, *Découverte*, v–vii.

32. Cited in Giolito, *Histoires de la philosophie avec Martial Gueroult*, 112n22.

33. Gueroult, *Descartes selon l'ordre des raisons* (1991), 1:19n12.

34. See Alquié, *Cahiers de jeunesse*, in particular Paule Plouvier's editorial introduction, 7–21.

35. Alquié, "Notes sur l'interprétation de Descartes par l'ordre des raisons," in his *Études cartésiennes*, 15–30.

36. Cf. Giolito, *Histoires de la philosophie avec Martial Gueroult*, 117.

37. Alquié, *Qu'est-ce que comprendre un philosophe?*, 76.

38. Ibid., 89–90, 26, 87, 87–88, 50.

39. Ibid., 52. See also Alquié, *Signification de la philosophie*, 241–43.

40. Alquié, *Qu'est-ce que comprendre un philosophe?*, 52–53.

41. Alquié, *La Nostalgie de l'être* (hereafter *Nostalgie*), foreword, 3.

42. Ibid., 12–13.

43. This also accounts for Alquié's general sympathy for Kant's philosophy. See Alquié, *Leçons sur Kant*. This position is also captured in the title of Alquié's *La Solitude de la raison*.

44. Alquié, *Nostalgie*, 13.

45. Ibid., 9.

46. Janicaud, *Heidegger en France 2*, 92. Presumably Alquié's charge was facetious.

47. Alquié, *Signification*, 247.

48. Alquié, *Nostalgie*, 148, emphasis added.

49. Gueroult, *Leçon inaugurale*, 22.

50. See Alquié, *L'Expérience*.

51. Alquié, "Expérience ontologique," 15. The French verb is *constater*.

52. Ibid., 13, 31.
53. See the "Discussion," 32–71.
54. Ibid.; all quotations come from page 32.
55. Ibid., 39.
56. Ibid., 42.
57. Ibid., 49.
58. Ibid., 56.
59. Goldschmidt, "A propos du 'Descartes selon l'ordre des raisons,'" 67.
60. Deleuze, "Spinoza et la méthode générale de Martial Gueroult," in *L'Île déserte*, 216. See also Parrochia, *La Raison systématique*, 27–29.
61. Cf. Brunschvicg, *Spinoza et ses contemporains*, 153–93. For the claim that Spinoza conceived his presentation of Descartes to be as critical as it was expository, see Israel, "Spinoza as an Expounder, Critic and 'Reformer' of Descartes."
62. Cf. Alquié, *Rationalisme*, 69.
63. The results were collected in Perelman, *Philosophie et méthode*.
64. Alquié, "Intention et déterminations dans la genèse de l'oeuvre philosophique," in Perelman, *Philosophie et méthode*, 28–42. Cf. Alquié, *Le Cartésianisme de Malebranche*.
65. Gueroult, "La Méthode en histoire de la philosophie," in Perelman, *Philosophie et méthode*, 17–27. The quotation comes from page 26. Nietzsche is deemed a case in point of this phenomenon, a philosopher whose own use of reason results in reason's detriment. See Gueroult's exchange with Gianni Vattimo following Gabriel Marcel's contribution in Deleuze, *Cahiers de Royaumont, no. VI: Nietzsche*, 121
66. Gueroult, "La Méthode en histoire de la philosophie," 27.
67. Gueroult was intent to maintain a sense of philosophizing reason as a "pensée en acte" (a "thought in action"), hence his preference for *raison* or *pensée philosophante* over *philosophique* (philosophical). Giolito, *Histoires de la philosophie avec Martial Gueroult*, 201n51. Cf. Gueroult, *Dianoématique: Livre II*.
68. The debate following Gueroult's and Alquié's respective contributions is in Perelman, *Philosophie et méthode*, 43–59, quotation from page 53.
69. Ibid., 55.
70. Ibid., 53.
71. Ibid.
72. Ibid., 52.
73. Ibid., 54.
74. Ibid.
75. Gueroult, *Spinoza I: Dieu*, 122–23. Further references to *Spinoza I* will be in the main text. The critique also extends to any "Thomist" distinction between "virtual" and "actual" (238n38). In this regard, Gueroult's account stands in contrast to Deleuze's efforts to reconcile Spinoza with Bergson, or indeed with Heidegger. See the discussion in Chapters 6 and 7.

76. See Spinoza, EIDef4: "By attribute I mean that which the intellect perceives of substance as constituting its essence." The evident discrepancy that results from Spinoza's speculative affirmation of an infinity of attributes and the fact that only two appear relevant to human experience will be central to Alquié's critique. For Spinoza's own most concise justification for why Thought and Extension are the only two attributes "the human mind can attain knowledge of," see Letter 64, to G. H. Schuller, in Spinoza, *Complete Works*, 918–19.

77. Spinoza, EIDef5. In order to follow Gueroult's reading, it is important to read the term "substance" as shorthand for "the idea of the infinity of substantially distinct attributes, each of which is substantial and infinite in itself."

78. The meaning of "cause" in this context is the one found in the formula *causa sive ratio*, "cause, that is, reason." This formula, first used by Descartes, will be codified as the Principle of Sufficient Reason in Leibniz's philosophy. For an account of Spinoza's philosophy that reads it as committed to the maximal application of this principle, see Della Rocca, *Spinoza*.

79. For this reason it is important for Gueroult to emphasize that Spinozism is not a philosophy concerned with the properties of discrete singularities. Cf. the circle example given previously.

80. Spinoza, EIP31. There is something deeply counterintuitive in what Gueroult is emphasizing here. Gueroult follows Spinoza's proposition to the letter. It reads: "The intellect in act, whether it be finite or infinite, as also will, desire, love, etc., must be related to *Natura naturata*, not to *Natura naturans*." Because of Gueroult's repeated emphasis on *pensée en acte*—i.e., *pensée philosophante*—we would expect an assimilation of present participles that would make intellect something active and thus on the side of *Natura naturans*. But what is vital here is the distinction between "intellect" as a *mode* and "Thought" as an *attribute*. In the proof to Proposition 31, Spinoza elaborates: "By intellect (as is self-evident) we do not understand absolute thought, but only a definite mode of thinking which differs from other modes such as desire, love, etc., and so (Def. 5) must be conceived through absolute Thought—that is (Pr. 15 and Def. 6), an attribute of God which expresses the eternal and infinite essence of Thought—in such a way that without this attribute it can neither be nor be conceived; and therefore (Sch. Pr. 29) it must be related to *Natura naturata*, not to *Natura naturans*, just like the other modes of thinking." In this regard, and to anticipate the later discussion of Deleuze, what takes place in the "intellect" is always *actual*; yet the differentiation constitutive of one intellect, or among many intellects, can be thought only in its relation to the formal process that goes by the name "Thought." For Deleuze, the "intellect" will be the actualization of "virtual" Thought, but in pursuing this reading, Deleuze effectively denigrates the "actual" intellect to the profit of "virtual" Thought—precisely the Thomist move that Gueroult proscribes. Indeed, since Gueroult insists that Spinoza abrogates this virtual/actual relation, he must remain consistent and insist as well that "effect" be stripped of all diminutive con-

notations; in other words, being on the side of *Natura naturata* in no way makes the "intellect" *less than* the Thought of *Natura naturans*. The point, rather, of this discussion of "intellect" is to demarcate its *qualitative* distinction from other modes of Thought (desire, love, etc.). But Thought is always *only* and *fully* existent *as modes*; there is no "excess" above or beyond the modal expressions. What we see here is Gueroult effectively prohibiting any effort to translate the terms of Spinoza's *natura naturans/naturata* into terms evocative of, or assimilable to, Heidegger's ontological difference, a phenomenon we will explore with regard to Deleuze later.

81. See Gueroult, "Introduction générale," 285–302.

82. Alquié, *Leçons sur Spinoza*, 206–10.

83. Alquié, *Rationalisme*, 326. Further references to *Rationalisme* will be in the main text.

84. See Levinas, *Otherwise Than Being*; and Marion, *God without Being*.

85. Cf. Hallward, *Out of This World*, where Deleuze is criticized for proffering a similar "theophany."

86. Alquié, *Rationalisme*, back cover (attributed to Alquié).

87. Ibid., 5.

88. Gueroult, *Spinoza I: Dieu*, 12, emphasis added.

CHAPTER 3

1. Desanti, *Introduction à la phénoménologie*, 20 (hereafter *IP*).

2. Desanti, *Un Destin philosophique*, 128–29 (hereafter *Destin*), and "A Path in Philosophy," 51 (hereafter "Path").

3. Desanti, *Destin*, 26–27.

4. Desanti, "Path," 53.

5. Ibid., 53. See also the "Souvenir de Jean Cavaillès" prepared by Desanti as a preface to Hermann's republication of Cavaillès's *Méthode axiomatique et formalisme*, where he refers to his mentor as "he who thought himself Spinozist," in *OC*, 6.

6. Desanti, *Destin*, 134–35.

7. Ibid., 256.

8. Ibid., 139.

9. Desanti, "Spinoza et la phénoménologie," 114.

10. See ibid., 113–15; and idem, *Destin*, 27, and "Path," 52–53.

11. Though varied in subject matter, Desanti's publication record was limited in its total output. Desanti was not a prolific writer, preferring instead to concentrate his energies on his teaching career. However, the lack of written output in Desanti's career is also arguably consistent with the ascetic turn that followed his years as a PCF ideologue. From 1957 to 1973, Desanti served as Althusser's counterpart at the ENS-Fontenay St. Cloud, west of Paris. See the chapter "Ulm or Saint Cloud: Althusser or Touky?," in Dosse, *The Rising Sign*, 284–92, for a

comparison of these two *caïmans*. In 1973, Desanti was elected to full professor at Paris I Panthéon-Sorbonne, where he would continue to teach and advise doctoral work well into the late 1990s (though his official retirement was in 1994). This chapter focuses on his writings from the 1950s and 1960s. These include his PCF writings; his 1956 study of Spinoza, *Introduction à la histoire de la philosophie* (hereafter *IHP*); and his published course on Husserlian phenomenology, *IP*. Desanti's many contributions to *La Nouvelle Critique*, the PCF's official intellectual journal, were collected in a single volume in 2008: Desanti, *Une Pensée captive* (hereafter *PC*). The discussion in this chapter also gestures forward to the arguments of his two major works, *Les Idéalités mathématiques* (1968) and *La Philosophie silencieuse* (1975), the latter of which is a collection of articles written around the time of *Idéalités* and bears on the methodological principles and theoretical implications of that work. The publication of *Destin* in 1982 inaugurated another phase of Desanti's philosophical output, which consisted primarily of published interviews. In 1976, Desanti had published a series of interviews with Pascal Lainé and Blandine Barrett-Kriegel, *Le Philosophe et les pouvoirs* (republished as *Le Philosophe et les pouvoirs et autres dialogues* in 2008), which effectively laid the groundwork for the auto-critique of *Destin*. Desanti was renowned for his talents as an orator, and the dialogical format allowed him to hold forth on topics ranging from the nature of time (*Réflexions sur le temps* [1992]), to the nature of philosophy (*Philosophie: Un rêve de flambeur* [1999]), to ethics (*La Peau des mots* [2004]).

12. Although there are no monographs devoted to Desanti's philosophy, there are two helpful volumes of collected essays: Ravis-Giordani, *Jean-Toussaint Desanti*; and Caveing et al., *Hommage à Jean-Toussaint Desanti*. Desanti's place in the history of French phenomenology is touched upon in Sebbah, *Testing the Limit*, 88–103.

13. Desanti, "Path," 66.

14. See Althusser, *The Future Lasts Forever*, 178–80, for Althusser's recollections. According to Dominique Desanti, the courses were conceived for those, like Althusser, who spent the war in the military or in prison camps (personal communication to the author, July 23, 2007).

15. See the contents of the folder ALT2-A56 for Desanti's lectures on Husserl and the "development of physics," with reference to ancient thought and modern events. See ALT2-60-09 for Desanti's course on Spinoza. These files are located in the Fonds Althusser at the Institut mémoires de l'édition contemporaine (IMEC).

16. Desanti's papers, though officially under the management of IMEC, are in the process of being catalogued and preserved at the campus of the ENS-LSH (formerly in Fontenay-St. Cloud, now in Lyon) at the Institut Jean-Toussaint Desanti. The institute's website (http://institutdesanti.ens-lsh.fr/) is a vital resource for research on Desanti.

17. Cf. Caute, *Communism and the French Intellectuals*. See also Kelly, *Modern French Marxism*. Though it devotes scant attention to the PCF ideologues,

the dated, though no less essential, resource for theoretical context is Lichtheim, *Marxism in Modern France*.

18. Caute, *Communism and the French Intellectuals*, 220.

19. "Science bourgeoise et science prolétarienne," *La Nouvelle Critique*, no. 8, 32–51, signed by M. Daniel, J. Desanti, and G. Vassails. Reprinted in Desanti, *PC*, 105–33. Desanti's contribution to the pamphlet that followed was titled "La Science: Idéologie historiquement relative," in *Science bourgeoise et science prolétarienne*, 7–14. On the Lysenko phenomenon, see Lecourt, *Proletarian Science?*

20. D. Desanti, *Les Staliniens*, 324–29.

21. Tony Judt describes Dominique Desanti's *Les Staliniens* as "a distinctly self-serving and misleading 'autocritique.'" He condemns as well her "hatchetwork" for the PCF, chiefly in the form of her condemnation of Tito (see her *Masques et visages de Tito et des siens*). See Judt, *Marxism and the French Left*, 186. Though it is true that *Les Staliniens* contains no unmitigated admission of political stupidity, it does take seriously the ethical errors and willful ignorance involved in the French indulgence of Stalinism. The apparent lesson of this "political experience," judging from Dominique Desanti's account, is one of chastened naïveté and an unequivocal renunciation of a concept of politics as the rational ordering of society.

22. "Un témoin: Jean-Toussaint Desanti," in D. Desanti, *Les Staliniens*, 361–69.

23. Ibid., 367.

24. Milosz, *The Captive Mind*. The title of the collection of Desanti's *Nouvelle Critique* writings—*Une Pensée captive*—is taken from a chapter title in *Destin*. The editors of this volume speculate as to whether Desanti intended to evoke Milosz's title. The circumstances of *Destin* are not without their own pertinence to recent French intellectual history. The book, though well over three hundred pages in length, takes the form of a long letter to Maurice Clavel, scholar of Kant, father figure to the "New Philosophers," and longtime friend of Desanti's. At the height of what Michael Scott Christofferson has dubbed the "antitotalitarian moment" of the 1970s, Clavel had begun a correspondence with Desanti in which he vented his frustration with the latter's apparent ease at claiming to be a materialist philosopher but having written a book titled *Les Idealités mathématiques*. Clavel died before receiving Desanti's full book-length response, although Bernard-Henri Levy would continue the task of soliciting the text from Desanti for publication in his own series with Éditions Grasset. Though irreducible to a renunciation of his Marxist past, Desanti's text fit well into the antitotalitarian publishing agenda of this series. On Clavel, see Bourg, *From Revolution to Ethics*, 261–65. On Grasset and Lévy, see Christofferson, *French Intellectuals against the Left*, 191–97.

25. Althusser, *For Marx*, 25–26.

26. Kelly, *Modern French Marxism*, 140–42.

27. Desanti "Hegel est-il père de l'existentialisme?," *La Nouvelle Critique*, nos. 56 and 57, 91–115, 163–87 (reprinted in *PC*, 279–332).

28. Moulier Boutang, *Ruptures et plis*, 277–80; D. Desanti, *Ce que le siècle m'a dit*, 568; Althusser, *The Future Lasts Forever*, 340–41.
29. Moulier Boutang, *Ruptures et plis*, 295–304.
30. Ibid.
31. "Notes retrouvées *Phénoménologie et praxis* de J.-T. Desanti. 2ff: 1 ms + dactyl," ALT2-A58-02.04, Fonds Althusser.
32. Desanti certainly had predecessors in Paul Nizan and Georges Friedmann, both of whom professed a hearty sympathy for Spinozism. Friedmann even produced a study, *Leibniz et Spinoza* (1946), geared toward showing the metaphysical superiority of the latter. But neither Nizan nor Friedmann attempted a systematic materialist reading of Spinoza's philosophy such as that undertaken by Desanti.
33. See Balibar, "Notice nécrologique de Jean-Toussaint Desanti."
34. Personal communication from Dominique Desanti, July 23, 2007.
35. See Desanti, "Matérialisme et épistémologie," in *La Philosophie silencieuse*, 133–53.
36. Kriegel, "Le silence de J-T. Desanti," 416–17.
37. Ibid., 417.
38. D. Desanti, "Un livre au destin imprévu," in Desanti, *IHP*, 7–16.
39. Ibid., 13–14.
40. The recent republication of Desanti's early writings has been accompanied by a weighty editorial apparatus that situates the texts in question. For example, in *Une Pensée captive*, each article is introduced by Maurice Caveing in order to provide the appropriate context in which it should be read. This editorial apparatus is immensely helpful and illuminating, but it raises some interesting interpretative questions in its own right. Two of the most distinctive features that set Desanti's post-Communist intellectual career apart from others of his generation are its *silence* (which, to be sure, was broken in several instances, though many years later) and the fact that Desanti's intellectual efforts in the 1960s and early 1970s turned as far away from political philosophy as possible. Some contrasts help make the point. When Merleau-Ponty sought to make amends for his indulgence in Stalinism (cf. *Humanisme et terreur* [1947]), he produced a philosophical critique of ultra-Bolshevism (cf. *Aventures de la dialectique* [1955]). When one of Merleau-Ponty's most devoted students, Claude Lefort, took leave of his early commitments to Trotskyism, the result was a protracted effort to develop a new theory of the political. For Desanti, it seems, the lesson was not simply that the political had been theorized in error but that *it was an error to theorize the political*, especially with tools borrowed from philosophy or the sciences, social or otherwise. In the editorial texts that accompany Desanti's early writings, there is not an effort to theorize them, but there does seem to be an effort to "explain" them. The ambiguities of this effort are more pronounced with regard to *IHP* than in the articles that compose *Une Pensée captive*. Whereas the insights offered by Dominique in her preface and Pierre-François Moreau in the afterword seem to be

largely justified by the text itself, certain readers might detect a tendency toward apologetics in the suggestion that Desanti's "break" with the PCF is already legible in the more sophisticated arguments of the book.

41. "Philosophie et singularité," in Desanti, *IHP*, 301–7.

42. Ibid., 306.

43. Ibid.

44. David Wittmann is the scholar currently in charge of Desanti's papers at the ENS-LSH in Lyon and the source of the speculation that this was the original intent behind the "Dieu ou Nature" piece. The document's contents are consistent with notes in Althusser's archive, and it is at least plausible that it was a written two-hour lecture that Althusser may have heard. Its composition date, 1948, and its length, approximately forty double-spaced typed pages, suggest as much. The analysis of the God/Nature polarity in Spinozism that we will pursue later is equally indebted to this document and *IHP*.

45. D. Desanti, *Les Staliniens*, 367; and Desanti, Desanti, and Droit, *La Liberté nous aime encore* (hereafter *Liberté*), 212.

46. Desanti, *IHP*, 28–29, 32–34, 34.

47. Althusser, *The Future Lasts Forever*, 176–80.

48. Desanti, *IHP*, 35–46.

49. Ibid., 37–38.

50. Ibid., 39–40. What formally distinguishes this worldview from the one on offer by Engels, or by Desanti for that matter, is not addressed.

51. Ibid., 43.

52. Ibid.

53. Ibid., 44.

54. Ibid., 92–93.

55. Cf. the opening paragraphs of "Science bourgeoise et science prolétarienne," in Desanti, *PC*, 105–10. The irony, of course, is that this case for science's "objectivity" was marshaled against the science "in the service of war" in the capitalist world but in defense of the dialectical materialist alternative to "genetics," Ivan Michurin's agronomics, which laid the groundwork for Trofim Lysenko's disastrous agricultural policies in the Soviet Union.

56. Ibid., 69–70.

57. Ibid., 70. What is most striking about this claim is that, much as Jean Hyppolite suggested to Cavaillès, even though it is put up as a critique of Hegelian idealism, this position is not without its own potential resources in Hegel's philosophy, specifically in *The Science of Logic*. On this score, it should be observed that Desanti had spearheaded the critique of Hegelianism and its complicity with existentialism several years earlier. The problem with Sartre and Merleau-Ponty both was that they made use of the *Phenomenology of Spirit* while forgetting the *Science of Logic*. Not only does this distinction foreshadow Althusser's later distinction between an early and a late Marx; it also suggests that what is being criticized

here under the name of "Hegelianism" is not so much Hegel's philosophy as a French cocktail of phenomenological existentialism consisting of equal parts Husserl, Heidegger, and Hegel, with a dash of Marx for good measure.

58. Desanti, *IHP*, 305.

59. Desanti, "Path," 57.

60. The book is an extended analysis of the development of the mathematical theory of real variables using a hybrid of phenomenological and rationalist methods. Desanti contends that the selection of this theory is arbitrary; he simply happened to be well acquainted with it. He deliberately chose a moment in mathematical history that had already been "surpassed" so to speak. His aim was to pursue the thought experiment of revisiting a moment, while bracketing knowledge of its outcome, in order to understand the liaison of necessity and contingency that happens in the production of a given "mathematical ideality."

61. See Desanti, "Path," 57–58.

62. Desanti's account anticipates Antonio Negri's *The Savage Anomaly* by twenty-five years but with one crucial difference. Negri reads Spinoza in his time to discover an alternative path for modernity to that which was taken. In marked contrast to the ostensible autonomy of the subject—be it Cartesian, Lockean, or Kantian, all are "bourgeois" to Negri—Spinoza's metaphysics gives us a concept of transpersonal power opposed to hierarchical and juridical models. Such a view, for all its historical determinations, was so untimely in its day that it could only be understood as "anomalous," hence Negri's title. For Desanti, who is acknowledged in Negri's study, Spinoza's importance draws from his status not as an anomaly but as an exemplar of the historical contradictions of the epoch. Cf. Negri, *The Savage Anomaly*, 250, 266.

63. Desanti, *IHP*, 102.

64. Ibid., 111–18.

65. Ibid., 119.

66. See Kolakowski, *Chrétiens sans église*; and Popkin, *Spinoza*.

67. Desanti, *IHP*, 135–45.

68. See Hardt and Negri, *Empire*, *Multitude*, and *Commonwealth*.

69. Desanti, *IHP*, 161–65.

70. Ibid., 167.

71. Note the following excerpts from Althusser's handwritten notes from a lecture of Desanti's on Spinoza given May 18, 1948: "contamination between religion and math . . . "; "mathematical knowledge means of salvation!"; "<u>this contamination</u> between physics-religion-math, <u>this interaction</u> requires an origin which is outside their level of reflection." "look for the <u>concrete link</u> among these [unequal] elements of culture of Spinoza's time? 3 elements represent the birth of the <u>bourgeoisie</u>." All punctuation and underlining in original. ALT2-A60-09, Notes sur Spinoza (2), Fonds Althusser.

72. See Negri, "Spinoza's Anti-Modernity," in his *Subversive Spinoza*, 79–93.

73. See Desanti, *La Philosophie silencieuse*, 151–52, 211.
74. Cf. Deleuze, *Logic of Sense*, 94–99.
75. Desanti, Desanti, and Droit, *Liberté*, 214.
76. See the introduction to the 1994 edition of *IP*, 10–44, for Desanti's reflections on the circumstances of its composition and publication.
77. Thao, *Phénoménologie et matérialisme dialectique*. Cf. Lyotard, *La Phénoménologie*.
78. See S. Bachelard, *A Study of Husserl's Formal and Transcendental Logic*, and *La Conscience de rationalité*. In addition to Derrida's introduction and translation of Husserl, *L'Origine de la géometrie*, published in 1962, see his 1952–53 *mémoire de maîtrise, Le Problème de la genèse dans la philosophie de Husserl*, published in 1990. For an overview, see Baring, *The Young Derrida*, 146–61.
79. The proximity of theoretical concerns can be seen in both thinkers' contributions to the conference on genesis and structure held at Cerisy in 1959 and published in 1965: Gandillac, Goldmann, and Piaget, *Entretiens sur les notions de genèse et de structure*. In his first attempt to return to mathematics after years of *Nouvelle Critique* writing, Desanti offered "Remarques sur la connexion des notions de genèse et de structure en mathématiques" (143–59), a piece that laid the groundwork for *Les Idéalités mathématiques*. Derrida's contribution, "'Genèse et structure' et la phénoménologie" (243–68) would find a wide readership after its inclusion in his *Writing and Difference*, 154–68. Cf. Baring, *The Young Derrida*, 161–90.
80. Desanti, *IP*, 18–20.
81. Ibid., 20.
82. It should also be noted that the sonorities and implications of the French word *déconstruction* are more evocative of Heidegger's *Destruktion* than any Husserlian principle, and that the provenance of Derrida's concept in Heidegger's thought distinguishes it from Desanti's project.
83. Desanti, "Path," 62.
84. Desanti, *IP*, 91–92.
85. See Cohen-Solal, *Sartre: A Life*, 159–78.
86. Ibid., 175.
87. Personal communication from Dominique Desanti, July 23, 2007.
88. Desanti, "'L'Être et le Néant' a cinquante ans," 31.
89. Ibid.
90. Desanti suggests that for all of his criticisms of Husserl, Sartre's project is consistent with a recurrent trope of phenomenology, that its use as a rigorous method often obscures the philosophical desires and intentions of the phenomenologist. The difference between Husserl and Sartre then is merely one of focus: for Husserl it is mathematics and logic; for Sartre it is the personal experience of the social world. See Desanti, "Sartre et Husserl." Lest Desanti himself be charged with duplicity in his recourse to phenomenology, his own use of it is perfectly consistent with his assessment of Sartre. In Desanti's case, phenomenological methods

are marshaled as a critical riposte to systematic philosophy and a call for epistemic modesty against totalizing ambition. See "Path" as well.

91. Here again the sites of comparison between Desanti's project and Derrida's are suggestive. There is no evidence that Desanti engaged with Derrida on the philosophical level, although Desanti was the senior jury member when Derrida presented a selection of his work for his doctoral degree in 1980. We would venture, however, that Desanti might subject Derrida to a similar critique, specifically focused on the issue or principle (though Derrida would never designate it as such) of *différance*. *Différance* is in effect the animus—in the sense of animating or energizing spirit—of Derrida's ontology. Desanti's ontology, insofar as it is present in his modest, technical writings, is among the most subtractive imaginable, chiefly in its efforts to think without recourse to *any* animating principle extrinsic to the scientific discourse itself. In this regard, it is striking to find Badiou—who endeavored in *Being and Event* to produce his own subtractive ontology of the "pure multiple"—refer to Desanti's efforts as "perhaps too restrictive" (483).

92. Desanti, "Path," 60.
93. Desanti, *IP*, 47.
94. Ibid., 60.
95. Ibid., 62.
96. Ibid., 70–71.
97. Husserl, *Méditations cartésiennes*, 122–23, emphasis in original.
98. Desanti, *IP*, 83.
99. Ibid., 149–50.
100. Ibid., 149.
101. Ibid., 150.
102. See Marion, *God without Being*. Of Marion's formidable trilogy on Descartes, the key work is the middle volume, *Sur la théologie blanche de Descartes*. The central volume of his phenomenological work is *Being Given*.
103. See the preface to Merleau-Ponty, *Signes*, 9–61, where Merleau-Ponty discusses his unease at the popularity of Spinozism among certain Communist peers, such as Paul Nizan, eager to reintegrate their "finite being" into an infinite productivity much greater than themselves (51). Note as well the comments at the end of the working notes compiled in *The Visible and the Invisible*, wherein Merleau-Ponty outlines the plan of his own future work, not to be compromised by humanism, naturalism, or theology, and claims that "precisely what has to be done is to show that philosophy can no longer think according to this distinction: God, man, creatures—which was Spinoza's division" (274).
104. Desanti, "Path," 53.
105. Merleau-Ponty, *The Visible and the Invisible*, xxv–xxvi.
106. *Les Piéges de la croyance* is the subtitle of Desanti's *Un Destin philosophique*.
107. Desanti, *La Philosophie silencieuse*, 149.
108. Ibid., 147.

CHAPTER 4

1. Althusser, *For Marx* (hereafter *FM*), 22.
2. In addition to Montag, *Althusser and His Contemporaries*, see the essays in Diefenbach et al., *Encountering Althusser*.
3. For an account of French Maoism, see Bourg, *From Revolution to Ethics*, 43–102. Though only tangentially connected to the Maoists, Jacques Rancière produced the most elaborate statement of the Maoist critique in *Althusser's Lesson*.
4. Dews, "Althusser, Structuralism, and the French Epistemological Tradition," 104–41.
5. E.g., Löwy, "Stalinist Ideology and Science," 180–82.
6. E.g., Judt, "Elucubrations: The 'Marxism' of Louis Althusser," in *Reappraisals*, 106–15.
7. Resch, *Althusser and the Renewal of Marxist Social Theory*, 24.
8. Supplementing Resch's theoretical exposition with a historical account of the French Communist Party, William S. Lewis pursues this line in *Louis Althusser and the Traditions of French Marxism*.
9. The original title of Althusser's memoir, *L'Avenir dure longtemps*, translates more accurately as *The Future Lasts a Long Time*, which is indeed the title of the UK edition of this book. Citations are from the American edition published by the New Press (hereafter *Future*), and I use that title as a result. It is possible that the distinction between "forever" and "a long time" is not without significance for a Communist philosopher insistent that the "the lonely hour of the 'last instance' never comes" (*FM*, 113).
10. Elliott, *Althusser: The Detour of Theory*.
11. Althusser, *Politics and History* (hereafter *PH*), 15.
12. Ibid.
13. Cf. the discussion of Gueroult's interpretation in Chapter 2, where Spinoza's rationalism was described as "a flight from the lived in the genesis of the work." See as well Granger, "Jean Cavaillès."
14. Althusser, *The Humanist Controversy* (hereafter *Humanist*), xvii–xviii. In a later essay Goshgarian suggests that, in the 1960s, Althusser belatedly discovers in Spinoza's texts themes that were already central to his 1959 book on Montesquieu, chiefly those pertaining to the historical singularity of political formations. The argument is convincing on its own terms, which are independent of the fact that Althusser's epistemology of the early 1960s was already Spinozist to the extent that it was indebted to a long-standing epistemological critique of phenomenology that was Spinozist in its essentials. See Goshgarian, "The Very Essence of the Object."
15. Cf. Eric Hobsbawm, "The Structure of *Capital*," in Elliott, *Althusser: A Critical Reader*, 1–9. Hobsbawm's review of *Pour Marx* and *Lire le Capital* was one of the first English-language assessments of Althusser's project, published in the *Times Literary Supplement*, before these works were translated into English.

16. Cited by Corpet and Matheron, in Althusser, *Humanist*, 34.
17. Althusser, "Ideology and Ideological State Apparatuses: Notes towards an Investigation," in *Lenin and Philosophy and Other Essays* (hereafter *Lenin*), 85–126.
18. Althusser, *Essays in Self-Criticism* (hereafter *ESC*), 125–41.
19. Althusser, *Philosophy and the Spontaneous Philosophy of the Scientists and Other Essays* (hereafter *PSPS*), 69–165. Althusser's fifth lecture from this seminar, "Du côté de la philosophie," is in Althusser, *Écrits philosophiques et politiques*, 265–310. The "annex" to this last lecture, "Sur Desanti et les pseudo 'problèmes de troisième espèce,'" remains unpublished but is accessible in ALT2-A12-02.01/02/03, Fonds Althusser.
20. Althusser, *Lenin*, 11–43.
21. Althusser, "The Only Materialist Tradition," 4. This text, pp. 3–19, was originally part of Althusser's memoir but was not included in the first French publication of this volume, which was the basis for the English translation.
22. See Tosel, "Hazards of Aleatory Materialism," 3–26; and Sotiris, "Rethinking Aleatory Materialism," 27–41. Cf. Lahtinin, *Politics and Philosophy*.
23. See Althusser, "The Underground Current of the Materialism of the Encounter," in Althusser, *Philosophy of the Encounter* (hereafter *Encounter*), 176.
24. There is even less poetry in the French. According to Gueroult, Spinoza "a décortiqué Dieu jusqu'au trognon." Personal communication from Pierre-François Moreau, May 24, 2007.
25. The emphasis on Spinoza's strategic appeal for Althusser along these lines is the guiding thread of Thomas, "Althusser and Spinoza." See also Williams, "Althusser and Spinoza."
26. Althusser, "Portrait of the Materialist Philosopher," in *Encounter*, 290–91.
27. Badiou, "Le (Re)commencement du matérialisme dialectique," 446, translated as "The (Re)Commencement of Dialectical Materialism," in Badiou, *The Adventure of French Philosophy*, 143tm. Note also the following observation from Althusser's biographer: "For Althusser, phenomenology was [in the 1950s] the most dangerous version of idealism, or of the always recurring school of French spiritualism." Moulier Boutang, *Louis Althusser, une biographie: La formation du mythe, 1946–1956: Ruptures et plis* (hereafter *Ruptures*), 458. When Moulier Boutang's biography of Althusser was first published in 1992, it was marketed as the first volume of a projected two-volume work. However, when the paperback edition appeared in 2002, this one volume was split into two. This explains why one sees "volume 1" cited in two different volumes: *La Matrice* and *Ruptures et plis*.
28. Althusser, *FM*, 213.
29. Althusser, *Lenin*, 5–7.
30. Althusser, *FM*, 229.
31. See Clive Cazeaux's remarks in his edited volume *The Continental Aesthetics Reader*: "French phenomenology, more so than Husserl's or Heidegger's, seeks to 'concretize' the phenomenological method, that is, to show how the structures

of experience can be derived from the 'feel' of lived experience" (74). Martin Jay addresses the equivocal status of lived experience for Husserl in "The Lifeworld and Lived Experience," noting that, in the progressive detranscendentalization of Husserl's original project, the vagaries of pre-predicative experience gained in importance for his investigations. It was these aspects of Husserl's project that would appeal most to Maurice Merleau-Ponty. For Althusser, as for Cavaillès, it was this telos of Husserl's effort in the supposed passivity of "simple experiences" that betokened his reliance on an increasingly interior, and increasingly figurative, "lifeworld," thus precipitating his project's collapse into the subjectivism that had been the bane of the psychologism he had originally sought to avoid.

32. Cf. Judt, *Past Imperfect*.

33. Arguably, aside from his PCF membership, it was Althusser's failure to accept "regret" as an adequate response for his and his cohort's support of Stalinism that most distinguishes him from other French Marxist intellectuals. Regret alone was no surrogate for understanding. See Althusser's introductory essay, "Unfinished History," in Lecourt, *Proletarian Science?*, 7–16.

34. "Letter to Jean Lacroix," in Althusser, *The Spectre of Hegel* (hereafter *Spectre*), 200.

35. Beyond Dominique Janicaud's 1990 polemic reprinted in *La Phénoménologie dans tous ses états*, see Moyn, *Origins of the Other*; and Baring, *The Young Derrida*, esp. 15–81.

36. In *Future*, however, Althusser would single out Merleau-Ponty as "a truly great philosopher" preferable to Sartre (178). Moulier Boutang also reports that Althusser had always preferred Merleau-Ponty to Sartre and that he regretted siding with Sartre for political reasons in the falling out over communism between the two philosophers in the 1950s. Moulier Boutang, *Ruptures*, 421.

37. Conversation with the author, March 2, 2005.

38. Althusser, *Spectre*, 36–169.

39. Cited by Matheron in Althusser, *Spectre*, 16.

40. Althusser, *Spectre*, 170–72.

41. This volume was translated and published in an abridged form as Kojève, *Introduction to the Reading of Hegel*.

42. Althusser, *Future*, 177.

43. Althusser, *Spectre*, 170.

44. See his remark in an interview with Maria Macciocchi: "My interest in philosophy was aroused by materialism and its critical function: for *scientific* knowledge, against all the mystifications of *ideological* 'knowledge.'" Althusser, *Lenin*, 1. Cf. Desanti's observation in 1970 that all materialisms "mobilize a certain form of rationality [. . .] in order to eliminate the mythic residues that haunt society [. . .] and propose a model of Reality such that these residues can no longer be effective. Each [materialism] realizes in its time and by its own methods, a

veritable *emendatio intellectus* [emendation of the intellect] in the Spinozist sense of the term." Desanti, *La Philosophie silencieuse*, 138.

45. Althusser, *Future*, 168.

46. Althusser, *Spectre*, 172.

47. One obvious resource for this perspective would be the author of *Materialism and Empirio-Criticism* (1908): Lenin. Although Lenin's scientism would prove useful to Althusser later on, Lenin does not figure as a theoretical reference in Althusser's early writings.

48. Althusser defended his master's thesis before Bachelard in the autumn of 1947. In a letter to Hélène Legotien recounting the experience and pondering his likely grade, Althusser averred, "I can't count on him [Bachelard], because he's not familiar with the questions that interest me." Bachelard clearly liked something in the thesis; he gave it an 18 out of 20, the French equivalent of an A+. See Althusser, *Spectre*, 15.

49. Althusser, *Future*, 333.

50. Ibid., 161.

51. ALT2-A56 and A60, Fonds Althusser.

52. ALT2-A56-12, Fonds Althusser.

53. ALT2-A56-11, Fonds Althusser.

54. One of Althusser's students, Yves Duroux, did his master's thesis on Cavaillès, according to Balibar. Conversation with the author March 5, 2008. Duroux, who began his tenure as a student at the ENS in 1960, recalls the prevalence of the Cavaillèsian slogan pitting a philosophy of the concept against that of consciousness in Ewald, "Elèves d'Althusser," 47. See as well Peden, "The Fate of the Concept."

55. Althusser, *Future*, 183.

56. This gloss comes from Yann Moulier Boutang, one of the few to have consulted the document, in his *Louis Althusser, une biographie: La Formation du mythe, 1918–1945: La Matrice* (1992; hereafter *Matrice*), 11–13. See as well Althusser, *Future*, 327. Balibar suspects that Martin had derived this concept in turn from his reading of Heidegger. Conversation with the author, March 5, 2008. Apparently, Martin's understanding of German was very good, which would have been necessary truly to engage with Heidegger's thought, as *Being and Time* was not yet fully translated into French. Of Martin's few published accomplishments were his translations into French of Hegel's *The Spirit of Christianity and Its Fate* and Hermann Hesse's *The Glass Bead Game*. See Moulier Boutang, *Ruptures*, 384–90.

57. Unlike Althusser, Martin did not serve in the French army nor did he spend the war in a prisoner-of-war camp, which Althusser's dedication may otherwise suggest, given *For Marx*'s opening reflections on the "terrible education of deeds" that was the Second World War. Martin declined to join the Resistance and spent 1943–45 as a laborer in Frankfurt after several years of conscripted factory work in France under the Vichy system of *Service du travail obligatoire*, which

he, unlike many *normaliens*, refused to evade. According to Moulier Boutang, the decision not to join the Resistance "weighed heavily" on Martin, a Germanist who nonetheless took advantage of his time in Germany to work through Hegel. Moulier Boutang, *Ruptures*, 384–85.

58. Ibid., 323.
59. Bourdieu, "Aspirant philosophe," 15–24.
60. Ibid., 19.
61. Cf. Althusser, *FM*, 25–27.
62. Ibid., 25.
63. Moyn, *Origins of the Other*, 21–56.
64. Althusser, *Future*, 340.
65. Conversation with the author, March 5, 2008.
66. Rancière, *Althusser's Lesson*, 42.
67. Adorno, *Negative Dialectics*, 382.
68. See Montag's illuminating discussion of Macherey's critique of Althusser's need for consistency and the role it played in precipitating shifts both in his recourse to Spinoza and his project more generally, in *Althusser and His Contemporaries*, 73–91.
69. Anderson, *Arguments within English Marxism*, 58.
70. Althusser, *FM*, 22.
71. Desanti, "Science bourgeoise et science prolétarienne," in *PC*, 105–33.
72. See Gregory Elliott's comments in his introduction to *PSPS*: "Althusser's original philosophical project—to secure the cognitive autonomy of theory—had been inspired by the counter-example of its instrumentalization during the Zhdanovism and Lysenkoism of the Cold War in Theory (with which Althusser's adherence to the PCF coincided)" (xviii–xix).
73. Althusser, *FM*, 28, emphasis in original. Thesis Eleven on Feuerbach states: "The philosophers have only *interpreted* the world, in various ways; the point, however, is to *change* it" (Tucker, *The Marx-Engels Reader*, 145).
74. Althusser, *FM*, 113.
75. Conversation with the author, March 2, 2005. Cf. Balibar's claim with the following: "I never thought as Sartre did that Marxism could be 'the untranscendable philosophy of our time'" (Althusser, *Future*, 176).
76. Althusser, *Future*, 181, and *PSPS*, 124–25.
77. Nizan, *Les Chiens de garde*.
78. See Martin Jay, "Vico and Western Marxism," in Jay, *Fin-de-siècle Socialism*, 67–81. Jay notes that Althusser's hostility to the *verum-factum* principle suggests a surprising commonality between his project and Adorno's critical ripostes to Lukàcs. Adorno and Althusser both are hostile above all to the subjectivism countenanced by this position. But whereas Althusser provides a Spinozist conception of truth in its stead, Spinoza was anathema to Adorno. In any event, their grievances about, even if they do not align exactly. For Adorno the key point was

the "negative dialectic" inherent in nature's resistance to the will of the subject, while Althusser's aim was to render nonsensical the notion that what is "created" is in any way the manifestation of a preexistent will or essence. On antihumanism and its historical relationship to a rejection of God more generally, see Geroulanos, *An Atheism That Is Not Humanist*.

79. In addition to "Feuerbach's 'Philosophical Manifestos,'" and "On the Young Marx," in *FM*, 41–48, 49–86, see "On Feuerbach," in Althusser, *Humanist*, 85–154.

80. Brunschvicg, *Les Étapes*, 142.

81. Popkin, *History of Scepticism from Savonarola to Bayle*, 251.

82. Dews, "Althusser, Structuralism," 115.

83. Hence Althusser's repeated positive references to Galileo and Galilean science, committed as it was to a mathematization of nature devoid of transient causes, origins, or goals. See, e.g., Althusser, *PSPS*, 66.

84. Dews, "Althusser, Structuralism," 120.

85. This was also Perry Anderson's judgment of Althusser's Marxism in *Considerations on Western Marxism*, 64–66, albeit one leveled in a more deliberately pejorative key. Still, it is difficult not to be struck by a footnote in which he remarks upon Althusser's later admission, in the 1970s, of his Spinozism: "[Althusser's] account of [his debt to Spinoza] remains vague and generic, characteristically lacking textual references and specific correspondences. It thus fails to reveal the true extent and unity of the transposition of Spinoza's world into his theoretical work. Further philological study would have little difficulty in documenting this" (66n38).

CHAPTER 5

1. "Conversation with Richard Hyland," cited by G. M. Goshgarian in his introduction to Althusser, *Encounter*, xiv.

2. Aron, *Marxismes imaginaires*. For Althusser's assent to the charge, see Althusser, "Correspondence about 'Philosophy and Marxism,'" in *Encounter*, 211, and *Future*, 148.

3. Althusser, *Encounter*, 3–4.

4. Ibid., 4.

5. Husserl, "The Origin of Geometry," 353–78. Jacques Derrida's introduction and translation of this short text was published in 1962. Though in his memoir Althusser claimed to be familiar only with the *Cartesian Meditations* and the *Crisis* from Husserl's corpus (*Future*, 176), he had been one of the very first to come in contact with Derrida's critical take on Husserl in the 1950s. Althusser was the primary reader of Derrida's master's thesis on Husserl, which was produced in 1954 but not published in French until 1990. See Derrida, *The Problem of Genesis in Husserl's Phenomenology*. On Derrida and Althusser, see Baring, *The Young Derrida*, 259–94.

6. Althusser, *FM*, 187. Further references to *For Marx* will be in the main text.

7. Cf. the discussion of the "knowledge effect" and the "meaning effect" in

Althusser and Balibar, *Reading Capital* (hereafter *RC*), 62–63. The problem with the bracketing procedure of the *epoché* is that, in moving toward pure subjectivity, it subsumes and conceptually forsakes the object. Theodor Adorno pursues a similar critique in his *Against Epistemology.*

8. Ricoeur, "Althusser's Theory of Ideology," 56.
9. Althusser, *Lenin*, 85–126.
10. Ricoeur, "Althusser's Theory of Ideology," 64.
11. Ibid., 59.
12. The concept of recognition is intimately linked to Jacques Lacan's concept of misrecognition (*méconnaissance*), which, as laid out in the parable of the mirror stage, is the phenomenon constitutive of subjectivity at the level of the imaginary. The impact of reading Lacan is palpable throughout Althusser's writings of the 1960s, especially the texts on ideology. But what Althusser finds in Lacan is largely consistent with a burgeoning critique of phenomenology whose development is anterior to Althusser's own theoretical engagement with psychoanalysis, which properly began with a seminar on Lacan in 1963–64. In this regard, what Lacan designates as an intrinsic fact of human existence—inaugural *méconnaissance*—is, in phenomenology, taken for granted as the rudimentary process of philosophical thought itself See Montag, *Althusser and His Contemporaries*, 118–30. Cf. as well Althusser and Balibar, *RC*, 56, where Althusser criticizes the conception of philosophy as a legal instance that legitimates the sciences, a motivation integral to Husserl's project: "This right is no more than the *fait accompli* of mirror recognition's stage direction, which ensures philosophical ideology the *legal recognition* of the *fait accompli* of the 'higher' instances it serves." For a discussion of Althusser's critique of ideology as a specular phenomenon, and its relation to Lacan, see Jay, *Downcast Eyes*, 370–80. See also Althusser, *Writings on Psychoanalysis.*
13. Althusser, *PH*, 21tm.
14. Ibid., 20.
15. Ibid., 38. Althusser's description of Montesquieu's agenda—"correcting errant consciousness"—echoes Spinoza's *Treatise on the Emendation of the Intellect.*
16. Althusser, *PH*, 107.
17. For an example of this approach, see Perry Anderson's *Lineages of the Absolutist State*. Anderson made a virtue of the relative autonomy of base and superstructure to show how absolutist ideology could operate independently of its original material support and produce effects on materials elsewhere in turn (e.g., absolutism emerges from the consolidation of wealth in France, and as a result of its success there absolutism as an idea and set of practices moves east to provoke a consolidation of serfdom). But the discordant relationship also illuminates developments within France alone. See Beik, *Absolutism and Society in Seventeenth-Century France.*
18. Althusser and Balibar, *RC*, 16–17. Further references to *RC* will be in the main text.

19. Part of the power of Althusser's critique comes from its linking the local to the historical, i.e., the "achievement" of one-to-one correspondence that is the goal of an empiricism in effect ad nauseam everyday is a synecdoche for the "goal" of history as such. Similarly, the phenomenologist's eidetic reduction, achieved via the bracketing maneuver of the *epoché*, is something to be performed repeatedly, yet the gesture bears synecdochal relation to the world-historical effort to return to the origin, origin being, in the famous words of Karl Kraus, the goal.

20. See Althusser's further remark: "The peculiar theoretical structure of Political Economy depends on immediately and directly relating together a homogeneous space of given phenomena and an ideological anthropology which bases the economic character of the phenomena and its space on man as the subject of needs (the givenness of the *homo oeconomicus*)" (Althusser and Balibar, *RC*, 162).

21. Anderson, *Arguments within English Marxism*, 7.

22. One of the more striking aspects of Althusser's contributions to the volume is the near equal importance, judging from number of references, attached to the 1857 Introduction to the *Critique of Political Economy* from the *Grundrisse* as to any particular volume of *Capital*. And not least among the scandals of Althusser's memoir was his claim not to have read all of *Capital*, and not to have read Volume One all that closely.

23. An anecdote suggests that reading Althusser in the context of a general heuristic of Western Marxism may not be the most illuminating. Shortly after the publication of E. P. Thompson's excoriation of Althusserianism as "Stalinism in Theory," in *The Poverty of Theory*, the editors of *New Left Review* contacted Althusser to see if he would be willing to publish a reply in their journal. Althusser's response was concise: "Who is E. P. Thompson?" Stewart Martin, "Rendezvous: Return(s) to Marx?," 54.

24. Cited by Elliott, in Althusser, *PSPS*, xi.

25. Spinoza, "The Principles of Cartesian Philosophy *and* Metaphysical Thoughts," in *Complete Works*, 108–212.

26. On the various purposes of Spinoza's volume on Descartes, see Israel, "Spinoza as an Expounder, Critic, and 'Reformer' of Descartes," 59–78.

27. Althusser, "Marx in His Limits," in *Encounter*, 7–162.

28. Althusser, *Humanist*, 1–18.

29. Ibid., 11, 14.

30. Ibid., 14.

31. Althusser, *Politique et histoire de Machiavel à Marx*, 13–25.

32. A glance at the blurb materials on his various English publications leads one to think that Althusser's position at the ENS was one of high reputation. It certainly was, but typically as a way station for philosophers en route to higher things. That Althusser remained the *caïman* for over thirty years was something of an anomaly, not unrelated to the fact that he never produced a major work of philosophy. Nonetheless, the length of Althusser's tenure meant that he came in contact with virtually every important French philosopher passing through the ENS

in those three decades. His influence certainly transcended "Marxist philosophy." See Clément Rosset's recollections in *En ce temps-là*, and the discussion in Baring, *The Young Derrida*, 234–39.

33. Althusser, *Humanist*, 3–4.

34. Althusser, *PSPS*, 141.

35. Vernière, *Spinoza et la pensée française*, 702.

36. Cf. Nathan Brown's efforts to develop the conceptual contents of a "rationalist empiricism" in a different but not unrelated context in his article "Absent Blue Wax (Rationalist Empiricism)."

37. See Althusser, "Materialism," in Bataille, *Visions of Excess*, 15–16. To be clear, the roots of Althusser's ideas on this score are more indebted to Cavaillès than to Bataille, the latter of whom seems to have played no role in Althusser's intellectual genealogy. The two figures of interwar French thought make for a stark contrast, but perhaps Cavaillès's notion that the connection of ideas is a material progress "between singular essences" (*LTS*, 90), that is, not an "idealist" progression, may find certain resonances in Bataille's writings.

38. Althusser, *Humanist*, 25. Further references to *Humanist*—which contains "On Lévi-Strauss," "Three Notes on the Theory of Discourses," and "The Historical Task of Marxist Philosophy"—will be in the main text.

39. The emphasis in this passage is Althusser's, but his exclamation points have been omitted.

40. This document is among the most exigent of Althusser's engagements with Lacan. The general point seems to be that since the theory of the signifier, insofar as it comes from linguistics, is itself originally a Regional Theory (RT), its status as the General Theory (GT) for another RT, that of psychoanalysis, is equivocal. This position is qualified and requalified throughout the essay. When Althusser shared these efforts with Franca Madonia, he cautioned, "Bear in mind that this writing exercise is research in the true sense, not an expression of things already known" (*Humanist*, 35). For more on the relation between Althusser and Lacan, see Hallward and Peden, *Concept and Form*. On the specific import of this document, see Hallward's introduction to volume 1, "Theoretical Training."

41. Cf. Tosel, "Hazards of Aleatory Materialism."

42. Althusser had a problematic and unclear relationship with the aesthetic, which he argued was not opposed to science but different from it. Art allows us to "see" the ideology from which it detaches itself and to which it inevitably "alludes." See Althusser, "A Letter on Art in Reply to André Daspre," in *Lenin*, 151–55. Clearly not one of his primary concerns, aesthetics in an Althusserian key were generally left to his collaborators. Cf. Macherey, *A Theory of Literary Production*.

43. By this period, 1966–67, Althusser was part of an internecine PCF quarrel with Roger Garaudy, the party's "official philosopher." Committed to the humanist Marx, and moving toward Christian socialism himself, Garaudy led the party charge against Althusser's heresies.

44. Althusser, *Lenin*, 34.
45. See Elliott, in Althusser, *PSPS*, xix.
46. Althusser, "Rousseau: The Social Contract," in *PH*, 113–60.
47. Lacan, *Écrits*, 726–45.
48. Derrida, "Nature, culture, écriture," 1–45.
49. "Généologie des sciences," *Cahiers pour l'Analyse*, no. 9 (Summer 1968): 5–44.
50. For more on the *Cahiers* and these specific contributions, see Hallward and Peden, *Concept and Form*.
51. See Rancière, *Althusser's Lesson*; and Badiou and Balmès, *De l'idéologie*.
52. See Montag's illuminating discussion of this text, in which he places it—theoretically and historically—in its context as part of a larger project, other portions of which were posthumously published in *Sur la réproduction*. Montag, *Althusser and His Contemporaries*, 131–51.
53. "In ideology, all questions are thus settled *in advance*, in the nature of things, since ideological discourse interpellates-constitutes the subjects of its interpellation by providing them in advance with the answer, all the answers, to the feigned question that its interpellation contains" (Althusser, *Humanist*, 55).
54. Althusser, *PSPS*, 107.
55. Lichtheim, *Marxism in Modern France*, 94.
56. See Yves Duroux's remarks in Ewald, "Elèves d'Althusser," 47–48. Another indicator of this course's popularity is that the recent Nobel laureate in biology, Jacques Monod of the Collège de France, attended the opening session. See the same issue of *Magazine littéraire*, 21.
57. Epistemology and ontology are typically understood to be branches of philosophy, or its component parts, not steps on the way to philosophy per se. But the point here is that, following Spinoza, learning to think "philosophically" means going through propaedeutic stages, which I have termed, no doubt anachronistically, "epistemological" and "ontological."
58. "Lenin and Philosophy," in Althusser, *Lenin*, is the companion piece to *PSPS*, presented as it was around the same time that Althusser was leading this seminar. The concept "spontaneous philosophy of the scientists" is an homage to Lenin's critique of spontaneity in politics.
59. Althusser, *PSPS*, 88. Further references to *PSPS* will be in the main text.
60. See Balibar, *Spinoza and Politics*; and Negri, *The Savage Anomaly*.
61. A more generous assessment of this slogan might run as follows: When Althusser speaks of the "class struggle in theory," it is an effort to universalize the concept of "class struggle" in such a manner that "class" loses any specifically economic, much less industrial, connotation. In this regard, Althusser himself is a participant in the "class struggle in theory" by virtue of his "class position" in French academia, the *caïman* at the ENS whose approach to philosophy consists of drawing lines of distinction, and revealing rifts and solidarities, rather than

producing a totalizing work of philosophy that, though it might procure him a "dominant" position, would ultimately be more ideological than philosophical in its essentials. In this Bourdieusian image, "class struggle in theory" acquires an existential depth and pathos. Still, to call this position "political" relies on a concept of the political expanded to such a degree that it threatens vacuity as a concept and lacks purchase, not necessarily on the polit*ical* as a quality, but on poli*tics* as an activity.

62. Clément Rosset, *En ce temps-là*, 39–40.

63. Ibid., 23; Althusser, *Future*, 169. This would be translated idiomatically as "to stop kidding yourself," but the literal sense of the French is pertinent here.

64. Ibid., 328.

65. Althusser, "The Only Materialist Tradition."

66. Althusser, *Machiavelli and Us*. For a discussion of this text and the persistence of anti-phenomenological themes within it, see Peden, "Anti-Revolutionary Republicanism," 34–37.

67. Althusser, *Machiavelli and Us*, 20.

68. Hallward said this during the Q&A of the conference on "Speculative Realism" held at Goldsmiths College, London, in April 2007, transcribed and published in Mackay, *Collapse*, 3:361.

69. Hallward, *Out of This World*.

70. Althusser, *Encounter*, 273–74.

CHAPTER 6

1. Deleuze, *Différence et répétition*, translated as *Difference and Repetition*, 388/304tm (hereafter *DR*). For this work, as with *The Logic of Sense*, *Spinoza and the Problem of Expression*, and *Desert Islands*, references will be to the page number in the French edition, followed by that in the English edition; tm = translation modified. Modifications are typically made to accentuate an aspect of my argument, not to correct an error.

2. Deleuze, *Masochism*, and *Francis Bacon*.

3. Deleuze's career can be divided into three more or less distinct phases. Between 1953 and 1968, he published five monographs on the following thinkers: Hume (1953), Nietzsche (1962), Kant (1963), Bergson (1966), and Spinoza (1968), the last of which was his minor doctoral thesis and is the most substantial of these studies. The major works *Difference and Repetition* and *The Logic of Sense*, published in 1968 and 1969, are the first studies where Deleuze claimed to be "doing philosophy in his own voice," and they serve as a hinge between his period as a historian of philosophy and his work with Félix Guattari pursued throughout the 1970s (*Anti-Oedipus* was published in 1974, and *A Thousand Plateaus* in 1980). The 1980s sees Deleuze's turn to aesthetics with the *Cinema* volumes, which followed his study of Francis Bacon first published in 1981. There are various excep-

tions to this framework—*Proust and Signs* was published in 1964, and *The Fold: Leibniz and the Baroque* was published in 1988—but it holds as a rough schematic. This chapter and the one that follows avoid Deleuze's collaboration with Guattari, which is a subject with many of its own unique features and an event unto itself in French intellectual history, quite apart from Deleuze's contribution to French philosophy. For an illuminating account of the gestation of *Anti-Oedipus* in particular, see Bourg, *From Revolution to Ethics*, 105–76.

4. Hoene-Wronski, *La Philosophie de l'infini*; Ruyer, *Éléments de psychobiologie*, and *La Genèse des formes vivantes*. Ruyer's renovation of gnosticism is clearest in his later work, *La Gnose de Princeton*.

5. Deleuze, *The Logic of Sense* (hereafter *LS*), 7–8/xiii–xiv.

6. Cf. Gutting, *French Philosophy in the Twentieth Century*, 331–41. "His approach was distinctive because he generally focused on thinkers who were not, at the time, particularly fashionable in France, and because he seems scarcely concerned with the dominant Germans, Husserl and Heidegger" (332–33).

7. "La Méthode de dramatisation," in Deleuze, *L'Île déserte: Textes et entretiens*, translated as "The Method of Dramatization," in *Desert Islands and Other Texts* (hereafter *ID*), 131–62/94–116.

8. Ibid., 135/97tm.

9. On the arguably metaphysical qualities of Kant's concept, and its debt to Newton, see Insole, "Kant's Transcendental Idealism and Newton's Divine Sensorium."

10. Deleuze, *Spinoza et le problème de l'expression*, translated as *Expressionism in Philosophy: Spinoza* (hereafter *SPE*). The formula used for the English title of this work was taken from the title of Deleuze's concluding chapter, which contrasted Spinoza and Leibniz as two exemplars of "expressionism in philosophy." Though the reasons for this change of title remain unclear, it is perhaps because the aesthetic connotations of "expressionism" were deemed a virtue at the time of the book's publication. Deleuze's study of Leibniz, which came much later in his career (1988), was published the same year in English with a direct translation of the French title: *The Fold: Leibniz and the Baroque*. This latter work is indeed an attempt to read Leibniz's philosophy in terms of the baroque aesthetic with which it was historically contemporaneous and is of a piece with Deleuze's efforts in the 1980s to explore the expressive relations between various arts and philosophy. There is nonetheless something slightly misleading in the intimation of this aesthetic concern in Deleuze's much earlier study of Spinoza. Also, the omission of the word "problem" from the title is itself unfortunate, given the attention devoted to the notion of problems in *SPE*'s accompanying work, *Difference and Repetition*. As a result, I have translated the French title literally when it is referred to in the main text.

11. Deleuze, *SPE*, 148/106tm.

12. Ibid., 149/106tm.

13. A note on capitalization: Deleuze usually capitalizes "the Idea" in the work of this period whenever he refers to it in the singular. I have followed suit in order to preserve Deleuze's unique account of "the Idea" as a concept. Similarly, I will capitalize the words "Thought" and "Extension" whenever used in reference to Spinoza's *Ethics*, Thought and Extension being the two attributes under consideration in Spinoza's tripartite distinction between substance, attributes, and modes.

14. Deleuze, *ID*, 144/103tm. At the time of this talk Deleuze was best known as an interpreter of Nietzsche. He had organized a colloquium on Nietzsche at Royaumont in 1964, the proceedings of which were published in 1967 as *Cahiers de Royaumont, no. VI: Nietzsche* and included contributions from Michel Foucault, Pierre Klossowski, and others. His own *Nietzsche et la philosophie* was published in 1962.

15. Deleuze, *ID*, 202–16/146–55tm. This review was originally published in *Revue de métaphysique et de morale* 74 , no. 4 (1969): 426–37.

16. Deleuze, *ID*, 216/155tm.

17. Ibid.

18. Ibid., 215/154tm.

19. Ibid., 216/154.

20. This subject was broached in Chapter 2, but it should be reiterated. This is one of the more controversial aspects of Gueroult's reading, and Deleuze's as well, because definition four of Book I of the *Ethics* reads: "By attribute I mean *that which the intellect perceives* of substance as constituting its essence" (emphasis added). For Brunschvicg and many an interpreter, this definition meant the attributes were mere formal categories of the understanding, artifacts of the mind's conception of things. Partially inspired by Gueroult, Pierre Macherey has insisted upon the semantic specificity of Spinoza's verb, "perceive" (*percipere*), because, in the terms of Spinoza's own lexicon, perception indicates "that the mind is passive with respect to the object." Consequently, what it receives from the object is in the object. According to Macherey, interpreters from Hegel to Brunschvicg would be on surer footing had Spinoza used the verb "conceive" rather than "perceive." Macherey, *Hegel or Spinoza*, 86–87. Deleuze, like Gueroult, accepts that the attributes are indeed formal categories, but they are categories of formal ontology and hence never without content. This argument is pursued by pointing to various points of the *Ethics* where the attributes are sutured to substance as its means of expression irrespective of the intellect's perception, e.g., EIP1XSch: "[B]y 'Natura naturans' we must understand that which is in itself and conceived through itself; that is, the attributes of substance that express eternal and infinite essence." Cf. Gueroult, *Spinoza I: Dieu*, 435.

21. Gueroult, *Spinoza I: Dieu*, 457.

22. The notion that Spinozism is best understood as the maximal application of the principle of sufficient reason is the guiding thesis of Della Rocca, *Spinoza*.

23. Cf. Olivier Revault d'Allones's remark "I always found Gilles to be a

great follower of Gueroult's," in Dosse, *Gilles Deleuze et Félix Guattari* (hereafter *GDFG*), 122. See also Clément Rosset's reflections on his fellow French Nietzschean in the short piece "Deleuze's Dryness" (Sécheresse de Deleuze), in Clément, *Gilles Deleuze*, 221–25. There Rosset observes that Deleuze's method seems strangely close to Gueroult's: "[W]ho knows if a philosophy is beautiful, if it is true, if it 'sounds good'; we first of all want to examine how it is made, to locate its mode of construction, to determine the solidity of its assemblage" (224).

24. Gueroult, *La Philosophie transcendantale de Salomon Maimon*; Vuillemin, *L'Héritage kantien et la révolution copernicienne*.

25. Janicaud, *Heidegger en France 2*, 92.

26. Janicaud, *La Phénoménologie dans tous ces états*.

27. Alliez, *De l'impossibilité de la phénoménologie*.

28. This is one of the key theses of Levi R. Bryant's *Difference and Givenness: Deleuze's Transcendental Empiricism and the Ontology of Immanence*. Bryant notes that the strange term "transcendental empiricism" Deleuze used in relation to Hume is a compacted expression of Deleuze's oft-repeated desire to develop a philosophy that gives us the conditions not of *possible* but of *real* experience (3). Alluding to Deleuze's call for a "reversal of Platonism," Bryant provides the following elaboration: "To be an anti-Platonist is not simply to reject the forms as determinative of being and what counts as real, but also to reject the thesis that the field of sensible givens is a rhapsody of unintelligible and irrational appearances. It is for this reason that Deleuze's transcendental empiricism is better conceived as a hyper-rationalism than as an empiricism" (9). More emphatically, "The opposition between the sensible and the intelligible is not even operative in Deleuze's ontology" (11).

29. See Giorgio Agamben's essay "Absolute Immanence," in his *Potentialities*, 220–39; and Badiou, *Deleuze*.

30. See Heidegger, *Being and Time* (hereafter *BT*), especially the celebrated tool analysis of division I, chapter 3, "The Worldhood of the World," 91–148. Heidegger's argument is that the entities of scientific analysis are ontically "present-at-hand" but that this "presence-at-hand" is itself rooted in a more primordial, ontological "readiness-to-hand." The static objects of the former instance are first encountered through their ontological existence as ways of being rather than as fixed entities. Heidegger provides the famous example of the hammer, which becomes "present-at-hand" only when it no longer functions properly, thus losing the ontological proximity of its readiness-to-hand. Heidegger's critique of science is that it "forgets" the ontological primacy of readiness-to-hand when it attempts to know objects in their ontic presence-at-hand. Deleuze's point is similar, insofar as he is claiming that when we regard static fixed objects in the world, we have "forgotten" the ontological process constitutive of their manifestation.

31. See, for example, de Beistegui, *Truth and Genesis*. Though remaining attentive to Deleuze's and Heidegger's differences, this volume effectively reads Deleuze as a necessary complement to Heidegger for contemporary philosophy: "By turn-

ing to Deleuze's thought [. . .] I hope to have shown that ontology can and must be as open to naturalism as to phenomenological intuitionism, as open to science as to art" (338). De Beistegui pursues the consequences of this conclusion in his *Immanence*.

32. By situating Deleuze's writings among those of his proximate influences, I am breaking with the predominant tendency to read Deleuze's development in terms of his monographs in the history of philosophy. Deleuze's focus on untimely thinkers, e.g., Hume and Bergson, is arguably something of a red herring in the historical appreciation of his thought. For example, while it is true that Hume was not the most popular thinker in French intellectual life in 1953, Deleuze's focus in his study of Hume is a theory of relationality and the constitutive nature of relations in the formation of the subject, a theme that is clearly consonant with the general thrust of French phenomenology at this time, even if the conclusions are presented as a critical rejoinder to these latter efforts. For a good example of the monograph-based approach, see Hardt, *Gilles Deleuze*. For an assessment of the contingency of state-run examinations in determining the publications of French pedagogues in philosophy, see Schrift, "The Effects of the *Agrégation de Philosophie*." Deleuze serves Schrift as an exemplary case.

33. Agamben, *Potentialities*, 225.

34. Deleuze, *Essays: Critical and Clinical* (hereafter *CC*), 91–98.

35. Badiou, "Gilles Deleuze, *The Fold: Leibniz and the Baroque*," 55.

36. See in particular the chapter "Univocity of Being and Multiplicity of Names," in Badiou, *Deleuze*, 19–29.

37. Dosse, *GDFG*, 21. On Beaufret and his emphasis on the need to understand Heidegger in his own words, see Kleinberg, *Generation Existential*, esp. 157–206, 281.

38. Deleuze, *ID*, 105–8/74–76.

39. Ibid., 106/75tm.

40. Jean-Pierre Faye remarks that "there was someone in Alquié's *khâgne* course who talked about Husserl's *cogito* at the highest level, and that was Deleuze." Dosse, *GDFG*, 121. On Deleuze's debt to Husserl in particular, see Hughes, *Deleuze and the Genesis of Representation*.

41. Deleuze, *Foucault*, 118.

42. Originally in *Poésie*, no. 28 (1945): 28–39, the piece appeared in *Angelaki* in 2002, translated by Keith W. Faulkner. See also Faulkner, "Deleuze in Utero," 25–43, in the same issue. For Deleuze's assessment of Sartre, and the inspiration he provided to a generation of young philosophers, see "Il a été mon maitre," first published in *Arts*, November 28, 1964, reprinted in *ID*, 109–13/77–80.

43. Deleuze, "Description of a Woman," 21.

44. Ibid.

45. The surviving notes for this course, totaling just over thirty thousand words, come from the hand of Pierre Lefebvre, a student in attendance. They are available

on Richard Pinhas's web archive of Deleuze texts and manuscripts: http://www.webdeleuze.com/php/sommaire.html. For a helpful assessment of this course, see Kerslake, "Grounding Deleuze," 30–36.

46. The first edition was published by Gallimard in 1938. Corbin's edition has been reprinted as the first half of Heidegger, *Questions I & II*.

47. Kerslake, "Grounding Deleuze," 35.

48. Quoted in ibid.

49. Kleinberg, *Generation Existential*, 69–71.

50. Geroulanos, *An Atheism That Is Not Humanist*, esp. 49–100.

51. Heidegger, *Qu'est-ce que la métaphysique?*, 12.

52. Ibid., 15.

53. See in particular chapter 2, "Repetition for Itself," in Deleuze, *DR*, 96–168/70–128.

54. See Deleuze, *DR*, 148–49/112–13; and *LS*, 178–79/151–52. Regarding Levinas's indirect influence on Deleuze via Blanchot, Ray Brassier writes, "[T]hough Deleuze may not have been aware of it, Blanchot derives this distinction [between death as personal possibility and dying as impersonal impossibility of possibility] more or less directly from Levinas, whose influence thoroughly pervades Blanchot's *oeuvre*." Brassier, *Nihil Unbound*, 255. Brassier emphasizes the importance of Levinas's 1948 text *Time and the Other*. Cf. Kleinberg, *Generation Existential*, 209–79.

55. Deleuze, *LS*, 350–72/301–21.

56. The provocation of Tournier's "retelling" is that it inverts Defoe's themes. Rather than re-create the world of modern man on the island, Crusoe reacquaints himself with primordial nature and effectively falls in love with the island, a sentiment consummated in an act of sexual congress with a tree and the surrounding grounds. At the novel's end, Friday leaves the island but Crusoe remains behind. One of the points of Deleuze's reading of this novel is to show how, since Crusoe encounters Friday only after he has abandoned the "other structure" of worldly existence, he experiences Friday not as an "other" within this world but as the opening onto a wholly other world itself: "non pas un autrui, mais un tout-autre qu'autrui" (*LS*, 368). Deleuze and Tournier became lifelong friends during their years at the Sorbonne in the late 1940s. See Dosse, *GDFG*, 112–34.

57. Deleuze, *LS*, 359/309. The denigration of the perceptive field in general in this essay and throughout the rest of *The Logic of Sense*, wherein it was reproduced as an appendix, helps accounts for why Michel Foucault described this volume, in his 1970 review in *Critique* of it and *Difference and Repetition*, as "the most alien book imaginable from [Merleau-Ponty's] *Phenomenology of Perception*." Foucault, "Theatrum Philosophicum," 347.

58. Deleuze, *LS*, 369/318.

59. Ibid., 370/318.

60. Ibid., 368/316.

61. Ibid., 372/320tm, emphasis added.

62. Deleuze, "Jean Hyppolite, *Logique et Existence*," in *ID*, 18–23/15–18. This review was originally published in the *Revue philosophique de la France et de l'étranger* 96, nos. 7–9 (1954): 457–60. Hyppolite's book was published by PUF in 1953; it appeared in English translation as *Logic and Existence* in 1997.

63. Deleuze, *ID*, 24/18tm.

64. According to Dosse's biography, this thesis, though formally submitted in 1968, "was almost completely finished by the end of the 1950s" (*GDFG*, 177).

65. Badiou, *Deleuze*, 22.

66. Deleuze, "Qu'est-ce que fonder?"

67. Deleuze, *Nietzsche and Philosophy*, 51–52, 205; and *DR*, 225–26/173–74, 253–54/196–97.

68. An excerpt from Vuillemin's book translated by Arthur Goldhammer appears as "The Kantian Heritage and the Copernican Revolution," in Balibar and Rajchman, *French Philosophy since 1945*, 7–10.

69. Vuillemin, *L'Héritage kantien*, 14.

70. Ibid., 306.

71. Deleuze, *La Philosophie critique de Kant*. This book was dedicated to Alquié, as "an expression of profound gratitude."

72. For an account of Maimon's Spinozism and its impact, see Melamed, "Salomon Maimon and the Rise of Spinozism in German Idealism." More generally, on Maimon as well as Spinozism and the pantheism controversy, see Beiser, *The Fate of Reason*, 44–126, 285–323.

73. Maimon, *Essai sur la philosophie transcendantale*, 50–51.

74. Ibid., 50. Deleuze cites this passage in *DR*, 225/174, wherein he provides his own translation of the original German. I have translated from Scherrer's edition.

75. Ibid., 216.

76. Deleuze, *ID*, 203/174tm.

77. Deleuze, *LS*, 342–43/295.

78. Cited by Henry Allison, in "Kant's Critique of Spinoza," 206.

79. Cf. Deleuze, *SPE*: "Spinoza's Method, in its opposition to Descartes, poses a problem closely analogous to Fichte's, reacting against Kant" (121/136). Deleuze's reference is Gueroult's study of Fichte.

80. On the metaphor of the black box, see Latour, *Pandora's Hope*. On Deleuze specifically, see During, "Blackboxing in Theory."

81. Spinoza, EIDef6. See as well Deleuze, *SPE*, 9/13, where Deleuze emphasizes "expresses."

82. Deleuze, *SPE*, 12–14/16–18. For a critical assessment of *SPE* that focuses on the concept of expression, see Howie, *Deleuze and Spinoza*. For a more generous view, see Wasser, "Deleuze's Expressionism."

83. Given Althusser's hostility to the concept of "expressive totality," in many ways the target of his own Spinozism, Deleuze's valorization of this concept may cause some confusion. That which is castigated as the "expressive" in Althusser's

project in fact goes by the name of the "emanative" in Deleuze's. In *SPE*, Deleuze attributes an emanative notion of being to the Neoplatonism of Plotinus. This is a model of being wherein all that exists emanates from a single original source, the very formula that Althusser criticizes under the name of expression in Hegel. Deleuze suggests that Spinoza moves beyond Plotinus by taking emanation and effectively detemporalizing it, making it fully immanent to, that is, coextensive with, being itself as expression. Though Deleuze does not use the formula, it is clear that what would be "expressive causality" in his system has its correlate in the "structural causality" of Althusser's. For Deleuze's own positive assessment of Althusser, see "How Do We Recognize Structuralism?," in *ID*, 238–69/170–92.

84. Deleuze, *SPE*, 21/27.

85. See the entire first part of *SPE*, "The Triads of Substance," 21–84/27–95. This is a technical but important point. To say that there is no actual distinction within the quantitative variations of one of the attributes is to state, in a baroque way, that a discrete moment dividing either Extension or Thought "in its kind" must always come from the outside, to wit, the other attribute. It is not a controversial proposition to say that matter is essentially continuous; there is no "real" or actual distinction within it. Any distinction discerned within it is the result of an act of Thought that imposes a distinction; indeed, this is Kantianism in a nutshell. This thesis seems much more troubling when it is applied to the attribute Thought, but in fact the logic is precisely the same. What is it that accounts for the *qualitative* or actual distinction between the Thought going on in my head and that in yours? It is precisely the intervention of matter itself that accounts for the distinction, the unbridgeable, material separation that results from embodiment. In the terms of a rationalist metaphysics, the rupture of continuity in Thought is a result of matter's permanent intrusion, just as the obviation of matter's intrinsic continuity is a result of Thought's intrusion. But this does not change the fact that when considered *wholly in their own terms*, Thought and Extension are each infinitely continuous, forming the common ground of their qualitative relation to one another. The first eight propositions of the *Ethics* seek to achieve this "proof," by showing how each substantial attribute "in its kind" can be interrupted only by a substance of a different nature. In actual existence, however, by the very same line of argumentation, Thought and Extension are *always* relating to one another; neither can exist alone. There is never an actual instance in which one could talk about "pure" Thought or "pure" Extension in any sensible way, yet rationally they must be understood in their real distinction from one another.

86. Hallward, *Out of This World*, 30.

87. Heidegger, *BT*, 127.

88. Ibid., 127.

89. Ibid., 153. The MacQuarrie and Robinson translation uses single quotation marks to distinguish Heidegger's use of scare quotes from citations of or allusions to the vocabulary of other philosophers.

90. Deleuze, *SPE*, 9/13.
91. Spinoza, EIP1.
92. Deleuze, *DR*, 388/304tm, emphasis added.
93. Deleuze, *SPE*, 173–298/191–320.
94. Ibid., 252–67/273–88.
95. Deleuze, *LS*, 178/152.

CHAPTER 7

1. Deleuze, "The Exhausted," in *CC*, 152.
2. Deleuze, *DR*, 95/69.
3. Ibid., 272–73/211.
4. Ibid., 234/220tm. Further references to *Difference and Repetition* will be in the main text.
5. That what is foundational would be named the third synthesis, rather than the first, may seem perplexing. But this is one example among many of the involuted nature of the argumentation throughout *Difference and Repetition*. This synthesis is third because it is the third one discovered in a philosophical consideration of the nature of time. But in this very discovery, what is discovered is the inaugural, grounding condition of time itself, thus leading to a repetition of the three tiers of time from the bottom up. This argumentative maneuver mimics Deleuze's own understanding of the nature of Nietzsche's eternal return and also echoes the genetic method employed by Gueroult to make sense of Spinoza. Cf. Deleuze, *Nietzsche and Philosophy*, 1–38.
6. Cf. the discussion of Pierre Klossowski's fictions in Deleuze, *LS*, 341/294: "Klossowski insists that God is the sole guarantor of the identity of the self and of its substantial base, that is, of the integrity of the body. One cannot conserve the self without also holding on to God. The death of God essentially signifies, and essentially entails, the dissolution of the self: God's tomb is also the tomb of the self."
7. See Deleuze, *Bergsonism*.
8. Heidegger, *BT*, 380.
9. Ibid., 379.
10. Ibid., 382.
11. Deleuze *LS*, esp. 74–82/58–65, 190–97/162–68. Further references to *The Logic of Sense* will be in the main text.
12. The reference is in fact to Lewis Carroll's text "What the Tortoise Said to Achilles," which Deleuze cites in French translation in Carroll, *Logique sans peine*.
13. For a critique that questions the accuracy of Deleuze's representation of Stoic theories of time, see Sellars, "Aiôn and Chronos." This appropriation is consistent with the more generalized ventriloquism in play whenever Deleuze discusses another philosopher (or philosophers).

14. See Deleuze, *ID*, 49, 141. Also see Deleuze, *DR*, 272–73/211. Gillian Rose, in her critique of "The New Bergsonism," in *Dialectic of Nihilism*, detects a sleight of hand in Deleuze's recuperation of Bergsonian *durée* as the medium of the virtual's actualization. Rose writes, "*Durée* is the movement from 'virtuality' to actuality which is not the formal Kantian separation of actuality and possibility, nor does it involve a mathematical notion of extension or space. 'Virtuality' is an alternative translation of Greek *dynamis* to the conventional Latinized 'possibility' or 'potentiality'" (100–101). Whatever is betrayed by the term's etymology, "virtuality" is indeed the term Deleuze mobilizes to develop an ontology that attempts to avoid all recourse to possibility.
15. Deleuze, *ID*, 58, 59–60/42, 43tm.
16. Worms, *Annales bergsoniennes II*, 155.
17. Heidegger, *BT*, 183.
18. Ibid., 309.
19. Spinoza, EIVP67.
20. Ibid., EVP23Sch.
21. Deleuze, *Negotiations*, 88–89.
22. Deleuze, *CC*, 152–74.
23. Dosse, *GDFG*, 217.
24. Ibid., 217–18. Dosse also notes another reason for the attenuated nature of Deleuze's doctoral defense; it was one of the very first defenses to take place after the May events of the preceding year, and Deleuze's committee was fearful of disruptions.
25. Ibid., 590–96. Dosse titles this section "Le Manque d'air jusqu'à la mort."
26. For a discussion of the role of the body, its weaknesses and strengths, in Deleuze's conception of thought, see Kaufman, *The Delirium of Praise*, 84–110. Breath was a running theme in Klossowski's thought and fiction, wherein its allegorical function was similar to Deleuze's concept of sense and events as singularities irreducible to corporeal states. See his 1965 novel, *Le Baphomet*. It is also significant that Klossowski's most substantive scholarly work was *Nietzsche and the Vicious Circle*. One of the major themes of this study, which was dedicated to Deleuze, is the relationship between Nietzsche's "valetudinary states" and his thinking.
27. Rosset, "Sécheresse de Deleuze," 224.
28. Rosset, *Schopenhauer*, 107.
29. Rosset, *L'Objet singulier*: "L'absence du manque signifie qu'il n'y a pas de 'ne pas': c'est-à-dire que ce que existe épuise toute possibilité d'existence, est à la fois parfait—pour ne manquer de rien—et essentiellement 'convenable' par ne rien laisser à désirer, ni à redire" (109).
30. Cf. Rosset, *Le Réel*, and *Le Démon de la tautologie*.
31. Spinoza, EIID6.
32. Dosse, *GDFG*, 112.

33. Kleinberg, *Generation Existential*, 209–79.

34. In this regard, Deleuze shares with the protagonists of Stefanos Geroulanos's account the conviction that, in the wake of catastrophe, only one promise is acceptable: "that of a world without promises." The distinguishing feature of Deleuze's effort from that of the generation Geroulanos considers is that this conviction is grounded not in destitution but affirmation. See Geroulanos, *An Atheism That Is Not Humanist*, 315.

35. Gueroult, *Spinoza I: Dieu*, 300.

36. Deleuze, *LS*, 342–43/295.

37. Deleuze, *Nietzsche and Philosophy*, 93.

38. Deleuze cites Sartre's essay "The Transcendence of the Ego" in support of his own position. Sartre's virtue was to introduce "the idea of a transcendental field, 'impersonal or pre-personal,' [the] producer of both the Je and the Moi." The error of Sartre's project is to read this transcendental field in terms of consciousness, that is, in terms of its unifying functions. See *LS*, 120n5/343–44n5.

39. Deleuze and Guattari, *Anti-Oedipus*, 112.

40. The vital work for Deleuze was Simondon's *L'Individu et sa genèse physico-biologique*.

41. The machinations of the human body are a case in point. Quantitative intensity is in a state of nonstop fluctuation, with blood in constant flow, and various other biophysical processes going on "unbeknownst" to waking consciousness. The moment a *qualitative* change has taken place is the moment that something about these quantitative intensities is *registered* in Thought, as either pain, or elation, or any other mode of discernment. If it is objected that qualitative change can occur even if it is not felt, e.g., the metastasis of cancer cells, the Spinozist response would be that the qualitative change still takes place only once it is registered, even if what does the registering is not the consciousness of the body wherein the metastasis takes place but the physician reading test results. For one of the rare instances where Deleuze gives an example of this process running in the opposite direction, i.e., quantitative intensity in Thought results in a qualitative change registered in Extension, see the discussion of the delirious fictions of F. Scott Fitzgerald and Malcolm Lowry in *LS*, "Porcelain and Volcano," 180–89/154–61, esp. 188/161: "It is true that the crack is nothing if it does not compromise the body, but it does not cease being and having a value when it intertwines its line with the other line, inside the body. We cannot foresee, we must take risks and endure the longest possible time, we must not lose sight of the grand health. The eternal truth of the event is grasped only if the event is also inscribed in the flesh."

42. Deleuze's reference is to Richard Dedekind, one of Cantor's main interlocutors (*DR*, 223/172).

43. Deleuze, *SPE*, 13/9. See also 128/113, where Deleuze addresses this issue with regard to Kant's charges in the *Critique of Judgment*, §73. Kant's error was to think Spinoza had not already considered this problem.

44. Brassier, *Nihil Unbound*, 195–98.

45. See part 2 of Deleuze, *SPE*, "Parallelism and Immanence," 87–169/99–186, and the following discussion.

46. The question "real or fictive?" refers to the status of infinitesimals, which Deleuze has addressed in the paragraphs preceding this excerpt. See the earlier discussion of the differential calculus as effectively shirking the question of the "status" of points on a line by positing the continuity constituted by the differential relation as primary.

47. Cavaillès, *LTS*, 78.

48. Lautman, "Mathematics and Reality" (1935), reprinted in Lautman, *Mathematics, Ideas and the Physical Real*, 12. This volume collects all of Lautman's published, and some unpublished, philosophical writings. Where relevant, I include reference to the original publications.

49. Lautman, "New Research on the Dialectical Structure of Mathematics" (1939), in ibid., 199. Deleuze cites the original publication of this short essay in the bibliography to *Difference and Repetition*. In its original incarnation, it was the first installment in a series titled "Essais philosophiques," edited by Cavaillès and Raymond Aron for Editions Hermann. Three other volumes appeared in the series: Sartre's *Sketch for a Theory of the Emotions* appeared in 1939 as well. Two posthumous publications appeared in 1949: Cavaillès's *Transfini et continu* and Lautman's *Symétrie et dissymétrie en mathématiques et en physique*.

50. Lautman, "New Research on the Dialectical Structure of Mathematics," 200.

51. Ibid., 224.

52. Benis-Sinaceur, "Lettres inédites de Jean Cavaillès à Albert Lautman," 125–26.

53. Ibid., 123–24.

54. Lautman, "New Research on the Dialectical Structure of Mathematics," 200–201.

55. Ibid., 202. Simon Duffy opts to translate *fonder* as "founding," but the resonances with the Heideggerian problematic of grounding that are also central to Deleuze's course "Qu'est-ce que fonder?" are clear, from the content of the discussion as well as Lautman's explicit invocation of *Begründung*.

56. Ibid.

57. Ibid., 203, emphasis added.

58. Ibid., 204. "For the sake of" renders *dessein*.

59. Ibid., 206.

60. "Darwin's great novelty, perhaps, was that of inaugurating the thought of individual difference. The leitmotiv of *The Origin of Species* is: we do not know what individual difference is capable of! [. . .] Natural selection indeed plays the role of a principle of reality, even of success, and shows how differences become connected to one another and accumulate in a given direction, but also how they

tend to diverge further and further in different or even opposed directions. Natural selection plays an essential role: the differenciation of difference (survival of the most divergent)" (Deleuze, *DR*, 319–20/248–49).

61. Deleuze's distinction between *différentiation* (with a *t*) and *différenciation* (with a *c*), the latter of which results in the English neologism differenciation, is an issue I have not broached in this chapter. In French, the version with the *t* refers solely to the mathematical operation, whereas *différencier* is the more general verb meaning to differentiate.

62. Deleuze and Parnet, *Dialogues*, 22.

63. Toscano, *The Theatre of Production*, 233n81, emphasis in original.

64. Deleuze, *Anti-Oedipus*, 129.

65. Beaulieu, *Gilles Deleuze et la phénoménologie*, 98–99.

66. Deleuze, *ID*, 364/261. There is some irony in this in that apparently *The Logic of Sense* was Guattari's favorite book of Deleuze's, the one that made him most eager to collaborate with him. In a letter written April 5, 1969, Guattari wrote to Deleuze, "A slow reading, with a fine-toothed comb, of *The Logic of Sense* leads me to think there is a kind of profound homology of 'point of view' between us." Cited in Dosse, *GDFG*, 15.

67. Deleuze, *Spinoza: Practical Philosophy*, 122–30; Deleuze and Guattari, *What Is Philosophy?*, 60.

68. Deleuze *Cinema 1*, and *Cinema 2*.

69. Deleuze and Parnet, *Dialogues*, 179.

70. Ibid., 180.

71. Ibid.

72. Ibid., 180–81.

73. Ibid., 181.

74. Cf. Hallward, *Out of This World*, 79–103.

75. Hallward often compares Deleuze with Corbin, who went on to have an illustrious career as an authority on Iranian philosophy and Islamic theology after his early translations of Heidegger. For example, "As Deleuze's contemporary Henry Corbin explains, absolute creativity (or God) 'cannot be an object (an objective given). He can only be known through himself as absolute Subject, that is, as absolved from all unreal objectivity,' from all merely 'creatural' mediation. Via Spinoza, Deleuze sets out from much the same point of departure" (57). Note also the observation that "along with his contemporaries Henry Corbin, Christian Jambet, and Michel Henry, Deleuze may eventually be remembered for the part he played in the late-modern revival of a post-theophanic conception of thought" (160). Though his influence on Jambet was indirect, Heidegger is the common denominator linking these thinkers. Indeed, we would argue that in many ways it is Spinozism that *mitigates* the Heideggerian elements Deleuze shares with Corbin, chief among them the theophanic notion that the task of thought is to permit

God (the virtual), as an absolute in *excess* of the world, to make himself (itself) known despite worldly creatural mediation.

76. Deleuze, "An Unrecognized Precursor to Heidegger: Alfred Jarry," in *CC*, 98.
77. Deleuze, *SPE*, 100/114.
78. Ibid., 106–7/121tm.
79. Ibid.,107/121–22, emphasis in original.
80. Spinoza, *TEI*, § 33.
81. Spinoza, EIIA2.
82. Spinoza, EIII, Definitions of the Emotions, 1: "Desire is the very essence of man in so far as his essence is conceived as determined to any action from any given affection of itself."
83. Alquié, *Qu'est-ce que comprendre un philosophe?*, 87.
84. Ibid., 87–88.
85. According to Dosse's biography, this book was completely written by Deleuze (*GDFG*, 27). Adding Guattari's name as coauthor was a kind of gift to Guattari, a way for Deleuze to recognize his fundamental debts to the past two decades of collaboration.
86. There is, however, a puzzling reference to Lautman wherein Deleuze and Guattari describe his account of mathematics' actualization of "virtual concepts" rather than ideas, which is perhaps best read as a simple error in Deleuze's recollection (ibid., 216). The fact that conceptual production is the predominant thematic of this work—a theme to be contrasted with the counter-actualization toward the virtual of *Difference and Repetition* and other later works—shows the extent to which Deleuze had come to hold the concept in higher philosophical regard than he did in the 1960s.
87. Spinoza, EIIP44Cor2.
88. Deleuze and Guattari, *What Is Philosophy?*, 60.
89. Deleuze, "He Stuttered," in *CC*, 112. Cf. as well the essay on Jarry and Heidegger cited previously, wherein the "tom-tom" of Jarry's language plays a role similar to the stutterer in this essay.
90. Deleuze, "G comme Gauche," in *L'Abécédaire de Gilles Deleuze*.
91. Deleuze and Guattari, *What Is Philosophy?*, 59–60:

We will say THE plane of immanence is, at the same time, that which must be thought and that which cannot be thought. It is the nonthought within thought. [. . .] Immanence [is] the incessant to-ing and fro-ing of the plane, infinite movement. Perhaps this is the supreme act of philosophy: not so much to think THE plane of immanence as to show that it is there, unthought in every plane, and to think it in this way as the outside and inside of thought, as the not-external outside and the not-internal inside—that which cannot be thought and yet must be thought, which was thought once, as Christ was incarnated once, in order to show, that one time, the possibility of the impossible. Thus Spinoza is the Christ of the philosophers. [. . .] Spinoza, the infinite becoming-philosopher: he showed, drew up, and thought the "best" plane of immanence—that is, the purest, the one that does not hand itself over to the transcendent or restore the transcendent, the one that inspires the fewest illusions, bad feelings, and erroneous perceptions.

Note here that the Christian model is linked with possibility/impossibility and transcendence. Spinoza's refusal to restore the transcendent is a refusal to countenance a model of possibility.

92. Spinoza, EVP42.

CONCLUSION

1. Nairn, "Make for the Boondocks."
2. Hardt and Negri, *Commonwealth*, vii.
3. Ibid., xiii–xiv. The citation is to Nancy, *The Birth to Presence*, 407n56.
4. Hardt and Negri, *Commonwealth*, xiv.
5. Deleuze and Parnet, *Dialogues*, 15.
6. See Badiou, *Being and Event*, 112–20, and *Court traité de l'ontologie transitoire*, 73–93. For evidence of Badiou's nonetheless high estimation for Spinoza's mathematical model of reasoning, see Badiou, "What Is a Proof in Spinoza's Ethics?," 39–49.
7. Brassier, *Nihil Unbound*, 116.
8. Deleuze, *Spinoza: Practical Philosophy*, 130.
9. On the nonnormative nature of Spinoza's metaphysics, see Verbeek, "Spinoza on Natural Rights."
10. Marion and Birnbaum, "Spinoza."
11. Brunschvicg, *Spinoza et ses contemporains*, 1.
12. Kolakowski, "The Two Eyes of Spinoza," 285.

Bibliography

ARCHIVAL SOURCES

Fonds Althusser. Institut mémoires de l'édition contemporaine. Caen, France.
Fonds Cavaillès. Bibliothèque de l'École Normale Supérieure. Paris, France.
Fonds Desanti. Institut Jean-Toussaint Desanti, École Normale Supérieure—Lettres et sciences humaines. Lyon, France.

BOOKS AND ARTICLES

Adorno, Theodor W. *Against Epistemology: A Metacritique. Studies in Husserl and the Phenomenological Antinomies.* Trans. Willis Domingo. Cambridge, MA: MIT Press, 1983.
———. *Negative Dialectics.* Trans. E. B. Ashton. New York: Continuum, 1973.
Agamben, Giorgio. *Potentialities: Collected Essays in Philosophy.* Trans. Daniel Heller-Roazen. Stanford: Stanford University Press, 2000.
Aglan, Alya. *La Résistance sacrifiée: Histoire du mouvement Libération-Nord.* Paris: Flammarion, 2006.
Aglan, Alya, and Jean-Pierre Azéma, eds. *Jean Cavaillès Résistant, ou la Pensée en actes.* Paris: Flammarion, 2002.
Ali, Tariq, ed. *The Stalinist Legacy: Its Impact on Twentieth-Century World Politics.* Boulder, CO: Lynne Rienner Publishers, 1984.
Alliez, Éric. *De l'impossibilité de la phénoménologie: Sur la philosophie française contemporaine.* Paris: Vrin, 1995.
Allison, Henry A. "Kant's Critique of Spinoza." In *Spinoza: Critical Assessments,* vol. 4, ed. Genevieve Lloyd. London: Routledge, 2001.
Alquié, Ferdinand. *Cahiers de jeunesse.* Ed. Paule Plouvier. Lausanne: Éditions L'Age de l'Homme, 2003.
———. *Le Cartésianisme de Malebranche.* Paris: Vrin, 1974.
———. *La Découverte métaphysique de l'homme chez Descartes.* Paris: PUF, 1950.
———. *Études cartésiennes.* Paris: Vrin, 1982.

———. "Expérience ontologique et déduction systematique dans la constitution de la métaphysique de Descartes." In *Cahiers de Royaumont, no. II: Descartes*. Paris: Minuit, 1957.

———. *Leçons sur Kant*. Paris: La Table Ronde, 2005.

———. *Leçons sur Spinoza*. Paris: La Table Ronde, 2003.

———. *La Nostalgie de l'être*. Paris: PUF, 1950.

———. *Qu'est-ce que comprendre un philosophe?* 1956. Reprint, Paris: La Table Ronde, 2005.

———. *Le Rationalisme de Spinoza*. Paris: PUF, 1981.

———. *Signification de la philosophie*. Paris: Hachette, 1971.

———. *La Solitude de la raison*. Paris: Le Terrain Vague, 1966.

Althusser, Louis. *Écrits philosophiques et politiques*. Vol. 2. 1997. Reprint, Paris: Livre de Poche, 2001.

———. *Essays in Self-Criticism*. Trans. Grahame Lock. London: New Left Books, 1976.

———. *For Marx*. Trans. Ben Brewster. London: New Left Books, 1969.

———. *The Future Lasts Forever*. Ed. Olivier Corpet and Yann Moulier Boutang. Trans. Richard Veasey. New York: Free Press, 1993.

———. *The Humanist Controversy and Other Writings (1966–67)*. Ed. François Matheron. Trans. G. M. Goshgarian. London: Verso, 2003.

———. *Lenin and Philosophy and Other Essays*. Trans. Ben Brewster. 1971. Reprint, New York: Monthly Review Press, 2001.

———. *Machiavelli and Us*. Ed. François Matheron. Trans. Gregory Elliott. London: Verso, 1999.

———. *Montesquieu: La Politique et l'histoire*. Paris: PUF, 1959.

———. "The Only Materialist Tradition, Part 1: Spinoza." In *The New Spinoza*, ed. Warren Montag and Ted Stolze, 3–19. Minneapolis: University of Minnesota Press, 1997.

———. *Philosophy and the Spontaneous Philosophy of the Scientists, and Other Essays*. Ed. Gregory Elliott. Trans. Ben Brewster, James H. Kavanagh, Thomas E. Lewis, Grahame Lock, and Warren Montag. London: Verso, 1990.

———. *Philosophy of the Encounter: Later Writings, 1978–1987*. Ed. François Matheron and Oliver Corpet. Trans. G. M. Goshgarian. London: Verso, 2006.

———. *Politics and History: Montesquieu, Rousseau, Hegel, and Marx*. Trans. Ben Brewster. London: New Left Books, 1972.

———. *Politique et histoire de Machiavel à Marx: Cours à l'École Normale Supérieure, 1955–1972*. Ed. François Matheron. Paris: Seuil, 2006.

———. *The Spectre of Hegel: Early Writings*. Ed. François Matheron. Trans. G. M. Goshgarian. London: Verso, 1997.

———. *Sur la reproduction*. Ed. Jacques Bidet. Paris: PUF, 1995.

———. *Writings on Psychoanalysis: Freud and Lacan*. Ed. Olivier Corpet and François Matheron. Trans. Jeffrey Mehlman. New York: Columbia University Press, 1996.

Althusser, Louis, and Étienne Balibar. *Reading Capital*. Trans. Ben Brewster. London: New Left Books, 1970.

Althusser, Louis, Étienne Balibar, Roger Establet, Pierre Macherey, and Jacques Rancière. *Lire le Capital*. Paris: Maspero, 1968.

Anderson, Perry. *Arguments within English Marxism*. London: New Left Books, 1980.

———. *Considerations on Western Marxism*. London: New Left Books, 1976.

———. *Lineages of the Absolutist State*. London: New Left Books, 1974.

Andler, Charles, ed. *La Philosophie allemande au XIXe siècle*. Paris: Alcan, 1912.

Aron, Raymond. *Marxismes imaginaires: D'une sainte famille à l'autre*. Paris: Gallimard, 1970.

———. *Mémoires*. Paris: Julliard, 1983.

Bachelard, Gaston. "Physique et métaphysique." In *Septimana Spinozana*. The Hague: Martinus Nijhoff, 1933.

Bachelard, Suzanne. *La Conscience de rationalité: Etude phénoménologique sur la physique mathématique*. Paris: PUF, 1958.

———. *A Study of Husserl's Formal and Transcendental Logic*. Evanston, IL: Northwestern University Press, 1968.

Badiou, Alain. *The Adventure of French Philosophy*. Ed. and trans. Bruno Bosteels. London: Verso, 2012.

———. *Being and Event*. Trans. Oliver Feltham. London: Continuum, 2005.

———. *Le Concept de modèle: Introduction à une épistémologie matérialiste des mathématiques*. Paris: Maspero, 1969.

———. *The Concept of Model*. Trans. Zachary Luke Fraser and Tzuchien Tho. Melbourne: Re.press, 2007.

———. *Court traité de l'ontologie transitoire*. Paris: Seuil, 1998.

———. *Deleuze: The Clamor of Being*. Trans. Louise Burchill. Minneapolis: University of Minnesota Press, 2000.

———. *Ethics: An Essay on the Understanding of Evil*. Trans. Peter Hallward. London: Verso, 2002.

———. *L'Être et l'événement*. Paris: Seuil, 1988.

———. "Gilles Deleuze, *The Fold: Leibniz and the Baroque*." In *Gilles Deleuze and the Theater of Philosophy*, ed. Constantin V. Boundas and Dorothea Olkowski, 51–69. New York: Routledge, 1994.

———. *Logics of Worlds*. Trans. Alberto Toscano. London: Continuum, 2009.

———. *Logiques des mondes*. Paris: Seuil, 2006.

———. *Metapolitics*. Trans. Jason Barker. London: Verso, 2005.

———. "Le (Re)commencement du matérialisme dialectique." *Critique* 23, no. 240 (May 1967): 438–67.

———. "What Is a Proof in Spinoza's Ethics?" In *Spinoza Now*, ed. Dimitris Vardoulakis, 39–49. Minneapolis: University of Minnesota Press, 2011.

Badiou, Alain, and François Balmès. *De l'idéologie*. Paris: Maspero, 1976.

Badiou, Alain, and Jean Birnbaum. "Aristote: La Prudence du juste milieu." *Le Monde des livres*, February 1, 2008.

Balibar, Étienne. "Notice nécrologique de Jean-Toussaint Desanti." *L'Annuaire de l'Association amicale de secours des anciens élèves de l'École Normale Supérieure* (Recueil 2004).

———. *Spinoza and Politics*. Trans. Peter Snowdon. London: Verso, 1998.

Balibar, Étienne, and John Rajchman, with Anne Boyman, eds. *French Philosophy since 1945*. New York: Free Press, 2011.

Baring, Edward. *The Young Derrida and French Philosophy, 1945–1968*. Cambridge: Cambridge University Press, 2011.

Bataille, Georges. *Visions of Excess: Selected Writings, 1927–1939*. Ed. and trans. Allan Stoekl. Minneapolis: University of Minnesota Press, 1985.

Bayle, Pierre. *Historical and Critical Dictionary: Selections*. Trans. Richard H. Popkin. Indianapolis, IN: Bobbs-Merrill, 1965.

Beaulieu, Alain. *Gilles Deleuze et la phénoménologie*. Paris: Vrin, 2004.

Beik, William. *Absolutism and Society in Seventeenth-Century France: State Power and Provincial Aristocracy in Languedoc*. Cambridge: Cambridge University Press, 1985.

Beiser, Frederick C. *The Fate of Reason: German Philosophy from Kant to Fichte*. Cambridge, MA: Harvard University Press, 1993.

Beistegui, Miguel de. *Immanence: Deleuze and Philosophy*. Edinburgh: Edinburgh University Press, 2010.

———. *Truth and Genesis: Philosophy as Differential Ontology*. Bloomington: Indiana University Press, 2004.

Benis-Sinaceur, Hourya, ed. "Lettres inédites de Jean Cavaillès à Albert Lautman." *Revue d'histoire des sciences* 40, no. 1 (1987): 117–28.

Benoist, Jocelyn. *L'à priori conceptuel: Bolzano, Husserl, Schlick*. Paris: Vrin, 1999.

———. "Bolzano et l'idée de Wissenschaftslehre." In *Les Philosophes et la science*, ed. Pierre Wagner, 659–78. Paris: Gallimard, 2002.

———. "Husserl et la fascination du 'formel.'" In *Les Philosophes et la science*, ed. Pierre Wagner, 679–711. Paris: Gallimard, 2002.

———. *Les Limites de l'intentionalité: Recherches phénoménologiques et analytiques*. Paris: Vrin, 2005.

Bloch, Olivier, ed. *Spinoza au XXe siècle*. Paris: PUF, 1993.

Boirel, René. *Brunschvicg: Sa vie, son oeuvre*. Paris: PUF, 1962.

Bolzano, Bernard. *The Mathematical Works of Bernard Bolzano.* Ed. Steve Russ. Oxford: Oxford University Press, 2004.
Bourdieu, Pierre. "Aspirant philosophe: Un point de vue sur le champ universitaire dans les années 50." In *Les Enjeux philosophiques des années 50*, 15–24. Paris: Éditions du Centre Georges Pompidou, 1989.
Bourg, Julian, ed. *After the Deluge: New Perspectives on the Intellectual and Cultural History of Postwar France.* Lanham, MD: Lexington Books, 2004.
———. *From Revolution to Ethics: May '68 and Contemporary French Thought.* Montreal: McGill-Queen's University Press, 2007.
Brassier, Ray. *Nihil Unbound: Enlightenment and Extinction.* Basingstoke, UK: Palgrave Macmillan, 2007.
Breckman, Warren. *Adventures of the Symbolic: Post-Marxism and Radical Democracy.* New York: Columbia University Press, 2013.
Brown, Nathan. "Absent Blue Wax (Rationalist Empiricism)." *Qui parle* 19, no. 1 (2010): 89–106.
Brunschvicg, Léon. *Les Étapes de la philosophie mathématique.* 1912. Reprint, Paris: Blanchard, 1981.
———. *L'Expérience humaine et la causalité physique.* Paris: Alcan, 1922.
———. *La Modalité du jugement.* 1897. Reprint, Paris: PUF, 1964.
———. *Le Progrès de la conscience dans la philosophie occidentale.* 2 vols. Paris: PUF, 1928.
———. *Spinoza et ses contemporaines.* 5th ed. Paris: PUF, 1971.
Bryant, Levi R. *Difference and Givenness: Deleuze's Transcendental Empiricism and the Ontology of Immanence.* Evanston, IL: Northwestern University Press, 2008.
Brykman, Geneviève. *La Judéité de Spinoza.* Paris: Vrin, 1972.
Canguilhem, Georges. "Hegel en France." *Revue d'histoire et de philosophie religieuse* 28–29, no. 1 (1948–49): 282–97.
———. *Vie et mort de Jean Cavaillès.* Paris: Allia, 2004.
Carroll, Lewis. *Logique sans peine.* Trans. Jean Gattégno and Ernest Coumet. Paris: Hermann, 1966.
———. "What the Tortoise Said to Achilles." *Mind* 4, no. 14 (April 1895): 278–80.
Cassou-Noguès, Pierre. *De l'expérience mathématique: Essai sur la philosophie des sciences de J. Cavaillès.* Paris: Vrin, 2001.
———. "The Philosophy of the Concept." In *The History of Continental Philosophy*, vol. 4, *Phenomenology: Responses and Developments*, ed. Leonard Lawlor and Alan D. Schrift, 217–34. Chicago: University of Chicago Press, 2011.
Caute, David. *Communism and the French Intellectuals.* New York: Macmillan, 1964.
Cavaillès, Jean. "Les deuxièmes Cours Universitaire de Davos." In *Die II. Davoser Hochshulkurser. Les IImes Cours Universitaires de Davos, 1929. 17 mars–6 avril 1929*, 65–81. Davos: Kommissionsverlag, Heintz, Neu, and Zahn, 1929.

———. "Lettres inédites de Jean Cavaillès à Albert Lautman." Ed. Hourya Benis-Sinaceur. In *Revue d'histoire des sciences* 40, no. 1 (1987): 117–29.

———. *Oeuvres complètes de philosophie des sciences*. Ed. Bruno Huisman. Paris: Hermann, 1994.

———. *Philosophie mathématique*. Paris: Hermann, 1962.

———. *Sur la logique et la théorie de la science*. 1947. Reprint, Paris: PUF, 1960.

Cavaillès, Jean, and Albert Lautman. "Mathematical Thought." Trans. Arthur Goldhammer. In *French Philosophy since 1945*, ed. Étienne Balibar and John Rajchman, with Anne Boyman. New York: Free Press, 2011. Original French publication 1946.

Caveing, Maurice, ed. *Hommage à Jean-Toussaint Desanti*. Mauvezin, France: TER, 1991.

Cazeaux, Clive, ed. *The Continental Aesthetics Reader*. New York: Routledge, 2000.

Christofferson, Michael Scott. *French Intellectuals against the Left: The Antitotalitarian Moment of the 1970s*. New York: Berghahn, 2004.

Clément, Catherine, ed. *Gilles Deleuze: L'Arc no. 49*. 1972. Reprint, Paris: Editions Inculte, 2005.

Cohen-Solal, Annie. *Sartre: A Life*. Ed. Norman MacAfee. Trans. Anna Cancogni. New York: Pantheon Books, 1987.

Cusset, Francois. *French Theory: How Foucault, Derrida, Deleuze, & Co. Transformed the Intellectual Life of the United States*. Trans. Jeff Fort. Minneapolis: University of Minnesota Press, 2008.

Dauben, Joseph Warren. *Georg Cantor: His Mathematics and Philosophy of the Infinite*. Princeton: Princeton University Press, 1990.

Delbos, Victor. "Husserl: Sa critique du psychologisme et sa conception d'une logique pure." In *La Philosophie allemande au XIXe siècle*, ed. Charles Andler, 25–42. Paris: Alcan, 1912.

———. *Le Problème morale dans la philosophie de Spinoza et dans l'histoire du spinozisme*. 1893. Reprint, Paris: Presses de l'Université de Paris Sorbonne, 1990.

———. *Le Spinozisme*. 1916. Reprint, Paris: Vrin, 1983.

Deleuze, Gilles. *L'Abécédaire de Gilles Deleuze, avec Claire Parnet*. Paris: DVD Editions Montparnasse, 2004.

———. *Bergsonism*. Trans. Hugh Tomlinson and Barbara Habberjam. New York: Zone Books, 1991.

———. *Le Bergsonisme*. Paris: PUF, 1966.

———, ed. *Cahiers de Royaumont, no. VI: Nietzsche*. Paris: Minuit, 1966.

———. *Cinéma 1: L'Image-mouvement*. Paris: Minuit, 1983.

———. *Cinéma 2: L'Image-temps*. Paris: Minuit, 1985.

———. *David Hume, sa vie, son oeuvre*. Paris: PUF, 1952.

―――. "Description of a Woman: For a Philosophy of the Sexed Other." Trans. Keith W. Faulkner. *Angelaki* 7, no. 3 (2002): 17–24. Original French publication 1945.

―――. *Desert Islands and Other Texts, 1953–1974*. Trans. Michael Taormina. Cambridge, MA: Semiotext(e), 2004.

―――. *Difference and Repetition*. Trans. Paul Patton. New York: Columbia University Press, 1994.

―――. *Différence et répétition*. Paris: PUF, 1968.

―――. *Essays: Critical and Clinical*. Trans. Daniel W. Smith and Michael A. Greco. Minneapolis: University of Minnesota Press, 1997.

―――. *Expressionism in Philosophy: Spinoza*. Trans. Martin Joughin. New York: Zone Books, 1992.

―――. *The Fold: Leibniz and the Baroque*. Trans. Tom Conley. Minneapolis: University of Minnesota Press, 1992.

―――. *Foucault*. Paris: Minuit, 1986.

―――. *Francis Bacon: The Logic of Sensation*. Trans. Daniel W. Smith. Minneapolis: University of Minnesota Press, 2005.

―――. *L'Île déserte et d'autres textes: 1953–1974*. Ed. David Lapoujade. Paris: Minuit, 2002.

―――. *The Logic of Sense*. Ed. Constantin V. Boundas. Trans. Mark Lester and Charles Stivale. New York: Columbia University Press, 1990.

―――. *Logique du sens*. Paris: Minuit, 1969.

―――. *Masochism: Coldness and Cruelty and Venus in Furs*. Trans. Jean McNeil. New York: Zone Books, 1991.

―――. *Negotiations, 1972–1990*. Trans. Martin Joughin. New York: Columbia University Press, 1995.

―――. *Nietzsche and Philosophy*. Trans. Hugh Tomlinson. New York: Columbia University Press, 1986.

―――. *Nietzsche et la philosophie*. Paris: PUF, 1962.

―――. *La Philosophie critique de Kant*. Paris: PUF, 1963.

―――. *Le Pli: Leibniz et le Baroque*. Paris: Minuit, 1988.

―――. *Pourparlers*. Paris: Minuit, 1990.

―――. *Proust and Signs*. Trans. Richard Howard. Minneapolis: University of Minnesota Press, 2000.

―――. *Proust et les signes*. Paris: PUF, 1964.

―――. *Spinoza et le problème de l'expression*. Paris: Minuit, 1968.

―――. *Spinoza: Practical Philosophy*. Trans. Robert Hurley. San Francisco: City Lights Books, 1988.

Deleuze, Gilles, and Félix Guattari. *Anti-Oedipus: Capitalism and Schizophrenia.* Trans. Robert Hurley, Mark Seem, and Helen R. Lane. Minneapolis: University of Minnesota Press, 1983.

———. *What Is Philosophy?* Trans. Hugh Tomlinson and Graham Burchell. New York: Columbia University Press, 1994.

Deleuze, Gilles, and Claire Parnet. *Dialogues.* 2nd ed. Paris: Flammarion, 1996.

Della Rocca, Michael. *Spinoza.* London: Routledge, 2008.

Derrida, Jacques. "Nature, culture, écriture (de Lévi-Strauss à Rousseau)." *Cahiers pour l'Analyse*, no. 4 (September–October 1966): 5–50.

———. *L'Origine de la géometrie.* Paris: PUF, 1962.

———. *Le Problème de la genèse dans la philosophie de Husserl.* Paris: PUF, 1990.

———. *The Problem of Genesis in Husserl's Philosophy.* Trans. Marian Hobson. Chicago: University of Chicago Press, 2003.

———. *Writing and Difference.* Trans. Alan Bass. Chicago: University of Chicago Press, 1978.

Desanti, Dominique. *Ce que le siècle m'a dit.* Paris: Plon, 1997.

———. *Masques et visages de Tito et des siens.* Paris: Pavillon, 1949.

———. *Les Staliniens: Une Expérience politique, 1944–1956.* Paris: Fayard, 1975.

Desanti, Jean-Toussaint. *Un Destin philosophique, ou les pièges de la croyance.* 1982. Reprint, Paris: Livre de Poche, 1984.

———. "'L'Être et le Néant' a cinquante ans." *Le Monde*, July 2, 1993.

———. *Les Idéalités mathématiques: Recherches épistémologiques sur le développement de la théorie des fonctions de variables réelles.* Paris: Seuil, 1968.

———. *Introduction à la phénoménologie.* Nouvelle édition revue. Paris: Gallimard, 1994.

———. *Introduction à l'histoire de la philosophie.* 1956. Reprint, Paris: PUF, 2006.

———. "A Path in Philosophy." In *Philosophy in France Today*, ed. Alan Montefiore, trans Kathleen McLaughlin, 51–66. Cambridge: Cambridge University Press, 1983.

———. *La Peau des mots.* Paris: Seuil, 2004.

———. *Une Pensée captive: Articles de La Nouvelle Critique (1948–1956).* Ed. Maurice Caveing. Paris: PUF, 2008.

———. *Le Philosophe et les pouvoirs et autres dialogues.* Paris: Hachette, 2008.

———. *La Philosophie silencieuse, ou critique des philosophies de la science.* Paris: Seuil, 1975.

———. *Philosophie: Un Rêve de flambeur.* Paris: Grasset, 1999.

———. *Réflexions sur le temps.* Paris: Grasset, 1992.

———. "Sartre et Husserl, ou les trois culs-de-sac de la phénoménologie transcendantale." *Les Temps modernes*, no. 531–33 (October–December 1990): 350–64.

———. "La Science: Idéologie historiquement relative." In *Science bourgeoise et science prolétarienne*, ed. Gérard Vassalis, 7–14. Paris: Éditions de la Nouvelle Critique, 1950.

———. "Spinoza et la phénoménologie." In *Spinoza au XXe siècle*, ed. Olivier Bloch, 113–28. Paris: PUF, 1993.

Desanti, Jean-Toussaint, Dominique Desanti, and Roger-Pol Droit. *La Liberté nous aime encore*. Paris: Odile Jacob, 2001.

Descombes, Vincent. *Modern French Philosophy*. Trans. L. Scott-Fox and J. M. Harding. Cambridge: Cambridge University Press, 1980.

Dews, Peter. "Althusser, Structuralism, and the French Epistemological Tradition." In *Althusser: A Critical Reader*, ed. Gregory Elliott, 104–41. Oxford: Blackwell, 1994.

Diefenbach, Katja, Sara R. Farris, Gal Kirn, and Peter D. Thomas, eds. *Encountering Althusser: Politics and Materialism in Contemporary Radical Thought*. London: Bloomsbury, 2013.

Dosse, François. *Gilles Deleuze et Félix Guattari: Biographie croisée*. Paris: La Découverte, 2007.

———. *History of Structuralism*. Vol. 1, *The Rising Sign, 1945–1946*. Trans. Deborah Glassman. Minneapolis: University of Minnesota Press, 1997.

———. *History of Structuralism*. Vol. 2, *The Sign Sets, 1967–Present*. Trans. Deborah Glassman. Minneapolis: University of Minnesota Press, 1997.

Duffy, Simon. "French and Italian Spinozism." In *The History of Continental Philosophy*, vol. 7, *After Poststructuralism: Transitions and Transformations*, ed. Alan D. Schrift and Rosi Braidotti, 149–60. Chicago: University of Chicago Press, 2010.

During, Elie. "Blackboxing in Theory: Deleuze versus Deleuze." In *French Theory in America*, ed. Sylvère Lotringer and Sande Cohen, 164–89. New York: Routledge, 2001.

Elliott, Gregory, ed. *Althusser: A Critical Reader*. Oxford: Blackwell, 1994.

———. *Althusser: The Detour of Theory*. 1987. Reprint, Leiden, Netherlands: Brill, 2006.

Everdell, William R. *The First Moderns: Profiles in the Origins of Twentieth-Century Thought*. Chicago: University of Chicago Press, 1997.

Ewald, François. "Elèves d'Althusser." *Magazine littéraire*, no. 304 (November 1992).

Eyers, Tom. *Post-Rationalism: Psychoanalysis, Epistemology, and Marxism in Postwar France*. London: Bloomsbury, 2013.

Fabiani, Jean-Louis. *Les Philosophes de la République*. Paris: Minuit, 1988.

———. "Sociologie et histoire des idées: L'Epistémologie et les sciences sociales." In *Enjeux philosophiques des années 50*, 115–30. Paris: Éditions du Centre Georges Pompidou, 1989.

Faulkner, Keith W. "Deleuze In Utero: Deleuze-Sartre and the Essence of Woman." *Angelaki* 7, no. 3 (2002): 25–43.
Ferrières, Gabrielle. *Jean Cavaillès: Un Philosophe dans la guerre, 1903–1944*. 1950. Reprint, Paris: Félin, 2003.
Flynn, Bernard. *The Philosophy of Claude Lefort: Interpreting the Political*. Evanston, IL: Northwestern University Press, 2005.
Foucault, Michel. "Critical Theory/Intellectual History." In *Critique and Power: Recasting the Foucault/Habermas Debate*, ed. Michael Kelly, 109–37. Cambridge, MA: MIT Press, 1994.
———. *Dits et écrits 1954–1988*. Vol. 3. Paris: Gallimard, 1994.
———. "Généalogie des sciences." *Cahiers pour l'Analyse*, no. 9 (Summer 1968).
———. "Life: Experience and Science." In *Aesthetics, Method, and Epistemology*, ed. James D. Faubion, 465–78. New York: New Press, 1998.
———. "Theatrum Philosophicum." In *Aesthetics, Method, and Epistemology*, ed. James D. Faubion, 343–68. New York: New Press, 1998.
Friedmann, Georges. *Leibniz et Spinoza*. Paris: Gallimard, 1946.
Gandillac, Maurice de, Lucien Goldmann, and Jean Piaget, eds. *Entretiens sur les notions de genèse et de structure*. Paris: Mouton, 1965.
Garrett, Don, ed. *The Cambridge Companion to Spinoza*. Cambridge: Cambridge University Press, 1996.
Geroulanos, Stefanos. *An Atheism That Is Not Humanist Emerges in French Thought*. Stanford: Stanford University Press, 2010.
Giolito, Christophe. *Histoires de la philosophie avec Martial Gueroult*. Paris: L'Harmattan, 1999.
Glucksmann, André, and Jean Birnbaum. "Platon: Penseur de la mondialisation." *Le Monde des livres*, January 25, 2008.
Goetschel, Willi. *Spinoza's Modernity: Mendelssohn, Lessing, and Heine*. Madison: University of Wisconsin Press, 2004.
Goldschmidt, Victor. "A propos du 'Descartes selon l'ordre des raisons.'" *Revue de métaphysique et de morale* 62, no. 1 (1957): 67–71.
Gordon, Peter E. *Continental Divide: Heidegger, Cassirer, Davos*. Cambridge, MA: Harvard University Press, 2010.
Goshgarian, G. M. "The Very Essence of the Object, the Soul of Marxism and Other Singular Things: Spinoza in Althusser, 1959–67." In *Encountering Althusser: Politics and Materialism in Contemporary Radical Thought*, ed. Katja Diefenbach, Sara R. Farris, Gal Kirn, and Peter D. Thomas, 89–111. London: Bloomsbury, 2013.
Granger, Gilles-Gaston. "Jean Cavaillès et l'histoire." *Revue d'histoire des sciences* 49, no. 4 (October–December 1996): 569–82.
———. "Jean Cavaillès, ou la montée vers Spinoza." *Les Études philosophiques*, n.s., 2, no. 3/4 (July–December 1947): 271–79.

———. *Pour la connaissance philosophique*. Paris: Seuil, 1988.
Grattan-Guinness, Ivor. *The Search for Mathematical Roots, 1870–1940: Logics, Set Theories and the Foundations of Mathematics from Cantor through Russell to Gödel*. Princeton: Princeton University Press, 2000.
Grene, Marjorie, ed. *Spinoza: A Collection of Critical Essays*. New York: Doubleday, 1973.
Gueroult, Martial. *Descartes selon l'ordre des raisons*. 2 vols. Vol. 1, *L'Âme et Dieu*; vol. 2, *L'Âme et le corps*. 1953. Reprint, Paris: Aubier-Montaigne, 1991.
———. *Dianoématique, Livre I: Histoire de l'histoire de la philosophie*. 3 vols. Vol. 1, *En Occident, des origines jusqu'à Condillac* (1984), vol. 2, *En Allemagne, de Leibniz à nos jours* (1988); vol. 3, *En France, de Condorcet à nos jours*. Paris: Aubier Montaigne, 1988.
———. *Dianoématique, Livre II: Philosophie de l'histoire de la philosophie*. Paris: Aubier-Montaigne, 1979.
———. *L'Évolution et la structure de la doctrine de la science chez Fichte*. Paris: Les Belles lettres, 1930.
———. *Leçon inaugurale*, faite le 4 décembre 1951, Collège de France, chaire d'histoire et de technologie des systèmes philosophiques. Nogent-le-rotrou, France: Daupeley-Gouverneur, 1952.
———. *La Philosophie transcendantale de Salomon Maimon*. Paris: Alcan, 1929.
———. "Le 'Spinoza' de Martial Gueroult: Introduction générale et fragment du premier chapitre du troisième tome du Spinoza." *Revue philosophique de la France et de l'étranger* 167, no. 3 (1977): 285–302.
———. *Spinoza I: Dieu*. Paris: Aubier-Montaigne, 1968.
———. *Spinoza II: L'Âme*. Paris: Aubier-Montaigne, 1974.
Guitton, Jean. *Notice sur la vie et les travaux de Ferdinand Alquié*. Paris: Institut de France, 1989.
Gutting, Gary. *French Philosophy in the Twentieth Century*. Cambridge: Cambridge University Press, 2001.
Hägglund, Martin. *Radical Atheism: Derrida and the Time of Life*. Stanford: Stanford University Press, 2008.
Hallward, Peter. *Badiou: A Subject to Truth*. Minneapolis: University of Minnesota Press, 2004.
———. *Out of This World: Gilles Deleuze and the Philosophy of Creation*. London: Verso, 2006.
Hallward, Peter, and Knox Peden, eds. *Concept and Form*. Vol. 1, *Key Texts from the* Cahiers pour l'Analyse. London: Verso, 2012.
———, eds. *Concept and Form*. Vol. 2, *Interviews and Essays on the* Cahiers pour l'Analyse. London: Verso, 2012.

Hammerschlag, Sarah. *The Figural Jew: Politics and Identity in Postwar French Thought*. Chicago: University of Chicago Press, 2010.
Hardt, Michael. *Gilles Deleuze: An Apprenticeship in Philosophy*. Minneapolis: University of Minnesota Press, 1993.
Hardt, Michael, and Antonio Negri. *Commonwealth*. Cambridge, MA: Harvard University Press, 2009.
———. *Empire*. Cambridge, MA: Harvard University Press, 2000.
———. *Multitude: War and Democracy in the Age of Empire*. London: Penguin, 2004.
Harris, Michael. "A Sometimes Funny Book Supposedly about Infinity: A Review of *Everything and More*, by David Foster Wallace." *Notices of the American Mathematical Society* 51, no. 6 (2004): 632–38.
Heidegger, Martin. *Being and Time*. Trans. John Macquarrie and Edward Robinson. New York: Harper and Row, 1962.
———. *Qu'est-ce que la métaphysique?* Ed. and trans. Henry Corbin. Paris: Gallimard, 1938.
———. *Questions I & II*. Trans. Kostas Axelos, Jean Beaufret, Walter Biemel, Lucien Braun, et al. Paris: Gallimard, 1990.
Heinzmann, Gerhard. "Jean Cavaillès und seine Beziehungen zu Deutschland." In *Entre Locarno et Vichy: Les Relations culturelles franco-allemands dans les années 1930s*, 2 vols., ed. Hans Manfred Bock, Reinhart Meyer-Kalkus, and Michel Trebitsch. Paris: CNRS Éditions, 1993.
Henry, Michel. *Généalogie de la psychanalyse: Le Commencement perdu*. Paris: PUF, 1985.
Hering, Jean. *Phénoménologie et philosophie religieuse*. Paris: Alcan, 1926.
Hoene-Wronski, Józef Maria. *La Philosophie de l'infini*. Paris: Didot, 1814.
Horkheimer, Max, and Theodor Adorno. *Dialectic of Enlightenment: Philosophical Fragments*. Ed. Gunzelin Schmid Noerr. Trans. Edmund Jephcott. 1947. Reprint, Stanford: Stanford University Press, 2002.
Howie, Gillian. *Deleuze and Spinoza: An Aura of Expressionism*. Basingstoke, UK: Palgrave, 2002.
Hughes, Joe. *Deleuze and the Genesis of Representation*. London: Continuum, 2008.
Huisman, Bruno. "Cavaillès et Spinoza." In *Spinoza au XXe siècle*, ed. Olivier Bloch, 77–83. Paris: PUF, 1993.
Husserl, Edmund. *Cartesian Meditations*. Trans. Dorion Cairns. The Hague: Nijhoff, 1960.
———. *Formal and Transcendental Logic*. Trans. Dorion Cairns. The Hague: Nijhoff, 1969.
———. *Méditations cartésiennes: Introduction à la phénoménologie*. Trans. Gabriel Pfeffer and Emmanuel Levinas. Paris: Vrin, 2001.

———. "The Origin of Geometry." In *The Crisis of European Sciences and Transcendental Phenomenology*, trans. David Carr. Evanston, IL: Northwestern University Press, 1970.

Hyppolite, Jean. *Logic and Existence*. Trans. Leonard Lawlor and Amit Sen. Albany: SUNY Press, 1997.

Insole, Christopher. "Kant's Transcendental Idealism and Newton's Divine Sensorium." *Journal of the History of Ideas* 27, no. 3 (July 2011): 413–36.

Israel, Jonathan. *Democratic Enlightenment: Philosophy, Revolution, and Human Rights, 1750–1790*. Oxford: Oxford University Press, 2011.

———. *Enlightenment Contested: Philosophy, Modernity, and the Emancipation of Man, 1670–1752*. Oxford: Oxford University Press, 2006.

———. *Radical Enlightenment: Philosophy and the Making of Modernity, 1650–1750*. Oxford: Oxford University Press, 2001.

———. "Spinoza as an Expounder, Critic, and 'Reformer' of Descartes." *Intellectual History Review* 17, no. 1 (2007): 59–78.

James, Susan. *Spinoza on Philosophy, Religion, and Politics: The* Theologico-Political Treatise. Oxford: Oxford University Press, 2012.

Janicaud, Dominique. *Heidegger en France 2: Entretiens*. Paris: Hachette, 2005.

———. *La Phénoménologie dans tous ses états*. Paris: Gallimard, 2009.

———. *Phenomenology and 'the Theological Turn': The French Debate*. New York: Fordham University Press, 2001.

Jay, Martin. *Downcast Eyes: The Denigration of Vision in Twentieth-Century French Thought*. Berkeley: University of California Press, 1993.

———. *Fin-de-Siècle Socialism and Other Essays*. London: Routledge, 1988.

———. "The Lifeworld and Lived Experience." In *A Companion to Phenomenology and Existentialism*, ed. Hubert L. Dreyfus and Mark A. Wrathall, 91–104. Oxford: Blackwell, 2006.

———. *Marxism and Totality: The Adventures of a Concept from Lukàcs to Habermas*. Berkeley: University of California Press, 1984.

Judt, Tony. *Marxism and the French Left*. Oxford: Clarendon, 1986.

———. *Past Imperfect: French Intellectuals, 1944–1956*. Berkeley: University of California Press, 1992.

———. *Reappraisals: Reflections on the Forgotten Twentieth Century*. London: Penguin, 2008.

Kadvany, John. *Imre Lakatos and the Guises of Reason*. Durham, NC: Duke University Press, 2001.

Kant, Immanuel. "What Does It Mean to Orient Oneself in Thinking?" In *Religion and Rational Theology*, ed. and trans. Allen W. Wood and George Di Giovanni, 7–18. Cambridge: Cambridge University Press, 1996.

Kaufman, Eleanor. *The Delirium of Praise: Bataille, Blanchot, Deleuze, Foucault, Klossowski*. Baltimore: Johns Hopkins University Press, 2001.
Kelly, Michael. *Modern French Marxism*. Oxford: Basil Blackwell, 1982.
Kerslake, Christian. *Deleuze and the Unconscious*. London: Continuum, 2007.
———. "Grounding Deleuze." *Radical Philosophy*, no. 148 (March–April 2008): 30–36.
Kleinberg, Ethan. *Generation Existential: Heidegger's Philosophy in France, 1927–1961*. Ithaca, NY: Cornell University Press, 2005.
Klossowski, Pierre. *Le Baphomet*. Paris: Mercure de France, 1965.
———. *Nietzsche and the Vicious Circle*. Trans. Daniel W. Smith. London: Continuum, 2005.
Kojève, Alexandre. *Introduction à la lecture de Hegel*. Paris: Gallimard, 1947.
———. *Introduction to the Reading of Hegel*. Ed. Raymond Queneau and Allan Bloom. Trans. James H. Nichols. Ithaca, NY: Cornell University Press, 1980.
Kolakowski, Leszek. *Chrétiens sans église: La Conscience religieuse et le lien confessionnel au XVIIe siècle*. Paris: Gallimard, 1987.
———. "The Two Eyes of Spinoza." In *Spinoza: A Collection of Critical Essays*, ed. Marjorie Grene, 279–94. New York: Anchor Books, 1973.
Koyré, Alexandre. *Études de l'histoire de la pensée philosophique*. Paris: Gallimard, 1971.
———. *Études de l'histoire de la pensée scientifique*. Paris: Gallimard, 1973.
———. *Études galiléenes*. Paris: Hermann, 1939.
———, ed. and trans. *Spinoza, Traité de la réforme de l'entendement*. 1937. Reprint, Paris: Vrin, 1994.
Kriegel, Blandine. "Le Silence de J-T. Desanti." In *Le Philosophe et les pouvoirs et autres dialogues*, ed. Jean-Toussaint Desanti, 403–38. Paris: Hachette, 2008.
Kristeva, Julia, and Jean Birnbaum. "Rousseau." *Le Monde des livres*, February 22, 2008.
Kusch, Martin. *Psychologism: A Case Study in the Sociology of Philosophical Knowledge*. London: Routledge, 1995.
Lacan, Jacques. *Écrits: The First Complete Edition in English*. Ed. and trans. Bruce Fink, in collaboration with Héloïse Fink and Russell Grigg. New York: W. W. Norton, 2006.
Lacroix, Jean. *Marxisme, existentialisme, personnalisme*. Paris: PUF, 1950.
Lahtinin, Mikko. *Politics and Philosophy: Niccolò Machiavelli and Louis Althusser's Aleatory Materialism*. Trans. Gareth Griffiths and Kristina Köhl. Leiden, Netherlands: Brill, 2009.
Laruelle, François. *En tant qu'un*. Paris: Aubier-Montaigne, 1991.
———. *Principles of Non-Philosophy*. Trans. Anthony Paul Smith and Nicole Rubczak. London: Bloomsbury, 2013. Original French publication 1996.

Latour, Bruno. *Pandora's Hope*. Cambridge, MA: Harvard University Press, 1999.
Lautman, Albert. *Mathematics, Ideas, and the Physical Real*. Trans. Simon Duffy. London: Continuum, 2011. Original French publication 2006.
Lawlor, Leonard. *Derrida and Husserl: The Basic Problem of Phenomenology*. Bloomington: Indiana University Press, 2002.
Lazier, Benjamin. *God Interrupted: Heresy and the European Imagination between the World Wars*. Princeton: Princeton University Press, 2008.
Lecourt, Dominique. *Proletarian Science? The Case of Lysenko*. London: New Left Books, 1977.
Levinas, Emmanuel. *Otherwise Than Being*. Trans. Alphonso Lingis. Pittsburgh: Duquesne University Press, 1998.
———. *Time and the Other*. Trans. Richard A. Cohen. Pittsburgh: Duquesne University Press, 1987.
Lévy, Benny. *Le Meurtre du pasteur: Critique de la vision politique du monde*. Paris: Hachette, 2002.
Lewis, William S. *Louis Althusser and the Traditions of French Marxism*. Lanham, MD: Lexington Books, 2005.
Lichtheim, George. *Marxism in Modern France*. New York: Columbia University Press, 1966.
Lilti, Antoine. "Comment écrit-on l'histoire intellectuelle des Lumières? Spinozisme, radicalisme, et philosophie." *Annales HSS*, no. 1 (January–February 2009): 171–206.
Longuenesse, Béatrice. *Kant et le pouvoir de juger*. Paris: PUF, 1993.
Lordon, Frédéric. *La Société des affects: Pour un structuralisme des passions*. Paris: Seuil, 2013.
Löwy, Michael. "Stalinist Ideology and Science." In *The Stalinist Legacy: Its Impact on Twentieth-Century World Politics*, ed. Tariq Ali. Boulder, CO: Lynne Rienner Publishers, 1984.
Luft, Sebastian, and Fabien Capeillères. "Neo-Kantianism in Germany and France." In *The History of Continental Philosophy*, vol. 3, *The New Century: Bergsonism, Phenomenology, and Responses to Modern Science*, ed. Keith Ansell Pearson and Alan D. Schrift, 47–85. Chicago: University of Chicago Press, 2010.
Lyotard, Jean-François. *La Phénoménologie*. Paris: PUF, 1954.
Macherey, Pierre. *Avec Spinoza*. Paris: PUF, 1992.
———. *Hegel or Spinoza*. Trans. Susan M. Ruddick. Minneapolis: University of Minnesota Press, 2011. Original French publication 1979.
———. *Introduction à l'Ethique de Spinoza*. 5 vols. Paris: PUF, 1994–98.
———. *A Theory of Literary Production*. Trans. Geoffrey Wall. London: Routledge, 2006.
Mackay, Robin, ed. *Collapse*. Vol. 3. Falmouth, UK: Urbanomic, 2007.

Macksey, Richard, and Eugenio Donato, eds. *The Structuralist Controversy: The Languages of Criticism and the Sciences of Man*. Baltimore: Johns Hopkins University Press, 1970.
Maimon, Salomon. *Essai sur la philosophie transcendantale*. Trans. Jean-Baptiste Scherrer. Paris: Vrin, 1989.
Marcel, Gabriel. *Le Mystère de l'être*. 2 vols. Paris: Aubier, 1951.
———. *Présence et immortalité*. Paris: Flammarion, 1959.
Marcel, Jean-Christophe. *Le Durkheimisme dans l'entre-deux-guerres*. Paris: PUF, 2001.
Marion, Jean-Luc. *Being Given: Toward a Phenomenology of Givenness*. Trans. Jeffrey A. Kosky. Stanford: Stanford University Press, 2002.
———. *Dieu sans l'être*. Paris: PUF, 2002.
———. *God without Being*. Trans. Thomas Carlson. Chicago: University of Chicago Press, 2012.
———. *L'Idole et la distance*. Paris: Grasset, 1977.
———. *In Excess: Studies in Saturated Phenomena*. Trans. Robyn Horner and Vincent Barraud. New York: Fordham University Press, 2002.
———, ed. *La Passion de la raison: Hommage à Ferdinand Alquié*. Paris: PUF, 1983.
———. *Reduction and Givenness: Investigations of Husserl, Heidegger, and Phenomenology*. Trans. Thomas A. Carlson. Evanston, IL: Northwestern University Press, 1998.
———. *Sur la théologie blanche de Descartes*. Paris: PUF, 1981.
———. *Sur le prisme métaphysique de Descartes*. Paris: PUF, 1986.
———. *Sur l'ontologie grise de Descartes*. Paris: PUF, 1975.
Marion, Jean-Luc, and Jean Birnbaum. "Spinoza: Un Complément à toutes les philosophies." *Le Monde des livres*, April 19, 2008.
Martin, Stewart. "Rendezvous: Return(s) to Marx?" *Radical Philosophy*, no. 115 (September–October 2002).
Massumi, Brian. *Parables of the Virtual: Movement, Affect, Sensation*. Durham, NC: Duke University Press, 2002.
Matheron, Alexandre. "A propos de Spinoza." Interview with Laurent Bove and Pierre-François Moreau. *Multitudes*, no. 3 (November 2000). Available at http://multitudes.samizdat.net/A-propos-de-Spinoza.html.
———. *Individu et communauté chez Spinoza*. Paris: Minuit, 1969.
Melamed, Yitzhak K. "Salomon Maimon and the Rise of Spinozism in German Idealism." *Journal of the History of Philosophy* 42, no. 1 (2004): 67–96.
Merleau-Ponty, Maurice. *Aventures de la dialectique*. Paris: Gallimard, 1955.
———. *Humanisme et terreur*. Paris: Gallimard, 1947.
———. *Phenomenology of Perception*. Trans. Colin Smith. London: Routledge, 1958.
———. *Signes*. Paris: Gallimard, 1960.

———. *The Visible and the Invisible*. Ed. Claude Lefort. Trans. Alphonso Lingis. Chicago: Northwestern University Press, 1969.
Milner, Jean-Claude, and Jean Birnbaum. "Marx: Espérer et expliquer sans prudence ni respect." *Le Monde des livres*, February 29, 2008.
Milosz, Czeslow. *The Captive Mind*. New York: Knopf, 1953.
Misrahi, Robert. *Le Désir et la réflexion dans la philosophie de Spinoza*. Paris: Gramma, 1972.
Montag, Warren. *Althusser and His Contemporaries: Philosophy's Perpetual War*. Durham, NC: Duke University Press, 2013.
———. *Bodies, Masses, Power: Spinoza and His Contemporaries*. London: Verso, 2009.
Montag, Warren, and Ted Stolze, eds. *The New Spinoza*. Minneapolis: University of Minnesota Press, 1997.
Moreau, Pierre-François. *Spinoza: L'Expérience et l'éternité*. Paris: PUF, 1994.
Moulier Boutang, Yann. *Louis Althusser, une biographie: Tome I, La Formation du mythe, 1918–1945: La Matrice*. 1992. Reprint, Paris: Livre de Poche, 2002.
———. *Louis Althusser, une biographie: Tome I, La Formation du mythe, 1945–1956: Ruptures et plis*. 1992. Reprint, Paris: Livre de Poche, 2002.
Moyn, Samuel. *Origins of the Other: Emmanuel Levinas between Revelation and Ethics*. Ithaca, NY: Cornell University Press, 2005.
Nairn, Tom. "Make for the Boondocks." *London Review of Books* 27, no. 9 (May 5, 2005).
Nancy, Jean-Luc. *The Birth to Presence*. Trans. Brian Holmes and others. Stanford: Stanford University Press, 1993.
Nancy, Jean-Luc, and Jean Birnbaum. "Nietzsche: Redécouvrir ce que 'sacré' veut dire." *Le Monde des livres*, March 7, 2008.
Negri, Antonio. *The Savage Anomaly: The Power of Spinoza's Metaphysics and Politics*. Trans. Michael Hardt. Minneapolis: University of Minnesota Press, 1991.
———. *Subversive Spinoza*. Manchester, UK: Manchester University Press, 2004.
Nizan, Paul. *Les Chiens de garde*. Paris: Rieder, 1932.
Oakeshott, Michael. *Rationalism in Politics and Other Essays*. 1962. Reprint, Indianapolis, IN: Liberty Fund, 1991.
Parrochia, Daniel. *La Raison systématique*. Paris: Vrin, 1993.
Peden, Knox. "Anti-Revolutionary Republicanism: Claude Lefort's Machiavelli." *Radical Philosophy*, no. 182 (November–December 2013): 29–39.
———. "The Fate of the Concept." In *Concept and Form*, vol. 2, *Interviews and Essays on the* Cahiers pour l'Analyse, ed. Peter Hallward and Knox Peden. London: Verso, 2012.
Perelman, Chaïm, ed. *Philosophie et méthode: Actes du colloque de Bruxelles*. Brussels: Éditions de l'Université de Bruxelles, 1974.

Popkin, Richard H. *The History of Scepticism from Savonarola to Bayle*. Oxford: Oxford University Press, 2003.

———. *Spinoza*. Oxford: Oneworld Publications, 2004.

Poster, Mark. *Existential Marxism in Postwar France: From Sartre to Althusser*. Princeton: Princeton University Press, 1975.

Racine, Nicole. "Les Années d'apprentissage." In *Jean Cavaillès Résistant, ou la Pensée en actes*, ed. Alya Aglan and Jean-Pierre Azéma, 13–78. Paris: Flammarion, 2002.

Rancière, Jacques. *Althusser's Lesson*. Trans. Emiliano Battista. London: Continuum, 2011. Original French publication 1974.

Ravis-Giordani, Georges, ed. *Jean-Toussaint Desanti: Une Pensée et son site*. Lyon: ENS Editions, 2000.

Regnault, François. "Dialectic of Epistemologies." In *Concept and Form*, vol. 1, *Key Texts from the Cahiers pour l'Analyse*, ed. Peter Hallward and Knox Peden, 119–50. London: Verso, 2012.

Resch, Robert Paul. *Althusser and the Renewal of Marxist Social Theory*. Berkeley: University of California Press, 1992.

Revill, Joel. "Taking France to the School of the Sciences: Léon Brunschvicg, Gaston Bachelard, and the French Epistemological Tradition." PhD diss., Duke University, 2006.

Ricoeur, Paul. "Althusser's Theory of Ideology." In *Althusser: A Critical Reader*, ed. Gregory Elliott. Oxford: Blackwell, 1994.

———. *Husserl: An Analysis of His Phenomenology*. Trans. Edward G. Ballard and Lester E. Embree. Evanston, IL: Northwestern University Press, 1967.

Rose, Gillian. *Dialectic of Nihilism: Post-structuralism and Law*. Oxford: Basil Blackwell, 1994.

———. *Hegel Contra Sociology*. 1981. Reprint, London: Verso, 2009.

Rosset, Clément. *Le Démon de la tautologie*. Paris: Minuit, 1997.

———. *En ce temps-là: Notes sur Louis Althusser*. Paris: Minuit, 1992.

———. *L'Objet singulier*. Paris: Minuit, 1989.

———. *Le Réel: Traité de l'idiotie*. Paris: Minuit, 1977.

———. *Schopenhauer: Philosophe de l'absurde*. Paris: PUF, 1967.

———. "Sécheresse de Deleuze." In *Gilles Deleuze: L'Arc no. 49*, ed. Catherine Clément. 1972. Reprint, Paris: Inculte, 2005.

Roth, Michael S. *Knowing and History: Appropriations of Hegel in Twentieth-Century France*. Ithaca, NY: Cornell University Press, 1988.

Roudinesco, Elisabeth. *Philosophy in Turbulent Times*. Trans. William McQuaig. New York: Columbia University Press, 2008.

Russell, Bertrand. *The Principles of Mathematics*. 1903. Reprint, London: Routledge, 1992.

Ruyer, Raymond. *Éléments de psychobiologie.* Paris: PUF, 1946.
———. *La Genèse des formes vivantes.* Paris: Flammarion, 1958.
———. *La Gnose de Princeton.* Paris: Fayard, 1974.
Schrift, Alan D. "The Effects of the *Agrégation de Philosophie* on Twentieth-Century French Philosophy." *Journal of the History of Philosophy* 46, no. 3 (2008): 449–73.
———, ed. *The History of Continental Philosophy.* 8 vols. Chicago: University of Chicago Press, 2010.
———. "Is There Such a Thing as 'French Philosophy'? or Why Do We Read the French So Badly?" In *After the Deluge: New Perspectives on the Intellectual and Cultural History of Postwar France,* ed. Julian Bourg, 21–47. Lanham, MD: Lexington Books, 2004.
———. *Twentieth-Century French Philosophy: Key Themes and Thinkers.* Oxford: Blackwell, 2006.
Sebbah, François-David. *Testing the Limit: Derrida, Henry, Levinas, and the Phenomenological Tradition.* Trans. Stephen Barker. Stanford: Stanford University Press, 2012.
Sebestik, Jan. *Logique et mathématique chez Bernard Bolzano.* Paris: Vrin, 1992.
Sellars, John. "Aiôn and Chronos: Deleuze and the Stoic Theory of Time." In *Collapse,* vol. 3, ed. Robin Mackay, 177–205. Falmouth, UK: Urbanomic, 2007.
Sharp, Hasana. *Spinoza and the Politics of Renaturalization.* Chicago: University of Chicago Press, 2011.
Simondon, Gilbert. *L'Individu et sa genèse physico-biologique.* Paris: PUF, 1964.
Sinaceur, Hourya. *Jean Cavaillès: Philosophie mathématique.* Paris: PUF, 1994.
———. "Philosophie et histoire." In *Jean Cavaillès Résistant, ou la Pensée en actes,* ed. Alya Aglan and Jean-Pierre Azéma, 205–24. Paris: Flammarion, 2002.
Skinner, Quentin. *Visions of Politics.* Vol. 1, *Regarding Method.* Cambridge: Cambridge University Press, 2002.
Smith, Steven B. *Spinoza, Liberalism, and the Question of Jewish Identity.* New Haven, CT: Yale University Press, 1998.
———. *Spinoza's Book of Life: Freedom and Redemption in the Ethics.* New Haven, CT: Yale University Press, 2003.
Sotiris, Panagiotis. "Rethinking Aleatory Materialism." In *Encountering Althusser: Politics and Materialism in Contemporary Radical Thought,* ed. Katja Diefenbach, Sara R. Farris, Gal Kirn, and Peter D. Thomas, 27–41. London: Bloomsbury, 2013.
Spiegelberg, Herbert. *The Phenomenological Movement: A Historical Introduction.* 3rd ed. The Hague: Nijhoff, 1982.
Spinoza, Benedict de. *Complete Works.* Ed. Michael Morgan. Trans. Samuel Shirley. Indianapolis, IN: Hackett, 2002.

———. *Éthique*. Ed. and trans. Bernard Pautrat. Paris: Seuil, 1988.
———. *Traité de la réforme de l'entendement*. Ed. and trans. Alexandre Koyré. 1937. Reprint, Paris: Vrin, 1994.
Stoetzel, Jean. *Notice sur la vie et les travaux de M. Gueroult (1891–1976)*. Paris: Institut de France, 1976.
Strauss, Leo. *Spinoza's Critique of Religion*. Trans. E. M. Sinclair. Chicago: University of Chicago Press, 1997.
Thao, Tran Duc. *Phénoménologie et matérialisme dialectique*. Paris: Minh-Tan, 1951.
Thomas, Peter. "Althusser and Spinoza: Philosophical Strategies." *Historical Materialism* 10, no. 3 (2002): 71–113.
Thompson, E. P. *The Poverty of Theory*. New York: Monthly Review Press, 1978.
Thompson, Kevin. "Historicity and Transcendentality: Foucault, Cavaillès, and the Phenomenology of the Concept." *History & Theory* 47 (February 2008): 1–18.
Tiles, Mary. *The Philosophy of Set Theory: An Introduction to Cantor's Paradise*. Oxford: Basil Blackwell, 1989.
Toscano, Alberto. *Fanaticism: On the Uses of an Idea*. London: Verso, 2010.
———. *The Theatre of Production: Philosophy and Individuation between Kant and Deleuze*. Basingstoke, UK: Palgrave Macmillan, 2006.
Tosel, André. "The Hazards of Aleatory Materialism in the Late Philosophy of Louis Althusser." In *Encountering Althusser: Politics and Materialism in Contemporary Radical Thought*, ed. Katja Diefenbach, Sara R. Farris, Gal Kirn, and Peter D. Thomas, 3–26. London: Bloomsbury, 2013.
———. *Spinoza, ou le crépuscule de la servitude*. Paris: Aubier, 1984.
Tournier, Michel. *Vendredi: Ou les limbes de la pacifique*. Paris: Gallimard, 1967.
Tucker, Robert C., ed. *The Marx-Engels Reader*. London: Norton, 1978.
Vardoulakis, Dimitris, ed. *Spinoza Now*. Minneapolis: University of Minnesota Press, 2011.
Verbeek, Theo. "Spinoza on Natural Rights." *Intellectual History Review* 17, no. 3 (2007): 257–75.
Vernière, Paul. *Spinoza et la pensée française avant la Révolution*. Paris: PUF, 1954.
Vuillemin, Jules. *L'Héritage kantien et la révolution copernicienne: Fichte-Cohen-Heidegger*. Paris: PUF, 1954.
———, ed. *Hommage à Martial Gueroult: L'Histoire de la philosophie, ses problèmes, ses méthodes*. Paris: Fischbacher, 1964.
———. *Physique et métaphysique kantiennes*. Paris: PUF, 1955.
Wagner, Pierre, ed. *Les Philosophes et la science*. Paris: Gallimard, 2002.
Wahl, Jean. *Vers le concret*. Paris: Vrin, 1932.
Wallace, David Foster. *Everything and More: A Brief History of ∞*. New York: Norton, 2003.

Wasser, Audrey. "Deleuze's Expressionism." *Angelaki* 12, no. 2 (August 2007): 49–66.
Webb, David. "Cavaillès, Husserl, and the Historicity of Science." *Angelaki* 8, no. 3 (December 2003): 59–72.
Williams, Caroline. "Althusser and Spinoza: The Enigma of the Subject." In *Encountering Althusser: Politics and Materialism in Contemporary Radical Thought*, ed. Katja Diefenbach, Sara R. Farris, Gal Kirn, and Peter D. Thomas, 153–163. London: Bloomsbury, 2013.
Worms, Frédéric, ed. *Annales bergsoniennes II: Bergson, Deleuze, la phénoménologie*. Paris: PUF, 2004.
Zac, Sylvain. *L'Idée de la vie dans la philosophie de Spinoza*. Paris: PUF, 1963.
———. *La Morale de Spinoza*. Paris: PUF, 1959.
———. *Spinoza et l'interprétation de l'écriture*. Paris: PUF, 1965.

Index

Adorno, Theodor: *Against Epistemology*, 300n7; vs. Althusser, 298n78; on consistency, 142; *Dialectic of Enlightenment*, 3; *Negative Dialectics*, 142

Agamben, Giorgio, 196; on Deleuze, 198–99

agrégation in philosophy, 43, 47, 96, 138, 165, 274n56, 308n32

Alembert, Jean le Rond d', 166

Alliez, Éric, 196

Alquié, Ferdinand: at Brussels colloquium of 1972, 68, 79–81, 91; as Cartesian, 65, 66, 281n6; on consciousness and Being, 75–76; on death, 91; on Descartes, 8, 66, 67, 68, 73, 74, 76, 76–81, 89, 90, 164; on Heidegger, 75–76, 195; on historicism, 68, 75; on history of philosophy, 66, 68; on Husserl, 81; on ideas, 145–46; on Kant, 81, 283n43; on Leibniz, 8; on Machiavelli, 187–88; on Malebranche, 8, 79, 81; on phenomenology, 67; on philosophy, 74–75, 76, 193, 254; relationship with Deleuze, 191, 192–93, 195–96, 248, 281n6, 308n40, 310n71; relationship with Gueroult, 14, 65–68, 73–81, 88–92, 98, 109, 164, 195–96; at Royaumont colloquium of 1955, 68, 76–79; at the Sorbonne, 195, 281n6; on Spinoza, 8, 66, 68, 81, 88–92, 98, 109, 110, 111; on theology, 68, 81, 90, 109; on truth, 74–75, 80–81, 91, 193

Alquié, Ferdinand, works of: *La Découverte métaphysique de l'homme chez Descartes*, 73, 74, 193; *Le Désir de l'éternité*, 193; *La Nostalgie de l'être*, 75–76, 90, 193; *Qu'est-ce que comprendre un philosophe?*, 74; *Le Rationalisme de Spinoza*, 66, 91; *La Solitude de la raison*, 283n43

Althusser, Louis, 4, 20, 22, 270n31, 274n57; on aesthetics, 302n42; vs. Bataille, 167, 302n37; on bourgeois juridical subject, 184, 185; on Brunschvicg, 33, 145; vs. Cavaillès, 8–9, 302n37; and changing circumstances, 127–28; on class struggle in theory, 130, 180, 186, 303n61; on concepts, 161, 169, 174; on consciousness, 130, 154, 155, 184; vs. Deleuze, 8–10, 11, 133, 189, 197, 219–20, 230, 310n83; on Descartes, 165–67, 184; on dialectical materialism, 148; on economism, 134, 141, 175; on empiricism, 158, 166–67, 177; at ENS, 47, 99, 101, 133, 135, 136, 139, 141, 142, 163, 164–65, 186, 282n8, 301n32, 303n61; on epistemological breaks, 128, 138, 145, 146–48; on Feuerbach, 141, 144, 145; on formalism, 164, 175; and Groupe Spinoza, 176, 177–78; vs. Gueroult, 8–9; on Gueroult, 282n8; on Hegel, 135, 136–38, 141, 155, 158, 165, 311n83; on Heidegger, 132, 158, 159, 165; on hermeneutics, 157; on historical materialism, 142, 143, 148, 149, 159–60, 167, 169–70, 174; on history and ideology, 154–57; on *homo oeconomicus*, 160, 301n20; on humanism, 11–12, 134, 137, 141, 151, 175; on Husserl, 121, 151–52, 158, 159, 165, 184, 296n31, 299nn5,7, 300n12, 301n19; on idealist rationalist empiricism vs. materialist rationalist empiricism, 166–68; on ideology, 130, 131, 132, 134–35, 143, 144, 147, 148, 151, 152–57, 160, 165, 169–72, 173–74, 175, 178–80, 181–82, 183, 184, 185, 186, 189, 219, 296n44, 300n12, 301n20, 303n53; on incommensurability of thought and object, 156, 158–59, 160, 179, 189;

on influences, 138, 141; on Kant, 184; on knowledge, 147–48, 151–52, 158–59, 161, 162, 163, 174, 189; on Lacan, 165, 167–68, 169, 175, 300n12, 302n40; on Lenin, 9, 130, 155, 173, 180, 183, 189, 303n58; on Lévi-Strauss, 165, 167–69, 175; on lived experience, 130, 132, 133, 134–35, 141, 142, 147, 151–53, 173, 175, 189, 296n31; on Marx and Feuerbach, 145; on Marx and Hegel, 137, 155; on Marx and historical materialism, 159–60; on Marx and Spinoza, 147–48; Marxism of, 6, 8, 9, 11–12, 81, 100, 101, 102, 115, 127–28, 129–30, 138, 139–40, 141, 142–45, 146–48, 149–50, 162–63, 164, 181, 186, 188, 190, 269nn25,30, 294n9, 296nn33,36, 299n85, 301nn22,23, 302n43; on Marx's early writings, 145, 154, 163, 290n57; on materialism, 132–33, 137–38, 166–67, 182, 185–86, 188, 189; on mathematics, 159; and May 1968, 130, 152–53, 176, 177, 178; on Montesquieu, 128–29, 154, 294n14, 300n15; on necessity, 168–69, 188; on overdetermination, 105, 139, 156; on phenomenology, 5, 8–9, 98, 101, 121, 129, 133, 134–36, 141–42, 143, 151–52, 153–54, 157, 158, 160, 161–62, 164, 165, 167, 177, 182, 185, 187, 188–89, 219, 230, 294n14, 295n27, 300n12, 301n19; "The Philosophical Conjuncture and Marxist Theoretical Research", 164–66; on philosophy, 127, 130, 130–33, 135, 137–38, 141, 143–45, 150, 158, 161, 162–63, 164, 165–66, 169, 173–75, 177, 179–85, 219, 257; on politics and philosophy, 173–76, 177, 180, 181, 182–87, 188–90; on politics and Spinozism, 9, 14; on practice, 172–75, 180, 183–84, 189; on problematic (*problèmatique*), 139; rationalism of, 5, 8–9, 92, 93, 98, 130, 131, 132, 138, 144, 145–46, 150–53, 165, 173, 174, 179, 185, 187, 188, 219; on relationality, 160; relationship to Sartre, 163–64, 296n36; relationship with Bachelard, 138, 146–47, 297n48; relationship with Canguilhem, 139; relationship with Cavaillès, 139, 140; relationship with Desanti, 9, 98–99, 100–102, 106, 116–17, 133–34, 135, 136, 138, 141, 143–44, 290n44, 291n71; relationship with Lacroix, 135–36, 138; relationship with Martin, 101, 136–37, 139–40, 187, 297nn56,57; relationship with Merleau-Ponty, 136–37, 140, 296n36; on relations of production, 160, 168; on science, 108, 127, 129–30, 131, 132, 133, 138, 142–44, 146–48, 150, 152–54, 155–56, 158, 159–60, 163, 165, 169–70, 172, 173–74, 175, 179, 180–87, 189, 219, 296n44, 298n72, 299n83, 302n42; on singularity, 132, 147, 148, 151, 154, 156, 164, 168–69, 172, 180, 181, 189; on solipsism, 121; on Spinoza, 131, 138, 145–46, 147–48, 149–50, 157, 161, 169, 170; Spinozism of, 7, 8, 12, 81, 92, 93, 98, 102, 115, 127, 129–33, 138, 143, 145, 149–50, 156, 160, 163, 166–67, 169, 170–71, 172, 173, 174, 175, 176, 177, 178, 179, 180–81, 182–83, 187, 188, 189–90, 219, 238, 259, 262, 263, 294nn14,25, 298nn68,78, 299n85, 310n83; on spontaneous philosophy of the sciences (SPS), 181–82; on Stalinism, 129, 133–34, 141–42, 143, 296n33; on structural causality, 169, 170; on structuralism, 131, 134; on subjectivity, 137, 138, 141, 171–72, 179, 184–85, 187, 188; on teleology, 144; on theology, 145, 154, 163, 182, 185–86, 187; on theoreticism, 128, 129, 130; on theory of history, 151; on truth, 145–46, 180–81, 182, 190, 298n78; on the unconscious, 156, 168, 170–71, 172; during World War II, 135, 297n57

Althusser, Louis, works of: *Eléments d'autocritique*, 178; *Elements of Dialectical Materialism*, 130; *The Facts*, 138; *For Marx*, 100, 128, 129–30, 132, 133, 139–40, 143, 151–57, 164–65, 169, 171, 179–80, 183, 294n15, 297n57; *The Future Lasts Forever*, 11, 128, 282n8, 294n9, 296n36, 301n22; "The Historical Task of Marxist Philosophy", 173–74, 180, 183–84; *The Humanist Controversy*, 294n14; ISA essay, 130, 152–53, 178–79, 188, 303n52; *Lenin*, 303n58; "Lenin and philosophy", 130; "Man, That Night", 137–38; "On Content in the Thought of G. W. F. Hegel", 136, 137; *Philosophy and the Spontaneous Philosophy of the Scientists*, 180–85, 298n72, 303n58; "Philosophy Course for Scientists", 130, 174, 180–81,

303n56; *Reading Capital*, 128, 129–30, 132, 133, 145, 147–48, 151, 157–65, 168, 169, 171, 177, 179–80, 294n15, 299n7; "Three Notes on the Theory of Discourses", 169–73, 302n40
Anderson, Perry: on Althusser, 142; on Althusser's Spinozism, 299n85; *Arguments within English Marxism*, 269n30; on relative autonomy, 300n17
Appuhn, Charles, 271n1
a priori intuition, 17, 31, 39
Aristotle, 2, 36; on actual vs. potential infinite, 40–41; on teleology, 112; on time, 224
Aron, Raymond, 140, 244; on Althusser, 149; on Cavaillès, 19–20, 22
art, 72, 73–74, 302n42, 305n10
Astier de la Vigerie, Emmanuel d', 18
Augustine, St., 166
Axelos, Kostas: *Vers un pensée planétaire*, 199

Bachelard, Gaston, 107, 140, 166, 270n1, 274n57; relationship with Althusser, 138, 146–47, 297n48; on scientific faith and Spinoza, 17
Bachelard, Suzanne, 115
Bacon, Francis, 191, 304n3
Badiou, Alain, 11, 20, 176, 177, 178, 269n25; on Althusser, 133; on Aristotle, 2, 267n2; *Being and Event*, 293n91; on Brunschvicg, 274n57; on Deleuze, 196, 198–99, 205; on Desanti, 293n91; on Spinoza, 261, 318n6; theory of the Event, 261–62
Balibar, Étienne, 7, 11, 130, 136, 176, 184, 269n25, 297n54, 299n7; on Desanti, 101–2; on Martin, 297n56; relationship with Althusser, 141, 144; on Sartre and Marxism, 298n75
Baring, Edward: *The Young Derrida*, 268nn12,22
Barthes, Roland, 5
Barth, Karl, 273n46
Bataille, Georges, 167, 302n37
Beaufret, Jean, 192; on Heidegger, 199
Beaulieu, Alain, 250
Beauvoir, Simone de, 24, 25
Beckett, Samuel, 231
Beistegui, Miguel de: on Deleuze and Heidegger, 307n31; *Immanence*, 308n31; *Truth and Genesis*, 307n31
Bergson, Henri, 10, 33, 37, 40, 70, 272n24, 274n57; vs. Deleuze, 212, 220, 224, 225, 228, 252; on *durée*, 313n14; on élan vital, 167, 231; and phenomenology, 25, 30, 72, 76, 106, 140–41, 167, 169; on Spinoza, 1; vs. Spinoza, 41, 83, 277n92, 284n75; on time, 224, 225
Berlinische Monatsschrift, 2
Blanchot, Maurice, 203, 204, 233, 309n54
Bolzano, Bernard, 39, 48, 50, 52, 53–54, 62, 279n125
Bordas-Demoulin, Jean, 236
Borne, Étienne, 30–32, 120
Bouglé, Celestin, 27, 34, 272n32
Bourdieu, Pierre, 140
Bove, Laurent, 282n8
Brassier, Ray: on Badiou, 261; on Deleuze, 240, 309n54
Bréhier, Émile, 34, 69, 73
Brentano, Franz, 72
Breton, André, 73
Brouwer, L. E. J., 37–38, 48, 52
Brown, Nathan, 302n36
Brunschvicg, Léon, 7, 32–38, 73, 95, 271n1, 274nn56,57; on Bergson, 272n24; on concepts, 33; on consciousness, 53, 278n111; critical idealism of, 146, 175; Desanti on, 106–7; *Les Étapes de la philosophie mathématique*, 35–36, 38, 47, 53, 145, 272n24; on Hegel, 33; on idea of the idea, 43, 52–53; on immanence of reason, 32; on intuition, 36, 37, 38; on Leibniz, 36; on mathematics, 35–37, 38, 47, 48, 52–53; neo-Kantianism of, 25, 32–33, 47, 53, 274n56, 275n58; on philosophy, 35–36; rationalism of, 25, 140; relationship with Cavaillès, 23, 29, 32, 34–35, 46–48, 52–53, 277n94; relationship with Husserl, 25; republicanism of, 32, 275n58; on Russell, 35, 36, 38; on science, 32–33, 36–37, 48, 50, 52, 53, 113, 146; on Spinoza, 32, 33, 36, 37, 46, 53, 67, 113, 145, 146, 264, 274n55, 276nn76,78, 306n20; on Spinoza and truth, 37, 145, 146, 276n78; on Spinoza's attributes, 306n20; on Spinoza's consciousness, 46; on Spinoza's originality, 37, 276n78; on Spinoza's

rationalism, 32, 33, 36, 53, 67, 113; on Spinoza's substance, 37; on thing-in-itself, 33; on truth, 36, 37, 276n78; on unity of judgment and will, 37; on the world, 53; during World War II, 34, 69
Bryant, Levi R.: on Deleuze, 307n28; *Difference and Givenness*, 307n28
Brykman, Geneviève: La Judéité de Spinoza, 67

Cadier, Jean, 280n129
Cahiers pour l'Analyse, 176, 177–78, 264
Calvinism, 111, 140, 273n46
Canguilhem, Georges, 48, 140, 166, 178, 314n42; on Cavaillès, 20–22, 62, 139; on Nazism, 21–22; on reason and history, 21–23; *Vie et mort de Jean Cavaillès*, 20–21
Cantor, Georg: continuum hypothesis, 39, 49; on cardinal and ordinal numbers, 39–40, 41; on infinity, 17, 31, 39–40, 41, 46; on set theory, 17, 31, 273n45
Carnap, Rudolf 36, 48–49, 56; on logical syntax, 50, 53
Carroll, Lewis: "What the Tortoise Said to Achilles", 312n12
Cartan, Henri, 35
Casanova, Laurent, 99, 135
Cassirer, Ernst: Davos encounter with Heidegger, 24, 27–28, 29, 244; as neo-Kantian, 24, 27
Cassou-Noguès, Pierre, 52–53, 276n81, 279n119
Cavaillès, Jean, 102, 125, 166; vs. Althusser, 8–9, 302n37; on Being, 31; on Bolzano, 53–54, 62, 279n125; Christianity of, 30, 273n46, 275n63; on the concept, 10, 18, 20, 24, 31, 45, 60–61, 65, 121, 139, 160, 243–44, 297n54; on consciousness, 10, 18, 20, 23, 29, 44, 49, 51–52, 53–54, 58–59, 60–61, 62, 114, 121, 125, 139, 297n54; at Davos, 27–28, 29, 244; vs. Deleuze, 106, 197, 241; on Descartes, 26; on *devenir*, 42, 43, 47; on dialectic, 60–61; at ENS, 19, 34, 47, 96, 272n32; on essence and existence, 29; and formalism, 31, 37–38, 42, 43, 54, 56, 61–63, 172; on Gödel, 43; vs. Gueroult, 42, 277n94, 281n8; vs. Hegel, 61, 280nn130,131; on Heidegger, 28–29, 31, 244–45; on *histoire*, 42; on

Husserl, 17–18, 20, 24, 26–27, 28, 29–30, 32, 44, 47–48, 52, 54, 57–61, 65, 114, 117, 120, 121, 139, 162, 279n116, 282n26, 296n31; at Husserl's Paris Lectures, 26–27, 29; on idea of the idea, 42–43, 52–53, 55, 108–9; on immanence, 28, 30–31, 32, 44; on intuition, 37, 38, 42; on Kant, 24, 48, 49, 50–52, 53, 56, 58, 59, 114, 279n123; on Leibniz vs. Spinoza, 34; on logic, 49, 50–52, 54, 59; on logical positivism, 48–49, 54–57, 58; on logical sense, 50; on logicism, 49, 67; on Marcel, 30–31; on mathematical experiment (*l'expérience mathématique*), 43, 44, 45, 47–48, 60–61, 92, 277n92, 278n102; and mathematics, 17, 19, 22, 23, 26, 28–29, 30, 31, 35, 36, 37–39, 40, 42, 43–44, 45–48, 49, 50, 52, 53–57, 58, 59, 60–61, 92, 172, 244, 273n45, 277n92, 278nn102,108, 279nn127,130; on necessity, 59, 169; on paradigmatization, 48–49, 54–55, 56; on Plato's *Parmenides*, 264; on rationality's immanence, 28, 30–31, 32; relationship with Borne, 30–32, 120; relationship with Bouglé, 27, 272n32; relationship with Brunschvicg, 23, 29, 32, 34–35, 46–48, 52–53, 277n94; relationship with Desanti, 8, 47, 95, 97–98, 108, 286n5; relationship with Lautman, 28–29, 31, 60–61, 242, 243–45, 246; relationship with Merleau-Ponty, 96, 97; relationship with Thao, 47–48, 279n116; on science, 46, 49, 50, 52, 53–57, 59–62, 105, 108, 125, 242, 263, 279nn119,125; on *sens posé* vs. *sens posant*, 50, 55, 56; on singularity, 54, 55, 60, 244; on solipsism, 24; on Spinoza, 18, 19–21, 31, 42, 43, 45, 46, 49–50, 62–63, 275n63, 280n130; on Spinoza and necessity, 19–21, 62–63; on Spinoza's God, 275n63, 280n130; on Spinoza's rationalism, 18, 19, 31, 42, 43, 45, 46, 49–50, 62–63, 65, 67, 108, 113, 117, 122, 143, 263, 273n46; Spinozism of, 18, 19–21, 31, 42, 43, 46, 49–50, 56–57, 62–63, 65, 95, 105, 108, 113, 117, 122, 140, 143, 145, 242, 243, 263, 273n46, 275n63, 279n127, 286n5; on subjectivity, 17, 27, 29, 59, 114; on synthesis, 51, 54–57; on thematization, 48–49, 50, 54, 55, 56, 108–9; on transcendental subjectivity, 17,

59, 114; on truth, 47; during World War II, 18–21, 22, 34, 37, 61, 62–63, 92, 139, 280n129, 281n8

Cavaillès, Jean, works of: *Méthode axiomatique et formalisme*, 38, 42, 276n81, 286n5; *Remarques sur la formation de la théorie abstraite des ensembles*, 38, 42, 276n81; *Sur la logique et la théorie de la science*, 22, 23–24, 42, 43, 46, 48–63, 108, 139, 242, 279nn126,127, 280nn130,131

Caveing, Maurice, 289n40
Cazeaux, Clive: on phenomenology, 295n31
Cercle d'Épistémologie, 177
Chomsky, Noam, 166
Christianity, 30, 135, 136, 141, 144, 182, 185, 318n91; Calvinism, 111, 140, 273n46
Christofferson, Michael Scott, 288n24
Clavel, Maurice, 288n24
cogito, the: Descartes on, 6, 26, 66, 73, 78, 80–81, 90, 122, 184, 201, 253–54; Husserl on, 18, 20, 26, 29, 61, 308n40
Cohen, Hermann, 33, 207, 275n58
Collège de France, 65–66, 67, 69, 70, 73
Comte, Auguste, 140, 166
concepts: Althusser on, 161, 169, 174; Brunschvicg on, 33; Cavaillès on the concept, 10, 18, 20, 23, 24, 31, 49, 60–61, 65, 121, 139, 160, 243–44, 297n54; Deleuze on, 192, 193, 198, 241, 243, 254, 306n13, 317n86; Desanti on, 108–9, 126; Descartes on, 77; Gueroult on the concept, 66, 78, 86–87; philosophy of the concept vs. philosophy of consciousness, 18, 20, 23, 24, 49, 60, 61, 65, 121, 139, 243, 297n54
consciousness: Althusser on, 130, 154, 155, 184; Brunschvicg on, 53, 278n111; Cavaillès on, 10, 18, 20, 23, 29, 44, 49, 51–52, 53–54, 58–59, 60–61, 62, 114, 121, 125, 139, 297n54; Deleuze on, 198, 235–36, 314n38; Desanti on, 134–35; Heidegger on, 196; Husserl on, 18, 20, 26, 49, 57–59, 72, 121, 134–35, 282n27; philosophy of the concept vs. philosophy of, 18, 20, 23, 24, 49, 60, 61, 65, 121, 139, 243, 297n54; Spinoza on, 46, 300n15. *See also cogito*, the
contextualist method, 13
Copernican Revolution, 112–13, 206–8

Corbin, Henry, 202, 204, 207, 248, 316n75; and *Qu'est-ce que la métaphysique?*, 200, 201, 245
Corpet, Olivier, 270n31
Cournot, Antoine Augustine, 166
Cousin, Victor, 140
Couturat, Louis, 166
Cuzin, François, 118, 281n8

Darwin, Charles, 3, 246, 315n60
death, 91, 203, 229, 230–31, 233, 309n54
Dedekind, Richard, 39, 40, 314n42
Delbos, Victor, 7; on Husserl, 24; on Spinoza, 274n55
Deleuze, Gilles, 5, 14, 38, 284n75; vs. Althusser, 8–10, 11, 133, 189, 197, 219–20, 230, 310n83; on Beckett, 231; vs. Bergson, 212, 220, 224, 225, 228, 252; on Bergson, 228–29, 231, 284n75, 308n32, 313n14; on causality, 227–28, 249–50; vs. Cavaillès, 106, 197, 241; on Chronos and Aiôn, 225–27, 228, 247, 249–50, 312n13; on common sense, 234–35; on concepts, 192, 193, 198, 241, 243, 254, 306n13, 317n86; on consciousness, 198, 235–36, 314n38; on contradiction, 205, 230; on Darwin, 246, 315n60; on death, 203, 230–31, 309n54; on differential calculus, 191, 236, 238–40, 241–42, 314n42, 315n46; on events, 175, 226–28; on expression, 205, 206, 210, 211–12, 214, 215, 216, 222, 240, 251, 305n10, 310n83; on expression as explication, 211, 213, 215, 222, 251; on expression as implication, 211, 213, 215, 222, 251; on Fichte, 206, 209, 310n79; on genesis and synthesis, 209–10, 222–23, 234; on God and self, 224, 312n6; on Gueroult, 193–95, 206, 208, 248, 280n3, 310n79; on Hegel, 228, 229; vs. Heidegger, 9–10, 195, 196–206, 210, 213, 214, 215, 216, 217, 220, 221, 223, 224–26, 229, 230, 246, 248, 251–52, 255, 257, 307nn30,31, 315n55, 316n75; on hermeneutics, 255–56, 257; on history of philosophy, 10; on Hume, 307n28, 308n32; on Husserl, 234–36, 237, 308n40; on the Idea, 193, 195, 237–38, 240–41, 243, 254, 306n13; idiosyncrasy of, 191, 305n6; on immanence, 220, 233, 250–51, 317n91;

on individuation, 236–37, 251, 314n40; on irrationalism, 234–35; on Jarry, 198–99, 205, 216, 252, 317n89; on Kant, 192, 193, 194, 202, 206, 208, 209–10, 220, 223–24, 228, 234–35, 237, 238, 239–40, 247, 310n79, 311n85, 314n43; on knowledge 222–23; vs. Klossowski, 232, 312n6, 313n26; vs. Lautman, 221, 238, 241–45, 247, 248, 251, 315n55, 317n86; vs. Levinas, 203–4, 206, 309n54; on lived experience, 220, 230, 232; on Maimon, 206, 209, 243; on the minor in music, 255–56, 257; on multiplicity, 195, 238–39; on negativity, 232; on Nietzsche's eternal return, 202, 223, 312n5; on ontology of excess, 105; on otherness, 203–4; on 'pataphysics, 198–99, 205; on phenomenology, 5, 133, 195, 196, 199, 219–20, 230; on philosophy, 193, 200, 254, 256, 263–64, 304n3, 317n91; on plane of immanence, 250–51, 317n91; on Plato, 243; on politics, 256, 257–58, 263; on possibility, 193, 198, 203, 204, 217, 219, 220, 221, 227–32, 233, 246–47, 248, 256, 313n14, 314n34, 317n91; on powers vs. attributes, 253–54; on quantitative intensity, 236–37, 258, 314n41; on quantitative vs. qualitative distinctions, 212, 216–17, 221, 236–37, 311n85, 314n41; rationalism of, 5, 195, 196, 197, 198, 205–6, 215, 217, 220, 221, 227, 234–36, 252, 307n28; relationship with Alquié, 191, 192–93, 195–96, 248, 281n6, 308n40, 310n71; relationship with Guattari, 10–11, 14, 82, 249, 250, 254, 304n3, 305n3, 316n66, 317n85; relationship with Gueroult, 191, 193–96, 197, 306n23; relationship with Vuillemin, 195, 197, 281n8; on Sartre, 199–200, 314n38; on singularity, 189, 198, 199, 205–6, 216–17, 232, 235–36, 237, 247, 251; on Spinoza, 111, 133, 191, 194, 204, 205, 206, 209, 211–13, 214–17, 219, 221, 222, 228–29, 234, 236–37, 238, 240–41, 248, 249, 251, 252–54, 256, 263–64, 284n75, 306n20, 310n79, 311nn83,85, 314n41, 317n91; on Spinoza's attributes, 194, 211–12, 214, 215, 216–17, 236–37, 240–41, 248, 251, 252–54, 306n20, 311n85, 314n41; on Spinoza's modes, 111, 191, 211–13, 214, 215–16, 222, 248, 251; on Spinoza's substance, 191, 211–13, 214–16, 221, 222, 228, 234, 240, 248, 251; Spinozism of, 7, 8, 9–10, 82, 92, 193–95, 196–98, 209, 210–17, 219–20, 221–22, 228–29, 230, 231, 232–34, 238, 241, 247–48, 249, 251, 252–56, 257–59, 262, 263–64, 267n7, 306n20, 316n75; on subjectivity, 221, 223–24, 247; on substance, 226; on thought, 198, 221–22, 225, 230, 237–38, 240–41, 247, 252–57, 285n80, 316n75, 317n91; on time, 202, 203–4, 221, 223–26, 228, 247, 249–50, 312nn5,12,13; on transcendental ego, 114, 210, 210–12, 234, 235, 314n48; on transcendental empiricism, 196, 307n28; on truth, 193, 232; on univocity, 82, 233–34, 252–53; on the virtual and the actual, 192, 193, 195, 198, 212, 220, 221, 225, 227, 228, 241, 242, 245–46, 247–51, 252, 254, 285n80, 313n14, 316n61, 317n86; on Vuillemin, 206

Deleuze, Gilles, works of: "The Actual and the Virtual", 250–51; *Anti-Oedipus*, 249, 304n3; "Bergson's Conception of Difference", 228; "By Creating Pataphysics Jarry Opened the Way for Phenomenology", 199, 317n89; "Capitalism and Schizophrenia" project, 10–11, 235; "Description of a Woman: For a Philosophy of the Sexed Other", 199–200; *Difference and Repetition*, 9–10, 191, 192, 197, 200, 202, 206, 209, 212, 216, 217, 220–21, 222–25, 227, 228, 230–34, 236–48, 249–50, 254, 256, 304n3, 305n10, 310n74, 312n5, 313n24, 317n86; "The Exhausted", 231; *The Fold*, 305nn3,10; "He Stuttered", 255–56, 257, 317n89; *The Logic of Sense*, 191, 197, 209–10, 217, 220–21, 225–28, 234–36, 249–50, 304n3, 309n57, 312nn6,12, 316n66; "The Method of Dramatization", 192–93, 195, 196; "Michel Tournier and the World without Others", 203, 231, 309nn56,57; *Nietzsche and Philosophy*, 206, 234, 306n14, 312n5; *Proust and Signs*, 305n3; review of Hyppolite's *Logic and Existence*, 204–5; *Spinoza: Practical Philosophy*, 249; "Spinoza and the General Method of M. Gueroult", 193–94; *Spinoza and the Problem of*

Expression, 192, 205, 209, 211–17, 221, 222, 228, 236–37, 240–41, 249, 252–54, 305n10, 310n64, 311nn83,85; "Spinoza and Us", 250; *A Thousand Plateaus*, 304n3; "An Unrecognized Precursor to Heidegger: Alfred Jarry", 198–99; "What is Grounding" course, 200–202, 207, 245, 308n45, 315n55; *What Is Philosophy?*, 250, 254, 255, 317n85

Della Rocca, Michael, 285n78, 306n22

Denjoy, Arnauld, 35

Derrida, Jacques, 67; on Alquié, 75, 195; on deconstruction/*déconstruction*, 3, 5, 292n82; vs. Desanti, 115–16, 292nn79,82, 293n91; on *différance*, 293n91; and Heidegger, 75, 132, 195, 292n82; on Husserl, 115, 299n5; *Of Grammatology*, 177; and phenomenology, 5, 176; *Writing and Difference*, 292n79

Desanti, Dominique, 287n14; on Althusser, 101, 134; on Jean-Toussaint Desanti, 99, 101, 103–4, 114, 115, 119, 289n40; and PCF, 99, 101, 288n21, 289n40; relationship with Sartre, 118; *Les Staliniens*, 288n21; as Stalinist, 99; on Tito, 288n21

Desanti, Jean-Toussaint: on Alquié, 106; asceticism of, 102–3, 124, 126; on Brunschvicg, 106–7, 272n24, 290n50; on Cavaillès and Hegel, 61; on concepts, 108–9, 126; on consciousness, 118, 134–35; vs. Derrida, 115–16, 292nn79,82, 293n91; on Descartes, 107; at ENS, 95, 98, 99, 101, 133, 286n11; on existentialism, 290n57; on Gueroult, 107; on Hegel, 100, 108, 290n57; on historical materialism, 101, 102, 103, 104, 109, 111, 113; on history of philosophy, 93, 106–8; on Husserl, 92, 93, 95, 106, 110, 111, 115–18, 119–26, 134–35, 141, 287n11, 292n90; on immanence, 117, 125–26; on logical positivism, 139; on Lysenkoism, 99, 143–44; Marxism of, 100, 108, 113, 114–15, 117, 133–34, 141, 288n24; on materialism, 109–11, 289n32, 296n44; and mathematics, 92, 95–96, 103, 109, 116, 124–26, 291nn60,71, 292n79; on method, 116, 117; on others/the world, 122; and PCF, 93, 99–100, 101, 103, 104, 106, 107–8, 114, 115, 119–20, 126, 133–34, 286n11, 287n11, 289n40; on phenomenology, 97–98, 101–2, 106, 110, 114, 120–22, 123–24, 126, 134–35, 287n11, 292n90; rationalism of, 95–96, 103–4, 118; relationship with Althusser, 9, 98–99, 100–102, 106, 116–17, 133–34, 135, 136, 138, 141, 143–44, 290n44, 291n71; relationship with Cavaillès, 8, 47, 95, 97–98, 108, 286n5; relationship with Merleau-Ponty, 96, 116, 118, 122–23; relationship with Sartre, 118–19; on Russell, 106; on science, 100, 107–8, 111, 112–13, 114, 120, 124–26, 139, 290n55; on singularity, 124; on Spinoza, 92, 93, 95–97, 98, 101, 103, 104–5, 107, 108–14, 116, 117–18, 122–24, 126, 138, 289n32, 290n44, 291nn60,62; on Spinoza as materialist, 109–11, 289n32; on Spinoza's God, 105, 110–11, 113, 118, 290n14; on Spinoza's principle *Deus sive Natura*, 105, 110–11, 113, 290n44; on Spinoza's rationalism, 95–96, 98, 105, 110, 122, 138; on Spinoza's substance, 110–11; as Stalinist, 93, 99–100, 102, 106, 126, 133–34, 135; on subjectivity, 106, 107, 109, 114, 117–18; on time, 120–21, 122; on transcendental ego, 97, 117–18, 121, 125–26; on transcendental fields, 125–26; during World War II, 118–19

Desanti, Jean-Toussaint, works of: "Bourgeois Science, Proletarian Science", 99, 288n19, 290n55; *Un Destin philosophique*, 100, 287n11, 288n24; "Dieu ou Nature", 105, 290n44; *Les Idéalités mathématiques*, 92, 108, 111, 116, 117, 124–26, 287n11, 288n24, 291n60, 292n79; *Introduction à la phénoménologie (Phénoménologie et praxis)*, 93, 95, 101, 115–17, 120, 287n11; *Introduction à l'histoire de la philosophie*, 101–2, 103–15, 116–17, 287n11, 289n40, 290nn44,57; "Materialism and Epistemology", 124; *Une Pensée captive*, 288n24, 289n40; *Le Philosophe et les pouvoirs*, 287n11; *La Philosophie silencieuse*, 116, 120, 126, 287n11; "Spinoza and Phenomenology", 96–97

Descartes, René, 35–36, 194, 281n7; on Aristotle, 112; on causality, 285n78; on certainty, 77–78; the *cogito* of, 6, 26, 66,

73, 78, 80–81, 90, 122, 184, 201, 253–54; on concepts, 77; *Discourse on Method*, 8, 163; on doubt, 73; dualism of, 77, 84; on extension, 77; on God, 89, 90, 163; on logic, 27; *Meditations*, 74, 163; and phenomenology, 25, 26, 67; rationalism of, 5–6, 25, 79, 89; vs. Spinoza, 6, 10, 61, 65, 66, 67–68, 78–79, 84, 89, 90, 130, 163, 284n61, 310n79; Spinoza on, 2; on substance, 213–14, 225; on thought, 77, 78–79, 159; on truth, 76–77

Descombes, Vincent, 162; *Modern French Philosophy*, 267n6

Dews, Peter, on Althusser, 146–47

D'Holbach, Baron, 269n28

Diderot, Denis, 166

Dilthey, Wilhelm, 70

Dosse, François: on Deleuze, 310n64, 313n24, 317n35; *History of Structuralism*, 268n9; *The Rising Sign*, 281n8

Dreyfus, Ginette, 282n17

Duffy, Simon, 315n55

Duhem, Pierre, 166

Duns Scotus, John, 10

Durkheim, Émile, 272n32

Duroux, Yves, 297n54

École Normale Supérieure (ENS): Althusser at, 47, 99, 101, 133, 135, 136, 139, 141, 142, 163, 164–65, 286, 282n8, 301n32, 303n61; Cavaillès at, 29, 34, 47, 96, 272n32; Desanti at, 95, 98, 99, 101, 133, 286n11; Lacan at, 177; Merleau-Ponty at, 47, 96

economism, 134, 141, 175

Ehresmann, Charles, 48

eidetic reduction, 80, 97, 99

Einstein's theory of relativity, 33

Elliott, Gregory, 128, 298n72

empirical verification, 46

empiricism, 158, 166

Engels, Friedrich, 106, 108, 290n50

Enlightenment, 182, 185, 269n28

ENS. *See* École Normale Supérieure

Entretiens sur les notions de genèse et de structure, 292n79

Epicurus, 109

existentialism, 5, 24, 30–31, 135, 290n57; and phenomenology, 106, 136, 138, 139, 176, 177, 195. *See also* Heidegger, Martin; Marcel, Gabriel; Sartre, Jean-Paul

Fabiani, Jean-Louis, 69

Faye, Jean-Pierre, 308n30

Ferrières, Gabrielle, 48

Feuerbach, Ludwig, 141; Marx's Thesis Eleven on, 144, 173, 190, 298n73

Fichte, Johann Gottlieb, 206, 208; absolute idealism of, 210; on Kant, 207; *Wissenschaftslehre*, 69

Fink, Eugen, 47, 60, 279n116

formalism: Althusser on, 164, 175; and Cavaillès, 31, 37–38, 42, 43, 54, 56, 61–63, 172; in mathematics, 31, 37–38, 42, 43, 54, 56, 172

Foucault, Michel, 20, 66, 136, 176, 177–78, 199, 206, 306n14; on Deleuze, 9–10, 231, 309n57

Frankfurt School, 177, 270n30

Fréchet, Maurice, 45

Frege, Gottlob, 36, 277n93; *Grundlagen der Arithmetik*, 39, 41; on truth, 39

French Communist Party (PCF): and Althusser, 11, 12, 100, 101, 127, 128, 133–34, 135, 296n33, 298n72, 302n43; and Jean-Toussaint Desanti, 93, 99–100, 101, 103, 104, 106, 107–8, 114, 115, 119–20, 126, 133–34, 286n11, 287n11, 289n40; and Dominique Desanti, 99, 101, 288n21, 289n40

Freud, Sigmund, 267n6

Friedmann, Georges: *Leibniz et Spinoza*, 34, 289n32

Galileo Galilei, 69, 112–13, 114, 299n83

Gandillac, Maurice de, 192

Garaudy, Roger, 100, 302n43

genesis and synthesis: Deleuze on, 209–10, 222–23, 234; Gueroult on, 46, 82–84, 86–87, 194–95, 208

Geroulanos, Stefanos, 201–2, 203, 314n34

Gilson, Étienne, 70

Giolito, Christophe: *Histoires de la philosophie avec Martial Gueroult*, 282n22

Glucksmann, André, 2

God: Deleuze on, 224, 312n6; Descartes on, 89, 90, 163; immanence of, 86, 89; Kant on, 3, 224; Spinoza on, 81, 84, 86, 87, 89, 90, 91, 110–11, 113, 114–15, 117–18, 132, 172, 194, 210–11, 214, 234, 260, 262, 274n46, 275n63, 280n130, 285n80, 293n103, 295n24. *See also* theology

Index   349

Gödel, Kurt, 49; incompleteness and undecidability theorems, 43
Goldhammer, Arthur, 278nn98,102
Goldschmidt, Victor, 78
Gordon, Peter E., 270n34, 275n58
Goshgarian, G. M., 129, 270n31, 294n14
Gramsci, Antonio, 144
Granger, Gilles-Gaston, 92, 279n126, 281n8; on phenomenology and mathematics, 49
Groupe Spinoza, 176, 177–78
Guattari, Félix: "Capitalism and Schizophrenia" project, 10–11, 235; relationship with Deleuze, 10–11, 14, 82, 249, 250, 254, 304n3, 305n3, 316n66, 317n85
Gueroult, Martial: vs. Althusser, 8–9; on Bergson, 70, 76, 277n92; at Brussels colloquium of 1972, 68, 79–81, 91; vs. Cavaillès, 42, 277n94, 281n8; on certainty, 76–78; at Collège de France, 65–66, 67, 69, 70, 73, 209; on the concept, 66, 78, 86–87; on creation, 82; on demonstration, 70, 76; Desanti on, 107; on Descartes, 8, 66, 68, 73, 74, 76–81, 87–88, 107, 194; on doctrine vs. system, 71; on Fichte, 69, 208, 209, 310n79; on Frege, 41–42, 277n93; on genesis and synthesis, 46, 82–84, 86–87, 194–95, 208; on Hegel, 71, 82; on Heidegger, 197, 206; on historicism, 68, 69, 70–71; on history of philosophy, 66, 68, 70–71, 72–73; on Husserl, 71–72, 121, 282n27; on incommensurability of idea and object, 86–87, 88, 91, 158–59; on infinity, 41, 83, 84–85; on intentionality, 72; on intuition, 83, 277n92; on Kant, 71, 194; on Leibniz, 8, 194; on Maimon, 195, 206, 208, 209; on Malebranche, 8, 194; on mathematics, 77–78, 277n93; methodology of, 69–70, 71–73, 74–75, 87, 107, 194, 281n8, 312n5; on phenomenology, 78, 79, 87, 121; on philosophical systems, 69, 70–71, 72, 73; rationalism of, 66, 68, 69, 70, 72–73, 79, 105, 107, 109, 150, 194, 206, 209, 248, 254, 263, 284n67; on reality, 71, 79–80; relationship with Alquié, 14, 65–68, 73–81, 88–92, 98, 109, 164, 195–96; relationship with Deleuze, 191, 193–96, 197, 306n23; at Royaumont colloquium of 1955, 68, 76–79; *savoir* vs. *connaître*, 87–88; on singularity, 70, 72, 73, 80, 90–91, 285n79; on Spinoza, 9, 41–42, 66, 68, 81–92, 105, 111, 119, 132, 156, 158–59, 193–95, 209, 211, 221, 233, 248, 263, 277nn92,93, 285nn77,79,80, 294n13, 295n24, 306n20; on Spinoza's attributes, 9, 83–85, 156, 158–59, 194, 211, 221, 277n93, 285nn77,80, 306n20; on Spinoza's God, 132, 295n24; on Spinoza's modes, 83–85, 111; on Spinoza's rationalism, 66, 68, 81, 82, 92, 105, 107, 109, 150, 194–95, 209, 248, 263, 294n13; on Spinoza's substance, 82–84, 132, 194, 233, 277n93; Spinozism of, 7, 8–9, 41–42, 78–79, 82, 87–88, 91–92, 98, 105, 107, 109, 119, 150, 164, 193–95, 248, 263, 281n8, 285n80, 306n20; on subjectivity, 72, 76; on theology, 68, 81, 91; on truth, 70, 71, 76–77, 80, 91–92
Gueroult, Martial, works of: *Descartes selon l'ordre des raisons*, 73, 74; *Dianoématique*, 66, 69–73, 80, 280n3, 282nn17,27, 283nn29,30; *L'Évolution et la structure de la doctrine de la science chez Fichte*, 206; *La Philosophie transcendantale de Salomon Maimon*, 206; *Spinoza I: Dieu*, 67, 81–82, 277n93, 281n8, 284n75; *Spinoza II: L'Âme*, 281n8
Guitton, Jean, 135, 281n6
Gutting, Gary, on Deleuze, 305n6

Hägglund, Martin: on Derrida, 268n12, 270n34; *Radical Atheism*, 268n12, 270n34
Halévy, Elie, 274n56
Hallward, Peter: on Deleuze, 189, 190, 212–13, 241, 316n75; on Spinozism and politics, 189
Hardt, Michael, 112; *Commonwealth*, 258–59, 267n7; *Empire*, 267n7; *Gilles Deleuze*, 308n32; on the multitude, 259–60; *Multitude*, 267n7; Spinozism of, 258–60, 261, 267n7
Hegel, G. W. F., 24, 267n6; on bad infinity, 83; vs. Cavaillès, 61, 280nn130,131; on contradiction, 155, 228, 229; on history, 155, 157; on history of philosophy, 71; on Kant, 207; on logic, 61, 280n130; and Marx, 137, 138, 155; *Phenomenology of Spirit*, 21–22, 100, 290n57; *Science of*

Logic, 100, 205, 290n57; on Spinoza, 13, 82, 306n20; on substance, 205; on thought, 159

Heidegger, Martin, 5, 24, 30, 70, 150, 159, 267n6; on Aristotle, 229; on authenticity, 229; Being/beings distinction, 28, 198, 213–14, 245, 248, 262–63, 285n80; on Bergson, 224, 225, 229; on consciousness, 196; on Dasein, 201, 202, 205, 214, 216, 217, 220, 229, 230; Davos encounter with Cassirer, 24, 27–28, 29, 244; on death, 229, 230–31, 233; vs. Deleuze, 9–10, 195, 196–206, 210, 213, 214, 215, 216, 217, 220, 221, 223, 224–26, 229, 230, 248, 251–52, 255, 257, 307nn30,31, 315n55, 316n75; on Descartes, 66, 213–14; on *Destruktion*, 292n82; on *ekstasis*, 202; on essence and existence, 28–29, 213–14, 244; on finitude, 205, 207, 217, 224–26, 229, 230, 231; on fundamental ontology, 9; on human freedom, 201; vs. Husserl, 3, 27; on infinity, 224–25; on Kant, 206, 207, 223, 247; on mathematics, 28; on metaphysics, 9, 75, 195, 200, 215, 217, 231; on modality, 215, 216, 217, 229; on negation, 229; ontological-ontic distinction, 28, 213–14, 215, 224–25, 245, 248, 262–63, 307n30; and politics, 4, 15, 262; on possibility, 220, 221, 229–30, 233, 248; on present-at-hand vs. readiness-to-hand, 196, 307n30; on science, 307n30; on substance, 213–14, 215; on time, 207, 214, 217, 220, 221, 224–26, 229, 230, 247; tool analysis of, 307n30; on transcendental subjectivity, 27, 201; on truth, 245

Heidegger, Martin, works of: *Being and Time*, 132, 200, 213–14, 230, 259, 297n56, 307n30; *Kant and the Problem of Metaphysics*, 200, 206; *Qu'est-ce que la métaphysique?*, 200, 201, 245; "Vom Wesen des Grundes", 200

Henry, Michel, 196, 281n6, 316n75

Hering, Jean: *Phénoménologie et philosophie religieuse*, 24

Hilbert, David, 37–38, 40, 42, 43, 54, 56

historical materialism: Althusser on, 142, 143, 148, 149, 159–60, 167, 169–70, 174; Desanti on, 101, 102, 103, 104, 109, 111, 113

historicism, 68, 69

Hitler's *Mein Kampf*, 21

Hobsbawm, Eric, on Althusser, 294n15

Hoene-Wronski, Józef Maria, 191, 236

Holocaust, 233

Horkheimer, Max: *Dialectic of Enlightenment*, 3

Huisman, Bruno, 279n125

humanism, 176, 177; Althusser on, 11–12, 134, 137, 141, 151, 175

Hume, David, 10, 161, 307n28, 308n32

Hungarian revolt of 1956, 99, 103

Husserl, Edmund, 23, 24, 39, 267n6; on acts of judgment, 57–58; on apophansis, 57–58; on categorial entities, 58; on the *cogito*, 18, 20, 26, 29, 61, 308n40; on consciousness, 18, 20, 26, 49, 57–59, 72, 121, 134–35, 282n27; on constitution of objects, 57–58; on Descartes, 25–26; on *epoché*/phenomenological reduction, 80, 120, 152, 282n27, 299n7, 301n19; on foundations, 115–16; vs. Heidegger, 3, 27; on intentionality, 26, 72, 184; on lifeworld, 152, 158, 295n31; and mathematics, 26–27, 31, 39, 92, 152, 292n90; on noema, 26, 58, 117; on noesis, 26, 57, 58, 117; Paris Lectures, 25–27, 29, 67, 272n22; on phenomenology as rationalism, 5–6; on philosophical evidence, 26; on psychologism, 24, 27, 296n31; relationship with Brunschvicg, 25; relationship with Fink, 47, 279n116; on science, 24, 48, 152, 279n119; on transcendental ego, 27, 28, 117–18, 121, 125, 184; on *Urdoxa*, 234–36

Husserl, Edmund, works of: *Cartesian Meditations*, 6, 25–27, 30, 67, 101, 115, 116, 120–21, 272n22, 299n5; *Formal and Transcendental Logic*, 29–30, 49, 57; *Ideen*, 282n27; *Logical Investigations*, 24, 26–27; "The Origin of Geometry", 115, 152, 168–69, 299n5

Hyppolite, Jean, 21–22, 25, 278n108, 290n57; on Cavaillès, 61, 280n130; *Logic and Existence*, 204–5

ideology: Althusser on, 130, 131, 132, 134–35, 143, 144, 147, 148, 151, 152–57, 160, 165, 169–72, 173–74, 175, 178–80, 181–82, 183,

184, 185, 186, 189, 219, 296n44, 300n12, 301n20, 303n53; and history, 154–57; ideological interpellation, 152–53, 178–79, 303n53; ideological state apparatuses (ISAs), 130, 152–53, 178, 303n52; and Spinozism, 1, 13–14
immanence: Cavaillès on, 28, 30–31, 32, 44; Deleuze on, 220, 233, 250–51, 317n91; Desanti on, 117, 125–26; of God, 86, 89; Lautman on, 242, 246; of reason, 28, 30–31, 32, 44, 46, 47, 49, 50
infinity: Cantor on, 17, 31, 39–40, 41, 46; Gueroult on, 41, 83, 84–85; Hegel on, 83; Heidegger on, 224–25; Spinoza on, 40–41, 83, 84–85, 89, 97, 109–11, 112, 253, 277nn92,93, 285nn76,77
intentionality, 26, 72, 87, 184
internalism vs. contextualism, 13
Israel, Jonathan, 4, 13, 269n28, 284n61

Jacobi, F. H., 264
Jambet, Christian, 316n75
James, William, 204
Janicaud, Dominique, 24, 195–96, 281n6
Jarry, Alfred, 198–99, 205, 216, 252, 317n89
Jay, Martin: on Althusser, 298n78; on Husserl, 296n31; *Marxism and Totality*, 269n30
Johns Hopkins symposium: "The Languages of Criticism and the Sciences of Man", 5
Judt, Tony, 288n21

Kanapa, Jean, 99, 135
Kant, Immanuel, 24, 35–36, 95, 147, 222–23; on categories of the understanding, 194; Copernican Revolution of, 206–8; *Course on Logic*, 50; *Critique of Judgment*, 314n43; *Critique of Pure Reason*, 2–3, 207; on form, 51; on God, 3, 224; on human freedom, 201, 207; on ideas and concepts, 192; on intuition, 51–52, 223; on logic, 27, 48, 50–52, 56, 62, 279n123; on mathematics, 36, 39; on noumenal self, 234; on noumenal sphere, 33, 201, 223; on reason, 2–3, 15, 21, 29, 50–52; on space and time, 51–52; on Spinoza, 2–3, 15, 33, 261, 264, 265, 269n28, 314n43; on Spinoza's God, 210; on synthetic a priori judgments, 39, 51–52, 71, 279n123; on thing-in-itself, 33, 209, 223, 234; on time, 223–24; on transcendental subjectivity, 80, 125, 184, 201, 202, 210, 234, 235–36, 239–40, 247; Vuillemin on, 206–7
Kerslake, Christian, 201
Khrushchev, Nikita, 99, 103
Kierkegaard, Søren, 202
Kleinberg, Ethan, 201, 203, 233, 272n19
Klossowski, Pierre, 306n14; vs. Deleuze, 232, 312n6, 313n26; on God and self, 312n6; *Nietzsche and the Vicious Circle*, 313n26
Kojève, Alexandre, 24, 141, 203; on Hegel, 205, 272n19; *Introduction à la lecture de Hegel*, 137–38, 296n41
Kolakowski, Leszek, 111
Koyré, Alexandre, 25, 30, 107, 140, 166, 278n97; on historicism, 69
Kraus, Karl, 301n19
Kriegel, Blandine: "The Silence of J.-T. Desanti", 102–3, 287n11

Lacan, Jacques, 5, 66, 114, 165, 169, 176, 274n57; *Écrits*, 177, 186; at ENS, 177; on misrecognition (*méconnaissance*), 300n12; on the unconscious, 171
Lacroix, Jean: *Marxisme, existentialisme, personalisme*, 135–36; relationship with Althusser, 135–36, 138
Lainé, Pascal, 287n11
Lakatos, Imre, 280n131
Laruelle, François: *Principles of Non-Philosophy*, 283n29
Lautman, Albert: vs. Deleuze, 221, 238, 241–45, 247, 248, 251, 315n55, 317n86; on dialectic, 60–61; on Heidegger, 28–29, 31, 244–46, 248, 251; on Ideas and concepts, 243–44; on Ideas and matter, 243; on immanence, 242, 246; on mathematics, 60–61, 241, 242–43, 244–46, 317n86; "New Research on the Dialectical Structure of Mathematics", 244–46; Platonism of, 242, 243, 244, 246; on problems and solutions, 241–42, 246, 248; relationship with Cavaillès, 28–29, 31, 43, 242, 243–45, 246; during World War II, 273n40
Lawlor, Leonard, 272n30
Lefebvre, Henri, 79
Lefebvre, Pierre, 308n45
Lefort, Claude, 123, 269n25, 289n40

Legotien, Hélène, 11, 12–13, 101, 297n48
Leibniz, Gottfried Wilhelm, 8, 33, 35–36, 169, 194, 275n63, 281n7, 305nn3,10; and principle of sufficient reason, 285n78; theodicy of, 233
Lenin, V. I., 11, 108, 142; and Althusser, 9, 130, 155, 173, 180, 181, 183, 188, 189, 303n58; *Materialism and Empirio-Criticism*, 297n47; on revolutionary theory and practice, 173, 180
Léon, Xavier, 274n56
Levinas, Emmanuel, 30, 90, 150, 272n22, 281n6; on death, 233; vs. Deleuze, 203–4, 206, 309n54; ethics of, 6; on Heidegger, 233; on Husserl, 24, 27; on time, 203–4; *Time and the Other*, 203–4
Lévi-Strauss, Claude, 5, 6, 165, 167–69, 175, 176; on kinship relations, 168
Levy, Bernard-Henri, 288n24
Lichtheim, George, 180
lived experience, 76–77, 88, 114; Althusser on, 130, 132, 133, 134–35, 141, 142, 147, 151–53, 173, 175, 189, 296n31; Deleuze on, 220, 230, 232; Husserl on, 152, 158, 295n31; vs. rationalism, 6, 17, 42, 44, 45, 53, 63, 67, 83; Spinoza on, 41, 42, 45, 63, 67, 83, 147, 179. *See also* subjectivity
logical positivism, 27, 35, 36, 37, 44, 47, 48–49, 54–57
logicism, 35, 36, 43, 49, 67
Longuenesse, Béatrice, 279n123
Lordon, Frédéric: *La Société des affects*, 268n7
Lucretius, 109
Lukács, Georg, 186, 280n131, 298n78
Lyotard, Jean-François, 68
Lysenkoism, 99, 143–44, 174, 185, 290n55, 298n72

Macciocchi, Maria, 296n44
Macherey, Pierre, 7, 176, 278n105, 298n68, 306n20
Machiavelli, Niccolò, 187–88
MacIntyre, Alasdair, 162
Madonia, Franca, 136, 302n40
Maimon, Salomon, 69, 236, 243; on differential calculus, 240; Gueroult on, 195, 206, 208, 209; on Kant's noumena, 209; Spinozism of, 208–9
Malebranche, Nicolas, 8, 79, 81, 159, 194

Marcel, Gabriel, 135; Cavaillès on, 30–31; *Être et avoir*, 30
Mardashvili, Merab, 149, 150
Marion, Jean-Luc, 90; early writings, 11; on ideology, 1; *Ontologie grise*, 281n6; as phenomenologist, 2, 3, 67, 122, 196, 281n6; on philosophy, 1–2; on reason, 1–2, 3; on Spinoza, 1–2, 3, 265; *Théologie blanche*, 281n6; on truth, 264
Martin, Jacques: relationship with Althusser, 101, 136–37, 139–40, 187, 297nn56,57; during World War II, 297n57
Marxism, 22, 24, 176, 177, 269n25; of Althusser, 6, 8, 9, 11–12, 81, 100, 101, 102, 115, 127–28, 129–30, 138, 139–40, 141, 142–45, 146–48, 149–50, 162–63, 164, 181, 186, 188, 190, 269n30, 294n9, 296nn33,36, 299n85, 301nn22,23, 302n43; of Desanti, 100, 108, 113, 114–15, 117, 133–34, 141, 288n24; Sartre on, 144, 298n75. *See also* French Communist Party (PCF); historical materialism; Lenin, V. I.; Stalinism
Marx, Karl, 108, 128, 131, 146, 267n6; early writings of, 145, 154, 163, 290n57; *1857 Introduction*, 163, 301n22; and Hegel, 137, 138, 155; and historical materialism, 159–60; on history, 137, 155; on reason, 3; and Spinoza, 147–48; Thesis Eleven on Feuerbach, 144, 173, 190, 298n73. *See also* materialism
Massumi, Brian: *Parables of the Virtual*, 268n7
materialism, 4, 269n28; Althusser on, 132–33, 137–38, 166–67, 182, 185–86, 188, 189; Desanti on, 109–11, 289n32, 296n44. *See also* historical materialism
mathematics: arithmetic, 38–39; axiomatization in, 31, 38, 42; Brunschvicg on, 35–37, 38, 47, 48, 52–53; cardinal and ordinal numbers, 39–40; and Cavaillès, 17, 19, 22, 23, 26, 28–29, 30, 31, 35, 36, 37–39, 40, 42, 43–44, 45–48, 49, 50, 52, 53–57, 58, 59, 60–61, 92, 172, 244, 273n45, 277n92, 278nn102,108, 279nn127,130; and Desanti, 92, 95–96, 103, 109, 116, 124–26, 291nn60,71, 292n79; differential calculus, 191, 236, 238–40, 241–42, 314n42, 315n46; dynamism in, 46–47, 59; formalism in,

31, 37–38, 42, 43, 54, 56, 172; geometry, 38–39, 95–96, 147, 276n83; Gueroult on, 77–78, 277n93; Heidegger on, 28; and Husserl, 26–27, 31, 39, 92, 152, 292n90; intuitionism in, 37–38, 38–39, 40, 41, 48; irrational numbers, 38, 40, 239, 276n83; Kant on, 36, 39; Lautman on, 60–61, 241, 242–43, 244–46, 317n86; necessity in, 46, 59, 278n108; and phenomenology, 26–27, 31, 39, 49, 59, 92, 152, 292n90; and philosophy, 8, 17, 23, 24–48, 35, 42, 46; relationship to physics, 46, 56, 159, 279n127; set theory, 17, 23, 31, 35, 38–39, 43, 273n45; Spinoza on, 40–42, 82–83, 89, 277n93, 291n60; transfinite mathematics, 17, 31, 38, 39–41, 49, 62

Matheron, Alexandre, 282n8; *Individu et communauté chez Spinoza*, 7

Matheron, François, 165, 270n31

May 1968, 130, 152–53, 176, 177, 178, 313n24

McLaughlin, Kathleen, 277n92

Merleau-Ponty, Maurice, 102, 289n40, 290n57; on chiasmic flesh, 162; at ENS, 47, 96; on Husserl, 25–26, 296n31; on *mathesis*, 123; on phenomenology, 26, 123, 136; *Phenomenology of Perception*, 309n57; relationship with Althusser, 136–37, 140, 296n36; relationship with Desanti, 96, 116, 118, 122–23; on Spinoza, 122–23, 140, 293n103; *The Visible and the Invisible*, 123, 293n103

Michurin, Ivan, 99, 290n55

Miller, Jacques-Alain, 177

Milosz, Czeslow: *The Captive Mind*, 100, 288n24

Misrahi, Robert, 7; *Le Désir et la réflexion dans la philosophie de Spinoza*, 268n17

Mitin, Mark Borisovich, 173, 174

Monde, Le, 1, 2, 3

Monod, Jacques, 303n56

Montag, Warren: *Althusser and His Contemporaries*, 12, 298n68, 303n52

Montesquieu, Baron de, 128–29, 154, 294n14, 300n15

morality, 2–3, 19, 263–64, 265

Moreau, Pierre-François, 282n8; on Desanti, 104–5, 108, 289n40; on singularity, 104–5; *Spinoza: L'Éxpérience et l'éternité*, 268n21

Morgan, Michael, 270n36

Moulier Boutang, Yann: on Althusser, 100–101, 134, 139, 295n27, 296n36, 297n56; on Martin, 139, 297n56, 298n57

Mounier, Emmanuel, 36, 135

Nairn, Tom, 258

Nancy, Jean-Luc, 259

Nazism, 3, 4, 21

necessity, 3, 62–63, 149–50, 154, 204; Althusser on, 168–69, 188; logical necessity, 27; Spinoza on, 19–21, 169, 188, 260–61

Negri, Antonio, 112, 184; *Commonwealth*, 258–59, 267n7; *Empire*, 267n7; on the multitude, 259–60; *Multitude*, 267n7; *The Savage Anomaly*, 291n62; Spinozism of, 7, 258–60, 261, 267n7, 291n62

New Left Review, 301n23

Newton, Isaac, 147, 201

Nietzsche, Friedrich, 3, 5, 10, 193, 267n6, 284n65, 306n14; on eternal return, 202, 223, 312n5

Nizan, Paul: on Brunschvicg, 25, 32, 145; *Les Chiens de garde*, 25; on Spinoza, 289n32, 293n103

Noether, Emmy, 40

Nouvelle Critique, La, 99, 100, 102, 287n11, 288n24, 292n79

Oakeshott, Michael: *Rationalism in Politics*, 3

pantheism, 68, 264

Parnet, Claire, 249, 251

Parrochia, Daniel: on Gueroult, 283n30

Pascal, Blaise, 153

Pautrat, Bernard, 270n36

PCF. *See* French Communist Party

Perelman, Chaïm, 79, 80

personalism, 30

Pfeffer, Gabriel, 272n22

phenomenology, 2, 3–5, 23; Alquié on, 67; Althusser on, 5, 8–9, 98, 101, 121, 129, 133, 134–36, 141–42, 143, 151–52, 153–54, 157, 158, 160, 161–62, 164, 165, 167, 177, 182, 185, 187, 188–89, 219, 230, 294n14, 295n27, 300n12, 301n19; and Bergson, 25, 30, 72, 76, 106, 140–41, 167, 169; Cazeaux on, 295n31; Deleuze on, 5, 133,

195, 196, 199, 219–20, 230; Desanti on, 97–98, 101–2, 106, 110, 114, 120–22, 123–24, 126, 134–35, 287n11, 292n90; and Descartes, 25, 26, 67; and existentialism, 106, 136, 138, 139, 176, 177, 195; and intentionality, 26, 72, 87, 184; and mathematics, 26–27, 31, 39, 49, 59, 92, 152, 292n90; Merleau-Ponty on, 26, 123, 136. See also Heidegger, Martin; Husserl, Edmund; Sartre, Jean-Paul
Philonenko, Alexis, 192
philosophy: agrégation in, 43, 47, 96, 138, 165, 274n56, 308n32; Alquié on, 74–75, 76, 193, 254; Althusser on, 127, 130, 130–33, 135, 137–38, 141, 143–45, 150, 158, 161, 162–63, 164, 165–66, 169, 173–75, 177, 179–85, 219, 257; Brunschvicg on, 35–36; of the concept vs. philosophy of consciousness, 18, 20, 23, 24, 49, 60, 61, 65, 121, 139, 243, 297n54; Deleuze on, 193, 200, 254, 256, 263–64, 304n3, 317n91; Gueroult on philosophical systems, 69, 70–71, 72, 73; history of, 8, 10, 66, 68, 70–71, 72–73, 93, 106–8; Marion on, 1–2; and mathematics, 8, 17, 23, 24–48, 35, 42, 46; and politics, 173–76, 177, 180, 181, 182–87, 188–90. See also genesis and synthesis; phenomenology
physics, 33, 46, 56, 147, 159
Picasso, Pablo, 103
Plato, 2, 28, 35–36, 66, 95, 109, 280n130; Lautman's Platonism, 242, 243, 244, 246; Parmenides, 264; vs. Spinoza, 102, 147; theory of forms, 242, 243, 307n28
Plotinus, 311n83
politics: Althusser on, 9, 14, 173–76, 177, 180, 181, 182–87, 188–90; Deleuze on, 256, 257–58, 263; and Heidegger, 15, 262; and phenomenology, 14–15, 26, 262; and philosophy, 173–76, 177, 180, 181, 182–87, 188–90; and Spinozism, 9, 14–15, 19–20, 23, 62, 81–82, 92–93, 103–4, 111–12, 114–15, 132–33, 182–83, 187–88, 189–90, 197, 256, 257–60, 261, 262–63, 264, 282n8. See also French Communist Party (PCF); Stalinism
Popkin, Richard, 111, 145
Port-Royal logic, 48, 51
possibility: Deleuze on, 193, 198, 203, 204, 217, 219, 220, 221, 227–32, 233, 246–47, 248, 256, 313n14, 314n34, 317n91; Heidegger on, 220, 221, 229–30, 233, 248
principle of sufficient reason, 195, 200, 285n78, 306n22
Protestantism, 111, 273n46, 275n63
Proust, Marcel, 225
psychologism, 33, 51; Husserl on, 24, 27, 296n31

Queneau, Raymond, 25

Racine, Nicole, 272n32, 273n46
Rancière, Jacques, 178; on Althusser, 142, 269n25; Althusser's Lesson, 269n25, 294n3
Ravaisson, Félix, 140
reason: Althusser's rationalism, 5, 8–9, 92, 93, 98, 130, 131, 132, 138, 144, 145–46, 150–53, 165, 173, 174, 179, 185, 187, 188, 219; Brunschvicg's rationalism, 25, 140; definition of rationalism, 6; Deleuze's rationalism, 5, 195, 196, 197, 198, 205–6, 215, 217, 220, 221, 227, 234–36, 252, 307n28; Descartes' rationalism, 5–6, 25, 79, 89; Gueroult's rationalism, 66, 68, 69, 70, 72–73, 79, 105, 107, 109, 150, 194, 206, 209, 248, 254, 263, 284n67; immanence of, 28, 30–31, 32, 44, 46, 47, 49, 50; limits of, 1–4, 15, 49, 78, 254, 264–65; lived experience vs. rationalism, 6, 17, 42, 44, 45, 53, 63, 67, 83; relationship to history, 21–23; Spinoza's rationalism, 18, 19, 31, 32, 33, 36, 42, 43, 45, 46, 49–50, 53, 62–63, 65, 66, 67, 68, 81, 82, 92, 93, 95–96, 98, 105, 107, 108, 109, 110, 113, 117, 122, 138, 143, 150, 194–95, 209, 248, 263, 264–65, 273n46, 285n78, 294n13, 306n22; universality of, 21, 22–23
Regnault, François: on sens, 264
Revault d'Allonnes, Olivier, 306n23
Revue de la métaphysique et de morale, 274n56
Ricardo, David, 160
Ricoeur, Paul: on Althusser, 152–53; on Husserl and rationalism, 5–6; "Ideology and Utopia", 152–53; on Lévi-Strauss's structuralism, 6; on masters of suspicion, 267n6
Rivaud, Albert, 271n1
Rose, Gillian, 313n14

Rosset, Clément: on Althusser, 186; on Deleuze, 232, 307n23; on negativity, 232–33, 313n29; *L'Objet singulier*, 232–33
Roudinesco, Elisabeth, 10, 66
Russell, Bertrand, 39, 106; logicism of, 35, 36, 43; *Principia Mathematica*, 36; theory of types, 36
Ruyer, Raymond, 191, 236, 305n4

Sacher-Masoch, Leopold von, 191
salvation, 90, 111–12; Spinoza on beatitude, 15, 88, 110, 112, 255, 256, 264, 270n36
Sartre, Jean-Paul, 3, 25, 67, 70, 106, 114, 140, 199–200, 203, 204, 290n57; *Being and Nothingness*, 119, 200; Deleuze on, 199–200, 314n38; on Husserl, 118, 292n90; on love, 200; on Marxism, 144, 298n75; on phenomenology, 24; on *pour-soi* and *en-soi*, 119, 162; on practice, 163–64; relationship with Althusser, 163–64; relationship with Desanti, 118–19, 292n90; *The Transcendence of the Ego*, 118, 119, 314n; during World War II, 118–19
Saussure, Ferdinand de, 87
Scholasticism, 36, 37, 82, 112, 114–15, 145, 166
science: Althusser on, 108, 127, 129–30, 131, 132, 133, 138, 142–44, 146–48, 150, 152–54, 155–56, 158, 159–60, 163, 165, 169–70, 172, 173–74, 175, 179, 180–87, 189, 219, 296n44, 298n72, 299n83, 302n42; Brunschvicg on, 32–33, 36–37, 48, 50, 52, 53, 113, 146; Cavaillès on, 46, 49, 50, 52, 53–57, 59–62, 105, 108, 125, 242, 263, 279nn119,125; Desanti on, 100, 107–8, 111, 112–13, 114, 120, 124–26, 139, 290n55; Heidegger on, 307n30; Husserl on, 24, 48, 152, 279n119; of the singular, 198–99; Spinoza on, 112–13, 114–15, 147
Sellars, John, 312n13
Serres, Michel, 79
Sharp, Hasana: *Spinoza and the Politics of Renaturalization*, 268n7
Shirley, Samuel, 270n36
Simondon, Gilbert, 236; *L'Individu et sa genèse physico-biologique*, 314n40
Sinaceur, Hourya, 274n51
singularity: Althusser on, 132, 147, 148, 151, 154, 156, 164, 168–69, 172, 180, 181, 189; Cavaillès on, 54, 55, 60, 244; Deleuze on, 189, 198, 199, 205–6, 216–17, 232, 235–36, 237, 247, 251; Gueroult on, 70, 72, 73, 80, 90–91, 285n79; Moreau on, 104–5
Skinner, Quentin: *Visions of Politics*, 270n32
Socialisme et liberté, 118–19
Société française de philosophie, 43, 45
solipsism, 29, 114, 118, 121, 220
Spinoza, Benedict de: on affect and emotion, 7, 9; on attributes, 56, 82, 83–85, 86, 89, 91, 156, 158–59, 170, 172, 181, 190, 194, 210, 211–12, 214, 216–17, 221, 236–37, 240–41, 248, 251, 252–54, 255, 261, 262–63, 277n95, 285nn76,77,80, 306nn13,20, 311n85; on beatitude, 15, 88, 110, 112, 255, 256, 264, 270n36; vs. Bergson, 41, 83, 277n92, 284n75; on biblical criticism, 157; on cause and effect, 85–86, 89, 260, 262; on concepts, 83, 161, 174; on consciousness, 46, 300n15; on death, 230; vs. Descartes, 6, 10, 61, 65, 66, 67–68, 78–79, 84, 89, 90, 130, 163, 284n61, 310n79; on desire, 254, 275n63, 317n82; equanimity of, 264–65; on essence, 84, 85, 86; on existence, 84; on Extension, 56, 82, 84, 85, 86, 156, 159, 170, 179, 194, 211–12, 215, 216–17, 221, 236–37, 240–41, 248, 251, 253, 255, 261, 262–63, 277n95, 279n127, 285n76, 306n13, 311n85, 314n41; on first causes, 260, 262; on God, 81, 84, 86, 87, 89, 90, 91, 110–11, 113, 114–15, 117–18, 132, 172, 194, 210–11, 214, 234, 260, 262, 274n46, 275n63, 280n130, 285n80, 293n103, 295n24; on idea of the idea, 42–43, 45, 50, 52–53, 108–9, 160, 279n127, 291n60; on imagination, 40–41, 83, 277nn92,93; on immediacy of thought, 78; on immortality, 110, 112; on infinity, 40–41, 83, 84–85, 89, 97, 109–11, 112, 253, 277nn92,93, 285nn76,77; on intellectual love of God, 110, 180; on intelligibility, 89–90; on intuition, 83, 110, 277n92; and Judaism, 67, 268n17; on knowledge, 15, 110, 147–48, 151–52, 158–59, 160, 180, 181, 189, 303n57; on lived experience/*vaga experientia*, 41, 42, 45, 63, 67, 83, 147, 179; on mathematics, 40–42, 82–83, 89, 277n93, 291n60; on method, 44–45, 46; on modes, 83, 84–85, 86, 89, 91, 105, 111, 191, 211–13, 214, 215–16,

248, 251, 253 261, 285n80, 306n13; on *natura naturata* vs. *natura naturans*, 50, 55, 56, 85, 212, 213, 215, 241, 251, 262, 285n80, 306n20; on necessity, 19–21, 169, 188, 260–61; parallelism thesis, 120, 158; principle of *Deus sive Natura*, 83, 111, 113, 117, 214, 263; and principle of sufficient reason, 195, 285n78, 306n22; rationalism of, 18, 19, 31, 32, 33, 36, 42, 43, 45, 46, 49–50, 53, 62–63, 65, 66, 67, 68, 81, 82, 92, 93, 95–96, 98, 105, 107, 108, 109, 110, 113, 117, 122, 138, 143, 150, 194–95, 209, 248, 263, 264–65, 273n46, 285n78, 294n13, 306n22; on reality and perfection, 233; on science, 112–13, 114–15, 147; on substance, 8, 9, 37, 40–41, 50, 82–83, 84, 85, 86, 87, 91, 110–11, 112, 114, 130, 132, 170, 171, 172, 191, 194, 195, 209, 210, 211–13, 214–16, 221, 228, 233, 238, 240, 248, 251, 262–63, 285nn76,77, 306nn13,20; *Theological-Political Treatise*, 258; on third kind of knowledge, 110, 147, 148, 151, 180, 181; on Thought, 56, 82, 84–85, 86, 156, 159, 170, 179, 194, 211–12, 215, 216–17, 221, 236–37, 240–41, 248, 251, 252–54, 255, 261, 262–63, 277n95, 279n127, 285nn76,80, 306n13, 311n85, 314n21; on tolerance, 111–12; on truth, 44–45, 47, 79, 86, 87, 97, 102–3, 109, 124, 145–46, 189, 190, 229, 232, 253, 264, 265, 276n78, 278n105, 280n130; on viewing things under the aspect of eternity, 13, 23, 215, 255; on the will, 146
Spinoza, Benedict de, works of: *Ethics*, 1, 2, 7, 8, 15, 42–43, 46, 82, 88, 89, 96, 112, 116, 130, 158–59, 160, 172, 180, 187, 194, 210, 216, 248, 256, 260, 270n36, 278n105, 281n7, 306nn13,20, 311n85; Letter 12, 40, 270n36; Letter 64, 285n76; Letter 78, 275n63; *Political Treatise*, 112, 258; *Tractatus Theologico-Politicus*, 111–12, 157, 258; translations, 270n36; *Treatise on the Emendation of the Intellect*, 8, 42, 43, 44–45, 46, 97, 130, 138, 147–48, 151, 197n44, 270n36, 278nn97,105, 300n15
Stalinism, 3, 11, 173, 185, 288n21, 289n40; Althusser on, 129, 133–34, 141–42, 143, 296n33; of Jean-Toussaint Desanti, 93, 99–100, 102, 106, 126, 133–34, 135; and economism, 134, 141, 175; and Lysenkoism, 99, 143–44, 174, 185, 290n55, 298n72
Stoicism, 225–26, 312n13
structuralism, 5, 6, 87, 90, 130, 131, 134, 165, 168–69, 175, 281n8
subjectivity, 20, 71, 137, 138, 141; Althusser on, 137, 138, 141, 171–72, 179, 184–85, 187, 188; Cavaillès on, 17, 27, 29, 59, 114; Deleuze on, 221, 223–24, 247; Desanti, 106, 107, 109, 114, 117–18; Descartes' *cogito*, 6, 26, 73, 78, 80–81, 90, 122, 184, 201, 253–54; Gueroult on, 72, 76. *See also* consciousness; lived experience; transcendental subjectivity
substance: Deleuze on, 226; Descartes on, 213–14, 225; Hegel on, 205; Heidegger on, 213–14, 215; Spinoza on, 8, 9, 37, 40–41, 50, 82–83, 84, 85, 86, 87, 91, 110–11, 112, 114, 130, 132, 170, 171, 172, 191, 194, 195, 209, 210, 211–13, 214–16, 221, 228, 233, 238, 240, 248, 251, 262–63, 285nn76,77, 306nn13,20
surrealism, 73
synthesis. See genesis and synthesis

Tarski, Alfred, 48–49, 50, 55–56
Telos, 269n30
Thales, 147
Thao, Tran Duc, 47–48, 279n116; *Phénoménologie et matérialisme dialectique*, 115
theology: Alquié on, 68, 81, 90, 109; Althusser on, 145, 154, 163, 182, 185–86, 187; Gueroult on, 68, 81, 91; negative theology, 82, 196, 215, 221, 234, 247, 248, 252, 255, 270n34
Third Republic, 20, 32, 69, 146, 275n58
Thomas, Peter, 295n25
Thomism, 166, 284n75, 285n80
Thompson, E. P., 142, 161, 270n30, 301n23
time: Bergson on, 224, 225; Chronos and Aiôn, 225–27, 228, 247, 249–50, 312n13; Deleuze on, 202, 203–4, 221, 223–26, 228, 247, 249–50, 312nn5,12,13; Desanti on, 120–21, 122; in differential calculus, 239–40; Heidegger on, 207, 214, 217, 220, 221, 224–26, 229, 230, 247; Kant on, 223–24; Levinas on, 203–4
Tort, Michel, 176, 177, 178
Toscano, Alberto, 249

Tournier, Michel: *Vendredi*, 203–4, 231, 309n56
transcendental subjectivity: Cavaillès on, 17, 59, 114; Deleuze on transcendental ego, 114, 201–2, 210, 234, 235, 314n48; Desanti on transcendental ego, 97, 117–18, 121, 125–26; Heidegger on, 27, 201; Husserl on transcendental ego, 27, 28, 117–18, 121, 125, 184; Kant on, 80, 125, 184, 201, 202, 210, 234, 235–36, 239–40, 247; Sartre on transcendental ego, 118, 119, 314n
truth: Alquié on, 74–75, 80–81, 91, 193; Althusser on, 145–46, 180–81, 182, 190, 298n78; Brunschvicg on, 36, 37, 276n78; Cavaillès on, 47; Deleuze on, 193, 232; Descartes on, 76–77; Frege on, 39; Gueroult on, 70, 71, 76–77, 80, 91–92; Heidegger on, 245; Marion on, 264; Spinoza on, 44–45, 47, 79, 86, 87, 97, 102–3, 109, 124, 145–46, 189, 190, 229, 232, 253, 264, 265, 276n78, 278n105, 280n130
Tschirnhaus, Ehrenfried Walther von, 253
Twentieth Party Congress of CPSU, 99, 103, 104

universality, 78, 79; of reason, 21, 22–23

Valéry, Paul, 106
Vardoulakis, Dimitris: *Spinoza Now*, 268n7

Vernière, Paul: on Spinoza, 166–67; *Spinoza et la pensée française avant la Révolution*, 166–67, 281n7
Vichy government, 297n57
Vico, Giambattista: *verum-factum* principle of, 145, 298n78
Vienna Circle, 67
von Neumann, John, 43
Vuillemin, Jules, 92; on finitude, 207–8; on Heidegger, 197, 206–7, 215; *L'Héritage kantien et la copernicienne révolution*, 195, 206–8, 281n8; *Physique et métaphysique kantiennes*, 281n8; on rationalism, 206

Weil, Simone, 19; on Cavaillès, 21
Wittmann, David, 290n44
Wolff, Christian, 33
World War II: Althusser during, 135, 297n57; Brunschvicg during, 34, 69; Cavaillès during, 18–21, 22, 34, 37, 61, 62–63, 92, 139, 280n129, 281n8; Desanti during, 118–19; French Resistance, 18–21, 22, 37, 61, 62–63, 92, 139, 233, 273n40, 281n8, 297n57; Lautman during, 273n40; Martin during, 297n57; Sartre during, 118–19

Zac, Sylvain, 7
Zeno's paradox of Achilles and the tortoise, 226, 312n12

Cultural Memory in the Present

Françoise Davoine, *Mother Folly: A Tale*

Elizabeth A. Pritchard, *Locke's Political Theology: Public Religion and Sacred Rights*

Ankhi Mukherjee, *What Is a Classic? Postcolonial Rewriting and Invention of the Canon*

Jean-Pierre Dupuy, *The Mark of the Sacred*

Henri Atlan, *Fraud: The World of Ona'ah*

Niklas Luhmann, *Theory of Society, Volume 2*

Ilit Ferber, *Philosophy and Melancholy: Benjamin's Early Reflections on Theater and Language*

Alexandre Lefebvre, *Human Rights as a Way of Life: On Bergson's Political Philosophy*

Theodore W. Jennings, Jr., *Outlaw Justice: The Messianic Politics of Paul*

Alexander Etkind, *Warped Mourning: Stories of the Undead in the Land of the Unburied*

Denis Guénoun, *About Europe: Philosophical Hypotheses*

Maria Boletsi, *Barbarism and Its Discontents*

Sigrid Weigel, *Walter Benjamin: Images, the Creaturely, and the Holy*

Roberto Esposito, *Living Thought: The Origins and Actuality of Italian Philosophy*

Henri Atlan, *The Sparks of Randomness, Volume 2: The Atheism of Scripture*

Rüdiger Campe, *The Game of Probability: Literature and Calculation from Pascal to Kleist*

Niklas Luhmann, *A Systems Theory of Religion*

Jean-Luc Marion, *In the Self's Place: The Approach of Saint Augustine*

Rodolphe Gasché, *Georges Bataille: Phenomenology and Phantasmatology*

Niklas Luhmann, *Theory of Society, Volume 1*

Alessia Ricciardi, *After La Dolce Vita: A Cultural Prehistory of Berlusconi's Italy*

Daniel Innerarity, *The Future and Its Enemies: In Defense of Political Hope*

Patricia Pisters, *The Neuro-Image: A Deleuzian Film-Philosophy of Digital Screen Culture*

François-David Sebbah, *Testing the Limit: Derrida, Henry, Levinas, and the Phenomenological Tradition*

Erik Peterson, *Theological Tractates*, edited by Michael J. Hollerich

Feisal G. Mohamed, *Milton and the Post-Secular Present: Ethics, Politics, Terrorism*

Pierre Hadot, *The Present Alone Is Our Happiness, Second Edition: Conversations with Jeannie Carlier and Arnold I. Davidson*

Yasco Horsman, *Theaters of Justice: Judging, Staging, and Working Through in Arendt, Brecht, and Delbo*

Jacques Derrida, *Parages*, edited by John P. Leavey

Henri Atlan, *The Sparks of Randomness, Volume 1: Spermatic Knowledge*

Rebecca Comay, *Mourning Sickness: Hegel and the French Revolution*

Djelal Kadir, *Memos from the Besieged City: Lifelines for Cultural Sustainability*

Stanley Cavell, *Little Did I Know: Excerpts from Memory*

Jeffrey Mehlman, *Adventures in the French Trade: Fragments Toward a Life*

Jacob Rogozinski, *The Ego and the Flesh: An Introduction to Egoanalysis*

Marcel Hénaff, *The Price of Truth: Gift, Money, and Philosophy*

Paul Patton, *Deleuzian Concepts: Philosophy, Colonialization, Politics*

Michael Fagenblat, *A Covenant of Creatures: Levinas's Philosophy of Judaism*

Stefanos Geroulanos, *An Atheism That Is Not Humanist Emerges in French Thought*

Andrew Herscher, *Violence Taking Place: The Architecture of the Kosovo Conflict*

Hans-Jörg Rheinberger, *On Historicizing Epistemology: An Essay*

Jacob Taubes, *From Cult to Culture*, edited by Charlotte Fonrobert and Amir Engel

Peter Hitchcock, *The Long Space: Transnationalism and Postcolonial Form*

Lambert Wiesing, *Artificial Presence: Philosophical Studies in Image Theory*

Jacob Taubes, *Occidental Eschatology*

Freddie Rokem, *Philosophers and Thespians: Thinking Performance*

Roberto Esposito, *Communitas: The Origin and Destiny of Community*

Vilashini Cooppan, *Worlds Within: National Narratives and Global Connections in Postcolonial Writing*

Josef Früchtl, *The Impertinent Self: A Heroic History of Modernity*

Frank Ankersmit, Ewa Domanska, and Hans Kellner, eds., *Re-Figuring Hayden White*

Michael Rothberg, *Multidirectional Memory: Remembering the Holocaust in the Age of Decolonization*

Jean-François Lyotard, *Enthusiasm: The Kantian Critique of History*

Ernst van Alphen, Mieke Bal, and Carel Smith, eds., *The Rhetoric of Sincerity*

Stéphane Mosès, *The Angel of History: Rosenzweig, Benjamin, Scholem*

Pierre Hadot, *The Present Alone Is Our Happiness: Conversations with Jeannie Carlier and Arnold I. Davidson*

Alexandre Lefebvre, *The Image of the Law: Deleuze, Bergson, Spinoza*

Samira Haj, *Reconfiguring Islamic Tradition: Reform, Rationality, and Modernity*

Diane Perpich, *The Ethics of Emmanuel Levinas*

Marcel Detienne, *Comparing the Incomparable*

François Delaporte, *Anatomy of the Passions*

René Girard, *Mimesis and Theory: Essays on Literature and Criticism, 1959–2005*

Richard Baxstrom, *Houses in Motion: The Experience of Place and the Problem of Belief in Urban Malaysia*

Jennifer L. Culbert, *Dead Certainty: The Death Penalty and the Problem of Judgment*

Samantha Frost, *Lessons from a Materialist Thinker: Hobbesian Reflections on Ethics and Politics*

Regina Mara Schwartz, *Sacramental Poetics at the Dawn of Secularism: When God Left the World*

Gil Anidjar, *Semites: Race, Religion, Literature*

Ranjana Khanna, *Algeria Cuts: Women and Representation, 1830 to the Present*

Esther Peeren, *Intersubjectivities and Popular Culture: Bakhtin and Beyond*

Eyal Peretz, *Becoming Visionary: Brian De Palma's Cinematic Education of the Senses*

Diana Sorensen, *A Turbulent Decade Remembered: Scenes from the Latin American Sixties*

Hubert Damisch, *A Childhood Memory by Piero della Francesca*

José van Dijck, *Mediated Memories in the Digital Age*

Dana Hollander, *Exemplarity and Chosenness: Rosenzweig and Derrida on the Nation of Philosophy*

Asja Szafraniec, *Beckett, Derrida, and the Event of Literature*

Sara Guyer, *Romanticism After Auschwitz*

Alison Ross, *The Aesthetic Paths of Philosophy: Presentation in Kant, Heidegger, Lacoue-Labarthe, and Nancy*

Gerhard Richter, *Thought-Images: Frankfurt School Writers' Reflections from Damaged Life*

Bella Brodzki, *Can These Bones Live? Translation, Survival, and Cultural Memory*

Rodolphe Gasché, *The Honor of Thinking: Critique, Theory, Philosophy*

Brigitte Peucker, *The Material Image: Art and the Real in Film*

Natalie Melas, *All the Difference in the World: Postcoloniality and the Ends of Comparison*

Jonathan Culler, *The Literary in Theory*

Michael G. Levine, *The Belated Witness: Literature, Testimony, and the Question of Holocaust Survival*

Jennifer A. Jordan, *Structures of Memory: Understanding German Change in Berlin and Beyond*

Christoph Menke, *Reflections of Equality*

Marlène Zarader, *The Unthought Debt: Heidegger and the Hebraic Heritage*

Jan Assmann, *Religion and Cultural Memory: Ten Studies*

David Scott and Charles Hirschkind, *Powers of the Secular Modern: Talal Asad and His Interlocutors*

Gyanendra Pandey, *Routine Violence: Nations, Fragments, Histories*

James Siegel, *Naming the Witch*

J. M. Bernstein, *Against Voluptuous Bodies: Late Modernism and the Meaning of Painting*

Theodore W. Jennings, Jr., *Reading Derrida / Thinking Paul: On Justice*

Richard Rorty and Eduardo Mendieta, *Take Care of Freedom and Truth Will Take Care of Itself: Interviews with Richard Rorty*

Jacques Derrida, *Paper Machine*

Renaud Barbaras, *Desire and Distance: Introduction to a Phenomenology of Perception*

Jill Bennett, *Empathic Vision: Affect, Trauma, and Contemporary Art*

Ban Wang, *Illuminations from the Past: Trauma, Memory, and History in Modern China*

James Phillips, *Heidegger's Volk: Between National Socialism and Poetry*

Frank Ankersmit, *Sublime Historical Experience*

István Rév, *Retroactive Justice: Prehistory of Post-Communism*

Paola Marrati, *Genesis and Trace: Derrida Reading Husserl and Heidegger*

Krzysztof Ziarek, *The Force of Art*

Marie-José Mondzain, *Image, Icon, Economy: The Byzantine Origins of the Contemporary Imaginary*

Cecilia Sjöholm, *The Antigone Complex: Ethics and the Invention of Feminine Desire*

Jacques Derrida and Elisabeth Roudinesco, *For What Tomorrow . . . : A Dialogue*

Elisabeth Weber, *Questioning Judaism: Interviews by Elisabeth Weber*

Jacques Derrida and Catherine Malabou, *Counterpath: Traveling with Jacques Derrida*

Martin Seel, *Aesthetics of Appearing*

Nanette Salomon, *Shifting Priorities: Gender and Genre in Seventeenth-Century Dutch Painting*

Jacob Taubes, *The Political Theology of Paul*

Jean-Luc Marion, *The Crossing of the Visible*

Eric Michaud, *The Cult of Art in Nazi Germany*

Anne Freadman, *The Machinery of Talk: Charles Peirce and the Sign Hypothesis*

Stanley Cavell *Emerson's Transcendental Etudes*

Stuart McLean, *The Event and Its Terrors: Ireland, Famine, Modernity*

Beate Rössler, ed., *Privacies: Philosophical Evaluations*

Bernard Faure, *Double Exposure: Cutting Across Buddhist and Western Discourses*

Alessia Ricciardi, *The Ends of Mourning: Psychoanalysis, Literature, Film*

Alain Badiou, *Saint Paul: The Foundation of Universalism*

Gil Anidjar, *The Jew, the Arab: A History of the Enemy*

Jonathan Culler and Kevin Lamb, eds., *Just Being Difficult? Academic Writing in the Public Arena*

Jean-Luc Nancy, *A Finite Thinking*, edited by Simon Sparks

Theodor W. Adorno, *Can One Live after Auschwitz? A Philosophical Reader*, edited by Rolf Tiedemann

Patricia Pisters, *The Matrix of Visual Culture: Working with Deleuze in Film Theory*

Andreas Huyssen, *Present Pasts: Urban Palimpsests and the Politics of Memory*

Talal Asad, *Formations of the Secular: Christianity, Islam, Modernity*

Dorothea von Mücke, *The Rise of the Fantastic Tale*

Marc Redfield, *The Politics of Aesthetics: Nationalism, Gender, Romanticism*

Emmanuel Levinas, *On Escape*

Dan Zahavi, *Husserl's Phenomenology*

Rodolphe Gasché, *The Idea of Form: Rethinking Kant's Aesthetics*

Michael Naas, *Taking on the Tradition: Jacques Derrida and the Legacies of Deconstruction*

Herlinde Pauer-Studer, ed., *Constructions of Practical Reason: Interviews on Moral and Political Philosophy*

Jean-Luc Marion, *Being Given: Toward a Phenomenology of Givenness*

Theodor W. Adorno and Max Horkheimer, *Dialectic of Enlightenment*

Ian Balfour, *The Rhetoric of Romantic Prophecy*

Martin Stokhof, *World and Life as One: Ethics and Ontology in Wittgenstein's Early Thought*

Gianni Vattimo, *Nietzsche: An Introduction*

Jacques Derrida, *Negotiations: Interventions and Interviews, 1971–1998*, ed. Elizabeth Rottenberg

Brett Levinson, *The Ends of Literature: The Latin American "Boom" in the Neoliberal Marketplace*

Timothy J. Reiss, *Against Autonomy: Cultural Instruments, Mutualities, and the Fictive Imagination*

Hent de Vries and Samuel Weber, eds., *Religion and Media*

Niklas Luhmann, *Theories of Distinction: Redescribing the Descriptions of Modernity*, ed. and introd. William Rasch

Johannes Fabian, *Anthropology with an Attitude: Critical Essays*

Michel Henry, *I Am the Truth: Toward a Philosophy of Christianity*

Gil Anidjar, *"Our Place in Al-Andalus": Kabbalah, Philosophy, Literature in Arab-Jewish Letters*

Hélène Cixous and Jacques Derrida, *Veils*

F. R. Ankersmit, *Historical Representation*

F. R. Ankersmit, *Political Representation*

Elissa Marder, *Dead Time: Temporal Disorders in the Wake of Modernity (Baudelaire and Flaubert)*

Reinhart Koselleck, *The Practice of Conceptual History: Timing History, Spacing Concepts*

Niklas Luhmann, *The Reality of the Mass Media*

Hubert Damisch, *A Theory of /Cloud/: Toward a History of Painting*

Jean-Luc Nancy, *The Speculative Remark: (One of Hegel's Bon Mots)*

Jean-François Lyotard, *Soundproof Room: Malraux's Anti-Aesthetics*

Jan Patočka, *Plato and Europe*

Hubert Damisch, *Skyline: The Narcissistic City*

Isabel Hoving, *In Praise of New Travelers: Reading Caribbean Migrant Women Writers*

Richard Rand, ed., *Futures: Of Jacques Derrida*

William Rasch, *Niklas Luhmann's Modernity: The Paradoxes of Differentiation*

Jacques Derrida and Anne Dufourmantelle, *Of Hospitality*

Jean-François Lyotard, *The Confession of Augustine*

Kaja Silverman, *World Spectators*

Samuel Weber, *Institution and Interpretation: Expanded Edition*

Jeffrey S. Librett, *The Rhetoric of Cultural Dialogue: Jews and Germans in the Epoch of Emancipation*

Ulrich Baer, *Remnants of Song: Trauma and the Experience of Modernity in Charles Baudelaire and Paul Celan*

Samuel C. Wheeler III, *Deconstruction as Analytic Philosophy*

David S. Ferris, *Silent Urns: Romanticism, Hellenism, Modernity*

Rodolphe Gasché, *Of Minimal Things: Studies on the Notion of Relation*

Sarah Winter, *Freud and the Institution of Psychoanalytic Knowledge*

Samuel Weber, *The Legend of Freud: Expanded Edition*

Aris Fioretos, ed., *The Solid Letter: Readings of Friedrich Hölderlin*

J. Hillis Miller / Manuel Asensi, *Black Holes / J. Hillis Miller; or, Boustrophedonic Reading*

Miryam Sas, *Fault Lines: Cultural Memory and Japanese Surrealism*

Peter Schwenger, *Fantasm and Fiction: On Textual Envisioning*

Didier Maleuvre, *Museum Memories: History, Technology, Art*

Jacques Derrida, *Monolingualism of the Other; or, The Prosthesis of Origin*

Andrew Baruch Wachtel, *Making a Nation, Breaking a Nation: Literature and Cultural Politics in Yugoslavia*

Niklas Luhmann, *Love as Passion: The Codification of Intimacy*

Mieke Bal, ed., *The Practice of Cultural Analysis: Exposing Interdisciplinary Interpretation*

Jacques Derrida and Gianni Vattimo, eds., *Religion*

The authorized representative in the EU for product safety and compliance is:
Mare Nostrum Group
B.V Doelen 72
4831 GR Breda
The Netherlands

www.ingramcontent.com/pod-product-compliance
Lightning Source LLC
Chambersburg PA
CBHW030518230426
43665CB00010B/662